# Critical Thinking

# Critical Thinking

Pseudoscience and the Paranormal

Second Edition

*Jonathan C. Smith*

*Roosevelt University, USA*

*Registered Office*
John Wiley & Sons, Inc., 111 River Street, Hoboken, NJ 07030, USA

*Editorial Office*
The Atrium, Southern Gate, Chichester, West Sussex, PO19 8SQ, UK

For details of our global editorial offices, customer services, and more information about Wiley products visit us at www.wiley.com.

Wiley also publishes its books in a variety of electronic formats and by print-on-demand. Some content that appears in standard print versions of this book may not be available in other formats.

*Library of Congress Cataloging-in-Publication Data*

Names: Smith, Jonathan C., author.
Title: Critical thinking : pseudoscience and the paranormal / Jonathan C. Smith.
Other titles: Pseudoscience and extraordinary claims of the paranormal
Description: Second Edition. | Hoboken : Wiley, 2017. | Rev. ed. of: Pseudoscience and extraordinary claims of the paranormal : a critical thinker's toolkit. 2010. | Includes bibliographical references and index.
Identifiers: LCCN 2017006793 (print) | LCCN 2017002367 (ebook) | ISBN 9781119029359 (pbk.) | ISBN 9781119029489 (Adobe PDF) | ISBN 9781119029373 (ePub)
Subjects: LCSH: Parapsychology.
Classification: LCC BF1031 .S635 2017 (ebook) | LCC BF1031 (print) | DDC 130–dc23
LC record available at https://lccn.loc.gov/2017006793

Cover images: © dem10/Gettyimages; © Dynamicfoto/Shutterstock; courtesy of the author
Cover design by Wiley

Set in 10/12pt Warnock by SPi Global, Pondicherry, India
Printed and bound in Malaysia by Vivar Printing Sdn Bhd

1  2018

*Lovingly dedicated to*

𝌆 ᚷᚱᚢ ᚾᛚᛚᛚᚲᛈᚤᛗ

# Contents

# Acknowledgments

I wish to acknowledge the generous support and contribution of Chicago's Roosevelt University, my home for decades. Special note to the University Research and Professional Improvement Leave Committee for all that they have done.

**Part I**

**Introduction**

# 1

# Critical Thinking: Your Survival Kit

---

**OUTLINE**

1) Critical Thinking Defined: *Critical thinking is the process of (1) evaluating a claim about objective reality and identifying support, and (2) considering alternative hypotheses.*
   a) Stating a Claim, Identifying Types of Support
      i) Appropriate sources
      ii) Logic and clear language
      iii) Science
   b) Alternative Hypotheses: Going Beyond Immediate Personal Experience and Intuition
      i) Oddities in nature and the world of statistics
      ii) Perceptual error or trickery
      iii) Memory error
      iv) Placebo effect
      v) Sensory phenomena, hallucinations, and psychiatric conditions
2) Bats, Balls, and Mind-Reading: Intuitive vs. Reflective Cognitive Thinking Styles
3) The Time and Place for Critical Thinking
4) Finding a Safe Practice Arena
5) The Four Challenges of the Open-Minded Critical Thinker
   a) Have the Courage to Pause and Reflect
   b) Question Fearlessly and Honestly
   c) Recognize that There May Be More to the World than Meets the Eye
   d) Admit You Might Be Totally Mistaken

---

Life can be a Pandora's box of problems and mysteries. This includes all things great and small. Everyday challenges like starting college, dating, and finding work. Threats to society, like war, poverty, disease, and environmental disaster. Yes, even frantic internet exposés of mind-controlling psychics, flesh-eating vampires, and invasions from other universes. In a world full of troubles, every student needs one important survival kit – a toolbox of powerful critical thinking skills.

Consider Alex, a college student who faces a rather complicated dating dilemma. The first few dates went well. What to do next? Please study this carefully:

> *I think I'm ready for sex. I'm dating Jesse, who is fun to be with. But I doubt Jesse has any interest in romance. I'm not quite sure what I want.*

> *I want to take Jesse to an art museum this weekend. There are two exhibits. I've seen both. Which has the more beautiful art?*

*Critical Thinking: Pseudoscience and the Paranormal*, Second Edition. Jonathan C. Smith.
© 2018 John Wiley & Sons, Inc. Published 2018 by John Wiley & Sons, Inc.

**Figure 1.1** What's in your Pandora's Box? Reproduced with kind permission of Shutterstock.

*I'm getting closer to both Jesse and Riley. I've gone out with both. It almost feels like I'm dating two people. Is that OK? Should I drop one and date the other? And what about Jamie, someone interesting I just met?*

*What does God want me to do? How can I tell the difference between God's will and my wishes?*

*Julian, my roommate wants me to take a drink he obtained from a store that specializes in alternative medicine. Citing personal experience, Julian says it works and will help me make choices more decisively. Should I try it?*

*All these questions! Last night I had a dream that I dropped out of school and took a hike on a long mountain path to clear my head. Out of nowhere, a sage on a vintage Harley rumbled to a dramatic stop in front of me. I was struck by what this person was wearing – a glowing ruby eye earring, delicate flowered silk scarf, and steel-studded leather arm band. As the dust settled, my Biker Sage whispered: "Think clearly!" blew me a kiss, and roared away. Should I take this premonition seriously?*

## Critical Thinking Defined

Fortunately, Alex is taking a course in critical thinking and hopes he can find some answers. He begins with some popular definitions. For example, his very first Google hit (out of 53,100,000 results) is a very popular definition:

> Critical thinking is the intellectually disciplined process of actively and skillfully conceptualizing, applying, analyzing, synthesizing, and/or evaluating information gathered from, or generated by, observation, experience, reflection, reasoning, or communication, as a guide to belief and action. In its exemplary form, it is based on universal intellectual values that transcend subject matter divisions: clarity, accuracy, precision, consistency, relevance, sound evidence, good reasons, depth, breadth, and fairness.
>
> *(Scriven & Paul, 2014)*

Such definitions are abstract and global and can be applied to a wide range of life's challenges. Think "clearly." Conceptualize "consistently." Evaluate "fairly." You could use these with just about any issue, whether it be one of romance, beauty, creativity, morality, God, science, the deeper mysteries of life, or even sex.

However, the majority of texts on critical thinking take a more focused approach. Put very simply, critical thinking boils down to two very simple questions:

*What are the facts? How do we know they're true?*

To elaborate:

*Critical thinking is the process of (1) evaluating a claim about objective reality and identifying support, and (2) considering alternative hypotheses.*

This needs a little unpacking. Let's examine each part of our definition.

### Stating a Claim, Identifying Types of Support

First, critical thinking involves stating and testing reality claims against three types of support:

- *Appropriate sources such as other people, groups, or institutions (Chapter 4);*
- *Correct use of the tools of logic and clear language (Chapter 5, Chapter 6); and*
- *Science (Chapter 7).*

### Alternative Hypotheses: Going Beyond Immediate Personal Experience and Intuition

Appropriate sources, logic and clear language, and scientific observation prompt us to be open to the possibility that there may be more than meets the eye, more to reality than what is apparent. They may suggest five alternative hypotheses. A mistaken conclusion that a paranormal claim is factual may be the result of:

- *Oddities in nature and the world of statistics (Chapter 8);*
- *Perceptual error or trickery (Chapter 9);*
- *Memory error (Chapter 10);*
- *Placebo effect (Chapter 11);*
- *Sensory phenomena, hallucinations, and psychiatric conditions (Chapter 12).*

This definition provides an outline of our text.

Critical thinking is reality checking. Thinking that masquerades as critical thinking, pretends to identify support, and fails to openly question personal experience and intuition is *pseudoscientific thinking*. A different way of looking at this is to consider the objectives. Is your goal to discover the facts (critical thinking) or protect your preconceived notions (pseudoscientific thinking)? Is your goal to put aside political, social, religious, or personal objectives in pursuit of the truth (critical thinking)? Or is it to "keep controversy alive" by sowing needless doubt and confusion in order to pursue another political, social, religious, or personal agenda (Oreskes & Conway, 2010)?

**Figure 1.2** Bats and ball. Reproduced with kind permission of Gettyimages.

## Bats, Balls, and Mind-Reading: Intuitive vs. Reflective Cognitive Thinking Styles

Stepping back, our definition is based on an important idea: the critical thinker takes pause and recognizes there may be more than *immediate personal experience and intuition*. First impressions and hunches, no how matter how vivid, may be misleading. One important area of cognitive research illustrates this idea. Consider these curious studies on the price of bats and balls.

An **intuitive thinking style** involves automatically going with one's first instinct. A **reflective thinking style** involves questioning such first instincts and considering other possibilities (Frederick, 2005; Stanovich & West, 1998). An intuitive thinker accepts what immediately seems to be true. A reflective thinker takes pause, questions first instincts, and considers other possibilities. As such, reflective thinking allows for counterintuitive conclusions. Importantly, a reflective thinker can suppress an intuitive and spontaneous wrong answer in pursuit of a less obvious answer that may be correct.

The Cognitive Reflection Test (CRT; Frederick, 2005) is a remarkably powerful and brief test that measures reflective and intuitive cognitive thinking styles. It consists of only three questions. Try this frequently cited example: "A bat and a ball cost $1.10 in total. The bat costs $1.00 more than the ball. How much does the ball cost?"

Is your answer $0.10? This is the intuitive answer, but it is incorrect. Reflective thinkers tend to suppress this automatic and intuitive answer because they are suspicious of the first thing that comes to mind. As a result, they are more likely to come up with the right answer, $0.05. (Ball = $0.05. Bat = $1.05. Bat + Ball total cost = $1.10. The bat costs $1.00 more than the ball; $1.05 − 0.05 = $1.00. Put differently, if the ball costs $0.10, and the bat costs a full $1.00 *more* than that, then the bat *alone* would have to cost $1.10. So the cost in total would have to be $1.10 + $0.10 or $1.20, not $1.10.)

Those who think intuitively are more likely to apply an emotionally appealing and immediately tempting paranormal explanation to an apparently paranormal event. In contrast, reflective thinkers are more likely to use critical thinking and take pause and look for a more complete explanation. While exploring a supposedly haunted house at night you may see a shadowy figure in a corner. Your shivering gut tells you it is a ghost. Or you may put aside your intuition and reflect that there might be other explanations, such as drifting cobwebs, window shades blowing in the wind, or simply scurrying mice.

The effects of intuitive and reflective cognitive thinking styles have been demonstrated in research. Bouvet and Bonnefon (2014) had students participate in what was described as an experiment in "telepathic transfer of information from one person to another." But the experiment was rigged to make it appear that extrasensory perception (ESP) was involved. Each student was paired with a "reader," someone who could presumably read minds. A student was given a stack of ESP Zener cards, each with a different symbol (star, plus sign, circle, wavy lines, square). He or she would then view one card completely hidden from the reader. The reader would attempt to use mind-reading to identify the viewer's card. Remarkably, the reader could do this successfully.

Actually the experiment was a trick. Unknown to the student, the reader was a plant working for the experimenter. During each session, the experimenter would secretly signal to the plant what card was being viewed.

Those who scored as intuitive (on the CRT) were more likely to say that ESP explained the odd results. This was true even if they did not particularly believe in ESP before the experiment. Reflective thinkers were more likely to explain the results as a statistical fluke. Both did find the results weird, suggesting that the reflective thinkers indeed could tell the results appeared to be paranormal.

In another experiment, Bouvet and Bonnefon gave students astrological horoscopes described as individualized personal descriptions. In fact, all were identical. Furthermore, all were actually fake horoscopes filled with meaningless generalities that could apply to nearly anyone (e.g., "You have a tendency to be critical of yourself."). Intuitive thinkers on the CRT were more likely to accept the "horoscopes" as personally accurate.

Yes, how people think (or fail to think) about bats and balls can tell us something important about open-minded critical thinking and the paranormal.

## The Time and Place for Critical Thinking

There may be a time and place for intuitive and reflective thinking. Some situations may be so complex that reflective analysis is not practical, and an immediate intuitive action is required. Perhaps at times intuition enables us to process a large amount of information unconsciously and quickly. Intuition may be highly desirable in considering questions not particularly amenable to critical analysis, for example, questions of love, beauty, morality, and God. On the other hand, intuitive thinkers may be at greater risk for fraudulent and deceptive manipulation, not only from unscrupulous psychics but for any type of persuasion that relies on a quick, unreflective response.

Concerning Alex's readiness for sex, one could consider claims about the objective risks of disease. However, objective reality checking may not apply to passions of the heart. Which museum has more beautiful art? A critical thinker might count the number of positive online reviews. But then beauty is in the eye of the beholder. What is the moral course of action? What is the will of God? A reality check may identify precise rules in a favored holy book or moral guide. Or one might rely on intuition or prayer. Some problems call for objective reality checking, others do not.

## Finding a Safe Practice Arena

If you want to become a master of critical thinking, you must do more than memorize a set of rules. A handy pocket list will be of little use in the battlefield of life. You need to practice. Where is the best place to practice? Where does a football player practice tackling a 250-pound receiver barreling at locomotive speed? Where does the rookie police officer practice nabbing a screaming terrorist wearing a suicide vest? Where does the surgeon practice slicing into one's chest to replace a heart valve? For future champions of critical thinking, what is the most appropriate practice arena? You want an arena that gives you a good workout, but one where there will be no bloody noses or broken bones.

One solution is to select a very limited subject area, for example repairing car mufflers, rearing children, writing college papers. Such targeted approaches work well for their restricted domains, but have limited generalizability. Skills for repairing a noisy car muffler may not always work for soothing a crying infant.

There are several arenas that work for most reality-testing skills, for example, science, politics, religion, journalism, and advertising. However, each has its drawbacks. Critical thinking applied to science can require specialized technical knowledge. Critical thinking applied to politics and religion can arouse distracting ideological passions. Journalistic critical thinking can be as dated as today's headline. Critical thinking applied to advertising can descend into the trivial.

There is one arena that has emerged as ideal, and indeed is the preferred choice for textbooks. Surprisingly, this is the world of ghosts, astrology, psychics, miracles, alien abductions, and magical cures. This is the world of the paranormal, the world of claims beyond science.

Think about it. Nearly everyone has at least one paranormal belief. And nearly everyone can identify a paranormal belief they reject as nonsense. Justifying either position requires sharp critical thinking skills. Paranormal claims have been around for millennia and permeate nearly every culture. You can find paranormal claims in science, politics, religion, journalism, and advertising – indeed just about every human endeavor. And frankly, the world of the paranormal is interesting. Applying and practicing our critical thinking skills can transform what might be a tedious exercise into something fun. And in this arena there should be few lasting bruises after our bouts of vigorous practice. In the following chapters, we will enter this arena with our saber and shield of critical thinking. In this book's final section, you can try your skills on more challenging claims. And I invite you to explore an extended sample of extraordinary claims in my companion text, *The Paranormal Sampler* (Smith, in press, createspace.com).

## The Four Challenges of the Open-Minded Critical Thinker

This book tries to make sense out of the strange and unexplained. We go beyond the ordinary, what we think is real. We will map the vast heavens of mysterious claims and explore reality-checking tools for determining which are true or false. My mission is not to convert you into a True Believer or True Skeptic. Instead, I invite you to take on the Four Challenges of the Open-Minded Critical Thinker.

**CHALLENGE 1: Have the courage to pause and reflect.**
**CHALLENGE 2: Question fearlessly and honestly.**
**CHALLENGE 3: Recognize that there may be more to the world than meets the eye, that things may be different than you wish.**

And perhaps most important:

**CHALLENGE 4: Admit you might be totally mistaken.** A true critical thinker can make this admission. In contrast, a True Believer cannot.

I invite you to apply these challenges to all life's mysteries, bright and beautiful, great and small.

## Study Questions

**1.1** *Definitions (Define, differentiate, and provide an example for each of the following)*
- A. Critical thinking
- B. Intuitive vs. reflective cognitive thinking style
- C. Practice arena
- D. Challenges of the Open-Minded Critical Thinker

**1.2** *Simple Thought Questions*
- A. What do you think is an area or topic that needs the application of critical thinking? Why? What are the possible consequences of uncritical thinking in this area or topic? What are some of the benefits of an intuitive thinking style?
- B. Is it possible to be a "closed-minded critical thinker"? What would it be like to engage in a discussion with such a person (perhaps about "the existence of ghosts")?

**1.3** *Essay Questions*
- A. Think of a question or choice in your life that cannot be satisfyingly answered through critical thinking? Why is that the case? What might be the costs of applying critical thinking? How might critical thinking help?
- B. *"How people think – or fail to think – about the prices of bats and balls is reflected in their thinking, and ultimately their convictions, about the metaphysical order of the universe"* (Shenhav, Rand, & Greene, 2011). Evaluate this observation using the concepts of this chapter.
- C. *"Perhaps one can be a reflective thinker and accept a paranormal claim reflectively"* (Tassi, 2012). What do you think?

**1.4** *Internet Search*
- A. Search "critical thinking" and find a definition that appears to differ from that of your text. What are the advantages and disadvantages of the term you discovered and the definition offered by your text?
- B. Search for definitions of "skepticism." How is skepticism similar to and different from our definition of critical thinking?

**1.5** *Conversation with a Classmate*

Most study guides include essay questions. Essay questions can be very valuable tools for teaching how to create and present an argument in textbook English. However, in real life our critical thinking skills are challenged, not by formal essays, but by what people say, text, and write in unexpected ordinary places – on the streets, by the water cooler, in the coffee house, over breakfast, and so on. Here one does not write essays.

I believe it is important to practice applying critical thinking in situations that resemble real life. Throughout this text we will attempt this through an exercise called "Conversation with a Classmate."

**Figure 1.3** A Klingon. Reproduced with kind permission of Fotolia.

In these exercises we begin with an email from a hypothetical classmate. He or she makes a challenging assertion. You reply with an email in which you explore and possibly question the assertion using textbook concepts. It is important that you write in the first person (*"Hi Student X. Thanks for writing. I disagree with your claim that vampires stole the cupcakes in the cafeteria, although I think I understand where you are coming from ...".*).

However, when creating this exercise I quickly discovered a problem. To make the exercise realistic, I wanted to use actual names (rather than "Student X," "A hypothetical person," or, God forbid, "John Smith.") But my editors noted that if I picked a real name I ran the risk of insulting someone who actually had that name, or perhaps some ethnic or national group. Here's my solution.

Klingons are a species of humanoid warriors in the famous science fiction series *Star Trek*. They are noted for their snarly personalities, rigid foreheads, spines, eight-chambered hearts, and multiple stomachs (all of which help them survive their frequent forceful encounters). The Klingon language is different from any human language. There is a Klingon dictionary (Okrand, 1992) and even a Klingon-English translator on the Bing search engine (which may prove useful for students exploring question 1.3C or the loving dedication on p. v). You can find a version of Shakespeare's Hamlet in the "original" Klingon (Nicholas & Strader, 2000), and translations of books of the Bible. "To be or not to be" in the original is *"taH pack taHbe."* (Note how Shakespeare was able to retain the alliteration and cadences of the original.) But we digress.

So, to avoid the possibility of insult, from this point on our examples will use Klingon rather than Human names.

Here is the complete list of students in our class of Klingons. These are actual Klingon names selected from a list of thousands available online (http://fantasynamegenerators.com/star-trek-klingon-names.php#.VVyg4FnBzGc):

| | |
|---|---|
| Gest Bimrat | Klong Pansato |
| Pelkewi Birc | Sasso Pondlil |
| Burf (the dog) | Dohla Qornang |
| Elana Emrem | Krorf Rrirdon |
| Eturd Ernoch | Obom Rrononn |
| Baltig Ev | Undun Sustradh |
| Durtid Ev | Jadoz Tassi |
| Yahi Firshack | Groshi Tharesbh |
| Otam Fistram | Bolkrom Thol |
| Ewith Gampazh | Jang Trenzaz |
| Urara Grolkolt | Dreth Ukrul |
| Yovon Haj | Lurinn Urni |
| Nemulo Hev | Drorf Vompaj |
| Ebek Hogur | Gil Vrunjol |
| Torkul Kadha | Borgh Wommruck |
| Yoho Krarang | Odros Xatzhog |
| Klurf K'tudij | Ovosi Zendloth |
| Tuss Lactaz | Chipolt Zolt |
| Ubaw Likirk | Jeska Zolt-Zonjag |
| Vinn Mennan | Ugrox Zonjag |
| Busti Mochirr | |

And now for our first email example, from one Chipolt Zolt.

TO: You
SUBJECT: Religion and doubt for Klingons
FROM: Chipolt Zolt

I think of myself as an intelligent critical thinker. For example, my culture teaches me that there are multiple gods; some have killed each other off. I believe it is honorable to question such claims, and I do so without fear. Indeed, only through such questioning does ones faith grow stronger.

Reply

TO: Chipholt Zolt
SUBJECT: Religion and doubt for Klingons
FROM: [Your name]

Hi Chipholt! It was good to read your thoughtful email. I always enjoy rowdy and civil discussions with my otherworldly classmates. Getting to your point: Religion is a very personal topic, and I think there are some religious ideas that aren't meant to be logically tested. I've read some of the accounts of battles of your gods, and some of them teach what it means to be courageous. But something you say confuses me. You see doubt as something very honorable. I get it. But doesn't that mean that you have to accept wherever your doubt takes you? What if in your open-minded search you conclude that Klingon gods never fought each other. But you say doubt is good because it strengthens belief. In this case doubt might lead you to change your belief. Aren't these paths contradictory?

Here's an example for you.

TO: You
SUBJECT: I saw it with my own eyes
FROM: Elana Emrem

Before we begin, I have to tell you about this incredible experience I had last week! My dear granny passed away last month. It was very sad. One night last week I went to her empty house to get some of my belongings. She had put them in her basement. As I walked down the stairs alone, the lights went out for about a minute. I heard a giggle that sounded like granny. She always liked to play jokes. I saw a misty figure next to her favorite chair. It looked like her, although very fuzzy. I felt a rush of cold air and the lights went on. At that instant I saw a blur moving from her chair to the window. It was her. I was terrified and walked to the chair. Sure enough, there were footprints in the dusty floor, right where I saw granny. I called for my sis, and she agreed that they were footprints. I saw granny's ghost. I know what I saw. Something was really there.

What is your civil reply?

TO: Elana
SUBJECT: I saw it with my own eyes
FROM: [Your name]

# 2

# The Paranormal Spectrum

*There are more things in heaven and earth, Horatio,*
*than are dreamt of in your philosophy.*

Hamlet (I, v, 166–167)

*All things bright and beautiful,*
*All creatures great and small,*
*All things wise and wonderful,*
*The Lord God made them all.*

Famous Anglican Hymn (Monk, 1875)

*'Extraordinary claims require extraordinary evidence'*

Popularized by Carl Sagan (Truzzi, 1976)

---

**OUTLINE**

1) Making Sense out of Mysteries: The Paranormal Spectrum
   a) Borderline and Gratuitous Paranormal Claims
   b) Simple Superstitions
   c) Paranormal Patterns
   d) Paranormal Powers
   e) Simple Life Energies
   f) Intelligent Forces and Entities
   g) Afterlife Entities
   h) Supernatural Entities
2) Extraordinary, Nonparanormal Mysteries
   a) A Theory in Search of a Fact
   b) Observations that Are Currently Unexplained

---

Have you ever made a wish that came true? Perhaps you carry a rabbit's foot or read the daily horoscope. Maybe you avoid walking under ladders, stepping on sidewalk cracks, or spilling salt, comforted by the thought that you are still alive and kicking. Nearly everyone has a habit or belief that others might call a bit superstitious.

Then there are the bigger mysteries. People spend millions on energy manipulation cures, psychic readings, and faith healing. Terrorists commit history-altering acts of suicide and murder driven by promised rewards in the afterlife. What are we to make of this world of extraordinary and strange claims? Why do they persist in the face of science? Is it possible some are true? Does it matter?

Decades ago, I started looking into things paranormal and supernatural. I was a teenager and my interests were not quite those of a scholar. My childish and magical wish was to become famous, build time machines, develop superhuman powers, or find a secret way to get good grades or hot dates. Before long I realized I had opened a treasure chest of claims, too many to fully understand. Overwhelmed, I turned to the more manageable study of psychology. But my curiosity about the mysteries of life never completely went away. In fact, it is difficult to avoid the world of the paranormal and supernatural. Like the proverbial gorilla, it sits conspicuously in the middle of the living room of life. If you ask the right questions, you will find that most of your friends and most professors, doctors, or preachers harbor at least one secret superstition.

## Making Sense out of Mysteries: The Paranormal Spectrum

What is the realm of the paranormal? This is a question of considerable interest to scholars. Clearly, mind-reading, astrology, and seeing into the future are paranormal claims. But what about acupuncture? Yoga? Space aliens? Silly mistakes of sloppy scientists? Dark energy? Typically, paranormal claims lie beyond science, that is, "normal" scientific observation and explanation. A paranormal event has not been observed, and if one were to be observed, any hypothesized scientific explanation would be inadequate.[1] This definition is not perfect, but it works quite well.

Consider the following:

*An invisible Flying Spaghetti Monster (FSM) creates everything, and hides all evidence of its existence.* This has never been observed (by definition, the FSM is not observable!).

*When playing the lottery, use the year of your birth and you are more likely to win.* If this were to really work, with no tricks, it could not be explained in any way by science. The claimed event is paranormal.

*A psychic can look at you and read what you are thinking. This is true, even if you are separated by a brick wall, the psychic doesn't know you, and you deliberately think of cards randomly selected from a deck.* This claim appears to rule out natural-world explanations such as reading body language and making good guesses based on what you are wearing. So it's a genuine paranormal claim.

*A nurse at a local hospital claims she can heal through therapeutic touch and cure your backache by gently waving her palm over your spine.* Such cures could be due to many things. People get over backaches on their own. Expectation can play a large role. Once you rule out these other explanations, you may have something paranormal.

Some mysteries are bigger than others. Cherishing a magic rabbit's foot isn't as dramatic as going to war over an astrological reading. I find it useful to organize paranormal and supernatural claims into eight groups placed on a *Paranormal Spectrum*

**Table 2.1** The Paranormal Spectrum.

| Lower-level paranormal claims | | | |
| --- | --- | --- | --- |
| **Borderline/gratuitous paranormal claims** | **Simple superstitions** | **Paranormal patterns** | **Paranormal powers** |
|  |  |  | 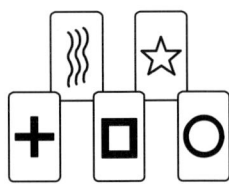 |
| • Bigfoot<br>• Loch Ness Monster<br>• Flying saucers<br>• Acupuncture<br>• Tai chi<br>• Firewalking<br>• Moon madness<br>• Many types of yoga and meditation | • Magic charms<br>• Rabbit's feet<br>• Stepping on cracks<br>• Number "13" | • Palmistry<br>• Tarot cards<br>• Reading entrails<br>• Tea leaves<br>• Some astrology<br>• Numerology<br>• Bible code | • ESP<br>• Psychokinesis<br>• Werewolves<br>• Fortune-telling<br>• Astral projection<br>• Out-of-body experiences<br>• Dowsing |

| Higher-level paranormal claims | | | |
| --- | --- | --- | --- |
| **Simple energies** | **Intelligent forces/ entities** | **Afterlife entities** | **Supernatural entities** |
|  |  |  |  |
| • Chi<br>• Magnet therapy<br>• Homeopathy<br>• Early chiropractic<br>• Traditional tai chi<br>• Traditional acupuncture<br>• Healing touch | • Yin/yang<br>• Spirits<br>• Karma<br>• Fate<br>• Comic book superhumans<br>• Vampires | • Reincarnation<br>• Ghosts<br>• Communication with dead | • Flying saucer cults<br>• Faith healing<br>• Organized supernatural religion with complex theologies, incorporating a literal heaven, hell, devil, angels, witches, saints, virgin births, resurrections, and fantastic miracles |

according to the degree to which they challenge what is or can be known by current science. Minor or *low-level paranormal claims* are on the left while *high-level paranormal claims* are on the right. You can see that higher-level claims are more *encompassing, complex,* and *organized.* More aspects of the natural world are brought into question, with greater diversity, and organized into an abstract belief system, itself divorced from the natural world. Claimed low-level processes have limited impact on our world, whereas high-level claims have greater potential impact.

It should be noted that all truly paranormal claims go beyond science. In that sense they are all equal. However, high-level paranormal claims are more elaborate than low-level claims. They more fully elucidate the implications and applications of a paranormal assumption, and posit additional parallel, perhaps equally improbable, assumptions. The belief that possessing a rabbit's foot will help you win the lottery violates what we know about matter and energy. Nothing about the chemistry and physics of a disembodied and dried piece of mammal anatomy should affect the random selection of winning lottery tickets thousands of miles away. If this could happen, then why not assume that wrinkle lines in the disembodied foot say something about your personality and future? Or that the foot possesses an energy that can cure warts? Or that the foot is indeed conscious and wants you to win the lottery and be wart-free? Or that the dead foot possesses the ghost of the recently deceased rabbit, a reincarnation of an ancient sage who is now your guardian angel and who wants you to be healthy, wart-free, and rich? All of these are equally improbable. All violate what science says we have observed or can explain. They differ primarily in their breadth, complexity, and organization.

Many paranormal claims come in several varieties each of which might be classified differently. For example, the claim that acupuncture releases brain endorphins or blocks pain gates is not paranormal. A vague claim that acupuncture opens blocked channels of unmeasurable life energy can be classified as a simple energy claim. A claim that the arrangement of stars at the time of one's birth contains information about one's personality and future is a paranormal pattern. However, it is an energy claim to state that the stars contain some mysterious force that can influence life on Earth.

### Borderline and Gratuitous Paranormal Claims

**Borderline paranormal claims** concern mysteries that need not violate the world of physics; nonetheless, true paranormal explanations are often entertained. For example, we have no clear evidence that flying saucers have visited Earth, but nothing in physics says that flying saucers from a different planet could not visit us. It might take a spaceship thousands of years using conventional rocket propulsion. Perhaps such a ship would be directed by robots or beings in hibernation. Or, to entertain a paranormal explanation, space aliens might slip from their home in the thirteenth dimension and instantly (and invisibly) appear on Earth. Such a paranormal explanation invokes a claimed phenomenon (travel from the thirteenth dimension) that runs counter to the physical world we know.

Closer to home, acupuncture is an ancient Chinese medical procedure that involves inserting needles in precisely defined points on the body. Acupuncture patients claim relief from a wide range of problems ranging from pain to hypertension. The traditional paranormal explanation is that acupuncture frees the flow of a mystical vital energy, chi, resulting in healing. Chi has never been detected and does not operate by the known laws of physics. A variety of contemporary nonparanormal explanations exists, including that the slight discomfort of inserting needles distracts one from pain, triggers the release of peaceful brain endorphins, reinforces expectations of cure, and so on. Thus, acupuncture represents a borderline paranormal claim.

Cryptozoology is the study of "hidden animals" ("cryptids"), claimed creatures whose existence is controversial (Heuvelmans, 1962). Examples include the Loch Ness Monster, Bigfoot, and various dragons of antiquity. Strictly speaking, there is nothing paranormal about cryptids because their existence would not violate the laws of physics. However, a few psychics have made additional paranormal claims, for example, that Bigfoot and Nessie are from some other dimension and can be conjured up psychically (Bauer, 1996). In such cases one might classify cryptozoology as a borderline paranormal claim.

**Gratuitous paranormal claims** offer a nonphysical explanation when there is no mystery to be explained. Why do leaves fall from trees? Because little fairies pluck them off. Why did you fail your exam when you didn't bother to read the textbook? Because Fate is punishing you for your irresponsibility. Why did your headache go away when you took the aspirin tablet? Because you unblocked the chi flowing to your brain. Why did your young nephew steal your cookies? The Devil made him do it. In each case there is no mystery to be explained, no need for a paranormal hypothesis.

Note the difference between pure, borderline, and gratuitous paranormal claims. Pure paranormal claims imply that an extraordinary event can be explained only by going beyond current basic science. No alternative explanations are sufficient. Borderline and gratuitous paranormal claims accept that current scientific explanations may work just fine and that paranormal explanations are simply alternatives. The remaining claims we consider are purely paranormal.

**Figure 2.1** Did flying saucers from another world, or from the future, once visit Earth? (borderline paranormal claim).

**Figure 2.2** Will possessing a rabbit's foot grant you good luck? (simple superstition).

**Figure 2.3** Do the creases in your palm reveal your personality, and future? (paranormal pattern).

### Simple Superstitions

Simple superstitions refer to everyday events that seem to violate the laws of physics. Generally, they are based on four types of support: (1) *coincidence*, (2) *folklore*, (3) "*similarities*," or (4) "*contagion*" (Frazer, 1911–1915). If you coincidentally won a card game

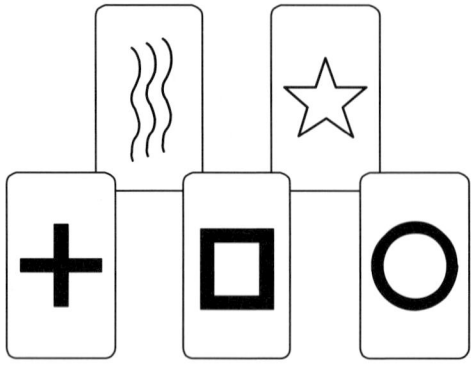

**Figure 2.4** Can psychics tell which of these special Zener ESP cards you are looking at ... with their eyes closed? (paranormal power).

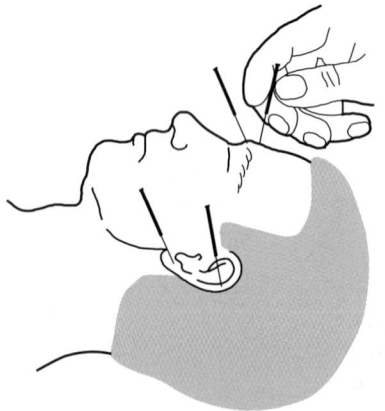

**Figure 2.5** Can acupuncture needle pricks release a powerful healing life energy? (simple paranormal energy).

while wearing a red shirt, you might wear this lucky shirt whenever playing cards. If your great-grandmother warned you never to peek at birthday presents, you might honor this rule because it is a bit of family folklore. Perhaps you think you are a bright and sunny person because of this similarity – you were born on a bright and sunny day. Maybe you shouldn't wear your great-grandfather's ring. After all, he wore it just before he died of a stroke and you don't want to "catch" his unfortunate, but contagious, luck. Perhaps bad luck can be like Ebola. And good luck can rub off on you. Simple superstitions are not encompassing, complex, and organized. Generally their broader implications are ignored or not elaborated. People do not devote careers to the risks of stepping on sidewalk cracks or avoiding the number "13." There are no rumors of secret Russian labs studying the feet of rabbits.

**Paranormal Patterns**

Are there secret messages embedded in the creases of your palm, tarot cards, tea leaves, entrails of sacrificial lambs, I Ching symbols, special combinations of numbers, the Bible code, and heavenly constellations? A relatively simple paranormal claim asserts that certain patterns contain special information that cannot be explained through any means consistent with contemporary physics. Palmistry claims that the wrinkles in the palm of your hand contain vast information about your history, personality, and future. There is no physical way this could be the case. Similarly, ancient tarot picture cards, particles of tea at the bottom of a tea cup, and the arrangement of intestines in a slaughtered lamb can be equally revealing. And, of course, astrology claims that the patterns of heavenly bodies present at the moment of your birth can say much about your life and future. Although such patterns may possess paranormal information, typically an individual with no paranormal ability can "read" the messages contained. Anyone with a book on palmistry can discover the secrets hidden in the wrinkles of a hand, and the message of a long "life line."

**Paranormal Powers**

Paranormal powers are limited human (and possibly animal) capacities that violate physics. However, few people possess or have cultivated such powers and these gifted individuals appear to be able to use them only in highly restricted circumstances. Examples include reading thoughts through extrasensory perception or bending spoons (or influencing the roll of a casino slot machine) through psychokinesis. People have devoted their careers to these topics. Libraries of books and articles have been written. And, of course, paranormal powers fuel a large part of the comic book universe.

### Simple Life Energies

Unlike paranormal powers, which may be limited and appear in select individuals at select times, simple life energies are enduring and more pervasive. Furthermore, they have the potential for affecting physical health and biological processes. For example, many practitioners of acupuncture believe that a mysterious paranormal energy, chi, permeates the human body and can be "unblocked" through the strategic insertion of needles. Unlike fate or karma, such forces do not guide, direct, or provide a purpose for actions. And unlike ghosts or spirits, they lack psychological characteristics such as thoughts, feelings, and intentions. However, simple life energies can be tapped and directed by individuals with paranormal powers. A skilled acupuncturist claims to use chi to heal.

**Figure 2.6** Does everything go well when "yin and yang," two principles that permeate the universe, are in balance? (intelligent force/entity). Reproduced with kind permission of Shutterstock.

### Intelligent Forces and Entities

Intelligent forces are also enduring and exist beyond the natural world. However, they have a complexity not possessed by life energies – an "intelligence" of their own that does not require the assistance of someone with a paranormal power. Such forces may be impersonal sources of guidance or direction, such as fate, yin/yang, the powers of prophetic astrology, karma, or some non-physical evolutionary principle that pushes toward "goodness" or "higher consciousness." Alternatively, intelligent forces may have psychological characteristics, such as consciousness, thoughts, feelings, and intentions, all internal complexities that enable us to call them **entities**. Examples include living objects possessed by spirits that wish us well.

**Figure 2.7** Are ghosts the spirits of dead people that can live in this world, and the next? (afterlife entity).

### Afterlife Entities

Afterlife entities are intelligent forces with one spectacular additional characteristic – they exist in this world and the world after death. They might include reincarnated souls as well as ghosts and some spirits. The existence of such entities permits communication with the dead.

### Supernatural Entities

The universe of the supernatural consists of paranormal claims that are exceptionally encompassing, complex, and organized. More aspects of the natural world are brought into question, with greater diversity. Supernatural beliefs are often organized into an

**Figure 2.8** Do some world religions – like Judaism, Islam, Christianity, Hinduism, and Taoism (represented here) as well as the Bahai faith, Buddhism, Pastafarianism, Shintoism, and Sikhism (not here) – make paranormal claims? (supernatural entities).

abstract conceptual system, itself divorced from the natural world. Supernatural entities have vast potential impact on our world.

Note that some purely supernatural entities may never intrude in the observable universe. Such a being would never make itself known, and would be forever unknowable. We do not know if there is one God (as in Christianity, Judaism, or Islam) or several (Hinduism, Greek and Roman religion), if God communicates with a flock of Angels, or if God created the Universe and retreated for the rest of eternity. Indeed, we may never know the private life of the great entity in the thirteenth dimension, why we've been dumped in a cosmic lunatic asylum (Hitchens, 2009), or who set the clockwork universe into motion and stood aside. Such *purely supernatural ideas* are off limits to science, but discussed extensively in various forms of literature, including personal accounts and diaries, Holy Scriptures, theology texts, science fiction and fantasy novels, and comic books. In contrast, some supernatural ideas claim a specific and measurable impact on the observable world. These are paranormal claims and are fair game for critical inquiry.

I am often surprised how vehemently practitioners of some religions object to the claim that some of their beliefs are paranormal. Yet they are perfectly comfortable identifying paranormal beliefs in other religions. Christians may object to labeling notions of the resurrection or virgin birth as paranormal, and yet fully accept as paranormal Hindu claims of reincarnation, that Allah dictated every word of the Qur'an, or that the Book of Mormon was inscribed on golden plates unearthed by Joseph Smith.

Should we be less critical of a paranormal religious claim that "serves an important social function" and "binds a community together"? Indeed this was the very opinion voiced by a review of the first edition of this work (PsycCRITIQUES, the comprehensive and authoritative database published by the American Psychological Association; Ludden, 2010). Are some supernatural paranormal claims off limits from critical inquiry? What do you think?

# Extraordinary, Nonparanormal Mysteries

A paranormal claim can be an extraordinary theory in search of an observation. A psychic might claim (correctly) that the science of quantum mechanics posits that two particles can be "entangled," in that the characteristics of one mirror those of another, even if they exist at opposite ends of the universe. He may proceed to claim that one person can read the thoughts of another, even if they are separated by a great distance (conceivably at opposite ends of the universe), providing their minds are "quantum entangled." This is an interesting theory, one that is indeed paranormal. However, there has never been an objective observation of such an event. The paranormal claim remains pure fantasy, *a theory in search of a fact.*

Another troublesome type of paranormal claim highlights the difference between the paranormal thinker and the Open-Minded Critical Thinker. These are scientific anomalies, observations for which there is no current explanation. However, it is unknown if science might eventually yield an explanation. The Open-Minded Critical Thinker takes a scientific stance and notes that this is an *observation that is currently unexplained*. The paranormal True Believer is more likely to invoke a *premature paranormal explanation.*

Sometimes an event seems mysterious simply because of our ignorance. I do not understand how flat screen televisions or laser pointers work, but I choose not to invoke a *premature paranormal explanation*. I am mystified by the feats of magicians, yet I know they are using sleight of hand.

But some phenomena are mysterious even to experts. Perhaps the most challenging is the notion of *dark energy*. Recently, astronomers discovered that the universe is expanding more rapidly than expected. There must be a type of "anti-gravity" or repulsive force to explain this mystery. Such dark energy is pervasive, making up the majority of the observable universe. Is this not a paranormal notion? First, most physicists agree that dark energy has been repeatedly observed. In that sense, it is not paranormal. Yes, science has no explanation for it, but given the current status of the science of physics, it is a good bet an explanation will be found.[2] So scientists use a special term, a **hypothetical construct** or **causal placeholder**, as a kind of **sticky note** to remind them that there's a mystery here that needs to be explained. The term "dark energy" is such a sticky note. The mysterious cause of the universe's expansion isn't actually *dark* and it may not actually be *energy* as we know it. However, it is easier to give it a name, "dark energy," rather than some boring code like "unexplained phenomenon # 325.112A."

Dark energy helps us define the paranormal. Indeed, we could provide a paranormal explanation for this repulsive force. "An entity in another dimension does not like matter and wishes to push it away using dark energy." Such an explanation is not supported by, indeed it contradicts, much of what science says. What dimension? What type of entity? Why would such an entity care about our dimension? Why would it (he or she) have "wishes"? It is much simpler to do what scientists have done for hundreds of years: simply acknowledge a mystery, and build upon what we already know in searching for an explanation.

To repeat, an Open-Minded Critical Thinker can tolerate the ambiguity of not knowing an answer; indeed, if there were no mysteries there would be no science.

The journey of science is paved with promises and sticky notes. A scientist has faith that the methods of reasonable and scientific inquiry can conceivably uncover the truth. The True Believer takes a bigger step and has faith in a specific explanation beyond science, even though natural-world explanations may eventually emerge.

Finally, I do not include as paranormal the millions of mistaken claims that stay within the boundaries of normal science. For example, you may believe that your gigantic gas-powered SUV gets 100 miles per gallon. As long as you do not claim your SUV uses a special miracle fuel, or runs on ghosts, you are simply mistaken. You may claim that eating nothing but rice and beans will cure all illness. For a known biological process to achieve this, a few laws of physics would have to be broken, and your claim would be paranormal. However, if you claim that the human body, and the physics on which it is based, can currently explain the curative powers of rice and beans, your claim is not paranormal. It is simply wrong.

There are many extraordinary claims that are the center of considerable controversy. Freud thought all men had latent homosexual urges. Is this true? How would you ever test this? Is Freud's long and tedious approach to psychoanalysis any better than simple 10-session therapies based on learning theory? Should evidence from lie detectors, and from hypnosis, be accepted in courts? Can graphologists really read your personality from your handwriting? Is the government really conspiring to hide the truth about UFOs, the Kennedy assassination, or 9/11? Is the medical community conspiring to hide evidence of simple and inexpensive cures available to everyone? Are childhood vaccinations dangerous? Controversial as these claims may be, none are paranormal. None require that we abandon physics.

## Study Questions

**2.1** *Definitions (Define, differentiate, and provide an example for each of the following)*
- A. Borderline paranormal claims
- B. Gratuitous paranormal claims
- C. Simple superstitions
  - Superstitious coincidence
  - Superstitious folklore
  - Superstitious similarity
  - Superstitious contagion
- D. Paranormal patterns
- E. Paranormal powers
- F. Simple life energies
- G. Intelligent forces
- H. Intelligent entities
- I. Afterlife entities
- J. Supernatural entities
- K. Extraordinary, nonparanormal mysteries
- L. Theory in search of fact
- M. Observations currently unexplained

### 2.2 *Simple Thought Questions*

- A. One of your classmates, Torkul Kadha (a Klingon, remember), claims that he can look at a stranger from a distance and make the person turn around. He can do this even if the other person doesn't know he is there and is totally unaware he is being watched. Do you think this is a paranormal claim? Why? Why not? If so, what type of claim?

- B. Elana (Torkul's friend) believes flying saucers may have visited Earth in the past. Is this a paranormal claim? Why? Why not? If so, what type of claim? What would make the claim paranormal?

- C. Deepak claims that he can converse with his departed great-grandfather through meditation. His great-grandfather often helps him out by answering questions. All Dreth has to do is ask, and changes happen. Is this a paranormal claim? Why? Why not? If so, what type of claim?

- D. Deepak elaborates his claimed ability to communicate with the dead. He says this happens in his dreams and fantasies. "My great-grandfather lives in my mind and is always with me." Is this a paranormal claim? Why? Why not?

- E. Rhodha has written a book that contains the secret to attaining health, happiness, love, and fortune. Simply visualize what you desire (like money coming in the mail), and like a magnet your positive thoughts will attract the positive outcome. "Similars attract – it's a law of physics." Is this a paranormal claim? Why? Why not? If so, what type of claim?

- F. Father Ebek Hogur makes a point of visiting the local hospital once a week. He visits a patient and brings good cheer. Sometimes he leads the patient in simple relaxation or prayer. He always encourages his patients to follow their doctors' orders and take their medications. The good Father believes that his efforts contribute to patient healing. Is this a paranormal claim? Why? Why not? If so, what type of claim?

- G. Otam drank 10 cups of coffee when cramming for an exam the next day. He passed the exam. His claim: "Coffee improved my performance." Is this a paranormal claim? Why? Why not? If so, what type of claim?

- H. Vinn observes that whenever he visits Mount Mennan, the starry sky and vast landscape make him "feel small and one with the universe." Is this a paranormal claim? Why? Why not? If so, what type of claim?

### 2.3 *Essay Questions*

- A. This chapter lists many paranormal claims. Some experts propose that to be paranormal a claim needs to violate some science, perhaps the science of biology, or chemistry, or even psychology. Identify and explain how any of our listed claims violates what we know about biology. Identify another claim and apply it to chemistry. Do it again for the science of psychology. Now, explain how each of these claims <u>also</u> violates what the science of physics says we have observed or can explain.

- B. Do you think religion is basically a paranormal phenomenon? Why or why not? (You might search the internet for "religion and the paranormal" or "secular religion.") What are the costs of viewing religion as paranormal? As viewing religion as not paranormal?

- C. Some paranormal claims can be classified in several categories. Think of one that covers at least three. Explain.

**2.4** *Field Exercise*

Find a friend or relative with a paranormal belief. Ask this person to describe their belief in detail. Where does it fit on the spectrum? Why? In what way does it contradict science?

**2.5** *Internet Search*

- A. You might be surprised to learn how many superstitions are out there. A simple internet search will give you an idea. Which are the most popular superstitions? Why?
- B. Do athletes have unique superstitions? What about different cultures or nationalities?

**2.6** *Conversation with a Classmate*

A classmate has just sent you the following email. What is your reply (using text-book concepts).

---

FROM: Eturd Ernoch
SUBJECT: Is "healing touch" paranormal?

---

Hi neighbor! Last week I injured my leg in a kickboxing debate tournament. Bad news! Fortunately, nothing was torn or broken, just a bit bruised and tense. I went to a local natural healing center and the nurse performed something she called "healing touch" on my aching legs. She slowly moved her hands up and down my calves, not quite touching them (her palms were always about half an inch from my skin). It was as if she was slowly brushing something away. She explained that she was sweeping away the "negative energy" in my leg and replacing it with "positive healing energy." I have to admit I could feel the warm energy coming from her hands, and my aching energy in my legs seemed to melt away every time her hands passed by.

Is the procedure my nurse performed paranormal? I'm confused because she said almost nothing about how it worked (except what I have described). She didn't say anything about the gods, other dimensions, spirits, or the like. What do you think?

---

TO: Eturd
SUBJECT: Healing touch

---

# 3

# What's the Harm? Why Study These Things?

*The unexamined life is not worth living.*

(Socrates, *Apology* 38a)

---

**OUTLINE**

1) Paranormal Claims Might Be True
   a) Meteors
   b) Hypnosis
2) The Costs of Unexamined Paranormal Claims
   a) Costs to Society
      i) Witchcraft
      ii) Nazi Holocaust
      iii) Political and social costs today
   b) Misguided Complementary and Alternative Medicine
   c) Superficial and Aggressive Religiosity
   d) Slamming Shut the Door of Critical Thinking: The Five Great Paths of Closed-Mindedness
      i) The Path of the Turtle
      ii) The Path of the Self-Appointed King or Queen of the Universe
      iii) The Path of the Magical Wonderland (subjective relativism)
      iv) The Path of the Paranormal Escape Hatch
      v) The Path of the Copout
3) The Costs of Closed-Minded and Uncritical Thinking
   a) The Path of Mistaken Belief
   b) The Path of Mistaken Helplessness

---

Why study the worlds of the paranormal? First, if you believe in such things you are not alone. Most people (73–76%) have at least one paranormal belief not derived from Judeo-Christian tradition (Moore, 2005; Newport & Strausberg, 2001) and 80–96% hold a religious-based paranormal belief (Bader et al., 2006). More people believe in astrology today than did so in the Middle Ages (Gilovich, 1991; Vyse, 1997). At the very least it is important to understand what our friends, neighbors, politicians, presidents, doctors, and preachers believe.

If you have a paranormal belief, surely it is valuable to know more about it. If you read the daily horoscope, do you really know how it was calculated? If you enjoy a good ghost story, do you know why some Christians are so opposed to Halloween (and Harry Potter), and why the United States government has officially recognized a witchcraft-based tax-exempt religion? If you go to an acupuncturist, did you know that this treatment is based on a form of energy which, if detected, could revolutionize physics?

*Critical Thinking: Pseudoscience and the Paranormal*, Second Edition. Jonathan C. Smith.
© 2018 John Wiley & Sons, Inc. Published 2018 by John Wiley & Sons, Inc.

## Paranormal Claims Might Be True

There is a deeper reason for exploring strange and extraordinary claims. Some might be true. A serious student of the paranormal should not have to waste time with unlikely claims, and should have the critical thinking tools for zeroing in on serious claims. History shows us many cases of disputed beliefs once considered crazy and then accepted as true. Two such phenomena are meteors and hypnosis.

### Meteors

In 1492, the year Christopher Columbus arrived in America, a 12-year-old boy in Ensisheim, Austria, heard a loud thunderclap and saw a stone fall from the sky and land in a field of wheat. He led townsfolk to the fallen rock, and quickly the excited crowd began chipping away the relic sent from God. Maximilian I, King of Austria, believed it was God's message that his battles against the French would succeed. (The Austrians did win.) This belief was typical. For millennia people had believed that meteorites were rocks from heaven and signs from God. Three hundred years later, about the time of the American Revolution, this thinking was to change.

In 1772, Europe's leading "think tank," the French Academy of Sciences, asked Lavoisier to take part in an investigation of rocks from the heavens. Lavoisier was

**Figure 3.1** The Ensisheim meteorite. Reproduced with kind permission of Science Source.

an excellent choice, having rejected the superstitions of alchemy and created the foundations for modern chemistry. He concluded that meteorites were produced by lightning (explaining their burned surface) and were not objects from the sky (Glenday & Friedman, 1999). Quickly the consensus among enlightened scholars was that meteors were impossible. Indeed Thomas Jefferson scoffed that rocks could not fall from the sky because there were no rocks up there (Hall, 1972). Museums throughout Europe tossed out their meteorites as superstitious rubble. The Austrian rock survived, probably because it was too heavy (280 pounds) to dislodge and survives to this day in a museum in Ensisheim (faithfully guarded by "The Brotherhood of St George of the Meteorite"). Of course, today we know that meteors come from space and burn as they fall through the atmosphere. Incidentally, Lavoisier lost his head to the guillotine during the French Revolution, but that is a different story.

Le Baquet de Mesmer.

**Figure 3.2** Mesmer's tub. Reproduced with kind permission of Wellcome images.

**Hypnosis**

Some still think of hypnosis as a paranormal phenomenon. However, today scientific hypnosis is respected and serious research has explored the application of hypnosis for treating problems such as pain, obesity, and smoking (Lynn & Kirsch, 2006). The lingering negative reputation of hypnosis can be traced again to seventeenth- and eighteenth-century France (with links to Lavoisier and the guillotine).

When people speak derisively of hypnosis, they often call it "Mesmerism," after Franz Anton Mesmer. Mesmer was a Viennese physician who won notoriety and popularity with his flamboyant sessions of "animal magnetism" (Pattie, 1994). In a darkened and colorfully draped chamber, Mesmer would utter hypnotic suggestions to willing female subjects as they touched magical iron rods embedded in large tubs of iron filings. These rods transmitted a special magnetic fluid, causing one to faint and fall into convulsions. Although many of Mesmer's subjects claimed spectacular cures, King Louis XVI was not impressed. The king appointed a learned panel that included commissioners from the Academy of Sciences, notably Lavoisier, Guillotin (responsible for the appliance used on Lavoisier), and the American Ambassador to France, Benjamin Franklin. Through a series of clever experiments, the commission concluded that Mesmer's treatment was nothing more than mere imagination requiring no special fluids. Mesmer was soundly discredited, and "Mesmerism" became synonymous with fraud and fakery, a connotation hypnosis carries even today. It is ironic that today the recognized clinical potential of hypnosis is often attributed to the healing power of imagination. As with meteorites, a phenomenon once discounted is now a legitimate topic of research (Gordon, 1967; Kroger, 1977).

So what if claims of the paranormal are true? If one paranormal claim were to be demonstrated beyond doubt, this could well be the most important discovery in the history of science. Such a discovery could easily justify the most massive international research effort ever, much larger than the program to create an atomic bomb or land a man on the Moon. Obviously, prematurely embracing such a project would be very costly.

For the student of paranormal claims, this extraordinary promise is an important reason to master the skills of open-minded critical thinking. It would be a tragedy to distract our attention with trivial claims. Critical thinking enables us to prioritize fantastic claims and pay serious attention to those that seem to hold the greatest promise. Why waste our time with werewolves and ghosts when some claim to have credible evidence that humans have the capacity to read thoughts or cure serious illness through simple touch?

## The Costs of Unexamined Paranormal Claims

One premise of this book is that extraordinary claims can have extraordinary consequences. Undeniable proof of a single superstition or single mysterious event that cannot possibly be rationally or scientifically explained could mean that the worldview of science has a defect. This in turn could require a new physics, a new astronomy, a new religion, and perhaps even a new appreciation of the ultimate mysteries of the universe. Yes, if your rabbit's foot worked, *really worked*, everything could change.

There is a dark side to this promise. Extraordinary claims can have extraordinary costs. For many years, I have been something of a recreational paranormalist. The paranormal has been a hobby, a treasure chest of curiosities. Then something happened.

Perhaps I encountered too many self-righteous psychic frauds, read too many foolish horoscopes, or witnessed too many casualties of misapplied alternative medicine. Perhaps it was the never-ending drama of medieval religious warfare and terrorism in the twenty-first century. Eventually it became abundantly clear that paranormal claims can do great harm. I see these potential dangers:

> *Costs to society*
> *Misguided complementary and alternative medicine*
> *Superficial and aggressive religiosity*
> *Slamming shut the door of open-minded critical thinking*

### Costs to Society

It is easy to find disaster stories of paranormal beliefs gone wild. Fanatical bombers kill thousands for bizarre supernatural beliefs and flying saucer cultists cheerfully commit

**Figure 3.3** Salem witchcraft trials. Reproduced with kind permission of Superstock.

suicide to prepare for promised alien rescue. However, murderous catastrophes in the name of the paranormal are nothing new. Perhaps the most spectacular examples in recent history are witchcraft trials and the Nazi Holocaust, both frequently cited in scholarly discussions of the paranormal.

### Witchcraft

In the early eleventh century, the Catholic Church considered belief in witches to be heresy. Witches simply did not exist. Gradually, the Church decided they did exist but were powerless in the face of God. However, in the fifteenth century, doctrine took a deadly turn. In 1494 Pope Innocent VIII issued a bull (named after the lead seal, "bulla," applied to the document.) proclaiming that witches cavorted with demons, destroyed crops, and aborted infants. He commissioned a study which yielded a text, the *Malleus Maleficarum* ("Witches' Hammer"). This document included stories of women having sex with demons, murdering babies, and stealing penises. The *Malleus* made it clear that Christians were obliged to hunt and destroy witches and gave judges and prosecutors torture-based tests. For the next three centuries it is estimated that over 200,000 witches were killed. With the dawn of the Enlightenment in the eighteenth century (about the time of Jefferson, Lavoisier, Franklin, and Guillotin), persecution of witchcraft subsided (Robbins, 1959). Scholars of the Enlightenment argued that there was no evidence for witches and that torture to elicit confessions was inhumane.

The most famous instance of witchcraft hysteria in America is the witchcraft trials in Salem Village, Massachusetts. In 1692 a group of young girls started behaving strangely, going into convulsions, screaming, and wandering about in trance states. Physicians could find nothing wrong, so city leaders concluded the girls were witches (today they would be rock stars). Village people began praying to chase the witches away. Eventually, the girls were forced to confess and 19 victims were tried and hanged. In addition, an 80-year-old man was crushed to death for refusing to be brought to trial.

One might discount witchcraft as a relic of unenlightened times. However, today roughly a quarter of Americans believe in witches and witchcraft. It wasn't until 2000 (on Halloween) that the state of Massachusetts officially exonerated the Salem witches, finally responding to centuries of tireless petitions of their desperate descendants (*New York Times*, November 2, 2001). Today Wicca is a recognized Earth-based religion that uses (only for good) some of the same paranormal practices of early witches.

### Nazi Holocaust

The degree to which paranormal thinking influenced Hitler and the Nazis in World War II is debated. Some of Hitler's top advisors consulted astrologers and used swinging pendulums over maps to locate enemy ships. The Nazis did hold a fanatical belief in a superior Aryan race, which was defiled when mixed with other, inferior groups (Niewyk & Nicosia, 2000). The claimed superiority may be derived from a fallacious borderline paranormal belief that Aryans were toughened by their harsh life in Northern Europe. Nazi beliefs supported the Holocaust and the extermination of six million Jews and countless minorities, disabled people, gay men, Jehovah's witnesses, non-Jewish Poles, and political prisoners. Again, most of these groups were reviled because of fictitious and borderline paranormal claims of blood inferiority.

### Political and Social Costs Today

Civilization has come a long way. The benefits of progress are obvious when we compare our lives with our ancestors 50, 500, or 5,000 years ago. Yet intolerable injustice and cruelty persist. Slavery, genocide, war, and terrorism continue for reasons that defy reason. I invite you to perform a thought experiment with the assistance of your favorite internet search engine. Pick a contemporary grotesque social atrocity. Alas, this should be relatively easy. I'm not referring to the latest hate crime or murder, but an act of terrorism, genocide, mass murder, or nationwide intolerance inflicted on thousands. Examine it closely. What justifications do the perpetrators offer? If we take the time to closely examine nearly any contemporary atrocity, we will often find some sort of paranormal belief, some guiding mistaken notion completely contrary to what science says. Notably absent will be any value of open-minded critical thinking. We will fail to discover any willingness to look at objective facts, question honestly and fearlessly, and admit one may be totally mistaken. Indeed, as part of your thought experiment, ask yourself what might happen if the perpetrators of your atrocity indeed questioned fearlessly and questioned honestly, and displayed a capacity to admit when they are completely mistaken.

### Misguided Complementary and Alternative Medicine

Complementary and alternative medicine (CAM), sometimes called "integrative medicine," includes a wide range of treatments not generally accepted as part of traditional medicine or taught in traditional medical schools. This includes a truly diverse assortment of approaches ranging from vitamin supplements, herbal treatments, and massage to yoga, acupuncture, tai chi, homeopathy, chiropractic, therapeutic touch, fasting, prayer, healing shrines, faith healing, and urine therapy. Saher and Lindeman (2005) sort these into approaches based on (a) paranormal claims, (b) inadequate or erroneous evidence, and (c) sound science. Up to 75% of the population believes alternative approaches are as effective as traditional approaches (Table 3.1) and over half the population uses alternative medicine (Barnes et al., 2004). The most common approaches (Clarke et al., 2015) are natural products (17.7% of the population uses), deep breathing (10.9%), yoga, tai chi, or qigong (10.1%), chiropractic or osteopathic manipulation (8.4%), meditation (8.0%), massage (6.9%), special diets (3.0%), homeopathy (2.2%), progressive relaxation (2.1%), and guided imagery (1.7%).

The medical establishment frequently warns of the dangers of alternative medicine (Angell & Kassirer, 1998; Fontanarosa & Lundberg, 1998) and questions their effectiveness (Bausell, 2007). Risks include the cost of ineffective interventions, safety (alternative approaches are generally unregulated), dangerous side effects, unexpected interactions with conventional treatments, and avoidance or delay in seeking traditional treatment. Tragically, the cost often falls on those least capable of defending themselves – children. Offit (2015) notes at least 200 cases of children who have died because they received healing prayer rather than standard medicine.

An understanding of the paranormal helps us understand and evaluate many of the claims of alternative medicine. Indeed, it may be the paranormal association that attracts many to such treatments (Saher & Lindeman, 2005). In chapters to come we will discover that often the same types of rationale given for voodoo spells, palm reading, and magic rabbit's feet have also been used to justify acupuncture, tai chi, and

**Table 3.1** Percentage of population who believe paranormal claims.

| Claim | Percentage |
|---|---|
| **Superstition and witchcraft** | |
| Witches | 28%[1] 26%[2] 26%[3] 23%[4] 26%[5] |
| Superstitious ("very or somewhat") | 24%[6] |
| **Spiritualism and ghostly experiences** | |
| Ghosts | 40%[1] 38%[2] 39%[3] 42%[6] 32%[7] 45%[8] |
| Haunted houses | 42%[2] 40%[3] 37%[7] 37%[9] 46%[10] |
| Spirit possession | 15%[2] |
| Communicating with dead | 28%[2] 16%[3] 21%[7] 20%[9] |
| Reincarnation | 21%[1] 25%[2] 14%[3] 25%[6] 5%[11] 20%[4] 24%[5] |
| **Fortune-telling and psychic readings** | |
| Psychics (etc.) foresee future, clairvoyance, prophecy | 32%[2] 13%[9] 14%[10] |
| Astrology | 25%[1] 28%[2] 17%[3] 33%[6] 25%[7] 26%[4] 29%[5] |
| Astrology impacts one's life and personality | 12%[9] 14%[10] |
| Dreams foretell future/reveal hidden truths | 52%[9] |
| Déjà vu | 69%[6] |
| **Scientific parapsychology** | |
| Telekinesis | 28%[9] |
| Extrasensory perception | 50%[2] 28%[3] 60%[6] 41%[7] |
| Telepathy | 36%[2] 24%[3] 31%[7] |
| Clairvoyance (psychic seeing) | 24%[3] 26%[7] |
| **Healing energies and faith cures** | |
| Psychic/spiritual healing | 54%[2] 56%[3] 59%[6] 55%[7] |
| Efficacy of alternative treatments | 75%[9] |
| Personally had illness cured by prayer | 34%[6] |
| **Space aliens and monsters** | |
| UFOs | 34%[1] 41%[6] 25%[9] 32%[4] 36%[5] 25%[10] |
| Aliens have visited Earth | 33%[2] 17%[3] 35%[6] 24%[7] |
| Bigfoot, Loch Ness Monster | 18%[9] 13%[10] |
| **Traditional religious beliefs** | |
| "God" (ambiguously defined) | 82%[1] 86%[12] 82%[4] 74%[5] |
| God (anthropomorphic plus non-anthropomorphic, see below) | 96%[9] |
| God (anthropomorphic – with human characteristics) | 70%[9] |
| God is male | 42% (2003) 36% (2006) 38% (2009) 39% (2013)[5] |

| Claim | Percentage |
|---|---|
| God is female | 1% (2003), 1% (2006), 1% (2009) 1% (2013)[5] |
| God is neither male nor female | 38% (2003), 37% (2006), 34% (2009), 31% (2013)[5] |
| God is both male and female | 11% (2003), 10% (2006), 11% (2009), 10% (2013)[5] |
| God controls what happens on Earth | 29% (2003) 29% (2006), 30% (2009) 29%(2013)[5] |
| Authoritarian paranormal entity involved in daily life and world affairs; God is quite angry and punishes unfaithful or ungodly | 31%[9] |
| Benevolent paranormal entity involved in daily life and world affairs; mainly a positive force and less willing to condemn or punish | 23%[9] |
| Critical paranormal entity who does not interact with the world; observes the world and views the current state of affairs unfavorably; justice is applied in the afterlife | 16%[9] |
| God observes but does not control what happens on earth | 50% (2003) 44% (2006) 43% (2009) 37% (2013)[5] |
| God neither observes nor controls what happens on earth | 6% (2003) 8% (2006) 8% (2009) 8% (2013)[5] |
| God (distant non-anthropomorphic paranormal (?) entity who is not active in the world and is not especially angry; God is a cosmic force which set the laws of nature in motion; God does not "do" things in the world or hold clear opinions about our activities or world events) | 24%[8] |
| Does not believe in God, not sure | 15% (2003) 18% (2006) 19% (2009) 25% (2013)[5] |
| "Heaven" (ambiguously defined) | 70%[1] 81%[12] |
| A person not of your religion can go to heaven | 79%[10] |
| Hell | 59%[1] 61%[4] 53%[8] 58%[5] |
| Devil possession | 41%[2] 40%[3] 59%[6] 42%[7] |
| The Devil | 61%[1] 70%[12] 60%[5] 47%[10] |
| Angels | 68%[1] 75%[12] 72%[5] |
| Creationism (Biblical account literally true) | 54%[1] 56%[6] 44% (1982) 47% (1993) 44% (1997) 47% (1999) 45% (2001) 45% (2004) 46% (2006) 43% (2007) 44% (2008) 40% (2010) 46% (2012) 42% (2014)[13] 40% (2013)[5] 36% (2013)[5] |
| Miracles | 73%[1] 76%[5] |
| Virgin birth of Jesus | 58%[1] 57%[5] |
| Resurrection of Jesus | 66%[1] 65%[5] |
| God literally answers prayers (most popular paranormal belief) | 83%[6] |
| Life after death | 70%[1] 72%[6] 71%[5] 64%[8] 64%[5] |

(Continued)

**Table 3.1** (Continued)

| Claim | Percentage |
|---|---|
| **Traditional religious beliefs and nonreligious paranormal beliefs** | |
| Believe in paranormal claims from traditional religion; do not believe in paranormal claims not from religion | 36%[6] |
| Believe in paranormal claims both from traditional religion and outside of religion | 40%[6] |
| Do not believe in paranormal claims from traditional religion, but do believe in paranormal claims outside of religion | 12%[6] |
| Do not believe in paranormal claims, either from or outside of traditional religion | 10%[6] |
| Percentage of Christians who believe in non-Christian paranormal claims (2009 Pew Forum) | Communication with dead 29%, Ghosts 17%, Psychics 14%, Spiritual energy in trees 23%, Astrology 23%, Reincarnation 22%, Yoga as a spiritual practice 21%, Casting of curses and evil eye 17%[14] |
| Percentage of general public who believe in non-Christian paranormal claims (2009 Pew Forum) | Communication with dead 29%, Ghosts 18%, Psychics 15%, Spiritual energy in trees 26%, Astrology 25%, Reincarnation 24%, Yoga as a spiritual practice 23%, Casting of curses and evil eye 16%[14] |

[1] Harris Poll, 2005 (Harris, 2005), 1,000 nationwide telephone poll. Retrieved February 4, 2017, from: http://www.prnewswire.com/news-releases/the-religious-and-other-beliefs-of-americans-2005-55544047.html

[2] Gallup Poll, 2001 (Newport & Strausberg, 2001). Retrieved February 10, 2017, from: http://www.gallup.com/poll/4483/Americans-Belief-Psychic-Paranormal-Phenomena-Over-Last-Decade.aspx

[3] Farha-Steward Poll, 2006 (Farha & Steward, 2006).

[4] Harris Poll, 2009 (Harris Interactive, 2015), 2,303 nationwide. Retrieved February 2, 2017, from: http://media.theharrispoll.com/documents/Harris_Poll_2009_12_15.pdf

[5] Harris Poll, 2013 (Harris Interactive, 2013), 2,250 nationwide. Retrieved February 2, 2017, from: http://www.theharrispoll.com/health-and-life/Americans__Belief_in_God__Miracles_and_Heaven_Declines.html

[6] Rice Poll (Rice, 2003), 1,200 random telephone interviews. Nationwide sample.

[7] Gallup Poll, 2005 (Moore, 2005), 1,002 nationwide sample, telephone interview. Retrieved February 12, 2017, from: http://www.gallup.com/poll/16915/Three-Four-Americans-Believe-Paranormal.aspx

[8] Omnibus YouGov Poll (2012), 1,000. Retrieved February 12, 2017, from: http://big.assets.huffingtonpost.com/ghosttoplines.pdf

[9] Bader et al. (2006). Retrieved February 20, 2017, from: http://www.baylor.edu/content/services/document.php/33304.pdf

[10] The Chapman University Survey on American Fears (Chapman, 2014), 1,500 Americans. Retrieved February 2, 2017, from: https://blogs.chapman.edu/wilkinson/2016/10/11/americas-top-fears-2016/

[11] Newsweek/Beliefnet Poll, 2005 (Newsweek/Beliefnet, 2005), 1,004 Americans. Retrieved February 12, 2017, from: http://www.beliefnet.com/story/173/story_17353_1.html

[12] Gallup Poll (Newport, 2007), 1,003 Americans. Retrieved February 12, 2017, from: http://www.gallup.com/poll/27877/Americans-More-Likely-Believe-God-Than-Devil-Heaven-More-Than-Hell.aspx

[13] Gallup Poll (Gallup, 2014), all polls involved about 1,000 Americans each. Retrieved February 12, 2017, from: http://www.gallup.com/poll/21814/Evolution-Creationism-Intelligent-Design.aspx

[14] The Pew Forum on Religion & Public Life (2009), 1,589 Christians. Retrieved February 2, 2017, from: http://www.pewforum.org/2009/12/09/many-americans-mix-multiple-faiths/

homeopathy. Proponents of alternative medicine often make the same logical and scientific mistakes made by those who claim to have been abducted by flying saucers or believe they are reincarnations of Cleopatra.

Unfortunately, alternative medicine is a catch-all category that lumps paranormal and borderline paranormal approaches with simple nutritional supplements, exercise, and relaxation. A patient may experience benefit from a relatively benign approach involving vitamins or exercise and conclude that alternative medicine has value. He or she may then feel comfortable exploring more risky borderline paranormal and paranormal alternative treatments. Knowing what's paranormal, and what's not, can help us navigate this medical minefield.

It is unethical and potentially dangerous for licensed health professionals to naively and uncritically accept paranormal treatments. Yet I have seen physicians and therapists embrace the mystery energies of chi, the curative power of prayer, and the healing magic of shamans – and pride themselves for their openness to alternative cultures, and sensitivity to non-Western wisdom. My wish is that all health professionals at least buy this book.

## Superficial and Aggressive Religiosity

Organized religion plays an important part in people's lives. Throughout history, paranormal claims have been sources of religious controversy. Jesus rejected temptations from Satan to turn stones into bread and fly off mountains to impress the masses. Buddha warned against meditation distractions of psychic powers. Mohammed condemned magic as deceptive evil contrary to God's will. Yet virtually every major world religion has devotees that are passionate advocates of the paranormal. Psychic powers are sometimes viewed as miraculous signs of God's intervention or of spiritual growth.

Bestselling polemics such as *The God Delusion* (Dawkins, 2006), *The End of Faith: Religion, Terror, and the Future of Reason* (Harris, 2004), *Waking Up* (Harris, 2015), and *God is Not Great: How Religion Poisons Everything* (Hitchens, 2007) argue that supernatural paranormal beliefs breed fanaticism, war, and oppression. Typically they cite the Crusades, ethnic cleansing, and a variety of religious wars, and more recently terrorists claiming Islam. People of faith counter with examples of genocide in atheistic countries such as the Soviet Union, China, and Cambodia, and that criticism of religion verges on bigotry. Skeptics respond that in such atheistic countries, leaders had become like gods, convinced of their god-like significance and privilege. At the very least, Stephen Jay Gould (1999) has suggested we note "… the stunning historical paradox that organized religion has fostered, throughout Western history, both the most unspeakable horrors and the most heartrending examples of human goodness." And Christopher Hitchens (2007) notes that throughout history atheists have been every bit as generous and self-sacrificing as believers.

Let me offer some hypotheses: (1) Any belief (either paranormal or skeptical) can become dangerous when embraced with dogmatic fervor, without honest and fearless questioning or the recognition that one may be completely mistaken. (2) High-level paranormal beliefs are more risky than low-level beliefs. More generally, I propose that religions tend to get combative when they apply paranormal claims of the supernatural to earthly politics and social policy. God wants your group to own or conquer this plot of land. God wants you to kill infidels. God wants you to love others by showing off your religion. God wants you to wear a hat in church, as long as it is not red or made of cloth of mixed fibers. It helps us gain perspective to realize that many of these holy injunctions are justified by the same type of thinking used to justify astrology, flying saucer cults, and witchcraft. However, as I noted in the previous chapter, I believe a sincere and careful contemplation of God must acknowledge and genuinely accommodate the tools of critical thinking. A truly religious person can question honestly and question fearlessly. An adult spirituality need not fear the reality check.

### Slamming Shut the Door of Critical Thinking: The Five Great Paths of Closed-Mindedness

If we open the paranormal box just enough to let one claim out, a world of unintended consequences may flutter out and cloud the skies of open-minded critical thinking.

If we accept one extraordinary paranormal claim that fails to meet a few sensible reality checks, we are intellectually obligated to accept all paranormal claims that have equivalent support. If you believe in ghosts, you must also believe in astrology, reincarnation, TV psychic superstars, prophetic pets, alien abductions, communication with the dead, fortune-telling, mental spoon-bending, and a Pandora's box of other treasures. Why? If you dig deeply enough, all have equally sincere, honest, sane, intelligent, educated, articulate, famous, and passionate proponents.

Think of how crazy your world would become if you indeed embraced every fantastic magical claim as true. Miracles, ghosts, angels, alien abductions, time travel, thought control, bending spoons, becoming invisible, seeing into the future, living forever. Everyone could become Superman, Wonder Woman, or both! Quite a world!

For paranormal researchers this can pose a problem. Which of many paranormal claims are worthy of study? If we waste our time with pointless claims we run the risk of missing those that might be true. We can view open-minded critical thinking as one of the best tools available for looking for diamonds in the rough. Conversely, a closed-minded person may well miss something truly remarkable. For these reasons, we conclude with the Five Great Paths of Closed-Mindedness:

1)  *The Path of the Turtle (Play Hide and Sleep)*
    Turtles pull their heads and limbs into their shells to hide from danger, and to sleep. This is a metaphor for our first closed-minded choice. "I believe it, and that's that. End of discussion. I don't want to discuss it any further. I may be wrong or right – I don't care. You may be able to point out flaws in my thinking, but it doesn't matter." This person hides and sleeps – hides from honest questioning and goes to sleep as an Open-Minded Critical Thinker.

2)  *The Path of the Self-Appointed King or Queen of the Universe*
    This path is similar to the path of turtle-like avoidance and sleep. However, your belief is not arbitrary. You can identify specific support for your claims. And you are willing to engage in civil discourse. However, you embrace your paranormal belief but reject other claims based on equivalent support. Ghosts are real, but werewolves, zombies, and angels are not. "I believe in ghosts because I saw one and I read an article by a professor. Other people are silly to believe in werewolves, zombies, and angels, even if this is what they've experienced, and even if they're professors."
    Rejecting claims based on types of support you accept makes you a very special person indeed. You are saying "my reality-checking rules are the only ones that are

valid." You are a kind of King or Queen of the Universe, exempt from the nuisances of open-minded critical thinking that plague the rest of us. More seriously, what gives you the right to cherry-pick how to use reality-checking rules, and deny that right to the rest of us?

3) *The Path of the Magical Wonderland (Subjective Relativism)*

One solution to our dilemma is called **subjective relativism** (or postmodernism). Here all truth is relative and personal. Reality depends on what you believe, not on what really is. It's OK to cherry-pick your paranormal beliefs as long as you grant others the same right to selectively believe what they want. This liberates you from the chore of thinking critically and questioning honestly and fearlessly. You get the additional benefit of appearing to be open-minded (being "open" to the beliefs of others). Taken to its extreme, you could think up quite a magical wonderland of delights.

Consider the following hypothetical blog between Dohla (a Klingon nurse) and her friend Vinn:

DOHLA:   I believe that when I touch people I can cure their arthritis.
VINN:    Why do you believe that?
DOHLA:   I took a nursing course on therapeutic touch and got continuing education credit for it. (http://www.healingtouchprogram.com/resources/faq) I've tried touching arthritic patients and they report they've been cured.
VINN:    Did you get any medical confirmation?
DOHLA:   No. I believe what my patients say. They're honest people.

Dohla is making a simple paranormal claim involving healing touch. It is typical of those who use this approach. Our blog continues:

VINN:    My grandmother is a nurse trained in voodoo and she says she can cure arthritis by sticking pins in dolls owned by her arthritis patients.
DOHLA:   Why does she believe that?
VINN:    Because her patients report they've been cured, and they are honest people.
DOHLA:   That's beautiful! Your grandmother comes from a culture that believes in voodoo pin cures. My culture believes in healing touch. See how our beliefs create our realities? Reality is relative.

Here's where things get interesting:

VINN:    So I'm thinking that your belief is totally false. I'm thinking "healing touch creates hives and rashes."
DOHLA:   Huh …
VINN:    That means you're having fun creating reality using your thoughts about the healing effects of healing touch. Then all of a sudden I destroy this reality by thinking opposing thoughts about healing touch and hives.
DOHLA:   Wha …
VINN:    You said your thoughts create reality. So there's a dollar bill in your pocket because you're thinking it. And I'm thinking that there's no dollar bill in your pocket. It's in my pocket. I'm thinking I took it. This could get ugly.
DOHLA:   You're just being mean! Give me my dollar back!

Prominent researchers of the paranormal often embrace subjective relativism as a new type of science, one that promises to uncover paranormal mysteries that have eluded old-fashioned science and logic (Irwin & Watt, 2007). However, such a fantasy begs for a reality check. First, subjective relativism has yet to produce a verified fact. More seriously, if we follow subjective relativism to its logical conclusion, we fall into an inevitable pit of absurdity. Consider these problems:

- Subjective relativism is *self-defeating*. If you can will something to be true, someone else can just as easily will it false. In our world it is logically impossible for something to exist and not exist at the same time.
- Subjective relativism is a logical contradiction and is *self-refuting*. The subjective relativist believes that in the real world there are no absolute truths because everything's subjective. If subjective relativism is a part of the real world, then it too is not absolutely true. If subjective relativism isn't always true, then there are indeed some absolute truths. But because everything is subjective, there aren't any absolute truths …
- Subjective realism can be a *science stopper*. Let's imagine that you have decided that the natural worldview is relative, and that one must consider alternative worldviews not based on what is scientifically observable or explainable. So, what's the harm of being open-minded and accepting an alternative worldview? Imagine you believed that studying the livers of butchered pigs enabled you to tell the future (some cultures once believed this). When it comes to liver-based fortune-telling, your alternative worldview may prohibit you from ever discovering for sure if it doesn't work. Every time a liver forecast fails, your alternative worldview can explain it away (evil spirits got in the way, the universal mystery energy blocked the forecast, you were fated to get a defective liver). In other words, subjective realism permits you to stop questioning and offer a never-ending torrent of excuses for any scientific test that fails to go your way. These include: "It works differently for different people," "You have to believe in it for it to work," and "It works in ways you might not detect." This is a pretty effective science stopper.

4) *The Path of the Paranormal Escape Hatch*

Many feel comfortable having one paranormal belief, reassured by the thought that they have perfectly reasonable criteria for rejecting others. You may believe in the power of acupuncture to modify chi, but reject astrology and ghosts. You may accept the biblical miracle of the virgin birth, but consider Noah's Ark to be a myth.

How might you pull this off? Create a *paranormal escape hatch,* a seemingly sensible rule that states clearly, if arbitrarily, what beliefs you can accept or reject. Here are some more examples: "Although I may have some beliefs that run counter to science, I will not abandon science when making important decisions." The constitutional separation of church and state is perhaps the most famous example of an institutionalized paranormal escape hatch. Your religion may require acceptance of a variety of paranormal claims. However, keep your religion separate from your vote. Here the US Constitution rules.

Acupuncture has been claimed to cure just about every ailment to afflict humankind. However, proponents frequently deploy the paranormal escape hatch of recommending you see a licensed physician if you have a serious illness. A faith healer may claim that her cures will invoke healing powers from an all-powerful deity.

However, just to be safe, see a doctor if you have a fever. Uri Geller, the famous psychic, claims to bend spoons with his thoughts – however, not when a qualified magician (with "negative energy") hands him the target kitchenware.

In sum, a paranormal escape hatch permits you to temporarily bail out of a paranormal belief when such a belief becomes difficult to defend or justify. They are magical in that you conveniently invoke or forget them whenever you want. Magically, you can even be an absolutist and relativist at the same time. Let's walk through this.

Consider this pair of assertions:

> *My special mystical chant invokes a powerful spirit that cures all illness.* (Thus: this is an all-powerful spirit.)
> *When I think I'm having a heart attack, I go to the emergency room.* (Thus: the chant-spirit is not all-powerful.)

This escape hatch permits you to have it both ways.

Magical paranormal escape hatches can work quite well. However, they ultimately postpone an uncomfortable moment of reckoning and set you on a path of costly hatch maintenance. How do you justify your escape hatch? What makes your escape hatch better than mine? Put differently, if you can accept one escape hatch, why not give yourself a blank check for all the hatches you desire? That way, you can safely believe anything. Why not grant everyone the right to create their own escape hatches? But this is just another way of jumping on the yellow brick road of subjective relativism. The paranormal escape hatch can be a very slippery slope.

5) *The Path of the Copout*
An argument similar to subjective relativism takes no stand concerning the validity of conflicting claims, but suggests that in the spirit of open-mindedness we consider them all. In many cases this is obviously a reasonable choice – but only when there is indeed a controversy. Otherwise to "consider the controversy" is to "consider the copout."

We will encounter such quasi-relativist thinking in our later discussion of the debate between creationism and evolution. Darwin's theory of evolution is taught in biology classes. Should we also teach the six-day biblical creation myth as theory? What about creation "theories" offered in other cultures, for example, those of the ancient Romans, Native Americans, Northern Europeans, and so on? Perhaps astronomy textbooks should grant equal time to astrology or the six-day theory of cosmic creation in the book of Genesis; chemistry texts should consider the alchemy of transforming lead to gold; history texts, the reincarnation of Cleopatra; medical texts, the evil spirit theory of disease; criminal justice texts, the devil-possession theory of crime; and family-planning texts, the stork theory of childbirth. Consider the controversies! Again, an Open-Minded Critical Thinker has to evaluate when to draw the line. To avoid this responsibility is to be closed-minded.

## The Costs of Closed-Minded and Uncritical Thinking

There are costs to carelessly embracing extraordinary claims. Stepping back, there are more general costs to choosing to close your mind and avoid the rigors of critical thinking. There are costs to becoming a True Believer and having absolutely no interest in or curiosity about the world as it is.

1) *The Path of Mistaken Belief*

   Honest and fearless questioning is the best way we have of getting things right, of seeing things as they really are. Refusing the question opens you up not only to the world of unproven alien abductions, pixies, and devil possession, but also to more ordinary factual errors. When sick, you may misdiagnose your symptoms and make deadly medical decisions. You may choose the wrong residence, the wrong school, the wrong home, the wrong spouse, the wrong pet. Put simply, by abandoning open-minded critical thinking you choose to drive the raucous highway of life with eyes firmly shut.

2) *The Path of Mistaken Helplessness*

   When you believe in something that is not factually true, obviously you limit your ability to change it. If you believe rain dances move the deity to make rain, then you set yourself up for the frustration of ineffective dancing. If you believe virtuous behavior will increase the length of day, again you will be frustrated. Furthermore, if you believe your actions are going to be ineffective, you will learn to be helpless. Sometimes this is a realistic facing of the fact ("Alas, I can't change the mind of God when it comes to rain." "Alas, I can't move the planets.") Sometimes it is undesirable and leads to inaction ("The government controls everything, so what's the use in voting?" "The government lies when it says there's climate change, so I won't conserve gas.") This is the cost of mistaken helplessness.

---

**Why Do You Believe?**

What paranormal claims do you believe? Maybe you are a firm believer. Maybe you believe just a little. Over the past decade I've been examining 12 claims commonly tapped in polls of paranormal and extraordinary belief:

1) Acupuncture and other Oriental treatments cure through an invisible and mysterious energy field
2) Angels are literally real
3) Astrology
4) Communicating with the dead
5) Dream prophecy
6) Flying saucers from other planets have visited Earth
7) Fortune-telling and seeing into the future
8) Ghosts and haunted houses
9) Herbal medicine
10) Psychic mind-reading and extrasensory perception
11) Prayer can heal people from a great distance, even when they don't know they're being prayed for
12) Reincarnation and past lives

Appendix A describes in detail research I have conducted with colleagues on these beliefs. I would like to share some highlights here.

**What Do You Believe?**

Most polls of the paranormal simply ask if you do or do not believe, using "yes/no" questions. Those that do ask for levels of belief (Bader et al., 2006) typically fail to report their differentiated data, and often lump categories together. Such studies at times provide extreme categories ("Strongly Agree, Agree, Disagree, Strongly Disagree, Undecided") that provide no option for the open-minded questioner or skeptic ("Believe slightly, Believe somewhat"). Using the data from such research, the popular press, as well as critical thinking texts, frequently proclaim the large number of believers in the paranormal, especially in highly educated societies. But I think my learned colleagues in the critical thinking community may be mistaken. Yes/no questions yield misleading answers.

My research asks, "To what extent do you believe? Do you (1) not believe, (2) believe a little, (3) believe somewhat, or (4) believe very much?" A rating of "1" or "4" reflects a rejection or embrace of a belief, disbeliever vs. believer. I hypothesize that levels "2" and "3" reflect "open-minded questioning belief," characterizing someone who has chosen less than total acceptance of a claim, presumably because of persisting questions about the claim. My way of asking belief questions reveals some surprising patterns.

Before continuing, pick your favorite claim, and indicate your degree of belief.

My Favorite Claim:

---

### Degree of Belief

○ I do not believe ○ I believe a little ○ I believe somewhat ○ I believe very much

How do you compare with undergraduates? We asked 554 undergraduates from a Midwestern university this very question. The results for each belief are shown in the chart below. I've shaded choices selected by at least 20% of our sample. Where do you fit?

This table reveals results obscured by generic polls. Four patterns characterize overall degree of belief or disbelief in the paranormal:

Pattern 1: Belief
Pattern 2: Open-Minded Questioning
Pattern 3: Polarization
Pattern 4: Skepticism

Patterns 2, 3, and 4 merit additional discussion.

*Open-Minded Questioning: Astrology, Acupuncture, Psychic Mind-Reading/ESP, Dream Prophecy*
Numerous polls show about 35.5% of the population believes in ESP, 55.2% in dream prophecy, and 23.1% in astrology. However, such polls miss that open-minded questioners constitute more than 70% for each of these groups. Believers actually constitute 12.2% or less.

*Polarization: Ghosts and Haunted Houses, Communicating with Dead, Reincarnation*
Numerous polls show 40.5% of the population believes in ghosts and haunted houses, 19.1% in reincarnation, and 21.3% in communicating with the dead. We find this may reflect the number of believers. More realistically, people may well be polarized, with sizable numbers believing and not believing in ghosts/haunted houses, communicating with the dead, and reincarnation.

**Table 3.2** What do college students believe?

| (Numbers in brackets show percentages of "believers" in generic polls) | I DO NOT BELIEVE (%) | I BELIEVE A LITTLE (%) | I BELIEVE SOMEWHAT (%) | I BELIEVE VERY MUCH (%) |
|---|---|---|---|---|
| PATTERN 1: BELIEF | | | | |
| Herbal medicine [75] | 5.6 | 19.4 | 38.6 | 36.4 |
| PATTERN 2: OPEN-MINDED QUESTIONING | | | | |
| Astrology [23.1] | 9.8 | 43.9 | 34.1 | 12.2 |
| Acupuncture [1.5 claim to use[1]] | 14.3 | 40.5 | 35.7 | 9.5 |
| Psychic mind-reading/ESP [35.5] | 16.7 | 40.5 | 35.7 | 7.1 |
| Dream prophecy [55.2] | 19.1 | 26.2 | 45.2 | 9.5 |
| PATTERN 3: POLARIZATION | | | | |
| Ghosts/haunted houses [40.5] | 9.3 | 34.9 | 18.6 | 37.2 |
| Reincarnation [19.1] | 30.5 | 22.2 | 30.6 | 16.7 |
| Communicating with dead [21.3] | 28.1 | 37.5 | 21.9 | 12.5 |
| Prayer at a distance [83.0] | 24.4 | 19.5 | 26.8 | 29.3 |
| PATTERN 4: SKEPTICISM | | | | |
| Angels [71.7] | 33.3 | 22.3 | 16.6 | 27.8 |
| Fortune-telling [22.8] | 42.1 | 36.8 | 15.8 | 5.3 |
| Flying saucers [34.8] | 50.0 | 15.6 | 28.1 | 6.3 |

[1] Clarke et al. (2015). Retrieved February 7, 2017, from: https://www.cdc.gov/nchs/data/nhsr/nhsr079.pdf

Generic polls show that the vast majority of the population (83.0%) believes that God literally answers prayers and that prayer-based miracle cures are real. In contrast to surveys of belief in psychics/ESP, reincarnation, and ghosts, polls on healing prayer appear to overstate the number of True Believers. We find that a different pattern emerges if we refine the question. Instead of asking if "faith cures," or "miracle cures are real," or "God answers prayers," we ask, "Does God answer healing prayers from a distance, even outside of the patient's awareness?" Here we see a polarized pattern: 29.3% are believers while 24.4% are nonbelievers.

*Skepticism: Flying Saucers/Fortune-Telling, Angels*

We find an average of 34.8% of the population believes in flying saucers. However, there are more flying saucer skeptics (50.0%) than for any other belief we've tested. The next most skeptical groups consist of those who don't believe in or believe very slightly in fortune-telling (total: 78.9%) or angels (55.6%).

**Why Do You Believe?**

If we further refine our belief questions, things get even more interesting. Over the years I have asked thousands of students why they accept various paranormal and extraordinary claims. My research has revealed nine "whys" or "justifications" people often use to support their beliefs.

1) Argument from ignorance ("This shows there's a lot science doesn't know about the world. This is real because there's no evidence against it. This is a mysterious truth science can't explain.")
2) Conspiracy theory ("The medical/scientific community doesn't want people to know about these things. The authorities are keeping this kind of information from us.")
3) Eyewitness testimonial ("This is something many people have experienced. This has been described in many eyewitness reports.")
4) Family and culture ("This is something my family has accepted for a long time. This is something I've been taught is true. This is something people in my culture generally believe.")
5) Faith and religion ("This is supported by my spiritual and religious teachers. This is supported by the existence of God. This is consistent with my faith.")
6) Media support ("This is supported on TV shows and documentaries. This has often been reported in the news media.")
7) Personal experience/intuition ("This is something I have personally experienced. This is true because it just feels right. This fits what my intuition tells me.")
8) Science ("This is supported by science. This is supported by research studies by scientists and experts.")
9) Test of time ("This has passed the test of time. If something has lasted this long, there must be something to it.")

These are assessed by my "Belief Justification Survey," which I invite you to take in Appendix B at the end of the book. Why do people believe? Once again, it is important to refine the question. What justifications become increasingly important as level of belief rises? Do believers use different justifications from those used by people who are more moderate in their belief? The answer is clearly "yes." The one justification most strongly associated with strength of belief is **personal experience**. This accounts for 34% of the differences in level of belief. Three additional contributors are **argument from ignorance** and **family and culture** (adds 5%) and **science** (adds 1%).

In sum, the stronger your belief, the more likely you will justify it with personal experience, supplemented by argument from ignorance, family and culture, and to a little extent, perceived scientific support.

These variables far outweigh other variables frequently cited in the paranormal literature, including conspiracy theories, eyewitness testimonial, faith and religion, media support, and perceived test of time.

When inviting others to consider paranormal beliefs, our research suggests offering alternative explanations for personal experience and intuition. One might also consider logical challenges to argument from ignorance (later in this book), as well as examples of open-minded critical thinking in one's family and culture.

It is perhaps a coincidence that each of these scientifically unearthed primary justifications for strength of belief is associated with a different section of this text:

| Justification | Chapter |
|---|---|
| Personal experience | Part 2: The Critical Thinker's Toolkit |
| | Part 3: Alternative Explanations |
| Argument from ignorance | Chapter 5, Logic |
| Family and culture | Chapter 4, Sources |
| Science | Chapter 7, Science |

## Study Questions

3.1 *Basic Concepts*
- A. Why were meteorites once considered to be paranormal?
- B. What is the Ensisheim meteorite? Why is it important?
- C. How was Benjamin Franklin an Open-Minded Critical Thinker?
- D. Explain what happened in the Salem witchcraft trials. Why were these trials important?
- E. Define complementary and alternative medicine.
- F. According to your text, when can religious beliefs be dangerous?
- G. Name the Five Great Paths of Closed-Mindedness.
- H. Define the Path of the Turtle.
- I. Define the Path of the Self-Appointed King or Queen of the Universe.
- J. Define the Path of the Magical Wonderland.
- K. Define subjective relativism.
- L. What are the problems with subjective relativism?
- M. Define the Path of the Copout.
- N. Define the Path of the Paranormal Escape Hatch.

3.2 *Simple Thought Questions*
- A. Pick any paranormal claim on the Paranormal Spectrum. If science demonstrated it was factually true, what might the consequences be? How might they be revolutionary, or catastrophic?
- B. If we accept even a simple paranormal claim we might have to accept others. Why? What would be the consequences of not accepting other claims?

**3.3** *Essay Questions*
- A. Describe an example in which you were engaged in a discussion with a person displaying closed-minded thinking. Explain which of the Paths of Closed-Mindedness were illustrated.
- B. According to public opinion polls, what paranormal beliefs are enduringly popular? Why? Which have changed over the years? Why?

**3.4** *Field Project*
Why do some people have paranormal beliefs, while others are disbelievers or ambivalent? Find a friend or relative who is willing to talk about their paranormal or supernatural beliefs. (Alternatively, you can simply discuss your personal responses.) Ask them if they are willing to answer a few simple questions. Use this script:

> *Hi! I'm interviewing some people for a class I am taking on the paranormal. This is not an experiment. Nearly everyone has a paranormal or supernatural belief. I'm trying to find out why people have their beliefs. What's your paranormal or supernatural belief? You may pick one from this list*

- *Acupuncture and other Oriental treatments cure through an invisible and mysterious energy field*
- *Angels are literally real*
- *Astrology*
- *Communicating with the dead*
- *Dream prophecy*
- *Flying saucers from other planets have visited Earth*
- *Fortune-telling and seeing into the future*
- *Ghosts and haunted houses*
- *Herbal medicine*
- *Prayer can heal people from a great distance, even when they don't know they're being prayed for*
- *Psychic mind-reading and extrasensory perception*
- *Reincarnation and past lives*

Then give your person the Belief Justification Survey.

Your assignment is to write an essay discussing your person's responses. What are the 4-8 main reasons your person gives for accepting their chosen paranormal/supernatural claim? How do your results compare with what is presented in the box "Why Do You Believe?" and information in Appendix A?

**3.5** *Internet Search*
Is witchcraft still practiced? Where? Is it practiced in any modern industrialized country? (Do not include "Wicca.")

**3.6** *Videos*
"Secrets of the Psychics" is a classic 1993 NOVA introduction to paranormal claims. The documentary "An Honest Liar" is a more recent version (2015). Both

documentaries are hosted by famous magician and founder of the critical thinking movement James Randi. Do an internet search of "Secrets of the Psychics James Randi" and view at least three segments. Which of the Five Great Paths of Closed-Mindedness can you find?

**3.7** *Conversation with a Classmate*

---

FROM: Ugrox Zonjag
SUBJECT: I believe! What's the harm?

---

Hi, friend! I think you're getting too upset. I am not a superstitious person! I see myself as very sensible and open-minded. But there's a long tradition in the Zonjag family of the "Power of Pebble-skipping." Go for a walk along the shore and find a pebble about the size of a hand. It must be flat, smooth, and shiny. Take a crayon and print your secret wish on the back of the pebble and fling it into the water so it skips. If it doesn't skip, that means your desire wasn't sincere enough, so try again. When you can finally get the pebble to skip at least twice, your wish will come true! I accept this belief because it always works for me. My friend, I see absolutely no harm in this little belief! Don't be so closed-minded!

---

TO: Ugrox
SUBJECT: Your pebble skipping. What's the harm?

---

Part II

The Critical Thinker's Toolkit

# 4

# Sources

---

**OUTLINE**

1) Ancient Wisdom
2) Testimonials and Anecdotal Evidence
3) Mass Media and the Internet
4) Popularity (and Common Use)
5) Groupthink
6) The Question of Authority
7) When Authorities are Never to be Trusted: Conspiracy Theories
8) Even the Experts Can Get It Wrong: The Importance of Replication
   a) Failure to Replicate
   b) Publication Bias and the File Drawer Effect
9) An Invitation to Question

---

Perhaps the easiest way to support a claim is to accept what others report. In most cases this involves trusting their logic and testing and evaluation of hypotheses and theories, or perhaps their sources. A good source uses the foundation of sound logic and science. An inappropriate source can lead to fallacious logical conclusions (see Chapters 5 and 6) or flawed scientific observation (Chapter 7). In this chapter we will examine some reality-checking precautions one needs to take when considering support from sources.

## Ancient Wisdom

Just because an idea is very old doesn't mean it's true. Some old ideas are downright silly. After all, we no longer talk to rocks or consult volcanoes for political advice. Some erroneously liken survival of an idea over time to a sort of informal "scientific test." Presumably, over the millennia people have tested astrological predictions and found them valid, otherwise they would abandon astrology. However, I doubt non-Babylonian systems such as Mayan astrology failed to gain worldwide acceptance because people over time found them less effective. As we will see throughout this text, there are many ways in which vast numbers of people can be fooled, even for millennia. And the survival of a belief system over history often has to do with the charisma of its proponents, and how well they wage war. If you accept astrology as valid because it is ancient, then you also have to accept the wisdom of witchcraft, the sadistic injunctions of the Old

*Critical Thinking: Pseudoscience and the Paranormal*, Second Edition. Jonathan C. Smith.
© 2018 John Wiley & Sons, Inc. Published 2018 by John Wiley & Sons, Inc.

**Figure 4.1** Head of bearded old man (Wenceslaus Hollar). Reproduced with kind permission of Metmuseum.

Testament, and voodoo, because all are equally ancient. And you would have to suspect Shakespeare, Lincoln, and Einstein because they are less ancient.

The world overflows with a special type of ancient wisdom, venerable inspirational texts rich with poetry and moral instruction. Such works have guided humankind for millennia and are often embraced without careful thought. Before accepting such sources wholesale, it is wise to ask a few questions:

- Are insights ambiguous and subject to various and contradictory interpretations?
- Do contradictory passages permit one to "cherry-pick" those that fit one's preexisting biases?
- Are there passages that make sense even in light of current knowledge?

## Testimonials and Anecdotal Evidence

If you ask enough friends, eventually you will find one who can testify to the accuracy of horoscopes. Such testimonials are often called anecdotal evidence. Testimonials and anecdotal evidence can be persuasive, especially if they are from credible and honest sources you know personally.

Even intelligent and honest people can be fooled. One case proves nothing. For every glowing testimonial, there may be thousands, even millions, of disappointed users (we may never know how many, given they probably don't speak out).

Carroll (2005) has offered a succinct evaluation of anecdotal and testimonial evidence:

> Anecdotes are unreliable for various reasons. Stories are prone to contamination by beliefs, later experiences, feedback, selective attention to details, and so on. Most stories get distorted in the telling and the retelling. Events get exaggerated.

Time sequences get confused. Details get muddled. Memories are imperfect and selective; they are often filled in after the fact. People misinterpret their experiences. Experiences are conditioned by biases, memories, and beliefs, so people's perceptions might not be accurate. Most people aren't expecting to be deceived, so they may not be aware of deceptions that others might engage in. Some people make up stories. Some stories are delusions. Sometimes events are inappropriately deemed psychic simply because they seem improbable when they might not be that improbable after all. In short, anecdotes are inherently problematic and are usually impossible to test for accuracy.

## Mass Media and the Internet

Some of the best newspapers and magazines in the world have published positive articles on astrology. Of the 30 million internet hits, some are pretty impressive.

Again, popularity isn't proof. Mass media and internet sources may or may not reflect authentic expert opinion. When considering articles and websites, use the criteria we considered for evaluating the qualifications of an expert. Note that the standards for getting something in the mass media are lower than for professional publication. And anyone can post any claim on the internet. Among the worst sources are slickly produced paranormal "documentaries" on cable networks that feature documentaries. Having subjected myself to over 100 shows on ghosts, flying saucers, psychic detectives, miracles, angels, and communicating with the dead, I must report that for every 10 unacceptable programs you may find one of quality. Programs on the paranormal are notorious for editing out disconfirming evidence, interviewing questionable and fraudulent sources, and engaging in outright deception. Remember that such programs are designed to be entertainment.

## Popularity (and Common Use)

It isn't particularly difficult to realize that the popularity of an idea doesn't mean it's true. Women used to be (and often still are) viewed as property. Various racial groups were once viewed as subhuman. Amazon.com lists twice as many books for astrology (70,000) as for the Ten Commandments (35,000).

## Groupthink

Groupthink occurs when the desire for group harmony or conformity impairs thinking and decision-making and leads to uncritical acceptance of group opinion. As such, it can be considered from various perspectives, including psychology and sociology. We will view groupthink as a complex of source errors. Consensus is valued over critical evaluation of alternatives and careful consideration of outside input. In terms of source errors, the inflated importance of the group and group loyalty leads to an unrealistic acceptance of in-group decisions (Janis, 1982; McCauley, 1989).

**Figure 4.2** How might a protest demonstration display groupthink? Reproduced with kind permission of Getty images.

Eight main symptoms of groupthink are frequently cited in the literature (Janis, 1982):

*Type 1: Group overestimation*
1) *Illusion of invulnerability.* Group members fail to note dangers and display excessive and risky optimism.
2) *Illusion of morality.* Members feel they are morally correct and even ignore or rationalize the negative consequences of their thinking and decisions.

*Type II: Closed-mindedness*
3) *Collective rationalization.* Members discredit and explain away potential problems or negative consequences of groupthink.
4) *Excessive stereotyping.* Group members establish rigid negative stereotypes of members of "outgroups."

*Type III: Pressures toward uniformity*
5) *Pressure for conformity.* Members pressure those who display critical thinking toward any group actions or opinions. Dissent is labeled disloyalty.
6) *Self-censorship.* Members refrain from critical thinking.
7) *Illusion of unanimity.* Members believe, often falsely, that everyone is in agreement; silence is consent.
8) *Mindguards.* Members appoint themselves minders of groupthink, protecting members from critical thinking and dissenting information.

Perhaps the best guard against groupthink is open-minded critical thinking, a consistent willingness to question.

## The Question of Authority

*Some of the most famous scientists in the world, indeed, even the founders of science, believed in astrology. If it was good enough for Copernicus, Tycho Brahe, Galileo, it's good enough for me.*

Just because someone is an expert in one field doesn't mean they are an expert in another. You wouldn't go to a "doctor" for cancer treatment if this "doctor" had a doctorate in insect physiology. Famous actors may know how to act, but they aren't necessarily experts in health and living. Just because a politician or religious leader is popular doesn't mean he or she is all-knowing. Everyone is ignorant about something.

When evaluating whether someone is an expert it is useful to consider if they are:

- educated and are trained from a relevant and up-to-date program or school;
- experienced and have accomplishments in their area of claimed expertise;
- current (ancient experts may no longer be relevant);
- respected among peers, other experts in their area.

Generally, when an authentic expert rejects a claim, or several experts disagree, there is good reason for us to doubt the claim. In my experience, the mainstream scientific community is often suspicious of claimed experts who:

- make exaggerated and unqualified claims and, for example, conclude that paranormal phenomena are conclusively and unambiguously supported by research (look for unqualified superlatives, such as "breakthrough," "revolutionary," "proven," or "pioneering");
- have a record of gullibility, for example, accepting as credible demonstrations of the paranormal clearly shown to be fraudulent or in error;
- fail to differentiate well-designed studies from those compromised by poor design, error, and the possibility of fraud;
- have a record of failing to report breaches in good design; and
- resort to ad hominem arguments (Chapter 5) when rejecting sincere criticisms of skeptics (accusing critics of being mean-spirited, narrow-minded, dogmatic, and the like). It is misleading to divide paranormal researchers into two groups, dogmatic believers and dogmatic disbelievers. There are many who are inclined to believe or not believe who are nonetheless willing to take an honest look at the evidence.

Finally, when considering the miraculous claim of a paranormal expert, it is useful to apply **Hume's Maxim**. David Hume was an eighteenth-century Scottish philosopher famous for his book *An Enquiry Concerning Human Understanding*. He argued: "That no testimony is sufficient to establish a miracle, unless the testimony be of such a kind, that its falsehood would be more miraculous than the fact which it endeavors to establish" (Hume, 1758/1958, p. 491). In other words, which is more miraculous? (1) That someone making a paranormal claim is deceiving or deceived, or (2) the claimed paranormal event actually happened. After making up your mind, reject the testimony of the greater miracle.

## When Authorities are Never to be Trusted: Conspiracy Theories

Given all the reasons we have provided for questioning sources, you might think it is best to reject all authorities. Perhaps they are all out to deceive us. Perhaps all are hiding something. This is the gist of conspiracy theory thinking.

A conspiracy theory is an attempt to explain big adverse events in terms of secret (and usually sinister) plots by powerful people or organizations. The conspirator seeks to change institutions, acquire power, hide truth, or gain influence at the expense of the common good (Uscinski & Parent, 2014). Conspiracy theories are popular, held by up to 63% of Americans (Seitz-Wald, 2013). Some recent examples include:

- The US government created AIDS.
- The 9/11 attacks were faked by the government to drum up support for the military.
- The medical community is suppressing evidence that cheap natural herbal remedies can cure a variety of diseases.
- Scientists fake temperature records to support the idea of global warming.
- The FBI is hiding evidence of who killed JFK or Martin Luther King.
- The Air Force is hiding evidence of extraterrestrial visitors.
- NASA faked the Moon landing using elaborate Hollywood sets.
- The British government murdered Princess Diana.
- The government is adding fluoride to drinking water to weaken the population.
- Bin Laden was never killed, but escaped.

To these we can add a wide range of generic conspiracy theories, for example that elections are stolen, that businesses design products to fail early, and that information about any current political or social crisis is being hidden.

Of course, some conspiracy theories prove to be true. The critically thinking citizen, consumer, patient, and student must be vigilant. How can one identify plausible conspiracies so as not to be distracted by false claims?

Rob Brotherton (2013) suggests that questionable conspiracy theories:

- lack evidence;
- are less plausible than alternative explanations;
- are sensational;
- assume global malign intent, in a black/white good/evil world;
- are beyond disproof.

Brotherton's final characteristic merits elaboration. A typical questionable conspiracy theory is unfalsifiable, a concept we will return to again and again throughout this book. Any contrary argument or evidence can be rationalized away, usually as further evidence of a conspiracy. For example, is the medical community hiding a natural and cheap cure for cancer in order to keep oncologists in business? You might argue that at least medical journals would jump at the chance of becoming famous and increasing sales by publishing a cheap cancer cure. But the medical community owns medical journals, and would quash any claims. But patients could try these cures on their own and broadcast their success through media interviews. But a conspiracy theorist could reply that these "cures" are not real, but planted by people who are against doctors. The argument can go on forever.

Wood, Douglas, & Sutton (2012) have found that people often embrace multiple and contradictory conspiracy theories. For example, an individual may claim that Osama Bin Laden is dead (secretly killed by the CIA), and the same individual may later claim that Bin Laden is still alive (secretly whisked away by the CIA). The government may be hiding information about possible impending epidemics (to minimize panic); the government may be leaking information about disease risk (to increase profits for drug companies selling flu remedies). How is this possible? Contradictory beliefs suggest an important feature of conspiracy theories: they are **monological** (Goertzel, 1994), that is, different conspiratorial notions are consistent with a central overarching belief in how the world works, as Brotherton suggests (2015), "the idea that somebody is always engaged in deception, there is always more to events than meets the eye, we are never told the whole story." Such people are *conspiracy minded* (Brotherton, 2015), prone to believe in conspiracies for everything. Research finds that the best predictor of whether you hold one conspiratorial belief is whether or not you hold another, regardless of what it is. Furthermore, this pattern may well be even more encompassing: beliefs in conspiratorial, pseudoscientific, and paranormal claims all seem to go together. The conspiratorial thinker is more likely to "accept a whole host of unconventional claims" (Brotherton, 2015). Goertzel suggests that the monological nature of conspiracy theories makes them self-perpetuating in that they support each other. If you accept one conspiratorial claim, this opens Pandora's box and you are open to others. Indeed, evidence for one theory can readily serve as evidence for others.

Who believes in conspiracy theories? Uscinski and Parent (2014) have found that gender, age, income, political affiliation, and occupational status do not matter. Republicans and Democrats are equally likely to believe in conspiracies. Liberals may believe that the media and political parties are controlled by capitalists and business, whereas conservatives that liberals and professors are in control. It may well be that nearly everyone accepts at least one conspiracy theory (Goertzel, 1994).

It is tempting to discount conspiracy theories as a type of personality disturbance. Perhaps the conspiracy theorist suffers from a "paranoid style," in which judgment is distorted (Hofstadter, 1964; Groh, 1987; Robins & Post, 1997). The paranoid style is not an incapacitating mental illness. Those who possess it may be perfectly normal and function well. However, it is a widespread condition waiting to be triggered by appropriate social conditions. The fruits are McCarthyism, The People's Temple of Jim Jones, and extreme nationalism. We see the rise of tyrants such as Hitler and Stalin.

Some have proposed that the paranoid style hypothesis goes too far. Perhaps a less severe aspect of paranoid thinking, a pervasive suspiciousness, is a key feature (Swami et al., 2013).

Recent research suggests that conspiratorial thinking may be activated whenever one perceives a threat or personal vulnerability, that is, when one's sense of control has been undermined. Such threats may emerge in times of conflict, economic uncertainty, social strife, illness, and environmental crisis. Shermer proposes a general human propensity to seek patterns, connect the dots, even to the point of preferring false alarms to missed threats (Shermer, 2011; see Chapter 9, Perceptual Error and Trickery). Under threat, one acquires a sense of control and understanding by connecting the dots in a perceived conspiracy.

Conspiratorial thinking may well be adaptive when occasional threats are real. At the very least, such thinking lessens the risk of missing a threat. Fearing a hidden bear lurking behind every tree increases the likelihood avoiding an actual bear. Today, sensitivity to conspiracies may well motivate people to demand more transparency in government as well as more discussion.

However, there is a dark side. Promoting a conspiracy theory can contribute to inaction and helplessness. Jolley and Douglas (2013) report that presenting individuals with information supporting a conspiracy theory actually increases powerlessness, uncertainty, and disillusionment, and reduces the propensity to take action (such as voting or changing behavior, for example by reducing one's carbon footprint). One way of inhibiting meaningful social action may well be to present information that appears to support conspiratorial thinking, especially when it is monological.

## Even the Experts Can Get It Wrong: The Importance of Replication

It seems to happen every month. A friend or student eagerly barges into my office proclaiming the "latest scientific finding." Or a journalist calls asking for a comment on the "latest psychological discovery" reported in a respected psychological journal. Alas, in most cases I find myself playing the sad and solemn role of Deflator of Balloons. A single study never makes a fact. Too much can go wrong. *A fact is a fact only when it is replicated, observed by different people using the same or better tools.*

### Failure to Replicate

How serious is the problem of lack of replication? A 2015 study provides a dramatic hint. In an extensive psychological study (Open Science Collaboration, 2015) no fewer than 270 researchers identified 100 prominent psychological studies from three very respected scientific journals. Each study was repeated, often using the very same materials and methods. The findings were shocking. Overall, "replication effects were half the magnitude of original effects, representing a substantial decline. Ninety-seven percent of original studies had statistically significant results. Thirty-six percent of replications had statistically significant results" (Open Science Collaboration, 2015). *To repeat, only thirty-six percent of the original studies could be replicated.* (However, even replications need to be replicated. Subsequent scholars have questioned the findings of the Open Science Collaboration; Gilbert et al., 2016).

Why do scientific studies fail to be replicated? Sometimes the answer is sloppiness or misuse of the tools of science, a topic we consider in Chapter 7. Perhaps a researcher fails to understand the laws of chance, and the fact that flukes can emerge, even in the halls of science. We consider oddities in the world of statistics and numbers in Chapter 8.

### Publication Bias and the File Drawer Effect

Scientists and scientific journals have a bias toward submitting and publishing positive results and discarding null or negative results. This is called **publication bias** or the **file drawer effect** (Rosenthal, 1979).

Consider the steps involved in getting a study published. First a scientist, usually employed by a university or medical establishment, conducts a study. He or she may have several under way. Grant funding, promotion, prestige, and even tenure may ride on publishing positive results. Given such incentives, a researcher could easily "put off until later" completing and writing up studies that seem to be producing negative results. (In other words, these studies die from loss of interest and end up in the recycle bin.) It appears that it is at this stage, when authors fail to write up and submit null findings, that most of the file drawer effect takes place (Franco, Malhotra, & Simonovits, 2014).

Once a study is submitted for publication, a journal has incentive to publish positive results. The editors may well have honorable intentions. Perhaps they want to encourage research in an unexplored area. Perhaps they want to help others recognize a positive result as having potential benefit for those in distress. Maybe they want to sell more copies of their journal, and unexpected positive results sell, especially when the paranormal is involved.

Malhotra and his colleagues at Stanford University (Franco, Malhotra, & Simonovits, 2014) have actually measured this problem. They examined 221 sociological studies from 2002 to 2012 initially approved for completion. Only 48% of the studies completed were eventually published. Which studies got published? For the null studies, those showing no effect, only 20% appeared in journals. Most (65%) were never even submitted. In contrast, about 60% of the studies with positive results were published. Researchers of the unpublished studies explained they did not submit their work because they felt journals would not consider them, or that the results were uninteresting. In general, publication bias and the file drawer effect are pervasive. Positive results are from three to 12 times more likely to be published than studies finding no effect (Dickersin et al., 1987; Dickersin & Min, 1993).

One way of protecting against publication bias and the file drawer effect is to examine the quality of a study. One of the strongest findings in scientific research on the paranormal is a negative correlation between study quality and obtained support for the paranormal (Bausell, 2007; Hines, 2003). Poorly designed and inexpensive studies are more likely to yield positive results. Good studies are much less likely to yield positive results. This is the opposite of what is found in all other areas of research. Ordinarily, the better the study, the more likely it will find an effect. Another tool is **study registration**. Researchers can publically announce or register completed plans to initiate research. Once the research plans are in the public domain, resourceful scholars can explore which were actually completed and what their results were. Perhaps the best protection is the replicated observation. The more replications, the better.

## An Invitation to Question

We could not function without taking the word of others we respect. We trust our drinking water is not poison, our vehicles will not collapse into piles of nuts and bolts, and our grocery stores will be stocked with food. We hope our children obey our rules not to play in streets, take candy from strangers, or eat yellow snow. However, there are times when we have to think for ourselves, ask questions, and perform reality checks. There are times when we have to take on the burdens of adulthood and not live as children. Perhaps one of the most important lessons of this book is that respected, honest, sincere individuals can get it wrong. Your professors, doctors, politicians, and preachers can suffer profound delusions. These delusions can persist for thousands of years. Never assume that the claims of your favorite authority are always based on the best of sources, logic, or science, or that their claims are immune from the errors of misinterpreting the oddities of nature; perception; memory; the placebo effect; or sensory anomalies and hallucinations. To begin, look at the logic and examine the science, topics we will consider in the following chapters.

## Study Questions

**4.1** *Basic Concepts*
- A. Define and explain:
  - Ancient wisdom
  - Testimonials
  - Anecdotal evidence
  - Mass media
  - Internet
  - Popularity
  - Publication bias
  - File drawer effect
  - Study registration
- B. What are the eight main symptoms of groupthink?
- C. Which of the "Four Challenges of the Open-Minded Critical Thinker" do those engaged in groupthink avoid?
- D. Define Hume's Maxim.
- E. What are the defining characteristics of a conspiracy theory?

**4.2** *Simple Thought Questions*
- A. Which of the eight categories of the Paranormal Spectrum are more likely to rely on authority as support? Why?
- B. Conspiracy theories are often monological. Explain.
- C. When is the tendency toward conspiratorial thinking adaptive?

**4.3** *Field/Internet Search Project*
- A. Ask a classmate, friend, or relative if they believe any of the following claims. Alternatively, conduct an internet search on the claim. Describe their sources using the terms in this chapter. Evaluate the quality of these sources.
  - The US government created AIDS.
  - The 9/11 attacks were faked by the government to drum up support for the military.
  - The medical community is suppressing evidence that cheap natural herbal remedies can cure a variety of diseases.
  - Scientists fake temperature records to support the idea of global warming.
  - The FBI is hiding evidence of who killed JFK or Martin Luther King.
  - The Air Force is hiding evidence of extraterrestrial visitors.
  - NASA faked the Moon landing using elaborate Hollywood sets.
  - The British government murdered Princess Diana.
  - The government is adding fluoride to drinking water to weaken the population.
  - The US Presidential election of 2016 was fixed.
- B. Search the internet for websites promoting Uri Geller ("Uri Geller") and Rhonda Byrnes' program *The Secret* ("the secret"). Analyze how both use sources in promoting their powers. Evaluate the quality of these sources.

- C. Ask a classmate, friend, or relative if they believe any of the following claims discussed throughout this book (alternatively, conduct an internet search on the claim):
  - ○ Acupuncture and other Oriental treatments cure through an invisible and mysterious energy field
  - ○ Angels are literally real
  - ○ Astrology
  - ○ Communicating with the dead
  - ○ Dream prophecy
  - ○ Flying saucers from other planets have visited Earth
  - ○ Fortune-telling and seeing into the future
  - ○ Ghosts and haunted houses
  - ○ Herbal medicine
  - ○ Prayer can heal people from a great distance, even when they don't know they're being prayed for (distant healing prayer)
  - ○ Psychic mind-reading and extrasensory perception (psychics/ESP)
  - ○ Reincarnation and past lives

What sources do they use to support their belief? Evaluate the quality of their sources.

**4.4** *Videos*
- A. View the famous movie, *12 Angry Men* (you can find selections on the internet). What examples of groupthink can you find?
- B. On November 13, 2008, 909 Americans were led to commit group suicide by drinking cyanide-laced Kool Aid in the South American country of Guyana. They were all members of the Peoples Temple church. The internet has a number of excellent brief documentaries on the "Jonestown Massacre." How was groupthink involved?

# 5

# Logic (Bonus: The Big Four Informal Logical Fallacies)

| OUTLINE |
| --- |
| 1) Basic Logic (Conclusions, Premises, Arguments) <br> 2) Pretend Logic and Make-Believe Arguments <br>   a) Circular Reasoning/Begging the Question <br>   b) Argument from Repetition <br> 3) Types of Logical Arguments <br>   a) Deductive Arguments and Formal Logical Errors <br>   b) Inductive Arguments and Informal Logical Errors <br>       i) Irrelevant <br>       ii) Insufficient <br>       iii) Factually incorrect <br>       iv) Ambiguous <br> 4) Untidiness in the House of Logic: The Big Four Informal Logical Fallacies <br>   a) Argument from Ignorance <br>       i) Argument from ignorance <br>       ii) Argument from confusion <br>       iii) Argument from incredulity <br>       iv) Argument from mystery <br>   b) Deflection <br>       i) Change the topic <br>       ii) Moving the goalposts <br>       iii) Red herring tactic <br>       iv) Poisoning the well <br>       v) Genetic fallacy <br>       vi) Appeal to hypocrisy <br>       vii) Appeal to motive <br>       viii) *Ad hominem* argument <br>   c) Appeal to Emotion <br>       i) Appeal to emotion <br>       ii) Appeal to flattery <br>       iii) Appeal to pride <br>       iv) Appeal to pity/sympathy <br>       v) Appeal to fear/threat |

*Critical Thinking: Pseudoscience and the Paranormal*, Second Edition. Jonathan C. Smith.
© 2018 John Wiley & Sons, Inc. Published 2018 by John Wiley & Sons, Inc.

d) Selection and Oversimplification
  i) Cherry-picking
  ii) Texas sharpshooter fallacy
  iii) Straw man fallacy
  iv) Either/or thinking
  v) False dilemma
  vi) Error of the excluded middle
  vii) Black/white thinking
  viii) Argument to moderation
  ix) False compromise
  x) False equivalency

Why do people believe in astrology? For many, astrology must be true because it is popular, ancient, and used by friends, celebrities, and authorities. Such thinking is logically fallacious in that it bases a conclusion on an unacceptable premise (the unquestioned truthfulness of what someone else says). Much pseudoscientific thinking is based on logical error. In this chapter we will take a deeper look at logic, or the process of drawing conclusions from premises, and examine how it can be a very useful reality-checking tool.

## Basic Logic

First we need to define some terms. A **conclusion** is a claim that something is true. Conclusions are often based on additional claims called **premises**. Together, conclusions and premises comprise a logical **argument** (not to be confused with a heated dispute). The first task of a student of logic is to develop the ability to identify a conclusion. This can be difficult because conclusions are sometimes hidden or buried in a forest of claims. Sort out all the claims you find in an argument and then identify what the arguer is trying to persuade you to accept. Once you've found the conclusion, it is easier to identify and analyze the premises.

**Figure 5.1** Rubik's cube. Reproduced with kind permission of Getty images.

Here are some arguments for astrology:

| *Premise* | | *Conclusion* |
|---|---|---|
| Astrology is very ancient | *therefore* | astrology is true |
| Many people believe in astrology | *so* | it must work |
| My priest says astrology's true | *thus* | it must be true |

One, somewhat imperfect, way to tell if someone is trying to make an argument is to look for **indicator words**, such as "prove," "because," "therefore," "so," "thus," and "leading one to conclude." These words often tell you that there's a conclusion present. But often this rule isn't enough. The following may look like an argument:

> *The ancients believed in astrology. We find astrological principles in cultures around the world. Astrology is truly timeless, used throughout history. Therefore, astrology has been accepted.*

Look carefully. This is nothing more than an assertion, a conclusion without a premise. It's just a list of claims. Overall, the assertion may or may not be true. But it proves nothing. Yes there is an indicator word "therefore," but the claim "astrology has been accepted" simply repeats what's been claimed. It is a conclusion with no support.

## Pretend Logic and Make-Believe Arguments

Before proceeding into the world of logic and its many erroneous manifestations, we consider statements and claims that do not even rise to the level of being fallacious. These are make-believe arguments that pretend to be logical. Such claims might superficially look like arguments, but they are not. No matter how interesting or informative, they prove nothing. Even when proclaimed with messianic passion in front of huge cheering crowds, they still prove nothing. You can rightly reply to such utterances with a simple statement: "Very interesting, but that is simply an unfounded claim, not an argument." Two examples are circular reasoning (or begging the question) and argument from repetition.

### Circular Reasoning/Begging the Question

Take a look at this argument:

> *You are healthy because you eat oats. How do we know this? Because eating oats makes you healthy.*

Note how the conclusion seems to be supported by the premise. But there's something wrong. The conclusion says exactly the same thing as the premise. Thus we have a circle. X is true because of Y. Why is Y true? Y is true because of X. Put differently, one is left begging the question, or asking "Where's your evidence? Where's the premise?" Our "argument" can be absurdly restated:

> *You are healthy because you eat oats. How do we know this? Because you are healthy because you eat oats.*

Take these examples:

> *My Holy Book is the word of God. Why? Because God says my Holy Book is his word, he says so in my Holy Book.*

> *I have the right of freedom of speech, therefore people shouldn't try to shut me up.*

People often use the phrase "begs the question" to mean "leads me to ask the question" or, of a claim, that "this claim leaves unanswered an important question." Technically, this is an incorrect usage of the term. Some continue to be upset over this frequent misuse. There's even a webpage to promote its correct use (begthequestion.info). However, the popular, if incorrect, use is so entrenched in our culture that we might as well accept how our language has evolved. I see no reason to make students sweat over such an issue. So, **circular reasoning** retains a rather limited meaning: the conclusion essentially restates or is a variant of the premise. **Begging the question** refers to this error as well as any claim that leaves an important question unanswered.

### Argument from Repetition

> *Many people have experienced ghosts. Ghost sightings are common. Everyone has had a ghost encounter. Probably all your friends and acquaintances have seen nonmaterial shadowy figures at night. It's common knowledge that ghosts have been seen by many people.*

Is this an argument? Where's the premise? The conclusion? This utterance is simply a repetition of statements. An **argument from repetition** simply repeats a claim over and over, without linking a premise to a conclusion. Each repetition may vary in choice of words, use substitute words with the same meaning, or rearrange words.

The argument from repetition is frequently used in advertising, politics, and in the realm of the paranormal. Later in this book we will see that such repetition can even have a deep impact on one's very beliefs.

Once again, statements that involve circular reasoning/begging the question and repetition may indeed be correct. However, they are not valid *arguments*. They are simply assertions, or conclusions without a premise.

## Types of Logical Arguments

There are two types of arguments, **deductive** and **inductive**. Each has its own potential for error.

### Deductive Arguments and Formal Logical Errors

Examine this classic deductive argument:

> *Premise*: All men are mortal.
> *Premise*: Socrates is a man.
> Therefore
> *Conclusion*: Socrates is mortal.

Here's another:

> *Premise*: If something's a vegetable, then it's a plant.
> *Premise*: A carrot is a vegetable.
> Therefore
> *Conclusion*: A carrot is a plant.

*In deductive arguments, if a premise is true, the conclusion must be true.* Such an argument is said to be **valid**. Note that if we assume the premises that all vegetables are plants and carrots are vegetables, then carrots must be plants. As long as we accept the premises, there is absolutely no room for debate, no need for further research or argumentation. A carrot is a plant, case closed. Socrates is mortal, no debate. This is a characteristic of all **deductive arguments**.

It is often useful to think of deductive arguments as going from the general to the particular. Here's an example:

> *Premise*: If a person is born when the Sun is the house of Pisces, he or she is athletic. [General]
> *Premise*: You were born in March and the Sun was in the house of Pisces. [Particular]
> Therefore
> *Conclusion*: You are athletic.

As long as you accept the premise, then the conclusion necessarily follows. If you accept the truthfulness of the general claim (people born when the Sun is in the house of Pisces are athletic), the specific claim (you are athletic if you were born in March and the Sun was in the house of Pisces) is also true. Valid deductive arguments follow this general form:

> *If A, then B.*
> *A is true.*
> *Therefore*
> *B is true.*

Arguments that violate this rule are not valid. They make a **formal logical error**. Note that the term "valid" has a very specific meaning – a deductive argument's logical structure has been correctly presented. A deductive argument may be internally **valid**, but not represent the real world. It may have false premises. For example:

> *Premise*: If a creature is an animal, it can write poetry.
> *Premise*: Fluffy, my cat, is an animal.
> Therefore
> *Conclusion*: Fluffy can write poetry.

Here the first premise is wrong: some living animals cannot, as far as we know, write poetry. But the argument is valid in that it follows the formal rules of deduction. Technically, its *form* is correct.

Here is a deductive argument that makes a *formal* logical error.

> *Premise*: If someone believes in ghosts and witches, they believe in a reality beyond the physical world.
> *Premise*: Bertha believes in a reality beyond the physical world.
> Therefore
> *Conclusion*: Bertha believes in ghosts and witches.

In fact, Bertha is a practicing Roman Catholic, very much believes in a higher power, and rejects the idea of ghosts and witches as heresy. The problem with this deductive argument is that it breaks the form rules. The first premise is an "if/then" claim with two parts, (A) If someone believes in ghosts and witches, (B) then they believe in a reality beyond the physical world. The first "if" part is called the **antecedent** and the second "then" part the **consequent**.

We have already seen that by affirming the "if," that is the antecedent, the consequent is automatically true. Every valid argument we have considered has done this. However, that's not what the Bertha argument does. Bertha's conclusion works backwards by initially **affirming the consequent**, thus concluding that the antecedent is true. Because it breaks the formal rules it is not valid. It is a logical error. To summarize, a valid argument **affirms the antecedent**, like this:

> *If A is true, then B is true.* [First Premise; antecedent – consequent]
> *A is true.* [Second Premise]
> *Therefore*
> *B is true.* [Conclusion]

In contrast, affirming the consequent proves nothing. The form of such a formal logical error is:

> *If A is true, then B is true.*
> *B is true.*
> *Therefore*
> *A is true.*

Arguments that affirm the consequent often appear in discussions of the paranormal. For example:

> *Premise*: If the stars and planets are aligned properly (A), you will recover quickly from your cold (B).
> *Premise:* You recovered quickly from your cold (B).
> Therefore
> *Conclusion:* The stars and planets are aligned properly (A).

> *Premise:* If a psychic can read your thoughts (A), he can tell if you are skeptical (B).
> *Premise:* The psychic you are visiting correctly observed that you are skeptical (B).
> Therefore
> *Conclusion:* The psychic can read your thoughts (A).

*Premise:* If a mystic has truly supernatural powers (A), she can perform stunts you cannot explain (B).

*Premise:* Maria, the mystic, has bent a spoon without touching it, a stunt you cannot explain (B).

Therefore

*Conclusion:* Maria has supernatural powers (A).

There is a different way of describing the mistake these examples illustrate. Whenever you affirm the consequent you have proven nothing because alternative explanations must be considered.

### Inductive Arguments and Informal Logical Errors

*For inductive arguments, premises support, but do not prove, the conclusion.* Unlike deductive conclusions, inductive conclusions are not absolutely true or valid, but simply **strong** or **weak**. If you conduct a survey of 1,000 Pisces and find that 80% are athletes (vs. 20% of the general population), you would have some evidence that Pisces are athletic. To repeat, you have not proven anything, but simply acquired strong, or weak, support for a conclusion or claim. Inductive claims are always probabilities, not certainties.

For example, an **inductive generalization** starts with a premise about a sample of cases and leads to a conclusion about the population of all cases. Thus, inductive arguments can be seen as going from the particular to the general.

*Premise*: 80% of the Pisces I randomly interview happen to be members of sports teams. [Particular cases summarized]

Therefore

*Conclusion*: 80% of the Pisces in the general population are probably members of sports teams. [General statement about the population]

Most logical fallacies do not involve errors in form and are thus called "in*formal* fallacies." Most experts consider such fallacies to have premises with the following *general attributes*:

**Irrelevant** premises may be true, but are irrelevant to the conclusion. Example: Astrology is true because astrologers are generally people without a criminal record. (Most astrologers may well not have a criminal record. However, not having a criminal record has nothing to do with accuracy of astrology.)

**Insufficient** premises might be relevant, but they are inadequate. Astrology is true because of documented cases of astrological predictions that have come true. Last week my local newspaper published four predictions that came true. (Four predictions are insufficient, especially when seen in light of the thousands made every day.)

**Factually incorrect** premises are presumed to be correct but in fact are not. There must be something to astrology because every US President has relied on the services of an astrologer. (Every US President? That's just not true.)

Finally, **ambiguous** premises (and conclusions) are unclear or confusing. It would surprise you how many educators look favorably on the symbolic richness of astrology; therefore, astrology must have its place. ("Educators" … what does that mean? "look favorably" …? "symbolic richness" …? "have its place" …?)

Students have little difficulty identifying the general attributes of informal fallacies. However, these attributes often overlap, and at times are unclear. It is useful to identify specific fallacies.

## Untidiness in the House of Logic: The Big Four Informal Logical Fallacies

It may surprise you that scholars of critical thinking have identified over 300 specific informal logical fallacies (Bennett, 2012). Which are the most important? Let me share with you a rather astonishing discovery I made while researching this book. I thought it would be a good idea to find which informal fallacies experts agree are most important. To this end, I reviewed over 30 texts on critical thinking and logic, and dozens of websites on skepticism. Indeed, most logic experts proclaim to have identified a list of the "most important" or "basic" fallacies. But each list is different. There is no consensus. Each expert has his or her handful of favorites based on little more than personal preference. I regret to report a degree of untidiness in the house of logic.

I devised a simple housecleaning strategy. Of the 300 or so logical fallacies in currency, *which are most widely used*? Which are most often identified as fallacies? How could one ever answer such questions? My approach was simply to perform repeated Google searches on each of 300 fallacies noted on the web and identify the number of "hits" for each. But there's a problem. For some fallacy titles we run the risk of getting hits that have nothing to do with logic. For example, consider the logical fallacy **cherry-picking** (unfairly selecting those facts that support one's conclusion). A search for "cherry-picking" will include examples involving logical fallacies as well as which farms grow the best cherries in Illinois. For potentially ambiguous searches, I used this format: "name of fallacy" AND *"irrational"* (for example, "'cherry-picking' AND 'irrational'" – 257,000 hits).

I repeated this type of search every other month for each of 300 fallacies over two years. Interestingly, although experts seem not to agree on which informal fallacies are most important, my internet searches were extremely consistent. I narrowed my list to 42 fallacies that yielded at least 30,000 hits.

Finally, I removed fallacies considered elsewhere in this text. To explain, we have already explored topics related to subjective relativism (wishful thinking) and source errors (appeal to tradition, argument from popularity). These were among the most frequent hits in my search and can be rightly termed informal logical fallacies. Given their importance, they merited special attention in separate chapters. The fallacy of argument from ambiguity, or using terms in ways that are unclear, forms the foundation of much illogical thinking and threatens how we view reality itself. Given its importance, we will consider ambiguity and language in the next chapter (Chapter 6). Confusing correlation with causality is an observational or scientific error, which we consider in our chapter on science (Chapter 7).

My quest produced an initial working list of 11 informal logical fallacies:

Appeal to fear (576,000 hits)
*Ad hominem* (503,000)
Red herring (320,000)

Cherry-picking (257,000)
Appeal to emotion (94,300)
Argument from ignorance (61,200)
Poisoning the well (58,800)
Appeal to pity (48,900)
False dilemma (46,900)
False equivalence (36,000)
Appeal to pride (30,000)[1]

I sorted these into four groups, which I term the "Big Four Informal Logical Fallacies."

*Ignorance*
Argument from ignorance

*Deflection*
*Ad hominem*
Red herring
Poisoning the well

*Emotion*
Appeal to fear
Appeal to emotion
Appeal to pity
Appeal to pride

*Selection*
Cherry-picking
False dilemma
False equivalence

Without further ado, here is an elaboration of the four "ides of error":

*Ignorance – Deflection – Emotion – Selection*

### Argument from Ignorance

In a very loose sense, all logical fallacies can be said to be ill-informed, unknowledge-able, or generally unenlightened. Someone who makes a claim on such thinking might be said to be "arguing from ignorance." Indeed, we might think of the entire enterprise of open-minded critical thinking as a campaign against ignorance. However, an **argument from ignorance** is also a very special and important type of informal logical fallacy. As noted earlier, our own research finds argument from ignorance to be the second strongest predictor of strength of one's belief in a paranormal claim, ranking just behind personal experience, and above perceived scientific evidence, eyewitness testimonial, faith and belief, family and culture, and perceived media support (See Appendix A).

You hope something is true. Yet there is an absence of evidence on which to base your hope. How might you cope with such "ignorance"? Under such conditions perhaps it is understandable that one might appeal to ignorance. Here one asserts that the lack of evidence against something:

- proves it is true;
- gives one permission to act as if it were true;
- removes any reason to deploy open-minded critical thinking;
- makes it more reasonable to believe; or
- makes the desire for something to be true sufficient reason to believe.

As we have seen earlier, the alternative is to simply accept lack of evidence for a claim for what it is, lack of evidence. Sometimes a mystery is just a mystery.

Here are some examples of arguments from ignorance:

> *There's a lot we don't know about the brain. Therefore, I believe in ESP. ESP exists.*

> *Just because scientists haven't examined whether rubbing moss on your head grows hair doesn't mean the treatment doesn't work. So you might as well try it.*

When overwhelmed by contradictory and conflicting factual claims and fake news, one may retreat from reality testing and simply accept as true what feels right. Such an **argument from confusion**[2] essentially states, "I'll ignore what people claim to be factual because we'll never know what's really true. I'll continue believing what I've been believing up until now, or what those closest to me believe." A variant is the **argument from incredulity**: "I can't conceive how this could be false (or true), therefore it must be true (or false)"

I wish to introduce a curious variant of the argument from ignorance, one that attempts to use a mystery to explain a mystery. I call this an **argument from mystery**, and it takes this form:

> *Premise*: Phenomenon X has been observed.
> *Premise:* Phenomenon X is a complete mystery. We do not fully understand and can't explain it.
> *Premise:* Phenomenon Y also cannot be explained.
> Therefore
> *Conclusion:* Phenomenon Y explains Phenomenon X.

Just because something can't be explained doesn't mean that it can explain something completely unrelated. As we noted in an earlier chapter, the notion of quantum entanglement is often used to explain numerous paranormal claims, ranging from miracle cures to mind-reading. Quantum entanglement is indeed a physical phenomenon that has been observed. In it, two distant particles, such as a photon split into two half photons, sent far in opposite directions, appear to have a mysterious connection. If you measure the property of one, say its "spin," you instantly set and know the complementary "spin" of its pair. Quantum physicists say these photons are "entangled," a phenomenon for which there is currently no explanation. Indeed, Einstein called it "spooky action at a distance," given that the particles are in no way connected. Indeed, it is a mystery.

Some paranormalists claim that psychics can read the minds of others because their thoughts are linked through "quantum entanglement." The mystery (for which we are "ignorant" of any explanation) explains another inexplicable mystery (which in the case of mind-reading is not only a mystery, but a phenomenon that has yet to be convincingly demonstrated.) Using this logic, we can have a lot of fun. How can yoga masters levitate above the ground while meditating (a mystery, which actually has never been demonstrated)? Dark energy is an apparent force that causes entire galaxies to fly apart and the universe to expand faster than the speed of light. We have no explanation for what this force is. It is a mystery. So, why not say that dark energy enables yoga masters to levitate? That should be an easy lift.

The argument from ignorance enables one to believe without evidence. This is the path of closed-mindedness. Simply because science has yet to find an explanation does not mean that it will never find one. The history of science can be described as a journey of discovering explanations for phenomena that initially appear to defy explanation (and tempt one to believe in the paranormal). Until such discoveries are made, scientists are content to assert: "We don't know." The absence of a normal explanation does not require an extraordinary explanation. Or as astronomer Carl Sagan popularized, "Extraordinary claims require extraordinary evidence" (Truzzi, 1976).

## Deflection

Our next informal logical fallacy is **deflection**, or simply changing the topic. Of course, the most direct way of doing this is indeed to abruptly **change the topic**. Another very simple strategy is to **move the goalposts**, or change previously agreed standards if they haven't been met.

One deflection strategy is a bit more colorful (or odoriferous). In 1807 English radical journalist William Cobbett wrote a story in which he as a boy tossed a smelly red herring into the path of hounds to divert them from chasing a hare (Oxford English Dictionary, 2015). Similarly, in logic the **red herring tactic** involves diverting an arguer by introducing an irrelevant topic. For example, if you wanted to argue that astrological horoscopes are paranormal, you might use this argument:

> *Premise*: An event that can't be explained through science might be paranormal.
> *Premise*: Astrologers have created horoscopes for me whose predictions I cannot explain through science.
> Therefore
> *Conclusion*: Astrological predictions may well be paranormal.

This is a perfectly fine argument. However, I might derail it by introducing an irrelevant topic:

> *Premise*: An event that can't be explained through science might be paranormal.
> *Premise*: Astrologers have created horoscopes for me whose predictions I cannot explain through science.
> *Premise*: Most astrologers completed their schooling before major scientific discoveries concerning the makeup of the universe and the stars. [Red herring]
> *Reply*: I think I understand science reasonably well. Now where were we?

In more general terms, when adverse discrediting information is presented before one makes an argument, one **poisons the well**.

*Premise*: Astronomers often criticize astrology.
*Premise*: Astronomers worship science and are closed to deeper human potentials. They are Godless haters and purveyors of negative energy. [Poisoning the well]
Therefore
*Conclusion*: We must be suspicious of the skepticism of astronomers.

Put more generally, when you question the source or origin of a claim, you commit a **genetic fallacy**.

*Premise*: I had a dream I should call my mother today.
*Premise*: Ideas from dreams are purely subjective and cannot be trusted. [Genetic fallacy]
Therefore
*Conclusion*: I should not trust my impulse to call my mother.

There are more subtle ways of changing the topic while seeming to stay with it. One might **appeal to hypocrisy**, also known as *"tu quoque."* Here one intends to discredit someone's conclusion by introducing the premise that the person making the conclusion has been inconsistent and hypocritical. If you discredit or divert an argument by questioning the specific intent one has in making that argument, your fallacy is an **appeal to motive**.

*Premise*: When many people observe the same phenomenon, we have evidence that the phenomenon might be true.
*Premise*: Most college students believe in fortune-telling.
*Premise*: Most college students simply want to impress their girlfriends and boyfriends. [Appeal to motive]
Therefore
*Conclusion*: We can discount the claims of college students concerning fortune-telling.

More generally, an ***ad hominem* argument** (Latin for "to the man") typically rejects a claim because of presumed negative characteristics of the person making the claim, rather than the claim itself. A claim may or may not be true, regardless of who is making it.

## Appeal to Emotion

An **appeal to emotion** uses emotion as an explicit or implied premise for an argument. Indeed, it is a form of deflection, one in which emotion diverts our attention. Such an appeal can be based on nearly any negative positive or emotional state, including fear, love, beauty, and spiritual states.

For example, scientists may well describe a certain theory or set of mathematical equations as "beautiful," suggesting this is evidence for their truthfulness. I found 375,000 Google hits for "beautiful" for "theory of relativity," 476,000 hits for "beautiful" and "quantum mechanics," 85,600,000 hits for "evolution" and "beautiful," and 446,000 hits for "creationism" and "beautiful." We often find the same argument for the existence of God. "Any experience as beautiful as God must be true." "The natural world is inconceivably beautiful. It is so beautiful there must be a God."

Of course, one could assert that a claim is true because of the presumed positive characteristics of the person receiving an argument. One might **appeal to flattery** or **pride**:

> *Premise*: Intelligent people understand what they read.
> *Premise*: You are intelligent.
> Therefore
> *Conclusion*: You understand this paragraph.

An **appeal to pity** attempts to argue a conclusion based on feelings of pity or sympathy. Advertisements showing photos of starving puppies may persuade you to give to animal shelters. If we break down their logic, it looks like this:

> *Premise*: When you encounter a distressed puppy, you should feel pity and sympathy. (An "if/then" premise)
> *Premise*: When you feel pity and sympathy, you should help. (Another "if/then" premise)
> *Premise*: You are reading about distressed puppies.
> Therefore
> *Conclusion*: You should help.

An **appeal to fear** incorporates scare tactics or the threat of force or injury in the premise to support a conclusion.

> *Premise*: People who don't believe in an afterlife go to hell.
> *Premise*: You do not believe in an afterlife.
> Therefore
> *Conclusion*: You will go to hell.

> *Premise*: Eating a vegetarian diet is the only way to prevent heart disease.
> *Premise*: You do not support eating a vegetarian diet.
> Therefore
> *Conclusion*: You do not want to prevent heart disease.

### Selection and Oversimplification

**Selection errors** involve rigging an argument in your favor by selecting only the evidence that supports your conclusion. This evidence may be true or false, but is asserted as factual. In general terms, this fallacy is also called **cherry-picking** and the **Texas sharpshooter fallacy**. In both one picks desired cherries, or bullet holes (the Texas sharpshooter fires bullets at a barn, draws a target around his biggest cluster of hits, and claims to be a "sharpshooter").

One of the most subtle and popular forms of selection and simplification is the **straw man fallacy**. In military training, soldiers might practice combat skills on straw men, or dummy soldiers' uniforms filled with bags of straw. Such opponents are cheap, easy to defeat, and don't talk back. A straw man argument distorts or oversimplifies an opponent's position so it is easy to refute. Note that the arguer has subtly rendered a position easily refutable through oversimplification, selection of weak elements, exaggeration (perhaps making the argument universal), blatant distortion, omission of key elements, or ignoring context. Like a military dummy, a straw man argument is easy to build, and requires little familiarity with the facts.

Perhaps you restrict your selection to only two alternatives, forcing a choice of one or the other. This is **either/or thinking**, also known as the **false dilemma**, **error of the excluded middle**, or **black/white thinking**. Example:

> *Premise*: You are either for us or against us.
> *Premise*: You are for us.
> Therefore
> *Conclusion*: You are not against us.

The opposite of the false dilemma is the **argument to moderation** or **false compromise**. Here one asserts that truth can be found only as a compromise between two opposite positions. The middle ground is always correct. Somewhat similar is a **false equivalency** in which two positions are argued to be essentially the same when in fact there are significant (but ignored) differences.

> *Premise*: Political candidate X has a foundation that accepts money (from terrorists).
> *Premise*: Political candidate Y has a foundation that accepts money (from friendly foreign countries).
> *Premise*: It is not ethical for political candidates to have foundations that accept money from groups outside of the country.
> Therefore
> *Conclusion*: Political candidates X and Y are equally unethical in the foundations they run.

## Study Questions

**5.1** *Definitions (Define, differentiate, and provide an example for each of the following)*
- A. Logic
- B. Argument
- C. Conclusion
- D. Premise
- E. Antecedent – Consequent

**5.2** *Definitions (Define each of the following logical errors and give an example for each)*
- A. *Ad hominem* argument
- B. Begging the question
- C. Black/white thinking
- D. Changing the topic
- E. Cherry-picking
- F. Circular reasoning
- G. Confusion, argument from
- H. Consequent, affirming the

- I. Either/or thinking
- J. Emotion, appeal to
- K. Error of the excluded middle
- L. False compromise
- M. False dilemma
- N. Fear/threat, appeal to
- O. False equivalency
- P. Flattery, appeal to
- Q. Genetic fallacy
- R. Hypocrisy, appeal to
- S. Ignorance, argument from
- T. Incredulity, argument
- U. Moderation, argument to
- V. Motive, appeal to
- W. Moving the goalposts
- X. Mystery, argument from
- Y. Pity/sympathy, appeal to
- Z. Poisoning the well
- AA. Pride, appeal to
- BB. Red herring tactic
- CC. Repetition, argument from
- DD. Straw man fallacy
- EE. Texas sharpshooter fallacy

**5.3** *The Logic Workout*

Instructors of clinical thinking frequently observe how difficult it is for students to master the basics of logic. I find skill develops through practice, and a lot of it. For this chapter we will immerse ourselves in a logic workout, practicing the basics. What follows is a list of sample arguments.

In this exercise, you have three tasks. For each sample argument, identify the:

1) premise(s) and conclusion;
2) antecedent–consequences;
3) type of logical error(s) committed.

- A. "The book, *Logic is Fun*, deserves the American Book Award. There are other good books, but nothing like *Logic is Fun*. Others might receive an honorable mention, but they aren't the best. The clothing accessories are fantastic! *Logic is Fun* is justifiably a best-seller. It truly deserves to be made into a movie in a 3D IMAX format. There is only one *Logic is Fun*. It wins and people like it the most."
- B. "If tuition is lowered, I will have more money to spend on books. This semester I discovered I have more money to spend. Therefore, tuition must have been lowered."
- C. After Baltig presents an eloquent and compelling case for delaying the midterm exam, Torkul throws a monkey wrench into the discussion and asks students if we should trust someone who has a poor grade point average, has missed a week's worth of classes, and eats animals others consider to be family pets.

- D. "The evidence that a fatty diet contributes to heart disease is very weak. My neighbor is a vegetarian and she has heart disease."
- E. Jeska didn't want to share her roommate's dinner of chopped liver and Brussel sprouts, but her mother admonished her to be more caring of the poor starving humanoids on other planets who have no food.
- F. Odros has been arrested for running over a skate-boarder on the streets. His defense: "If the skate boarder had been wearing a helmet, he would have survived the crash. The court should cut my sentence in half because the accident was half his fault."
- G. SENATOR LIKIRK: "I propose we cut funding for universities."
  SENATOR BIRK: "And what is your argument?"
  SENATOR LIKIRK: "It's very simple. Either we cut educational funding, or we will be forced to live with a deficit that is driving us to bankruptcy."
- H. "There may be some merit in Senator Likirk's tax plan. But if we as the loyal opposition party are to survive, we must show that we are as tough as Senator Likirk's party and come up with what the public wants."
- I. "You know, Professor Smith, I really need an A in this class to graduate. May I stop by your office and talk about my grade? I will be visiting the Dean anyway (who is my dad). Has your tenure vote come up this year?
- J. INTERVIEWER: "Your resume looks impressive but I need another reference."
  ODROS: "Ms Durtig can give me a good reference."
  INTERVIEWER: "Good. But how do I know that Ms Durtig is trustworthy?"
  ODROS: "That you don't have to worry about! I can vouch for her totally."
- K. "I thought you were a good person, but I didn't see you at church this month, and I don't think you ever went to confession."
- L. "Congress is considering a law to restrict the use of the internet in hospitals or clinics that access confidential patient records. This law was proposed by Senator Zendloth, an intelligent man with good ideas about agriculture and defense, but with no college training or work experience in the internet."
- M. The Potato Chip Foundation has studied chip consumption in various countries, states, cities, and neighborhoods. They report: "Science shows that communities that consume more potato chips have fewer crimes against the homeless. Therefore, our potato chips reduce crime."
- N. "You keep insisting that I stop smoking. But last night I noticed you were smoking, and had an ashtray full of butts."
- O. The biological properties of the human brain are not sufficient to explain consciousness and free will. Therefore, there must be a nonmaterial soul or spirit.
- P. "You claim that my boyfriend is cheating on me only because he turns you on and you want to date him yourself!"
- Q. "My opponent is not only a physician, but an official of the American Medical Association. Obviously he is against any research that finds simple green tea cures cancer. He'll lose business."
- R. "Yes, I dated your boyfriend behind your back. But I was terribly lonely and depressed and desperately needed companionship."

- S. "My sister says I hook up too much. But that's normal. It is healthy to exercise hormones. I'm only 19 and it's good to have contacts in college. And I'm learning."
- T. YOHO: "I think our family should buy vegetables only from the farmer's street market down the street. Their vegetables come directly from the farm."
  ELENA: "I think that's a bad idea. Farms are full of insects, bacteria, and worse, fertilizer from animal waste. If you ate all those insects, bacteria, and animal waste, you would get very sick!"
- U. "It's unfair for you to accuse me of lying. All I did was spend the money you lent me on beer, when I said I was buying dinner. After all, last week you said you would meet me at noon and in fact you met me at 1 p.m."

**5.4** *Group Exercise: Identify the Fallacy*
In this exercise, divide into two teams. Each team selects an example of a logical fallacy (from this chapter) from one of these websites:

- Logicallyfallacious.com
- Yourlogicalfallalcyis.com
- Logfall.wordpress.com
- Nizkor.org
- Rationalwiki.org
- Philosophypages.com

Team 1 presents its example to Team 2. Team 2 has five minutes to identify it and explain. If the explanation is acceptable to the moderator, Team 2 gets a point.
  Repeat for Team 2. Continue until each team has a chance to identify five logical fallacies. The team correctly identifying the most fallacies wins.

**5.5** *Blogs*
Below are some popular blogs. Select one blog (or pick one you already read) and find a posting that makes an argument. Describe the argument, identifying the premise and conclusion (if they exist). Evaluate the argument using the terms in this textbook.

- advocate.com
- businessinsider.com
- bestspiritualblogs.com
- cheezburger.com
- collegefashion.net
- deadspin.com
- engadget.com
- espn.com
- gizmodo.com
- huffingtonpost.com
- jezebel.com
- kotaku.com
- lifehacker.com

- mashable.com
- nakedpastor.com
- perezhilton.com
- randi.org/swift
- skeptic.com/insight
- style.com
- techcrunch.com
- thedailybeast.com
- theverge.com
- thestranger.com
- tmz.com
- queerty.com

**5.6** *Videos*

- A. What fallacies are demonstrated in the following PBS video: "Five fallacies/ idea channel/PBS digital studios." What is their explanation of how each is fallacious? Can you identify any examples that illustrate more than one logical fallacy? https://www.youtube.com/playlist?list=PLtHP6qx8VF7dPql3ll1 To4i6vEIPt0kV5
- B. Find examples of fallacies from advertising, politics, and popular culture. Start with this link: https://www.youtube.com/watch?v=fXLTQi7vVsI

# 6

# Logic and Language: Fallacies of Ambiguity

<table>
<tr><td>

**OUTLINE**

1) Sloppy Language
   a) Weasel Words
   b) Meaningless Jargon and Technobabble
2) Types of Argument from Similarity
   a) Argument from Similarity
   b) Analogies
      i) False analogy
      ii) Dangling analogy
   c) Fallacy of Composition
   d) Fallacy of Division
3) Messing with Reality: Ontological Errors
   a) Category Errors
   b) Ontological Fusion and Core Knowledge Confusion
   c) Emergent Properties and Reductionism
   d) Reification
   e) Truth, Reality, The Answer, and Faith
4) Conclusion

</td></tr>
</table>

**Fallacies of ambiguity** involve using a key word or phrase with an unclear meaning or multiple meanings. As such they add an important new element to our discussion of logic, and therefore merit a special chapter. The logical fallacies considered in the preceding chapter may lead to erroneous conclusions. However, their premises leave, or can leave, important pieces of reality intact. For example, you may argue from ignorance that absence of any evidence of alien flying saucer invasions permits us to speculate that such invasions have occurred. The lack of evidence is an unchallenged fact. You may use deflection and appeal to motive when you argue that we should reject a greedy physician's claim of a cure for cancer. However, the fact remains that the claim has been made. You may appeal to emotion and question your despised former husband's claim that you are overweight. However, alas, facts are facts. And you may cherry-pick from thousands of scientific studies those few that support your belief in alien abductions. However, the fact is that those few studies indeed make the claim.

Fallacies of ambiguity draw into question reality itself. Sometimes, this is achieved through the distorting lens or mirror of sloppy language. Or one might treat a "similarity"

*Critical Thinking: Pseudoscience and the Paranormal*, Second Edition. Jonathan C. Smith.
© 2018 John Wiley & Sons, Inc. Published 2018 by John Wiley & Sons, Inc.

as an "equivalency." Ambiguity can involve transforming the very "ontological status" of a topic under discussion. Fallacies of ambiguity fool us into thinking something is other than what it really is.

## Sloppy Language

Sometimes the imprecise or vague use of words constitutes a logical fallacy of ambiguity. The most common examples are perhaps weasel words, meaningless jargon, and technobabble.

### Weasel Words

We will devote considerable attention to this fallacy, given its importance in worlds of the paranormal. A **weasel word** has more than one meaning or a meaning that is so sufficiently vague that various interpretations can apply. Because of this ambiguity, an arguer can make one claim (based on one implied meaning), and then switch meanings when the claim is challenged. Such a word behaves like a weasel.

A weasel is a thin squirrel-like mammal known for its ability to slither out of trouble and sneak into the burrows of other animals and eat tasty victims or their eggs (Nowak & Walker, 2005). Perhaps author Steward Chaplin was the first to use the expression "weasel word" in his short story "Stained Glass Political Platform" (Chaplin, 1900):

> [...] weasel words are words that suck the life out of the words next to them just as a weasel sucks the egg and leaves the shell. If you heft the egg afterward it's as light as a feather, and not very filling when you are hungry, but a basketful of them would make quite a show, and would bamboozle the unwary.
>
> *(p. 305)*

Many weasel words can be divided into three groups (Ganter & Strube, 2009). Some are numerically vague expressions ("some … people in the know … many … most"). Some incorporate the passive voice to avoid identifying a source or responsible person ("it is claimed that … it is well-known that …"). Finally, weasel adverbs weaken or dilute the impact of their referent ("often … likely … commonly").

More serious are weasel words that have more than one meaning, depending on the context. As such, a weasel word gives you an "out" in case your claim is challenged. For example, examine the claim: "Some scientists challenge the notion that using alcohol hand wipes reduces the chance of catching a cold." Here the word "some" is a weasel word. On close examination, we might find that "one percent of scientists challenge the value of alcohol hand wipes in preventing transmission of the cold virus."

Some people engage in weaseling by their use of the word "healing." "Healing" generally means "returning to physiological health." When a broken leg is healed, you can walk again. Healing can also mean "returning to psychological well-being." Even if your leg is broken, you are "healed" if you have recovered from the initial distress of breaking your leg and are more or less happy. Because of these two meanings, faith healers can weasel out of promises. They may claim to "heal" your arthritis, take your "donation" ("healing" your wallet of excess weight), and then praise the Lord that your "spirit" has been healed. Who are you to challenge such a demonstration of piety?

A similar and clever weasel word is the verbal construct "dis-ease." Of course, when spoken, it sounds like "disease," a medical condition, whereas the written phrase "dis-ease" should refer to something like "discomfort." A healer can claim a worthless potion cures your "dis-ease" and convey the impression of offering a medical treatment when in fact he is simply making you feel good. What is clever about this weasel word is that the healer has a backup rationalization, the idea that psychological well-being ("ease") is important for physical health, and that his nostrum removes obstacles to such good feelings ("dis-ease").

Just as weasels can sneak into uninvited places, weasel words can introduce unintended and confusing meanings into a discussion. The words "controversial" and "debatable" are popular weasels in paranormal literature. Let's take a simple example. Uri Geller is one of the best-known contemporary psychics, world-renowned for his claimed ability to bend spoons with thought alone. However, magicians routinely bend spoons through simple sleight of hand (Randi, 1982). Randi has claimed that whenever Geller attempts to bend a spoon in the presence of a magician, he fails, and that he can bend spoons only in settings where deception or sleight of hand cannot be ruled out. In sum, few credible scientists question the overwhelming rejection of Geller's spoon-bending claim. Here there is no serious "debate" or "controversy" (Randi, 1982).

Yet, consider what Irwin and Watt (2007) conclude in what is perhaps the most widely respected serious paranormal textbook written by believers:

> The authenticity of Geller's performance is a matter of much debate (as it must be with folk who derive their living from such performances).
>
> *(p. 119)*

To be fair, Irwin and Watt duly note the challenges of skeptical magicians. However, they try to have it both ways. They do not conclude that Geller's claim has weak scientific support. Instead, it is "a matter of much debate." Furthermore, the primary reason given for the "debate" is the potential for financial gain, a potentially compromising circumstance that must be faced by many paranormal researchers and skeptics, including myself.

Weasel words can have consequences. Weaseling can mean the difference between a recommendation to stop or continue researching a topic. One might argue that a logical assessment of the scientific consensus concerning Geller would lead to a recommendation to stop inviting him to participate in expensive scientific studies. This is not what Irwin and Watt conclude. Instead:

> Without adequate testing in properly controlled conditions it is impossible to validate Geller's psychic talents.
>
> *(p. 119)*

Implication? If we could only amass sufficient resources for adequate testing, then perhaps we could attempt to finally validate Geller's talents. This implies that the "controversy" or "debate" is far from settled, the evidence at hand is not sufficient to challenge Geller's claims, and future research on Geller is merited. See where this innocent bit of weaseling gets us?

Let me put this in a slightly different way. The words "controversial" and "debatable" can imply that there is good evidence on both sides of a question, or that a plausible claim has minimal evidence. John claims that he can turn rocks into gold through touch.

This claim is "controversial" and "debatable" because he has never demonstrated it to others. John believes, others do not. Joe claims that eating chocolate reduces blood pressure. His claim is also "controversial" and "debatable" because one or two studies offer suggestive support, whereas others do not. In other words, there are two ways in which a claim can be controversial or debatable. It might not be supported by evidence, but stir argument. Or it might have inconsistent empirical support. A careless scholar may report that a paranormal claim is "controversial" or "debatable," meaning "no support, much argument." He or she may then engage in weaseling and treat the claim as having achieved at least a limited level of respectability (implying "mixed support").

### Meaningless Jargon and Technobabble

At times technical jargon cannot be avoided. However, **meaningless jargon** is language that appears to be specialized and meaningful but in fact communicates nothing. Just because a claim uses difficult language doesn't mean it is logical support. It may well be pure pseudoscience. "Quantum entanglement" is a legitimate technical phrase with precise meaning. "Dental oscillatory friction device" is a pointlessly complex phrase for an electric toothbrush. "Fallacy of ambiguity" means something whereas "Fallacy of reverse error" has no meaning. Pointless jargon can be introduced into an argument (valid or invalid) to make it appear more plausible and respectable even though it may be weak or meaningless.

**Technobabble** goes further and incorporates scientific-sounding jargon in an extended argument. Because a claim is scientific-sounding, it must accurately reflect reality. Often those who use technobabble do not understand the very point they are trying to make, or are deliberately trying to be unclear or deceptive.

The use of technobabble can quickly rise to the realm of the absurd. In a famous example, Alan Sokal fooled the prestigious professional journal *Social Text* into publishing as a serious article his technobabble spoof, "Transgressing the boundaries: Towards a transformative hermeneutics of quantum gravity" (Sokal, 1996). This parody is so good that it provides a more convincing quantum-based rationale for parapsychological phenomena than the currently popular notions of "quantum consciousness." But it is pure and deliberate nonsense.

My all-time favorite example of pseudoscientific technobabble is holographic urine treatment. Because human urine initially resides in the body, it comes in contact with healthy and diseased or damaged tissue and thereby acquires a holographic memory of health and disease. Thus, by consuming one's own urine, one can activate the body's natural healing potential. One might elevate holographic urine theory as the "gold standard" for technobabble.

**Science fiction** goes one step beyond technobabble. Here one begins with scientifically accepted fact and theory and then extrapolates new scientific-appearing fictions that have no bases in reality. For example, science fiction writers often have their characters travel from galaxy to galaxy in a matter of hours. This is physically impossible. To get around this inconvenience, writers may invent wormholes that serve as rapid long-distance transit portals. The rationale may begin with the correct observation that black holes exist throughout the universe (fact supported by theory) and that the laws of physics may not apply deep within black holes (also proposed by current science). When two black holes in different parts of the universe connect, what happens between them also violates the laws of physics (so far this also fits current theory) so they form a tunnel (yes, this indeed would also violate the laws of physics; but it's science fiction) through which people can travel nearly instantaneously (science fiction).

The notion of quantum consciousness (Radin, 1997, 2006) is a popular explanation for many claimed paranormal phenomena, including reading thoughts at a distance and influencing objects through thoughts. Here is a reality check. The notion of quantum consciousness begins with the accurate observation that under certain conditions some subatomic particles seem "entangled," that is, at the subatomic level an esoteric characteristic of one may immediately appear in a sister particle far away (see Chapter 1). This may seem strange, but it is fact. Quantum consciousness states that the human brain is made of atoms, which in turn are made of subatomic particles (fact). The subatomic particles in the brain follow the rules of quantum physics (fact). Human thought is generated by the human brain (fact) and may follow the same quantum rules as subatomic particles in the brain (science fiction). Therefore, the thoughts of one person can immediately influence the thoughts of another far away (science fiction), a process that may seem like thought reading or thought control.

However popular, quantum explanations of thought reading and control make no more sense than various other possible science fiction explanations. Let me offer a few. String theory, a popular notion that says that subatomic strings permeate the universe, requires the existence of almost a dozen dimensions (actual theory). One might then reflect one's thoughts off a fifth or sixth dimension in order to communicate telepathically with someone else (science fiction). Here's another: some quantum theories state that gravity is the only force that can leak between dimensions. All atoms possess some gravity (fact). Our brains are made of atoms (fact). Thoughts are generated by activity in the brain (fact). One might then imagine that thoughts travel by means of gravity waves (science fiction) through other dimensions and return to our dimension instantaneously (science fiction), resulting in telepathic communication. And another: a mysterious dark energy forces some galaxies apart, at times approaching and maybe exceeding the speed of light (an apparent fact). When human thoughts come in contact with dark energy, they can travel very rapidly to others, permitting telepathy (science fiction). Obviously science fiction explanations are partly based on fact. However, those who believe in such make-believe typically have a very poor understanding of underlying science and therefore make the logical error of confusing fact with fiction.

## Types of Argument from Similarity

Errors of ambiguity that incorporate weasel words, meaningless jargon, technobabble, and science fiction most generally rely on fallacious similarities (for example, between a true scientific term and a scientific-sounding term). Errors of similarity in themselves constitute a popular logical fallacy. Similarity is both a specific type of logical error, and a general class of error.

### Argument from Similarity

An argument based on similarities assumes that if two things are similar in one way they are similar in other ways. Positing a similarity necessarily distorts reality. If two things are similar, by definition they are not identical. They are different. In this sense, a similarity is always factually incorrect. However, often a similarity can be instructive and we can ignore the obvious fact of lack of equivalency. In contrast, a **false similarity** claims that if two things are alike in one way, they are also alike in a way in which they are not:

*Premise*: Cats have nervous systems that enable them to feel pain.
*Premise*: People have nervous systems that enable pain to be felt.
*Premise*: When people are in pain, they take aspirin.
*Therefore*
*Conclusion*: Give aspirin to a cat that is in pain. *(FACT: This could kill the poor cat!)*

Two things can be similar in various ways. They may be linked through analogy, composition, or division. When incorrectly applied, we have the errors of false analogy, dangling analogy, fallacy of composition, and fallacy of division.

## Analogies

An argument from analogy starts with the premise that things that consistently share some major similarities possess other similarities:

*Premise*: Water pumps and hearts both move fluids.
*Premise*: Water pumps and hearts are impaired when pipes are blocked. In a water pump this would be a clog, in a heart, a heart attack.
*Premise*: Water pumps and hearts are more likely to clog with fluids saturated with dissolved solids.
*Premise*: Cholesterol is like grease that clogs pipes in a water pump.
*Therefore*
*Conclusion*: Given the analogy between water pumps and hearts, lowering cholesterol should be like reducing grease in a water pump, leading to a reduction in heart disease.

### False Analogy

An analogy can be an extremely useful tool in science. Rats are similar to humans in many ways, so testing out medications in rats may help us determine which may work in humans. A good analogy is grounded in a solid explanation. A **false analogy** is based on a weak or irrelevant similarity:

*Premise*: "Taurus" is a constellation of stars that looks like a bull.
*Premise*: Bulls are aggressive.
*Therefore*
*Conclusion*: The constellation "Taurus" is associated with aggressiveness.

Or consider this:

*Premise*: Any system that looks like the science of astronomy must be true.
*Premise*: Astrology looks like astronomy because it is complicated, mathematical, and considers the stars.
*Therefore*
*Conclusion*: Astrology must be true.

### Dangling Analogy

Sometimes the fallacy of similarity or analogy takes the form of a colorful and metaphorical explanation. Always be suspicious when you encounter a **dangling analogy**, an analogy that is not explained or grounded in a solid logical argument. Put differently, a dangling analogy is a simple, unelaborated illustration. Here are some examples:

> Students are like horses. They learn best when subjected to strong discipline.

> Prayer is like soap. Its bubbles lift you up and burst into a different realm.

> You can travel faster than light across the universe. Einstein says the space-time continuum can be warped (true). So, the space-time continuum is like a giant sheet of paper, which you can fold over on itself. This way, two spots, which might be at opposite ends of the sheet, are now adjacent. So instead of traveling a vast distance, one only need jump a little distance to move from one end of space to another, apparently faster than the speed of light. In the center of black holes the laws of physics break down (apparent fact), so two black holes adjacent on a folded space-time sheet should easily punch through and connect, forming a tunnel.

> When my priest blesses a glass of wine it turns to blood. Of course it still tastes and looks like wine, but it is really blood. It's like this. When we have an infection, we take an antibiotic. We can't see what the drug is doing to the bacteria in our bodies, but it still works. There are things that are true that we cannot see. *(Carroll, 2006)*

Here are some questionable analogies presented by various paranormal advocates. See if you can figure out the problems. (If you give up, check www.skepdic.com):

> Research on psychics is like studying baseball players. When Mickey Mantle gets one hit out of three, that's good. So when a psychic guesses what you're thinking one time out of three, that's equally good.

> The body reacts to medicine like a piano string resonates to the vibrating string of another piano. If you strike "C" on one piano, the "C" string of a nearby piano will resonate and vibrate.

> Homeopathic medicines involve extremely small dilutions of substances that supposedly have an impact on the human body. Medical science says the substances are so diluted that they couldn't conceivably have any effect on the body. However, small things can have big effects. Just because atoms are very small doesn't mean that they have no effect when they collide in an atomic bomb.

### Fallacy of Composition

The **fallacy of composition** erroneously claims that what is true for component parts must by definition be true for the whole. Put differently, this fallacy assumes at least one essential equivalency between part and whole. (Note that this is not a generalization error, as is the case for errors of selection and oversimplification.)

> *Premise*: The church has a few priests who are immoral.
> *Premise*: You can judge a whole by component parts.
> Therefore
> *Conclusion*: The church is immoral.

### Fallacy of Division

Division is the opposite of composition. The **fallacy of division** erroneously states that what is true for the whole must be true for all component parts. The Urni family line is notoriously irritable. Lurinn is a member of the Urni family. Therefore Lurinn must be irritable. Here's another one:

> *Premise*: The church is immoral.
> *Premise*: Our local priest is a part of the church
> *Premise*: The whole defines its parts.
> Therefore
> *Conclusion*: Our local priest is immoral.

## Messing with Reality: Ontological Errors

Ontology is the branch of philosophy concerned with what kinds of things can be said to be "real" or to "exist." Sometimes when we commit errors of ambiguity we are messing with the very nature of reality, that is, making ontological errors.

### Category Errors

If you claim that "rocks have thoughts and feelings," you are doing more than committing a false analogy by claiming an inappropriate similarity between rocks and humans. You are positing an attribute of physical reality itself that does not apply. This is a **category error**. In most general terms, a category error involves giving something a property it cannot logically have (Ryle, 1949). Rocks can't have "feelings."

### Ontological Fusion and Core Knowledge Confusion

To elaborate, think of the world as consisting of three basic types of realities or "ontological categories," each with their own attributes: *psychological realities* (thoughts, feelings, intentions), *biological realities* (birth, life, reproduction, death), and *physical realities* (matter, energy). **Ontological fusion** involves applying an attribute of one type of reality to another (Lindeman & Aarnio, 2007). Rocks (a physical entity) think (a psychological attribute). Emotions (psychological) can be transmitted through electrical wires (physical). Ontological fusion reflects **core knowledge confusion** about how the world works (Svedholm, Lindeman, & Lipsanen, 2010). Those who have such core confusion tend to think of metaphor as literal fact:

- "Stars live in the sky" (Lifeless natural objects are living)
- "Planets know things" (Lifeless objects are animate)
- "Flowers want light" (Living inanimate objects are animate)
- "A home knows its inhabitants" (Artificial objects are animate)
- "Force can sense a human being" (Force is living and animate)
- "The mind falls apart when ill" (Mental states are material)

Svedholm, Lindeman, and Lipsanen (2010) have found that those who are prone to making basic errors about how the world works are much more likely to embrace paranormal claims. Furthermore, different types of confusion are highly correlated; if you are prone to one error, you are likely to make others.

### Emergent Properties and Reductionism

The notion of **emergent properties** states that various levels of analysis have their own theories and explanations. Quantum physics, Newtonian physics, chemistry, biology, psychology, sociology, and economics each refer to different realms. The laws that may explain one realm may not at all apply to another. In physics, two objects with the same "charge" may repel each other. Yet in psychology, two people with similar characteristics or "energy level" may attract one another. Taking this notion further, one cannot propose that a thorough understanding of one level will permit an understanding of another. No matter how well we understand the movement of sub-atomic particles, or how gravity affects time, or the laws of chemistry that permit hydrogen to bond with oxygen to form water, these laws will not explain the unconscious in psychology, mob behavior in sociology, or the stock market in economics. To apply such cross-realm explanations is to commit **reductionism**, an error of mistakenly applying explanations appropriate for one level of analysis to another. It is an error similar to ontological fusion.

### Reification

**Reification** is a category error that involves taking an abstraction, belief, or hypothetical construct, and treating it as if it were a concrete entity, something real. ("Reify" is based on the Latin word *res*, which means "thing.") For example, "government" is an abstract idea. The statement "Government wants you to prosper" treats government as a person. "The universe guides every action" reifies the universe as a being with intentions. "Religion tries to lead people down the path of virtue" again treats religion as a person. The notion that "Good and evil are the two forces driving the universe" treats ideas as forces. In sum, when we reify, we turn something that is not a thing into a thing.

### Truth, Reality, The Answer, and Faith

What is truth? Reality? The "Answer"? Such terms point to some of the most important questions of life. They can also be weasel words that can cause considerable mischief.

Consider a topic we discussed previously – subjective relativism. Subjective relativism is the perspective that the beliefs you and I possess create our realities, even though they may be quite different. As we noted, this stance poses many logical problems (*all* perspectives cannot be true; everyone cannot be masters of the universe.)

A subjective relativist might complain that there are *realities* science cannot detect. Just because something can't be measured by science doesn't mean it's not *true*. Science doesn't have all the *answers*. At the very least, just have *faith*.

Of course, there are many "realities," "truths," and "answers" beyond the domain of science. Among these are subjective states such as emotions and urges; judgments of beauty and morality; and symbolic expressions and stories based on metaphor and myth. Anyone can claim that their feelings of love, opinions concerning what is beautiful or righteous, or favorite fairy tale are "real," "true," or some sort of "answer." Evaluating such claims simply isn't the job of science. Indeed, such utterances may legitimately involve a degree of subjective relativism. Beauty is in the eye of the beholder.

However, here is where such questions get into trouble. Words such as "reality," "truth," and "answers" have a certain ambiguity in that they can also refer to objective facts as determined through the scientific method. An "objective fact" is by definition based on reliable and public observation. The only way to show that something is publicly and reliably observable is to *subject it to public and reliable observation*, that is, scientific inquiry.

So when someone says, "Paranormal Phenomenon X (God, chi, the wisdom of the stars, a ghostly presence, the eternal now, the magic energy from crystals, fate, universal mind, quantum interconnectedness, etc.) is real, true, the answer" and tries to shut down any discussion by asserting "there is more to the world than science," it is not impolite to ask for clarification:

> *Is this Paranormal Phenomenon X some sort of inner feeling or urge, like love or feeling "high"? Is it a metaphor or story? Perhaps it's an aesthetic or moral "reality, truth, or answer"? If so, you're right and science has nothing to say, and my perspective may be just as valid as yours. But if you are claiming that Paranormal Phenomenon X is objective fact, then by definition you are claiming that it is scientifically demonstrated. Objective facts are scientific facts. So we are entitled to a civilized discussion of the evidence.*

If an advocate friend persists by asserting that Phenomenon X is not something that can be subjected to scientific scrutiny, yet is not a subjective emotional state or urge, metaphor or fairy tale, or something of beauty or a moral principle, you can rightly wonder if your friend knows what he or she is talking about.

Here's another example. Consider the word "faith." Physicist and cosmologist Paul Davies (2007) argues that both science and religion rely on faith. The religious believer accepts God without evidence. The scientist accepts an unexplained set of basic physical laws as "just there." Nobel Prize winner Charles Townes (2005) agrees that many people don't realize that science basically involves faith. From this one might conclude that a scientist risks hypocrisy when he or she chides a supernaturalist for accepting paranormal claims without logic or evidence. But this oversimplifies things. A scientist is perfectly open to testable explanations for physical laws, even though none may be present. Yes, he or she may have "faith" that such laws will eventually be found. But this "faith" is different from the "faith" of a God-fearing individual (Park, 2008).

To elaborate, the word "faith" is a potential weasel word with at least two meanings: (1) confident belief in the truth, value, or trustworthiness of a person, idea, or thing, and (2) belief that does not rest on logical proof or material evidence (*American Heritage Dictionary of the English Language*, 2003). A scientist may claim confidence in the "truth, value, or trustworthiness" of the idea that explanations for basic physical laws will eventually be found through logic and empirical investigation. This confidence is based on the success of scientific explanations over history. However, such confidence or "faith" is not chiseled in stone. If some future observations show that current perspectives of physics are inadequate, the faith of the scientist would change. In direct contrast, the faith of the religious does not rest on and simply cannot be challenged by logic or evidence. Yes, the True Believer may have "faith." But the faith of a scientist is a different animal.

## Conclusion

The misuse of sources, logic, and language can impair our ability to separate fact from fiction and discern things as they really are. However, there is one strategy for directly conducting a reality check, science. We consider this in the following chapter.

## Study Questions

**6.1** *Definitions (Define, differentiate, and provide an example for each of the following)*
- A. Fallacy of ambiguity
- B. Meaningless jargon
- C. Technobabble
- D. Science fiction
- E. Weasel
- F. Weasel words
- G. Argument from similarity
- H. False analogy
- I. Dangling analogy
- J. Fallacy of composition
- K. Fallacy of division
- L. Category error
- M. Ontological fusion
- N. Core knowledge confusion
- O. Reductionism
- P. Reification

**6.2** *Using the list of logical fallacies provided in 6.1, identify which fallacy or fallacies are illustrated in the following comments.*

- A. "You may disagree with the theory of evolution. However, let's agree to disagree, and at least share the controversy in biology class."
- B. "Our new healing modalities incorporate and functionally integrate current concepts of fluid dark energy in the multiverse."
- C. "Basically, the US government is a business. So our primary concern must be the bottom line."
- D. "Green tea is like the golden rays of the Sun, warming and healing you with energy from the inside."
- E. "Thoughts are generated by the brain. Thoughts are conscious. The brain consists of cells. Therefore brain cells are conscious. Brain cells consist of organic molecules. Therefore even molecules have consciousness."
- F. "It is not healthy to consume the element chlorine or sodium. Therefore any combinations of chorine and sodium should not be eaten."
- G. "This new veggie burger has got to be delicious. It is brown, crispy, and dripping with ketchup. Looks like real."
- H. "Women get paid less than men. Therefore female CEOs of top corporations get paid less than male CEOs."

- I. "If you are open to love, love will come to you. If you visualize prosperity, prosperity will embrace you."
- J. "All members of our school baseball team contribute to school spirit. Where is it? I don't see the 'spirit.'"

KEY:

A: Weasel words; B: Jargon/technobabble; C: False analogy; D: Dangling analogy; E: Ontological fusion; F: Fallacy of composition; G: Argument from similarity; H: Fallacy of division; I: Reification; J: Category error.

**6.3**  *False Analogies*

Identify how each of these is an analogy. How is each fallacious?
- A. "People are like horses. Both respond best to strong discipline."
- B. "This herbal tea is like a dream. It elevates you to the world of ghosts."
- C. "Our university is like a corporation. What it needs most is an aggressive competitive strategy that focuses entirely on profit and the bottom line."
- D. "Good lawyers know how to go to reference books to research difficult cases. Therefore students in law school should be permitted to take all of their tests in libraries where they can look up answers to test questions."
- E. "It is silly to say that humans can live forever. That's like saying that automobiles are immortal."
- F. "We can't pass a law requiring that people register their guns. That's the first step for any dictatorship. Making people register their guns, then their possessions, then their names."
- G. "It is not wise to limit your sexual experiences to your spouse. If you ate just one type of food, it would eventually become tasteless. By having sex with many different people you guarantee that sex is always interesting and fresh."
- H. "Religious groups that do not become actively involved in politics eventually die. It's like any living organism. Use it or lose it."
- I. "The way we treat cows and chickens is horrible, like the Nazis treated Jews."

**6.4**  *Essay Questions*

- A. How do the following claims illustrate ontological fusion?
  - "Playing Mozart for potted roses will help them grow."
  - "Do not wear the shirt of someone who has passed away. Their bad Karma will rub off."
  - "The planet Earth is so complex that it can best be viewed as a living organism."
  - "Today's computers can play chess and perform simple medical diagnoses. They must be conscious."
  - "The human brain consists of electrical, chemical, and mechanical parts, just like a computer. Therefore it is nothing more than a computer."
  - (ADVANCED QUESTION). "Two subatomic particles, smaller than atoms, can become entangled in a remarkable way. If a particle of light is split into two half-photons that fly away at the speed of light, the 'spin' characteristic of one will always be reflected in the 'spin' characteristic of the other – even if the parts are billions of miles apart. Therefore, two minds, which consist

of atomic and subatomic particles, can be linked and share the same thoughts even if they are separated by great distances."

- B. Evaluate this claim: "*All* paranormal claims are based on ontological fusion. Indeed, one can define as paranormal any claim that ontologically fuses constructs."

- C. How might core knowledge confusion and an impulsive thinking style reinforce each other and contribute to premature acceptance of paranormal claims? How might reflective thinking counteract core knowledge confusion.

- D. According to Professor Gary Schwartz (Schwartz, 2004; Schwartz & Russek, 1999), Einstein came up with his famous theory of relativity by engaging in a thought experiment in which he imagined himself riding a beam of light. Inspired by this idea, Schwartz decided to imagine himself riding vibrations. Imagine two adjacent tuning forks. If you strike one, it will hum and the second fork will also hum in resonance. Furthermore, the first fork will pick up the hum of the second fork and resonate in a new way reflecting both the original hum and the reflected hum. There are three parts to this system. The first tuning fork, the second fork, and the vibrations that travel between them. Take the forks away, and the vibrations continue through the air containing the information from each fork. (When you finally hear a lightning bolt, the lightning is actually over.) Through such feedback the recurrently interactive behavior of photons and electrons enables them to store information. Therefore, any two things (electrons, cells, organs, people) that maintain an ongoing relationship evoke a dynamical info-energy system, a memory of their interactional history. Just as the photons of a dying star travel through the universe millennia after the star's demise, the informational loop between electrons, atoms, organs, and even people exists independently. Homeopathy works because such information contains memory concerning bodily systems. Psychics can read "minds" by actually tapping into information feedback loops. Life after death exists, because information loops continue even after one's demise. Systemic Memory Theory also explains out-of-body experiences, reincarnation, chi, aromatherapy, crystal healing, distant healing, spirit medicine, acupuncture, the kabala, and karma. People have their own dynamical info-energy systems, which are actually living and evolving after death. So Jesus, and Elvis, still live. This synopsis has not done justice to the subtleties of Professor Schwartz's theory. Analyze in terms of concepts introduced in this chapter.

**6.5** *Internet Search*
- A. Scientific hoaxes have been used to demonstrate the pseudoscientific use of jargon and technobabble. Select and describe one of these hoaxes. Which logical errors do they illustrate?
    - o Dihydrogen monoxide hoax
    - o Turboencabulator hoax
    - o Blond hair will be extinct in a century
    - o Archaeoraptor bird dinosaur
    - o Check the following postmodernism hoax generator:
      http://www.elsewhere.org/journal/pomo/
      Find and explain an interesting hoax from this site.

- B. On the web you will find a number of "technobabble generators," "Star Trek technobabble generators," and "jargon generators." Search and find one. Describe a gem you have unearthed.
- C. Find examples of jargon, weasel words, ontological fusion, and reductionism in internet discussions of:
  o Quantum consciousness
  o Quantum healing
  o Rain dances
  o The Secret
  o Uri Geller

# 7

# Science

---

**OUTLINE**

---

1) Science in Action
2) Observational Science
    a) Operationalized Definitions
    b) Public and Replicable Measures
    c) Reliable and Valid Measures
3) Experimental Science
    a) Independent and Dependent Variables
    b) The Ambiguities of Temporal Contiguity
        i) *Post hoc* fallacy
        ii) Pragmatic fallacy
    c) Ask the Right Question
        i) The falsifiability criterion and the "F-Question"
        ii) Burden of proof
    d) Rule Out Alternative Explanations
        i) Control groups
        ii) Double-blind procedures
        iii) Stimulus leakage
    e) Test the Right People
        i) Representative sample
        ii) Random sample
4) Theories
    a) Falsifiability
    b) Productivity
    c) Comprehensiveness
    d) Simplicity and Occam's Razor
        i) Anomaly
        ii) Paradigm shift

---

Science is one of our best reality-checking tools. When you test an idea, often you use science. When you try to find out what works and what doesn't work, you use science. When you take a pragmatic or practical approach to solving a problem, you use science. Doctors use science to diagnose illness and prescribe treatment. Detectives use science to solve crimes. Auto mechanics use science to fix cars. Students use science to decide on courses, career paths, and even weekend dates.

*Critical Thinking: Pseudoscience and the Paranormal*, Second Edition. Jonathan C. Smith.
© 2018 John Wiley & Sons, Inc. Published 2018 by John Wiley & Sons, Inc.

## Science in Action

Science is not technology or the production of devices and gadgets. Science is not religion because science holds no dogmas. Indeed science is no more religious, or atheistic, than dentistry. But science is not without values; a scientist treasures discovering things as they are, and questioning honestly and fearlessly. A true scientist is an Open-Minded Critical Thinker.

Here are some everyday scientists in action:

Yoho is camping with his friends and one night comes across a patch of mushrooms. He wonders if they are edible or poisonous. He looks in his camper's guide of edible forest plants for pictures and characteristics of poisonous mushrooms. The book warns against mushrooms covered with scaly warts. It notes that these spots can be hard to detect in low light and when the mushrooms are covered with dust or due. Yoho asks his fellow campers if what he's found looks like the pictures in the book. He decides to wash the mushrooms and take another look in daylight. Just to be careful, he takes a quick photo with his phone and texts it to his best friend, a camping expert.

Vinn is a basketball player looking for a new pair of shoes to improve her game. She notes that the best brands are not made of cloth, but of real or synthetic leather. Her friends recommend real leather. Her coach wears synthetic leather. She decides to find out for herself which is best and goes to the sports store. There Vinn picks the best real and best synthetic leather shoe, wears each for 10 minutes and walks around the store, jumps a few times, and stretches. After each trial she asks herself if the shoe was comfortable and seemed to fit right for a good game.

Gil (a carnivore) is cooking a special dinner for his vegetarian friend Yoho (who has just left the hospital having had food poisoning). He is trying out a new soup made with water, soy beans, onions, celery, salt, and garlic. The problem is that Gil thinks this concoction tastes terrible. Something is missing. He guesses that the soup is too bland and needs something to add spice and tang. So he tries adding a tomato, and then a green pepper. Yoho is happy with the mix. (Gil secretly plops some bacon in his own serving.)

Dreth is very excited about his new computer. Unfortunately, it is not working. The screen simply flashes all the time and typing does nothing. Perhaps it needs a new battery. Maybe he just has to unplug and plug the set in again so it resets. So Dreth pops in a new battery, pushes the "start" button, and nothing happens. But performing a simple reset does the trick.

How are these examples of the scientific method? Although philosophers disagree as to the precise elements of scientific investigation, most would agree that a narrow definition includes the following: observe, test, and explain through theory. By applying these tools, ideas are added and rejected, and knowledge grows. When these tools are not applied, our knowledge is likely to remain static and unchanging. Indeed, one of the best signs of whether a theory is scientific, or pseudoscientific, is whether it has changed and grown over time. We will look at two types of scientific research, observational and experimental.

# Observational Science

Observation is at the heart of scientific inquiry. One asks, "What is there?" Using good observational science, a hiker finds a spotted mushroom, an astronomer discovers a new planet, a biologist identifies a new type of frog, and a physicist uncovers a new subatomic particle.

### Operationalized Definitions

Any scientific study must use words with clear definitions. Specifically, key terms must be **operationally defined**. An operationalized definition specifies how a concept can be measured. For example:

> *Measure "heat" using a "thermometer."*
> *Measure "weight" using "scales."*
> *Measure "friendship" in terms of number of Facebook "likes."*

### Public and Replicable Measures

Years ago I conducted a study on the psychological effects of meditation and various techniques. One part of the design involved observing how practitioners responded to various anxiety questionnaires. Near the end of the study I met with those assisting in technique instruction and asked how the participants were doing. Without hesitation, their leader closed her eyes and after a few thoughtful seconds reported, "You have nothing to worry about. They are doing fine." I assumed she was recalling her meeting with my trainees. I was wrong. How did she operationalize what she was measuring? She used her presumed psychic powers to contact each participant and psychically assess their well-being. I was not convinced. Her observations were not public because I could not see what she was doing in her head. And they were hardly replicable because there was no way I could do exactly the same thing in my head. A scientific observation must be **public** and **replicable** in that others can witness it when given precise instructions. Have your friends examine the mushrooms.

### Reliable and Valid Measures

Our measures must be **reliable** and **valid**. Reliability and validity have precise scientific meanings which may differ from everyday use. In science, a reliable test yields a similar score over and over. A reliable scale for weight will give you consistent readings over different days. A valid test agrees with other tests of the same thing, or works well in testing out hypotheses. A valid set of scales will give you the same weight as, say, the scales used in your doctor's office. Invalid scales may be calibrated incorrectly and consistently under- or overstate your weight.

# Experimental Science

When we make observations, we may encounter a question about causes. We may detect a pattern that prompts us to ask, "What's going on." In an experimental study you look for the causal relationship between something and something else. "Does extra sleep lead to higher grades?" "Does sexual abstinence before a game increase one's score?" "Do zinc lozenges shorten a cold?" With these questions we are examining things that change (less or more sleep … lower or higher grades; less or more abstinence … lower or higher game scores; less or more zinc … long or short colds). Things that change are variables, the basic focus of all experimental science.

### Independent and Dependent Variables

An **independent variable** (IV) is something that isn't changed by other variables you might measure. It is independent. If you are interested in whether one's height is related to success at playing basketball, the number of basketball games one wins is not going to change a player's height. Therefore height is the independent variable. A **dependent variable** (DV) depends on other factors. For example, if you changed the height of basketball team members, game performance might increase. Games won is the dependent variable.

Sometimes students get confused at this point. Imagine visitors from another planet, perhaps Klingons from Star Trek, are trying to figure out the mysterious Earth kitchen faucet. They note two things, a movable knob and water flowing out of a spout. To figure out how this device works, they grab the handle and turn it. They discover water flow increases or decreases, revealing how the faucet works. Here the independent variable is the knob, the variable one "grabs," the variable under direct control of the observer. The DV is the stream of water. Manipulating the IV causes changes in the DV.

Generally, the independent variable causes a change in the dependent variable: IV → DV; CAUSE → EFFECT. Indeed, you can test this out by simply switching the terms in a sentence using both. "Player height (IV) leads to higher basketball scores (DV)" makes sense. However, switching the terms makes no sense: "Scoring higher in basketball (IV) increases player height (DV)."

There are times when the IV and DV are genuinely unclear. For example, two variables may occur together, that is, be temporally contiguous or correlated. For example, active pet dogs may eat more dog food. But what is the causal relationship? Maybe activity makes dogs more hungry, so they eat more. Or perhaps dogs that are fed more have more energy, and are more active. Here we simply do not know the cause or effect between the IV and DV.

### The Ambiguities of Temporal Contiguity

One of the most common observational errors is also an informal logical fallacy, the ***post hoc*** ("after this") or ***post hoc ergo propter hoc*** ("after this, therefore because of this") **fallacy**. It is a very popular fallacy (I get 440,000 Google hits). Here one argues that just because event X comes before or occurs at the same time as Y does not prove that X caused Y. Technically, X is the predictor while Y is the criterion, nothing more. It would be just as valid to say that Y is the predictor and X is the criterion. The false presumption is that correlations prove causality. For example, astrology may well have developed when early humans figured out that when the stars appear in a certain part of the sky, spring will soon arrive. Of course, the stars do not cause the seasons to change. But this did not prevent the development of astrology.

Similar to the *post hoc* fallacy is the **pragmatic fallacy**, the belief that because something appears to work, the presumed causal assumptions must be true.

*Premise*: Whenever my psychic healer places his hands over a sore muscle, it feels better. He says that electromagnetic energy from his aura normalizes the flow of my life energy.
Therefore
*Conclusion*: There must be something to his explanation because his treatments do work.

In order to identify and sort out a causal relationship we must test it, beginning with a hypothesis.

## Ask the Right Question

A useful experimental hypothesis specifies a cause–effect relationship between an IV and a DV. In addition it proposes how we might conduct a replication to rule out alternative hypotheses. In our examples, Vinn was comparing two hypotheses: real leather shoes are best for her feet vs. synthetic leather shoes are best. Gil hypothesized that adding tomatoes or green peppers would add spice and tang to a bland soup. Dreth hypothesized that a new battery, then a reset, would make his new computer work. It may seem obvious, but each of these experimental hypotheses makes sense because you know how to test them out. But sometimes this isn't the case.

### The Falsifiability Criterion and the "F-Question"
One of the most powerful tools in critical thinking is the "**F-Question**." Simply ask: "*What would it take to reject your claim?*" If your hypothesis can't be tested, or disconfirmed, it is generally useless for establishing the facts. In general terms, this is the **falsifiability (or testability) criterion**, one of the most frequently cited tools of critical thinking. Philosopher Carl Popper (1959) proposed that no hypothesis can be considered scientific if there is no way of proving it false. For example, Freud says that all men have latent homosexual tendencies. If you are male, and have no homosexual urges, then you are repressing them. If this claim irritates you, your irritation is evidence of your underlying homosexual urges. If you're getting confused, that's evidence that your repressed homosexual tendencies are interfering with your brain. You can't win. There's no test to show this idea is wrong.

To repeat, if a hypothesis is not falsifiable, it fails the "F-Question."

Sometimes a hypothesis is effectively not falsifiable if its proponent simply refuses to accept any evidence, no matter how good. Put differently, the proponent uses ***ad hoc*** (improvised "for this purpose") reasoning to explain away any observed empirical support:

ASTROLOGER: You are a Pisces. Therefore, you are sensitive.
SKEPTIC: But my friends tell me I am tough and unfeeling.
ASTROLOGER: That's because the Moon and Sun are in conflict for your sign.

### Burden of Proof
Repeated use of unfalsifiable and *ad hoc* claims is often symptomatic of another problem. In the real world, especially the world of extraordinary claims, the burden of proof

resides with the claimant. Imagine how our legal system would work if the target of every grievance had to prove their innocence! A frustrated husband might accuse his wife of cavorting with each of his 10 office mates. In our new world, each person accused would have to prove his innocence, regardless of the absence of evidence. Imagine the police claimed you drove through 10 red lights, and required you prove you did not.

In the world of open-minded critical thinking, **the burden of proof** is with the claimant. If someone claims that little pixies pluck leaves off trees each autumn, it is not up to the scientific community to spend millions of dollars showing that this is not true. It is the responsibility of the person who believes in pixies to prove that it is true. Sometimes we see advocates of the paranormal use this strategy. Can you see how the following claims do not play by the rules?

> *I can read my grandmother's thoughts. Prove I can't.*
> *Astrological horoscopes can predict the future. Prove they can't.*
> *Drinking urine is good for you. Prove it isn't.*
> *God is female. Prove this isn't true.*

In sum, the burden of proof requirement is perhaps our best way of ensuring that questions are asked well.

### Rule Out Alternative Explanations

We have noted that a good test specifies how we might perform observable public replications that rule out alternative explanations. This is often done through careful experimental design, which often involves **control groups**, **double-blind procedures**, and **controls for stimulus leakage**.

#### Control Groups

Imagine you are testing the effects of green tea on memory. You give a group of people green tea and then test their memory. If memory scores improve, there could be alternative explanations. For example, perhaps their belief that tea increases memory resulted in their improved scores. The tea-drinkers became so motivated and enthusiastic that their performance improved. To control for this, one would have to test a control group designed to rule out the explanation that expectation and motivation improved performance. Such a control group would be identical to the experimental group in every way except that green tea would not be used. They might get green tap water spiked to taste somewhat bitter, like tea. Such a fake treatment, designed to look exactly like an experimental treatment, but with the active ingredient removed, is called a **placebo** (Chapter 11). If the placebo control group scores worse than the tea group, then one has support for the hypothesis that green tea improves memory.

#### Double-blind Procedures

Often the enthusiasm and beliefs of an experimenter can rub off on participants. Perhaps the experimenters who gave the real green tea were excited about the powerful memory elixir they were about to test. Perhaps the participants unconsciously picked up on this excitement and became more motivated and excited. The only way to absolutely control for this alternative explanation is to introduce a **double-blind** control.

In a double-blind study, neither the experimenter nor the participants know what treatments they have. Those giving and receiving the green tea or green tap water have no way of knowing which. Therefore, neither group of participants has reason to be more enthusiastic or motivated than the other.

### Stimulus Leakage

When a study has inadequate double-blind controls, the possibility exists for **stimulus leakage**. Here key elements of a research design may be detected by participants, biasing their results. A psychic may claim to be able to magically read through a sealed envelope. Unknown to you, when the psychic holds the envelope to the light she can actually see faint impressions of its contents leaking through the translucent paper. Stimulus leakage can be very difficult to detect and may require the assistance of an expert trained in deception, distraction, and subliminal control – a magician. This suggestion is actually now accepted by the majority of paranormal researchers (Irwin & Watt, 2007).

### Test the Right People

Finally, a study might have an excellent experimental design and fail because research participants were poorly sampled. It is impossible for a researcher to include everyone in a study.

### Representative Sample

Researchers attempt to select a **representative sample** that resembles the population in which one is interested and is not biased to favor a preferred research outcome. A study about the female population should include women. A study about heart patients should include heart patients.

### Random Sample

One way to increase representativeness is to select a **random sample** from the population. If you are interested in why people stand in lines to buy the latest smart phone, it would be unwise to interview the first five people in line. One might pick names out of a giant hat, have a monkey point at names in a phone book, or use more systematic statistical tools.

## Theories

Once you have made observations and tested a hypothesis, or series of hypotheses – again, all public and replicable – you might generate an encompassing theory that explains an observed phenomenon. A good theory shows how different ideas are related and thereby systematizes and unifies what we know. "Green tea can improve memory" is a simple explanatory hypothesis. A theory is encompassing and complex, and includes confirmed hypotheses. This could be a green tea memory theory:

> The antioxidants in green tea help prevent the deterioration of brain cells, and stimulate the flow of blood to the brain. This combined effect results in improved memory.

Many philosophers and scientists have proposed long lists of rules for judging the adequacy of theories (and hypotheses). The essentials can be reduced to four criteria: falsifiability, productivity, comprehensiveness, and simplicity (Schick & Vaughn, 2005).

### Falsifiability

We have already encountered falsifiability as a characteristic of a good hypothesis. Falsifiability is also one of the most frequently mentioned criteria for theory adequacy. It is also one of the most hotly debated (Hartshorne & Weiss, 1932). An unfalsifiable explanation is a string of empty words. As Vaughn (2008) has quipped: "It is equivalent to saying that an unknown thing with unknown properties acts in an unknown way to cause a phenomenon – which is the same thing as offering no explanation at all" (p. 351).

There is another way of saying all of this: a good testable theory predicts something we don't already know. We might not know if something's false; a theory should enable us to increase our knowledge of the universe a bit by finding out if it is indeed false. In the fifteenth century, witches were hypothesized to be possessed by the devil. If you admitted (after augmented interrogation) that you were a witch, the case would be closed and you would be burned at the stake. If you denied being a witch, this would be evidence that the devil was causing you to lie, and again you would be burned at the stake. We know you are either going to deny or admit to being a witch. Hypothesizing that you are a witch adds nothing because our minds are already made up. We already know you're guilty.

Theories about the objective world can become unfalsifiable when they are based on personal motives and emotions, realms that have the potential for telling us little about objective fact. These justifications include *morality*, *aesthetics*, *intuition*, or just *arbitrary opinion*. Consider these examples:

*Morality*: "Killing is immoral. Therefore capital punishment desensitizes society to immorality and leads to violence and crime."
*Aesthetics*: "I find beauty in the idea that there is no supreme being, and that everything is due to chance. Therefore there is no God."
*Intuition*: "Maybe it's a gut reaction, or maybe God's trying to tell me something, but I have to marry Dreth."
*Arbitrary opinion*: "I've decided candidate X will make the best mayor. She's my choice. I don't know why, but I've decided she's right for the job."

For such claims, the presence or absence of evidence is irrelevant, so there is no way of proving the claim false. Again, that's because the claim is embraced, not because of its objective reality, but because of other more personal reasons.

### The Saber and Shield of Unfalsifiability

For those seeking objective truth and fact, an unfalsifiable claim is of little value, something akin to wishful thinking. After all, if you believe something is objective fact, your claim should be empirically testable and open to potential refutation. You should be willing to engage in open-minded critical thinking.

Friesen, Campbell, and Kay (2014) have proposed that unfalsifiability can have "offensive" and "defensive" payoffs, serving as both saber and shield. Armed with unfalsifiable arguments, believers can promote and protect their convictions with intractable fervor. As a result they can more readily criticize, marginalize, and polarize skeptics.

A series of elegant experiments demonstrated how this process can work. One experiment tested if people change their beliefs to be unfalsifiable when these beliefs are challenged. One hundred seventy-four participants were selected, 124 who supported and 50 who opposed same-sex marriage. All participants were given a passage that reported research (fabricated) on the effects of same-sex and opposite-sex parents on child career success, criminality, and intelligence. Some of the passages reported an adverse effect, whereas others stated that same-sex marriage had no effect. Again, the research was fake.

Participants then rated whether the issue of whether same-sex marriage should be legalized is opinion-based (and thus unfalsifiable) or fact-based (effect on children).

Something interesting happened when supporters and opponents of same-sex marriage were given facts that appeared to contradict their position. One might expect they would change their position. Instead, they maintained their support or opposition, but retreated to an unfalsifiable justification ("opposition/support for same-sex marriage is a matter of moral opinion"). In other words, they protected their political beliefs by framing the issue as more unfalsifiable. It is interesting that opponents and proponents of same-sex marriage have used a variety of unfalsifiable arguments in state and federal court. Opponents have argued that same-sex marriage will "weaken the institution of marriage," and "lead down a 'slippery slope' giving people in polygamous, incestuous, bestial, and other nontraditional relationships the right to marry." Proponents have argued that same-sex marriage will "reduce discrimination in other areas," "enhance the financial health of state and local governments," and "reduce divorce rates." (gaymarriage.procon.org)

Friesen et al. speculate that such beliefs do not stay dormant, but have great potential for unconstrained growth. An unfalsifiable belief is protected from challenge, so when it is part of a worldview containing both falsifiable and unfalsifiable beliefs, the unfalsifiable beliefs are more likely to survive and rise in prominence. The encompassing worldview becomes increasingly defined by a mix of unfalsifiable beliefs and in turn provides increased protection and justification for unfalsifiable components. Worldviews become more rigid, intolerant, aggressive, and anti-scientific.

Unfalsifiability frees believers to promote their convictions with fervor and intolerance. At the very least, fervor and intolerance are not discouraged. The contest of ideas becomes something of a siege, aggressors resistant to change attacking a vulnerable resistance. The matchup is one-sided unless the rules change and falsifiability itself becomes a mandatory ticket for admission to the game.

One can hypothesize that this pattern may contribute to the fervor and prevalence of paranormal beliefs. Belief in astrology, witchcraft, ghosts, and zombies has persisted for thousands of years. Indeed, today more people believe in astrology than was the case a millennium ago. It is easy to find True Believers for nearly every paranormal claim. Books promoting such claims far outsell objective and skeptical reviews.

Friesen et al. conclude:

> These results and speculations suggest that unfalsifiability may be a dangerous force in society at large. Though it might benefit individuals psychologically or groups socially, unfalsifiability might also lead people and societies to continually

> make truth-defying decisions. To the extent that the success of a society largely depends on its ability to respect good data and change behavior accordingly ..., a devotion not just to ideas but to testing those ideas is necessary for the welfare and improvement of the society.
>
> *(p. 11)*
>
> A note of optimism. In another study, these same researchers found that asserting that a claim may indeed be subject to falsifiability reduced the fervor with which one holds a belief. Perhaps this introduces an element of reflective thinking. A critical thinker accepts the possibility of being mistaken.
>
> What do you think? Can you apply the Friesen speculation to any current extremist movement?

It's worth repeating the costs of unfalsifiable theory. Most basically, such a theory is a science-stopper. Some paranormal theories are falsifiable, whereas others are less so. Although there are many systems (or theories) of astrology, one can usually generate a testable hypothesis based on the time of your birth. In contrast, quantum theory of extrasensory perception (ESP) states that thoughts are interconnected at a subatomic level. How could this be falsified? If everyone is connected, shouldn't everyone have access to everyone's thoughts all the time? Or are connections between thoughts random, like the flickering of electrons? If so, we could never predict when any one person randomly picks up the thought of another, and when this does appear it would be indistinguishable from a nonparanormal random coincidence. And then there is the creationist theory of the origin of the universe which states that the story of Genesis is factually correct. God created the universe 6,000–10,000 years ago. This would seem to permit some easy tests. We can determine the age of rocks and fossils through carbon dating and the age of stars through an analysis of the light they emit. Unfortunately, creation theory permits a convenient additional feature – God may hide evidence of His handiwork in order to test our faith. This is indeed the position of some followers of Islam, Christianity, and Pastafarianism (Chapter 8).

Unfalsifiable theories have caused considerable mischief and misery throughout history. The Nazis believed that they were a race with superior blood. God wills that a particular plot of land belongs to our people, and we must die (and commit genocide) to keep it. God doesn't directly answer our prayers because that would compromise our free will. Mind-reading works only when negative scientists (and skeptical magicians) are kept away. Ghosts are shy and tend to hide when ghost-detecting equipment (or scientists and magicians) are present. Many paranormal phenomena in this text are unfalsifiable.

Unfalsifiability is not always undesirable. Aristotle correctly hypothesized that all material was comprised of atoms. However, because he didn't have a cyclotron or nuclear reactor, he couldn't test it out. (Aristotle also incorrectly proposed that all elements were combinations of four basic elements – fire, earth, air, and water – another untestable idea that contributed to hundreds of years of alchemy.) So, a theory that can't be falsified may not be wrong, but simply ahead of its time.

Furthermore, in real science, researchers at times go to great lengths generating *ad hoc* hypotheses so that preferred theories can survive assaults of falsifying evidence.

Sometimes, as is the case with many paranormal phenomena, such a patchwork represents a refusal ever to discard a theory. The theory is embraced with dogmatic fervor. However, at other times such efforts stimulate good research. At first, those who postulated that the Earth orbits the Sun didn't know how to test this idea against the prevailing and apparently obvious notion that the Sun orbits the Earth. But they persisted and eventually won out. How do we know when it's time to give up a theory? We need to see how it stands the tests of productivity, comprehensiveness, and simplicity.

### Productivity (Predicting Something New)

How do you select between two theories that are testable? Two of the greatest scientists of the world had different theories about gravity. Newton thought that gravity instantly pulled masses together and kept planets in orbit. Einstein thought that gravity was a curve in space and time that bent the movement of whatever passed through. Newton's theory worked well. By examining the tug of planets, astronomers could predict the existence of the planet Neptune. Something was pulling on Uranus, probably an undetected planet. Einstein's theory also worked to predict planets. However, it predicted something extraordinary that Newton never considered. Heavy objects could actually bend light like a lens. Indeed, massive galaxies far away bend space and time so much that, like a telescope, they magnify what is beyond so that we can see what might otherwise be too small to detect. Einstein's theory of gravity is more **productive** than Newton's theory. It predicts the unexpected.

Because good theories are productive, they are always changing and growing, always on the move. One good way to determine if an explanation is not science is to ask if it has evolved over time. Ideas of witchcraft, zombies, astrology, ghosts, and communication with the dead have remained essentially unchanged for millennia.

### Comprehensiveness

How much of the world does the theory explain? Good theories have wide scope. Einstein's theory of relativity explains not only why heavy objects bend light, but the fact that time slows down when one travels very fast. This hypothesis has actually been verified in research. Clocks in fast-moving satellites actually run slower than clocks on Earth. (Yes, this is true. You can test it out. All you need is a $1 million atomic clock and a jet.) His theories also state that as objects go faster, they get heavier. A particle moving at the speed of light would get extremely heavy. This too has been shown in carefully controlled experiments. (To test this you need a particle accelerator, costing millions of dollars.)

### Simplicity and Occam's Razor

Occam's razor states that the best explanation is the one that requires the fewest assumptions. To elaborate, a weak theory implies additional untested questions (often answered with *ad hoc* assumptions). In addition, the links between parts of a theory are not simply explained. And the theory conflicts with "background knowledge," what we already have observed to be true.

William of Occam was a fourteenth-century English logician and Franciscan friar who, according to lore, is said to have proposed that an explanation should assume as little as possible (actually there is little evidence that Occam actually invented the razor bearing his name; however, it's a great story). Superfluous assumptions should be discarded or "shaved off" (as with a razor) because they add nothing. Put differently, avoid using one unexplained/unobserved phenomenon to explain another unexplained phenomenon.

Imagine a church group performs a rain dance, and the next day it rains. One explanation might be that the Rain Gods were pleased by the dance performed in their honor, and granted rain as a gift. Another explanation might be that the rain was a random event, perhaps expected because of the changing seasons. Which is simpler? Count the assumptions. This can be a little tricky. After all, it might seem simple to say the Rain Gods did it. However, this claim makes many questionable assumptions. Do supernatural entities exist? How do we know Rain Gods exist? Are they invisible? Why don't they make their presence known? How do we know this is true? What kinds of dance work on Rain Gods? Ballet? Belly dancing? Do the Rain Gods create rain out of thin air, or do they manipulate global weather patterns to eventually create rain over your dry field? What if all the churches prayed for rain at the same time, how could it possibly rain everywhere at once? Who gets the rain and who doesn't? How do we know? We could go on and on for centuries, or simply apply Occam's razor, conclude that the rain was a random weather event caused by conflicting weather systems, and go on with living.

Lack of simplicity is not always undesirable. As stated by Thomas Kuhn (1970) in *The Structure of Scientific Revolutions*, science progresses when one discovers a certain type of complexity, an **anomaly** that does not fit the prevailing **paradigm** or worldview of facts and investigative methods. When anomalies persist and cannot be explained away, the scientific community is forced to change what it believes is true. Such changes are called **paradigm shifts** and have occurred throughout history. For example, there was a time when people believed that diseases arose spontaneously (Black, 1996). This seemed to fit everyday observations that people fall ill for no apparent reason. However, some observations could not be explained. People living in isolation from those suffering an epidemic were less likely to fall ill. People living under hygienic conditions seemed more protected from disease. A new investigative tool, the microscope, enabled scientists to discover the presence of microorganisms in spoiled food and diseased tissue. Eventually these observations led to a paradigm shift in medicine that linked disease with germs, and used microscopes as an investigative tool (Metchnikoff & Berger, 1939).

---

### Is Science Bad?

Unfortunately, calling something "science" can cause problems. Believers in the paranormal and supernatural often display hostility toward science, accusing scientific thinkers of narrow-mindedness and Godlessness. Christian creationists warn against the "godless religion" of science. Non-Christian advocates of complementary and alternative medicine speak of deep mystical energies that science cannot detect. Movies and television often portray scientists as sexless geeks wearing white lab coats, isolated from the real world in windowless laboratories. Scientists are eccentric, if not outright mad.

It is easy to test the depth of this misperception of science. The next time you are with a group of friends, say at a party, wait for someone to utter an extraordinary paranormal claim. (You can "stir the pot" by mentioning the latest TV or movie hit on ghosts, miracles, flying saucers, or psychic detectives.) A friend comes up with this:

> "Last week I was thinking about you, and you called! I think I can see into the future! I'm psychic! I'm going to be famous!"

Imagine what would happen if you replied:

> "Let's be scientific and systematically apply the scientific method to your extraordinary claim. How many times do you think about your friends? Probably many times. Psychologists would say that it is highly likely you forgot most of the times. When I call, you are more likely to remember that you just thought about me. It's just chance and selective recall."

I think your friend would be rather annoyed, and not inclined to pursue this line of discussion. Now imagine you made the same observation without using the "S word" (or "P word").

> "Get a grip, friend! Let's do a reality check. You use your phone a lot. Eventually you are bound to think of me just before I call. That's simply an everyday coincidence."

As biologist Thomas H. Huxley, perhaps the most important defender of Darwin's theory of evolution, remarked (Huxley, 1880): "Science is simply common sense at its best – that is, rigidly accurate in observation, and merciless to fallacy in logic." More recently, Albert Einstein said pretty much the same thing: "The whole of science is nothing more than a refinement of everyday thinking" (Einstein, 1936; Paydarfar & Schwartz, 2001).

---

### Project Alpha, Sagan's Balance, and the FEDS Standard

Research on the paranormal has been plagued with fraud, error, deception, and sloppiness. Project Alpha is possibly the most famous attempt to demonstrate what can go wrong (Randi, 1982, 1983). I recommend viewing the documentary of James Randi's life, "An Honest Liar."

In 1979, James S. McDonnell (Chairman of McDonnell Douglas Aircraft) gave Washington University in St Louis a half-million-dollar grant to establish the McDonnell Laboratory for Psychical Research. Specifically, the lab was interested in investigating psychokinetic metal bending (PKMB) by children. Magician James Randi ("The Amazing Randi") saw an opportunity to conduct an experiment he had contemplated for quite some time.

Randi selected two teenage magicians, Steve Shaw (Banachek) and Mike Edwards (aged 18 and 17, respectively), trained them to perform a variety of tricks, and sent them off to the lab.

#### The Deception

After screening 300 applicants, the McDonnell lab selected Shaw and Edwards. For four years the two young men fooled a variety of scientists in more than 160 hours of experiments. They bent spoons as well as aluminum rods securely embedded in blocks of plastic, identified pictures sealed in envelopes, made digital clocks stop working, caused

**Figure 7.1** James Randi.

fuses to burn out, rotated a paper propeller isolated inside a glass dome, psychically created pictures on film inside cameras, linked two closed wooden rings, and magically drew mystical symbols out of piles of dry coffee grounds in a locked aquarium. They achieved all of these using nothing more than standard magician's tricks easily found and explained on the internet (search "Project Alpha").

Amazingly, Randi wrote to the director of McDonnell lab, Dr Peter Phillips (a physics professor) outlining 11 "caveats" they should be wary of and what to do to avoid being tricked. Randi also offered to serve as a consultant and witness for free, and to even help set up "trick-proof" experiments. Dr Phillips refused, claiming he was quite capable of detecting deception. However, he decided to videotape many of the experiments.

Shaw and Edwards succeeded in fooling the McDonnell lab researchers and quite a few other scientists. Dr Phillips and the paranormal community were enthralled with his "gifted psychics." Lab researchers could see no evidence of deception in the video tapes, although outside viewers found the tricks amusingly obvious. When Randi leaked stories that the talented psychics might be plants, Phillips laughed it off as a joke. Of course, eventually all was revealed. Some researchers still refused to believe. One even claimed that Steve and Mike actually had psychic powers, and were lying when they claimed to be magicians. Another scientist complained that Randi's experiment had "set parapsychology back 100 years." McDonnell lab soon closed in disgrace.

Project Alpha is perhaps the best example of how a professional magician can identify deceptions that scientists and sincere psychics miss.

### Sagan's Balance and the FEDS Standard
Astronomer and popular critical thinker Carl Sagan is famous for advocating a rule, known as "Sagan's Balance": *"Extraordinary claims require extraordinary evidence."* This is an idea

that skeptics and many believers accept for evaluating paranormal claims. Project Alpha helps us understand what Sagan's Balance requires. I propose an elaboration.

Research on extraordinary claims of consequence requires *expert independent and impartial supervision and replication to eliminate **F**raud, **E**rror, **D**eception, and **S**loppiness.* I call this the **FEDS Standard**.

*1. Fraud*
The investigator makes up or changes data, reports only positive results, fails to report compromising design features, or claims to have done something that was in fact not done.

*2. Error*
The investigator misuses experimental tools, methods, or statistics.

*3. Deception*
Research participants, assistants, or colleagues trick the investigator.

*4. Sloppiness*
The investigator does not take into account such research problems as stimulus leakage, submission of positive studies for publication (the file drawer effect), untrained and careless assistants, arbitrarily stopping a study when positive results emerge (arbitrary stop points, Chapter 8), or failing to rule out any of the five "alternative explanations" discussed in this text.

## Study Questions

**7.1** *Definitions (Define, differentiate, and provide an example for each of the following)*
- A. Observational science
- B. Operationalized terms
- C. Public observation
- D. Replicability
- E. Reliability
- F. Validity
- G. Experimental science
- H. Independent variable
- I. Dependent variable
- J. Temporal contiguity
- K. *Post hoc* fallacy
- L. Pragmatic fallacy
- M. Operationalized definition
- N. Falsifiability criterion
- O. *Ad hoc* reasoning
- P. Burden of proof
- Q. Control group
- R. Double-blind
- S. Stimulus leakage

- T. Representative sample
- U. Random sample
- V. Theories
- W. Falsifiability
- X. Unfalsifiability
- Y. Theory productivity
- Z. Theory comprehensiveness
- AA. The simplicity criterion
- BB. Occam's razor
- CC. Scientific anomaly
- DD. Paradigm
- EE. Paradigm shift
- FF. Sagan's Balance
- GG. The FEDS Standard

**7.2** *Simple Thought Questions*
- A. Give an example of an everyday activity in which you use observational or experimental science.
- B. How can inductive reasoning involve hypotheses testing?
- C. Give an example of when a moral decision is unfalsifiable. Can you think of an example of a moral decision that is based on a falsifiable claim?
- D. How is an unfalsifiable theory a science-stopper? What are the possible costs of this?

**7.3** *Essay Question*
One source of knowledge about the physical world is your own anecdotal evidence, that is, your personal experience and intuition. Can you think of times when personal experience and intuition cannot conceivably pass the test of science? Does this mean that your personal experience and intuition are worthless? Why? Why not?

**7.4** *Internet Search*
- A. One of the more challenging tasks facing students of the paranormal is figuring out what theoretical notions underlie a paranormal claim. Astrology is a good example. You will not find a single, coherent, agreed-upon "theory" of how astrology might work. However, if you browse through various astrology websites, you can collect bits and pieces of theory. What can you find? Do any of these notions contradict each other? How could this be a logical problem? Which theory fragments are unfalsifiable?
- B. Many paranormal websites claim to present scientific evidence for their claims. However, often they misuse science and are actually examples of pseudoscience. Search the internet for scientific evidence for any paranormal or extraordinary claim. Look for two types of evidence: scientific observation and scientific experimentation. For example, a claim of evidence for "the Flying Spaghetti Monster" would likely be observational (perhaps a photograph). A claim that "the Flying Spaghetti Monster can answer your sincere requests for money" might be experimental (copies of email you sent

to the FSM followed by a large check from this entity). Evaluate the evidence using the concepts of this chapter.

What questions do your selected websites leave unanswered? When they describe "scientific support," can you identify a measurable (operationalized) independent and dependent variable? Is there a hypothesis that is falsifiable? Then examine critical websites such as www.skepdic.com; web.randi.org; csicop.org, skeptic.com, or quackwatch.com. Describe the type of evidence that proponents offer. Evaluate this evidence in terms of the criteria for good science. What scientific mistakes do your proponents make? If you can't think of a claim to research, consider any of the following (from the nearly 800 listed in skeptic.com):

- Acupuncture
- Alien abductions
- Angel therapy
- Astral projection
- Astrology
- Auras
- Bermuda triangle
- Bible code
- Bigfoot
- Celestine prophecy
- Chakra
- Chi
- Channeling
- Clairvoyance
- Cold reading
- Communicating with the dead
- Crop circles
- Creationism
- Crystal power
- Déjà vu
- Demon possession
- Ectoplasm
- Exorcism
- Extrasensory perception
- Faith healing
- Feng shui
- Flying saucers
- Ghosts
- Graphology
- Haunted houses
- Homeopathy
- I Ching
- Kirlian photography
- Intelligent design
- Law of attraction

- o Life after death
- o Magnet therapy
- o Moon madness
- o Near-death experiences
- o Nostradamus
- o Oracles
- o Ouija boards
- o Out-of-body experiences
- o Palmistry
- o Past-life regression
- o Prayer healing
- o Precognition
- o Premonitions of death
- o Prophetic dreams
- o Psychic staring effect
- o Psychic surgery
- o Psychics
- o Psychokinesis
- o Ramtha
- o Reflexology
- o Reich, Wilhelm
- o Reiki
- o Reincarnation
- o Remote viewing
- o Repressed memory therapy
- o Retrocognition
- o Roswell
- o Santa Claus
- o Sasquatch
- o Satan
- o Shamanism
- o Succubus
- o Synchronicity
- o Tai chi
- o Tarot cards
- o Telepathy
- o Telekinesis
- o Talisman
- o The Flying Spaghetti Monster
- o Therapeutic touch
- o Trance writing
- o UFOs
- o Urine therapy
- o Werewolf
- o Witch
- o Zombies

**7.5** *Correlations and Causality Workshop*

Just because two events appear together and are correlated doesn't mean that one caused the other. Events A and B might occur at the same time for four reasons: (1) A may be the IV and cause B, (2) B might cause A, (3) some unknown variable C might cause A and B, or (4) the paired appearance of A and B was a fluke. Professor Jonathan Mueller has posted some wonderful articles from the popular press that illustrate the need to think clearly about correlations (Mueller, 2007). I've screened his many examples and have added some. For each of the following, perform a reality check and see if you can identify an alternative explanation. Identify a plausible independent variable (the one you can deliberately fix or set up) and then a plausible dependent variable (the one that may or may not change once you've set the IV).

*Get up and move. It may make you happier (New York Times, 2017)*

The *New York Times* reported an extensive study on everyday activity and happiness. 10,000 men and women downloaded a special android smart phone app that rang at random times throughout the day and asked how happy one felt at the time of the ring. The phone's motion detector recorded how active one was. The study lasted 17 months and found a correlation between happiness and activity. People were more likely to report being happy when they were active. The *New York Time*'s happy headline: "Get up and move. It may make you happier." However, did activity lead to happiness? Or did happiness lead to more activity? In other words, when people are feeling happy, are they more likely to decide to engage in some activity? Or maybe some third IV contributes to both happiness and activity. For example, people who are sick are likely to be less active and less happy. Here inactivity did not cause unhappiness, and unhappiness did not cause inactivity. The IV illness is the causal agent. Or drinking a lot of coffee may make one feel happier and more active. Again, the causal IV is not activity or happiness.

*Pill changes women's taste in men (BBC News, 2003)*

Women who take contraceptive pills are more likely to prefer "macho types" with strong jaw lines and prominent cheekbones. Women who do not take contraceptive pills like sensitive men with traditional masculine features. Explanation: Women taking the pill (IV) can't become pregnant and are therefore subconsciously liberated to feel sexually attracted to men (DV). If they marry someone while on the pill, they might realize they made the wrong decision when they are off the pill.

*Nightlight may lead to nearsightedness (CNN, 1999)*

Children who go to bed with a night light on in their room are significantly more likely to be nearsighted when they get older. Nightlights cause eye strain and eventual nearsightedness.

*Video games improve surgery skills for surgeons (Science Daily, 2007)*

A study of 33 surgeons and surgical residents found those who had more experience playing video games did better at performing laparoscopic surgery on a simulation test. The authors concluded that medical schools should consider including video games in their training.

*Housework cuts breast cancer risk (BBC News, 2006a)*

Research on 200,000 women from nine European countries found that housewives who did housework were less likely to contract cancer than those playing sports or having a physical job. Housework included 16–17 hours a week cooking, cleaning, and doing the wash.

*Sexual lyrics prompt teens to have sex (Fox News, 2006)*

Teens who say they listen to music with degrading sexual messages are almost twice as likely to have sexual intercourse the following two years as teens who say they listen to music with little or no sexually degrading content. The music makes them less inhibited.

*Sex cuts public speaking stress (BBC News, 2006b)*

Sex helps reduce stress. But only penetrative sex works. Forty-six men and women kept diaries on when and what they did in bed. Then they were asked to take a stress test that involved public speaking. Those who had the most penetrative sex displayed more rapid reductions in blood pressure than those who did not. Abstainers had the highest blood pressure during stress. Penetrative sex may stimulate the vagal nerve, which can produce relaxation.

*Eating breakfast makes girls slimmer (Peer trainer, 2007)*

In a 10-year study of 2,400 girls, girls who ate breakfast every day had lower average body mass than those who did not. It didn't matter what the girls ate. Not eating breakfast is the worst thing you can do for your weight.

*Your name influences your future (Brooks, 2007)*

People named Dennis and Denise are more likely to become dentists. Those named Lawrence and Laurie are more likely to become lawyers. People are drawn to professions that remind them of their names.

*Panic attacks may raise women's heart, stroke risk (Associated Press, 2007)*

A panic attack is often characterized by rapidly pounding heart, sweating, trembling or shaking, and shortness of breath. The symptoms are very similar to those of an actual heart attack, although just having a panic attack doesn't mean you are having a heart attack. A study of more than 3,000 older women found that women who reported at least one full-blown panic attack during a six-month period were three times more likely to have a heart attack or stroke over the next five years than women who didn't report a panic attack. Perhaps having a panic attack releases stress hormones that can cause a heart attack.

*Make your bed, save your brain* (Springen, 2007)

In 1994 researchers studied 997 older Catholic priests, nuns, and monks (average age: 75) who did not have dementia. The subjects rated themselves on a "conscientiousness scale" answering such questions as "I am a productive person who always gets the job done." Over the 12 years of the study, those who developed Alzheimer's had initially rated themselves as less conscientious.

*Societies worse off 'when they have God on their side'* (Gledhill, 2005)

According to *The Times*: "Religious belief can cause damage to a society, contributing to high murder rates, abortion, promiscuity and suicide, according to research published today."

"According to the study, belief in and worship of God are not only unnecessary for a healthy society but may actually contribute to social problems. The study counters the view of believers that religion is necessary to provide the moral and ethical foundations of a healthy society."

In the largest study of its kind, using the best survey data available, researchers looked at all of the world's 18 most prosperous democracies (with a combined population of 800,000,000) and found a nearly perfect correlation between negative societal health/societal dysfunction and religiosity (belief in God, frequency of prayer, church attendance, biblical literalism, and creationism).

For more see Burns (1997) and Carroll (2007).

**7.6** *Operationalized Definitions*
Convert each of the following into proper operationalized definitions. We start with two examples.

A student is interested in finding out if being more sociable is a way of making friends. His original definitions: "I define sociable as 'getting along well with others.' I define making friends as 'feeling wanted by others.'"
*Comment:* These definitions are too vague and do not indicate how variables are to be measured.
*Better:* "I define sociable as 'the number of times I introduce myself to a stranger in class.' I define 'making friends' as 'the number of times a new contact calls me up the following seven days.'"

A coffee house owner is trying to increase her profits. Her original definitions: "I wonder if making my coffee house more home-like will increase traffic."
*Comment:* Too vague. How are the variables measured?
*Better:* "I define 'home-like' as 'adding chairs with cushions and amber lights.' 'Traffic' means 'number of cups of coffee sold during a day.'"

Now try to improve these definitions.

- A. Accessing inner healing powers decreases the likelihood you will suffer illness.
- B. Establishing empathic contact with another person helps you read their thoughts.
- C. Releasing the healing warmth from your heart to another person can cure disease.
- D. Eating natural food increases psychic energy.
- E. The government has a system for controlling our access to information about the unexplained.
- F. My astrologer very effectively sees into my deepest secrets.
- G. Simply wishing something hard enough, and with enough sincerity, will cause it to come true.

**7.7** *Internet Search*

Paranormal phenomena may seem like magic. Indeed, at times unscrupulous magicians have used their skills at trickery to fool people into believing they have paranormal powers. Search the internet for "magic" and view some of the best tricks you can find. How might they be presented as paranormal phenomena? What tests would you require to determine they are genuine?

**7.8** *Conversation with a Classmate*

| |
|---|
| FROM: Gest Bimrat |
| SUBJECT: A theory is just a hunch |
| Our professor claims that dietary cholesterol contributes to heart disease. He presents that as if it were something like "scientific fact." How arrogant! It's just a theory, and a theory is just a hunch, a guess. Of course he might be right, but let's put things in perspective. Maybe people get heart disease because of random genetic factors. It's in your genes. Just because his bacon-eating uncle died of heart disease proves nothing. I know many bacon eaters who are just fine. I eat bacon and I'm in great condition. And I think the professor is just feeding into what's politically correct in some circles. I see the pattern: "Eating bacon increases cholesterol. Diet increases cholesterol. Diet contributes to heart disease. We have to have more government involvement in what foods get to our grocery stores to reduce heart disease. We need more government control." I know where this leads. Fascism. Loss of freedom. |

| |
|---|
| TO: Gest |
| SUBJECT: A theory is just a hunch |
| |

# Part III

# Alternative Explanations

We have completed our survey of the basic three reality-checking tools for finding support for a claim. We considered how to select sources, think logically, and test and evaluate scientific observations. We now turn to what may be a more basic question.

We have seen (Chapter 3, "Why Do You Believe"; Appendix B) that the most powerful justification people give for a paranormal belief is personal experience and intuition. This is a category of support that is more direct than sources, logic, or science. It reflects our first encounter with the world, and perhaps the world of the paranormal.

In the following five chapters we examine five ways in which immediate personal experience and intuition can be mistaken. Put differently, we consider five questions, alternative hypotheses for apparent paranormal events. Sometimes things aren't what they seem because of a misunderstanding of unexpected oddities of nature and numbers; perceptual errors and trickery; memory errors; the placebo effect; and sensory anomalies and hallucinations.

*Critical Thinking: Pseudoscience and the Paranormal*, Second Edition. Jonathan C. Smith.
© 2018 John Wiley & Sons, Inc. Published 2018 by John Wiley & Sons, Inc.

# 8

# Oddities of Nature and the World of Numbers

---

**OUTLINE**

1) Probability Estimates and Bias
   a) Availability Error
   b) Unreasonable or Illusory Optimism
2) Math Ignorance (and the Famous Birthday Paradox)
3) Coincidences
   a) Synchronicity
   b) People Underestimate Coincidences
      i) The clumpiness of randomness
      ii) The law of very large numbers
         1) Death premonitions
         2) Prophetic dreams
         3) Littlewood's Law of Miracles
4) Science and Chance
   a) Sample Size
   b) Arbitrary Stop Points and Data Mining
   c) How to Tell When a Scientific Finding is "Significant"
5) Psychic Bias

---

The world is full of surprises. You need only consult the latest edition of the *Guinness Book of World Records* or *Ripley's Believe It or Not* to uncover a wealth of bizarre and unusual facts. Lizards that walk on water, frogs with two heads, fish that rain from the sky, housewives lifting automobiles – there's enough to entertain for hours. In a previous age, many such oddities might have been viewed as evidence of the paranormal. Today, paranormal researchers do not embrace the *Guinness* and *Ripley* books as evidence. Most people recognize that their contents are natural phenomena.

Yet the world serves up too many oddities to fit the record books. Many tempt us to consider paranormal interpretations. A slender slimy form bobs above the surface of Loch Ness. Is it the Loch Ness Monster (perhaps from another dimension) or a log? A hand placed on an electrically charged photographic plate leaves a glowing hand-shaped image. Is it a photograph of spiritual energy or an artifact of electrical discharge? A digital camera records a shining orb in a haunted house. Is it a ghost or a lens reflection? A marble statue of the Virgin Mary weeps. Or is it condensation, water drawn from humid air to cold stone? Years ago, Native Americans witnessed gigantic paranormal entities (gods) arriving on their shores. Or were these simply Spanish ships?

*Critical Thinking: Pseudoscience and the Paranormal*, Second Edition. Jonathan C. Smith.
© 2018 John Wiley & Sons, Inc. Published 2018 by John Wiley & Sons, Inc.

UFO (unidentified flying object, or alternatively "unexplained aerial phenomena" or UAP) sightings are perhaps the best known and most enduring examples of wide-scale misinterpretation of natural oddities as paranormal or borderline paranormal phenomena. The UFO era began in 1947 when Kenneth Arnold, a private pilot, reported seeing nine airborne objects that looked like saucers. Around the world others began seeing flying saucers. Then came the famous alleged 1947 UFO crash near Roswell, New Mexico, later revealed to be a government crashed balloon radar array. To this day UFO sightings persist, complete with expert anecdotal accounts and photographic evidence, and are repeatedly broadcast in television "news" documentaries. All can conceivably be explained as natural phenomena (planets, stars, reflections of the Moon, ball lightning, aircraft, missile launches, satellites, balloons, searchlights, test clouds, flares, St Elmo's fire, optical camera distortions, simple fraud) or as examples of perceptual and memory error and sense anomalies (McGaha, 2009). For an excellent review, see the January/February 2009 issue of *Skeptical Inquirer* (Frazier, 2009).

It is beyond the scope of this book to catalog all of the unusual natural phenomena that have at one time or another inspired paranormal beliefs. Our concern is more basic: the world of numbers and how a misunderstanding of statistics can fool us and lead us to make pseudoscientific mistakes.

## Probability Estimates and Bias

We misjudge probabilities because of lack of experience with the unusual. Sometimes this simply involves not knowing an esoteric statistic. Here are some examples. Are you more likely to die on a motorcycle or on a bicycle? The odds of dying on a motorcycle are 1 in 938, and on a bicycle 1 in 4,472. What about on a bus or train? Your odds on a bus are 1 in 94,242 and on a train 1 in 139,617 (www.NSC.org). Drowning in a swimming pool or bath tub? 1 in 6,031 vs. 1 in 9,377. What about winning the jackpot in a slot machine vs. a "mega millions" lottery? 1 in 16,777,216 vs. 1 in 175,711,536 (casinogambling.about.com/). For more odds see www.veegle.com.

### Availability Error

However, people tend to make consistent errors when estimating probabilities. A simple example is the **availability error** in which one notices, remembers, and overestimates the probability of evidence that stands out (Tversky & Kahneman, 1973). For example, imagine you could not get to sleep last night because the new neighbor's dog barked twice. The next morning, tired and upset, you complained to your neighbor that the dog was barking all night. Your frustration made two barks stand out, leading you to overestimate the actual frequency of barks. A friend shares with you a remarkable newspaper horoscope. It says she will come upon some money, and the same day she finds $5. This event sticks in your mind, prompting you to comment on "all the evidence for astrology." Because of the availability error, we often make hasty conclusions and over-generalize from a few cases.

### Unreasonable or Illusory Optimism

Conversely, people underestimate the probability of rare negative events, for example, the likelihood that they will get injured in a car accident, or experience an illness from smoking, until the unexpected actually hits and they have an accident or get sick. Ask someone who is not reading this book the following question: "Compared to others, how likely is it that you will get sick next month? Less likely, equally likely, or more likely?" Most people will answer "less likely" even though the law of averages states that the probability that the average person will get sick next month is, of course, average. Try asking the same question to a group of 50 people. Statistically, the mean answer should be "average"; in fact researchers find that "less likely" is what most people will claim. This common mistake illustrates **unreasonable**, or **illusory optimism** (Weinstein, 1980; Weinstein & Klein, 1996), the tendency to perceive yourself as more likely than your peers to have something good happen to you (a raise, new friend, solve a problem, win the lottery), and less likely than your peers to have something bad happen to you. Similarly, gamblers tend to overestimate the probability of winning, especially when the stakes are high (Sanbonmatsu, Posavac, & Stasney, 1997).

Unreasonable optimism can be one reason why smokers think they are less at risk than other smokers, why teenagers think they are less likely than others to contract AIDS, why many people do not use seat belts, or why many stay in relationships that aren't working. Fortunately, there are strategies to minimize the risk of such distorted thinking, including having an unfortunate experience. Those who have been in a car accident are more likely to wear seat belts (McKenna & Albery, 2001). Nonetheless, unreasonable optimism is a general process in which we misjudge probabilities. An unscrupulous psychic or astrologer who knows this human tendency can comfortably predict that you will have more good fortune, and less misfortune, than others. It is likely you will agree.

## Math Ignorance (and the Famous Birthday Paradox)

Psychic Madam Urni is very popular on the lecture circuit. Each week she addresses groups of about 75 eager listeners. She begins each lecture with a dramatic demonstration of her paranormal abilities. As the lights dim, she closes her eyes, stretches her arms upward, and in a hushed tone pronounces, "I hereby determine that there are two people in this room who have exactly the same birthday. The same day and month." She then asks everyone to write down their birthday, and has three audience volunteers tabulate the results, to be announced at the end of her hour-long presentation. Remarkably, Madam Urni has made this prophecy for hundreds of groups and her success rate is nearly 100%. Recently, a local newspaper reporter decided to check the psychic out. Convinced the Madam was a fraud, he attended several sessions in disguise, and each time volunteered to tabulate the collected birthday reports. He was astonished to discover that indeed her success rate was 99%. Before publishing his findings, he went to a local junior college and found a professor interested in paranormal phenomena. After the reporter had explained Urni's claims and his experiences, the professor offered several hypotheses. Perhaps the psychic had retroactive psychokinetic abilities, a claimed paranormal power to use one's thoughts to change events in the past. That is, perhaps Madam Urni used her psychic skills to change the actual birthdays of two audience members. Alternatively, he suggested she may have used her psychokinetic powers to attract two people with the same birthday to her sessions. Or perhaps she used mind control to make two participants

**Figure 8.1** Birthday cake. Reproduced with kind permission of Getty images.

unconsciously write down the same birthday. The professor suggested testing Madam Urni in controlled conditions in which she would perform for random groups of 75 students at his college. Urni was more than willing to comply. As a check, birthdays would be obtained from university records before students attended the psychic's lecture. Astonishingly, the psychic maintained a near perfect hit rate. In just about every group, two participants had exactly the same birthday. Which hypothesis is supported? Have we missed anything?

Sometimes we misjudge probabilities because we are unfamiliar with a mathematical rule or haven't done our math homework. Let's begin with an example very popular in textbooks of critical thinking. In a room of 23 individuals, what is the probability that two will have the same birthday (day and month)? Most people guess that the probability of this should be low, maybe one out of 20. Actually, the chances are 50/50. Furthermore, the probability that two in a group of 75 will have the same birthday is 99.9%, a probability often called the **birthday paradox**, one of the most popular math anomalies cited in critical thinking textbooks, sometimes cited as "one of math's greatest hits" (Bellos, 2014). In other words, there was nothing spooky going on in Madam Urni's sessions.

Before proceeding, it is important to address a mistake students often make. *If you walk into a room of any number of individuals, what is the probability another person will be born the same month and day as you?* Correct answer: 365/365. Obviously, this is not the birthday paradox. The birthday paradox refers only to the likelihood that *someone, anyone* in a room of 23 (you plus everyone else), will have the same day and month of birth as *someone, anyone else*, in the room.

Here's how it works. Again, imagine there is only one person in a room. What is the probability that the birthday of this person is unique in that room, and there is no one else in the room with that birthday? This question is actually a little silly; because there is no other person in the room, logically she can't share a birthday. The probability is 365/365, 100%. If there are two people in the room what is the probability that person No. 2 does not have the same birthday as Person No. 1? If No. 1 has taken one birthday, there are 364 left, any of which would be different from No. 1's birthday. Therefore, No. 2 has 364 chances out of 365, or 364/365, of having a birthday different from that of No. 1.

Let's continue. When we get to person No. 3, assume for the sake of argument that two birthdates have already been taken, so there are 363 birthdays left untaken and the probability that No. 3's birthday will be one of these is 363/365. Following this logic, each time we add a person, we reduce by one his or her chances of having a birthday not already taken. Now, to obtain the overall probability that none of the three share a birthday the statistical rule is to multiply the individual probabilities, $365/365 \times 364/365 \times 363/365$. The answer is .992. It's almost certain that in a room of three, no two will share birthdays. Note that the statistical multiplication rule yields the very result you might have predicted. You can trust the rule, it works fine.

Now, for a room of 23, we simply apply the same rule 23 times:

$$365/365 \times 364/365 \times 363/365 \times 362/365 \times 361/365 \times 360/365 \times 359/365 \times 358/365 \times 357/365 \times 356/365 \times 355/365 \times 354/365 \times 353/365 \times 352/365 \times 351/365 \times 350/365 \times 349/365 \times 348/365 \times 347/365 \times 346/365 \times 345/365 \times 344/365 \times 343/365$$

and get 0.493. Rounding things out, the chances are about 50/50 that in a room of 23 people, no two will share the same birthday. But we were interested in the probability that two people *would* share the same birthday. If the chances are 50/50 that no two have the same birthday, logically the chances are 50/50 that two will indeed share the same birthday. Using the same process, the probability is 99.9% that two people in a group of 75 will have the same birthday.

If this confuses you, google "birthday paradox" for a variety of fun and lucid explanations.

## Coincidences

Coincidences involve events that unexpectedly occur together in an apparently meaningful way, without any apparent causal link. A present–future coincidence might be seen as a prophecy, an event that correctly follows an omen or prediction. A present–present coincidence might suggest a set of events that are remarkably linked by some paranormal process outside of the world of causality.

### Synchronicity

Popular paranormalists have made much of coincidences. Carl Jung, Freud's famous breakaway disciple, invented a term, **synchronicity**, to refer to remarkably meaningful coincidences. Synchronicity refers to the simultaneous occurrence of events that appear to be causally related, but are not (Jung, 1960). Instead, synchronous events are connected by an "acausal connecting principle." For example, imagine you had a dream about winning the lottery, and later you actually won. What a coincidence. However, this is not any ordinary coincidence, but one with meaning and significance. Jung would say that your dream did not cause you to win the lottery (nor did the future lottery win retroactively cause your present dream). But he would also say that your win was not random. Your win was the result of some third mysterious "acausal connecting principle."

Students of critical thinking often find the term "synchronicity" confusing, so let me offer my simple explanation. We begin with the basics. Science permits two fundamental explanations for any pairing of events, say event A and event B. They are either causally related or their appearance is random. We have already defined as *paranormal* any event that is "beyond science," that is, cannot be explained by current science, which again states that all events are either caused or random. If your premonition of a lottery win neither caused you to win, nor was a random event, there is only one explanatory option left. Your dream was paranormal. It was beyond science. Jung's notion of synchronicity is nothing more than a paranormal claim dressed up in considerable technobabble. Synchronicity belongs in the same spooky house as ghosts, witches, fortune-telling, and urine therapy.

Perhaps because of its scientific connotations, the term "synchronicity" is popular in paranormal discussion. Redfield (1993), in *The Celestine Prophecy*, counsels us to look at strange coincidences as somehow fated and willed, and to use them as spiritual guides. SQuire's [sic] silly but very popular *God Winks* books argue that there are no coincidences because all are messages from the divine.[1] And then there is Deepak Chopra (2003), who advises that coincidences enable us to connect with the underlying field of infinite possibilities, *synchrodestiny*, where it becomes possible to achieve the spontaneous fulfillment of our every desire. Such a notion begs for a reality check.

**People Underestimate Coincidences**

Let's stand back and take a deep breath. What do uncanny coincidences mean? In fact, *coincidences happen all the time and usually mean nothing.* If you want meaning, go to Shakespeare. *For just about any topic, if you look hard enough, you will find a coincidence.* Those intrigued by such things often point to presidents (Leavy, 1992), starting with Lincoln and Kennedy. Examine these strange facts. Lincoln was elected in 1860, Kennedy in 1960; both were assassinated on a Friday while with their wives; both were involved in civil rights; both had lost a child while in office; both were killed by a bullet shot to the head; Lincoln was killed in Ford's theater, and Kennedy was killed in a Lincoln, a car made by Ford. According to some, Booth (Lincoln's assassin) was born in 1839, Oswald (Kennedy's assassin) was born in 1939. There seems to be a lot of synchronicity going on with Lincoln and Kennedy. What are the deep forces of life trying to tell us?

Why stop with Lincoln and Kennedy? Why not look at two other assassinated presidents, William McKinley and James Garfield? Sure enough, both were Republicans, both born and raised in Ohio (as was the author of this book!), both were veterans of the civil war, both served in the House of Representatives, both supported the gold standard, both names have eight letters, both were replaced by vice-presidents from New York

City, both of their vice-presidents had mustaches, both were shot in September at the onset of their terms, Garfield named his cat "McKinley" and McKinley named his cat "Garfield" (this latest claim is hotly disputed; Schick & Vaughn, 2005).

One could write a small volume on coincidences involving the terrorist attack of 9/11. Both New York City and Afghanistan have 11 letters. The terrorist who first threatened the Twin Towers, Ramsin Yuseb, has 11 letters. George W. Bush has 11 letters. The eleventh state is New York. Two flights hit the twin towers, Flights 11 and 92; $9 + 2 = 11$. Flight 77 has 65 passengers ($6 + 5 = 11$).

What most people don't realize is that if you look deep enough, you can always dig up a coincidence for just about anything. If you were to take all of the words in the Bible and circle every tenth letter, some of the circled letters would form words, and some of the words might seem to convey a message, a sort of Bible code (Drosnin, 1997). Indeed, you can do the same thing with just about any large book.

---

**Coincidence and the Flying Spaghetti Monster**

**Figure 8.2** Professor Smith's Rendering of the Flying Spaghetti Monster.

Let me share with you an uncanny coincidence I uncovered before starting the first edition of this book. It nearly changed my career, and is perhaps the closest I have ever come to an actual paranormal encounter.

In 2005, a college student and slot-machine engineer, Bobby Henderson, had just unleashed onto the world a new religion, Pastafarianism. Its core belief is that 4,000 years ago the *Flying Spaghetti Monster* created the universe. This revelation of an invisible deity made of spaghetti and meatballs was quickly reported in major publications such as the *New York Times* and *Scientific American*. The term "Flying Spaghetti Monster" became a popular symbol for "unfalsifiable assertion." "Pastafarianism" became an alternative religious option for critical thinkers.

Inspired by this instructive satire, I decided to probe deeper using a new tool I had just acquired, a computer-based anagram analyzer. An anagram arranges the letters of one word or phrase to form another, as in *"Elvis"="Lives," "slot machines"="Cash lost in 'em," "Dormitory"="Dirty Room," "Rich at sin"="Rich saint,"* and *"Skeptic"="It pecks."* Throughout history, mystics, Kabbalists, and even Nostradamus have used anagrams to uncover deep mysteries (Curl, 1996). Indeed, perhaps *"anagrams are true"* (= *"as a rare argument"*).

Using my new analyzer, I searched for all legal anagrams of the word combination "Flying Spaghetti Monster" (Smith, 2011a, 2011b). To my astonishment, I discovered 128 that form an epic poem, which I call the Pastafarian Quatrains.

The Quatrains depict a timeless battle between simple truth and obfuscating illusion (remarkably the story of the book you are reading). It is a story with two stars, the "Serpent" (Illusion), and the "Angel." The Angel of Truth is manifest on Earth as a Flying Pig, a traditional symbol of skepticism ("I'll believe that when pigs fly"). Note James Randi's famous "Pigasus Award," given annually to expose paranormal and pseudo-scientific fraud.

The Quatrains are remarkable in their complexity, beauty, and detail. We find a beginning confrontation followed by a stirring battle. Truth, the Flying Pig, prevails in these concluding Spaghettigrams:

*Fine Piggy halts torments.*
*Oh! Finest Pig – gently smart.*

There's more. We find advice on how to study ("*Fragment this tiny gospel.*" "*Forget anything misspelt*"), dealing with skeptics ("*The angry simpleton's gift*"), and how to meditate ("*Forget simplest anything*"). If you are still a doubter, consider the following three quatrains (remember that each line is a legal anagram of the word combination "*Flying Spaghetti Monster.*" So, in a sense, each comes "Directly from the deity").

### Direct from the FSM …

*Finest might, sporty Angel,* (1:1)
*Mostly fighting a Serpent.* (1:2)
*Petty mangler of insights,* (1:3)
*Floating pestering myths.* (1:4)

*"Angel's" snotty, prime fight.* (3:1)
*Fight gentlest parsimony.* (3:2)
*Myth-generating flip-toss,* (3:3)
*Petty sign of this mangler.* (3:4)

As in many classic holy books, The quatrains even get a little racy:

*This frosty pig gentleman,* (13:1)
*Tormenting shapely gifts.* (13:2)
*Phony flirt gets steaming,* (13.3)
*Then flings petty orgasm.* 13.4)
*Self-pitying tenth orgasm.* (15.3)

The meaning of some passages is fairly clear. The "Sporty Angel fighting a Serpent" obviously refers to Truth and Illusion. The Serpent, the great creator of illusion, "mangles insights," "floats myths," and "fights parsimony". These phrases are poetic depictions of acts of obfuscation. Parsimony is often seen as a characteristic of clear logical and scientific thinking, something the Serpent opposes. "Myth-generating flip-toss"? Here we find a remarkably artful depiction of one of the Serpent's main missions, and indeed the message of the Quatrains – to take something that is simply random coincidence ("flip-toss," like a coin or dice) and read great meaning into it ("myth-generate").

What about the last troubling quatrain, "This frosty pig gentleman"? Some passages are so profound that they are open to multiple interpretation. Here I chose not to rush in where angels fear to tread.

Time to take pause. Did I indeed make a fantastic mystical discovery? Did I have a magical tool that defies the laws of science? Could I use my anagram powers to win at the stock market? Predict the future? Alter the course of history? Was I, in Pastafarian theology, "touched by His Noodly Appendage"? But wait, are not anagrams arbitrary rearrangements of letters, about as meaningful as a claim that "*Elvis*" indeed "*Lives*"?

Alas, this is all a lesson in probabilities. The word combination "Flying Spaghetti Monster" yields over 3,000,000 legal anagrams. In this massive pool, meaningful phrases are inevitable, although due to chance. They can be readily cherry-picked to form a story of apparent profound spiritual significance. As another famous pig concludes, "That's all folks."

We could go on and on. Indeed, it is difficult for most students, and many professors, to get their arms around the idea that coincidences are more common than they think. Often I deploy the technique of "immersion therapy" to counter this tendency. Here, I simply introduce a never-ending torrent of coincidences until one gets the point. One can achieve a similar outcome by simply googling "remarkable coincidences."

It would be truly remarkable if there were no coincidences. Two processes involved are the inherent **clumpiness of randomness** and the **law of very large numbers**.

### The Clumpiness of Randomness

Random lists rarely appear random. You will always find clumps or streaks that seem unexpected, and even meaningful. This contributes to the **clustering illusion**. Imagine you tossed a coin 51 times and your sequence of heads (H) and tails (T) was spread evenly, like this:

HTHTHTHTHTHTHTHTHTHTHTHTHTHTHTHTHTHTHTHTHTHTHTHTHT
HTHTH

Does this look random? Of course not, it's too regular. You can see that any random sequence has to have a few clumps to be convincing. What people underestimate is the frequency and size of clumps that will appear in a random sequence. For example, Myers (2004) flipped a coin 51 times and got this sequence of heads (H) and tails (T):

HTTTHHHTTTTTHHTTTHTTTHHTTTHTTTTHTHTTTTTTTHTTTHTHHHHTH
HTTTT

Remember, this is a purely random sequence, nothing more. Now imagine I told you that this sequence contained a secret and profound message. Once I planted this seed, what could you find? I discovered there are 19 "TT" pairs but only eight "HH" pairs. In addition, there are five "TTTT" combinations and only one "HHHH" combination. And "TTTTT" appears twice while "HHHHH" never appears. There is even one "TTTTTT" combination. The Myers Randomized Sequence prefers even-numbered T combinations. "T" stands for "Tails." It can also stand for "Truth." "H" stands for "Heads." It is clear that if you are looking for truth in your life, don't use your head too much. To discover truth you must turn what you think about probabilities on its "tail."

We see such clumpiness all the time in gambling. A poker player wins three times in a row. Friends conclude he has a **hot hand** or winning streak, and bet on him. Conversely, a gambler might identify a slot machine that hasn't paid out for a full day. It's time for a win, so she plays the machine. This too is a mistake. If the slot machine isn't defective, your chances of winning are the same with other similar machines. To believe that the chances of a random event are influenced by, or can be predicted from, other independent events is the **gambler's fallacy**. Imagine you purchase three lottery tickets today. Your first, second, and third tickets win. Should you assume you've been blessed with a winning streak and buy more tickets, or stop buying tickets because you figure the probability of winning again after three wins is reduced? The only reasonable answer is to realize that you misunderstand probabilities and that your chances of getting a fourth winning ticket have nothing to do with your previous winnings. It's pure chance.

Statisticians refer to a phenomenon called **regression to the mean** (Gilovich, 1991). Put simply, it means that if you have an extreme run of bad or good luck, chance alone says this won't continue. In the long run, scores average out. In Chicago, the average temperature for March may be 50 degrees. Some days will be warmer, and some colder. And there will always be a few extreme days. But generally, temperature will average out to 50 degrees. So if it is freezing in Chicago in March, and you pray for warmer weather, the odds are that the extreme temperature will not continue – just through regression to the mean.

### The Law of Very Large Numbers

Given a large enough sample, you are bound to find something odd, surprising, or even "miraculous." Someone has to win the lottery. Occasionally someone does get hit by lightning. After thousands of dreams, eventually one might come true. This is generally called *the law of very large numbers.* Such a remarkable event or coincidence can be even more impressive if you forget the thousands, or even millions, of ordinary nonmiracles that preceded it.

*Death Premonitions.* Here's a happy thought to start your day. Holt (2004) has calculated the probability of having a death premonition, just by chance. Let's walk through the logic. *Think of all the living people you know, know of, and have thought about at least once over an entire year.* This includes your family, friends, distant relatives, authors, teachers, movie actors, politicians, and so on. Of this long list, perhaps 10 will die each year. (If this seems excessive, do a Google search for "people who died this year" and pick a year. How many do you recognize? Probably more than 10.)

We started with the assumption that over a year you have at least one thought about each of the people on the list (while they are still alive). That's a given. So, if the Pope is on your list, we would assume that you thought about the Pope at least one time over the last 12 months. How long is a thought? For the sake of argument, let's say a thought lasts five minutes. In a year there are 105,120 five-minute intervals. Statistics show that there are 10 chances in 105,120 that you will have a "thought" about one of these people five minutes before you hear of his or her death. Put differently, that's about one chance in 10,000, not very likely. Ho hum.

Now look at the big picture. There are over 300 million people in the United States, and each person has one chance in 10,000 of thinking about the passing of someone they know of five minutes before their death. That changes the numbers considerably. Specifically, over 25,000 people a year, over 70 a day, will think of someone dying five minutes before their death. This is by chance alone, with nothing spooky going on. In this day and age when most people have access to the internet, what is remarkable is that there are so few premonitions of death reported. We should be hearing about hundreds every month. Psychics should be enjoying a nonrandom run of field days.

*Prophetic Dreams.* Most people can remember a dream that came true. Perhaps you had a dream of meeting a friend, and the next week you met your friend. Perhaps you had a dream of getting a raise, and you got one. Are prophetic dreams coincidences, or extraordinary evidence of the paranormal? (For an interesting discussion of how our motivations affect the extent to which we think our dreams are prophetic, see Morewedge & Norton, 2009).

Paulos (2001) has looked at the numbers. Most people have about 250 dreams a night. This is not so hard to believe if you consider how many thoughts you have during the average day. After all, dreams are thoughts we have while sleeping. Of course, we remember very few of these dreams. However, a memory cue might help you remember. Perhaps last week one of your 1,750 ($7 \times 250 = 1,750$) dreams involved a small furry dog. There is no reason you would remember such a trivial dream, unless you nearly drove your bicycle over a small furry dog. This could readily trigger a memory of your furry dog dream, and provide you with false evidence for your paranormal powers, at least concerning small furry dogs. A much more conservative estimate of dreams leads to the same conclusion. Imagine that everyone remembers only one dream every day, or 365 dreams a year. In a country of 300 million, there are 109,500,000,000 remembered dreams a year. By chance alone, some are bound to coincidentally precede some remarkable event (Schick & Vaughn, 2005). Statistics suggest that for every dream that comes true, there are billions that don't.

To actually test if dream prophecies come true, one would have to actually obtain dreams before a prophesied event. Furthermore, the prophecy and event would have to be unambiguous, not fortune-cookie platitudes. One remarkable study pulled this off. In 1937 Charles Lindbergh's baby was kidnapped, causing national outrage. Famous Harvard psychologist Henry Murray placed a newspaper advertisement asking people to send in their dreams concerning the fate of the baby. Of course, the baby's body was eventually discovered. But before this gruesome event, Murray (Murray & Wheeler, 1936) had obtained about 1,300 dreams and could analyze them for unambiguous predictions, such as whether or not the baby was dead. Many dreams simply repeated speculations that had appeared in newspapers. Only 5% indicated the baby was dead and only 7% predicted concrete conditions associated with the murder. Only four people correctly predicted that the baby was dead and buried near trees.

*Littlewood's Law of Miracles.* These examples illustrate Littlewood's Law of Miracles (Bollobás, 1986): *a person can by chance expect one miracle a month.* How can this possibly be? For the sake of argument, Littlewood begins by defining a "miracle" as an event so extraordinary that its probability is one in a million. How often have you heard someone use that informal statistic, "A miracle ... one chance in a million"? Statistically, there's at least one chance in a million that you will (figuretheodds.org):

- toss a coin 20 times and get tails every time;
- win the California Lotto if you buy 40 tickets;
- get killed by a poisonous snakebite;
- get struck and killed by lightening;

- get killed by bees;
- get chickenpox.

Remember, one chance in a million is by chance alone with nothing paranormal going on. If you collect a million pebbles, by chance alone one is going to be remarkable (perhaps shaped like the face of someone you know).

Now, back to Littlewood's Law. For the sake of argument, let's assume that a human will experience one thing per second (this sentence, the next sentence, the sound of a fan, the binding of a book, the color of the sky …). One thing per second computes to over a million things a month. Just as we'll probably find a really remarkable pebble if we amass one million pebbles, so too we are likely to encounter a really remarkable event among the one million events we experience in a month. With so many events, it's very likely one event is going to seem very strange, unexpected, paranormal, and "miraculous." By chance alone with nothing paranormal going on. So many pebbles. What was your "miracle" this month?

## Science and Chance

Scientific experiments are designed to rule out chance as an alternative explanation. Informally, we can use the same methods. In statistics and research we have a system of rules, procedures, and "checks and balances" to help us sort things out.

### Sample Size

It is illogical and unfair to generalize from one example. The bad apple you got from the store might be an exception. Similarly, one scientific study does not convincingly prove a claim. Too much can go wrong. Researchers can be dishonest. Sometimes the unexpected happens. To guard against this, scientists require additional studies (from different unbiased researchers and labs) to confirm any finding. Any single study must include a sufficient number of participants to be powerful enough to yield a significant result. Generally, data from one or two individuals are not enough, and are akin to anecdotes.

### Arbitrary Stop Points and Data Mining

We have seen that purely random phenomena happen in clumps or streaks. You can cheat in research by stopping a study just at the point you seem to be getting the results you want. This is establishing an **arbitrary stop point**. If you were studying a purely random phenomenon, for example the relationship between foot size and grades, you would inevitably run into a streak of cases of short-footed individuals with high grades. This would likely even out in the long run, possibly by a streak of short-footed individuals with low grades. So what would happen if you stopped your study right after your first streak of short-footed, low-grade individuals? This would be cheating, and your study would seem to confirm that foot size is related to grades. So you can't run a study over and over, and apply an arbitrary stop point once you get the results you want.

**Data mining** is a similar problem. Here you apply numerous analyses to your data until one analysis yields the result you want. A good scientist states before beginning what analyses will be applied. In a famous example, the noted astrology researcher Gauquelin

(1974) claimed to have found that those born under the planet Mars were more likely to be top athletes. The problem is that he continuously worked his data until he finally found a pattern, a somewhat obscure relationship between two appearances of the planet Mars in two points in the sky and athleticism. Actually he mined many patterns to find one that worked. Perhaps athleticism is related to being born under Jupiter, Venus, or Mercury. Perhaps your Sun sign. There are hundreds of astrological variables in a 5,000-year-old astrological chart. By chance alone, one is going to relate to athleticism.

### How to Tell When a Scientific Finding is "Significant"

When do you take a scientific finding seriously? When is it "significant"? Statistics gives us a tool. We begin with the default hypothesis that a claimed phenomenon does not exist. This is called the **null hypothesis**. You can think of the null hypothesis as the skeptic's position that there is no effect (green tea didn't increase your IQ), no difference (girls do not run faster than guys), or no correlation (how much protein you eat doesn't correlate with your basketball scores). Imagine you are the only person in your dormitory to win a local lottery. Is that just a fluke (the skeptic's position or null hypothesis), or indicative of some special power you may have? If the null hypothesis is true, then any effect, difference, or correlation you observe is the result of meaningless random fluctuations or error. In the world of the null hypothesis, anything special is just a fluke, luck, or chance occurrence.

A **P value** is the probability you would get an observed set of results by chance alone. Here's an example that addresses the question of the effect of weekend study sessions on grades. Students in one class study weekends, while those in another class study weekdays. Imagine the weekend students receive an average grade of B, and the weekday students get an average of A. Imagine scientists find this difference is statistically significant, with a P value of .01 (or "$p = .01$"). That means there is one chance out of 100 the difference in grades was due to chance alone, that the null hypothesis is true. This increases our confidence in concluding that weekday studying works better. (Of course, a careful researcher would have to look at other factors like sleep time, hours reading, pizza and beer consumption, amount of recreation, and so on. A P value doesn't automatically tell you what variables other than chance may be in operation.)

The following example illustrates the proper way of stating the significance of a study, and its P value:

A study compares the effectiveness of a vaccine for the common cold with a fake drug, a placebo. Two hundred people got the vaccine, and 200 the placebo. At the end of the study, five vaccinated individuals caught a cold compared with 15 of those who were not vaccinated. Is this difference significant? The obtained P value was .03 ($p = .03$), lower than our selected threshold of ($p = .05$). Interpretation: If we assume the null hypothesis that the vaccine has no effect, the probability that we would obtain our results by chance alone is only .03 (three times out of 100). Since our threshold was $p = .05$, we have some confidence that the vaccine works. Put simply, it's unlikely we would obtain these results just by chance.

In sum, P values show how well a study supports the skeptic's position of the null hypothesis (of no effect, difference, or correlation). If an obtained P value is high (perhaps over .20), your study probably reflects a true null hypothesis, the fact that there's nothing going on. If a P value is low (by convention, lower than .05), your results would be unlikely if in fact there were nothing going on.

Calculating P values can be tricky. For example, conducting the same study many times can pose a special problem, sometimes ignored by paranormal researchers. Any study in itself is like a throw of dice. If you toss dice many times, eventually by chance alone you might get a hoped-for result. If you ask 1,000 psychics to predict a winning lottery number, by chance alone a few would get it right. Similarly, if one repeats a scientific study hundreds of times, by chance alone a few might yield results with low P values. Students sometimes have a hard time understanding this. Aren't scientific studies supposed to be immune from false results? Aren't they protected from flukes, luck, or chance occurrence? No. Random error permeates even the most pristine scientific laboratory. It is impossible to completely wash away all error. Error sticks around, like Lady Macbeth's "damned spot."

To correct for this problem, some apply a test invented by Carlo Emilio Bonferroni (1935). The Bonferroni correction is a very simple tool you can apply whenever you read about a study. Simply divide a reported target P value by the number of hypotheses made. The new P value becomes your "corrected target," one that compensates for the fact that you are increasing the chances of winning by repeatedly tossing dice. For example, imagine you searched the web and found 100 studies that looked at psychic predictions. Most reported a P value of about .05. Are these findings statistically significant? This is a serious question given the large number of studies conducted. Apply the Bonferroni test, and the new corrected threshold P value becomes .0005. You would accept only those studies that report a P value of .0005 or less.

Below is a hypothetical report of a study on green tea. Can you see why it is misleading?

> We examined the effects of green tea as a way of increasing classroom performance. In a double-blind placebo study, 20 students were given green tea, and 20 flavored water made to look like green tea. Participants drank their tea or water every day for a month. We looked at five variables: grade point average, grades on final exams, grades on written reports, classroom participation, and class attendance. On written reports, green tea drinkers received an average grade of "A" whereas water drinkers received an average grade of "B." The difference is significant, $p = .02$, which beats our threshold of .05. We conclude these results are not consistent with the null hypothesis of no effect.

Here's the same report applying the Bonferroni correction:

> We examined the effects of green tea as a way of increasing classroom performance. In a double-blind placebo study, 20 students were given green tea, and 20 flavored water made to look like green tea. Participants drank their tea or water every day for a month. We looked at five variables: grade point average, grades on final exams, grades on written reports, classroom participation, and class attendance. Green tea worked best on written reports. Here green tea drinkers received an average grade of "A" whereas water drinkers received an average grade of "B." We found that the grades were different, at $p = .02$. However, because we looked at five variables we

applied the Bonferroni correction. Our corrected new threshold P value was .01, which was not met. We conclude these results are consistent with the null hypothesis of no effect.

## Psychic Bias

Yes, it is easy to be tricked by the numbers. Nearly everyone has mistaken ideas about how probable various events are. We may perceive a perfectly ordinary coincidence as something more than random, perhaps as evidence of the paranormal. Some people are more prone to this type of error than others. Blackmore and Troscianko (1985) have found that people who believe in paranormal abilities are especially prone to make mistakes in probability judgments, a phenomenon we might call **psychic bias**. One study involved an automatic coin-flipping test in which believers and nonbelievers were instructed to use their thoughts to influence the results of automated coin-flipping. In one part of the experiment, the researchers asked paranormal believers and disbelievers to guess the number of "heads" one might expect by chance alone. Believers, but not disbelievers, displayed an interesting bias called *chance baseline shift*. Specifically, they *underestimated* the number of heads one might get from chance alone. Why is this important? Because when Blackmore and Troscianko asked participants to use their thoughts to influence the outcome of coin tosses, and got perfectly random results, paranormal believers thought they were nonrandom (of course they were from the believers' distorted perspective). Because of their bias, they were more likely to believe they had used their paranormal powers to influence the coins. In more general terms, such a bias illustrates how our beliefs and expectations can influence perception, a topic we consider in the next chapter.

## Study Questions

**8.1** *Definitions (Define, differentiate, and provide an example for each of the following)*
- A. Availability error
- B. Unreasonable/illusory optimism
- C. Birthday paradox
- D. Coincidence
- E. Synchronicity
- F. Clumpiness of randomness
- G. Gambler's fallacy
- H. Regression to the mean
- I. Law of very large numbers
- J. Death premonitions
- K. Prophetic dreams
- L. Littlewood's Law of Miracles
- M. Replication
- N. Sample size
- O. Arbitrary stop points

- P. Data mining
- Q. Psychic bias
- R. Chance baseline shift
- S. Statistical significance
- T. P value
- U. Null hypothesis
- V. Bonferroni correction

**8.2**   *Essay Questions*
- A. How might availability error, illusory optimism, math ignorance, and the clustering illusion enhance psychic bias?
- B. Professor Vinn Mennan teaches two courses in critical thinking every semester. Over the past decade he has taught 20 sections. He begins each term with a small class experiment. Before class, he has a colleague randomly toss a coin in another room. The coin is tossed in a sealed can, so that no one can see the results. And both the coin can and the coin tosser remain isolated from Professor Mennan and his students until the completion of the experiment. In the experiment, students close their eyes and try to guess whether the toss was heads or tails. Note, they are at all times isolated from the coin tosser and the coin can. This semester, for the first time, over half the class correctly guessed the coin toss. Statistically, this result was significant, $p = .05$. Given the size of the class (120 students), and the caution given to control for stimulus leakage, Dr Mennan decides to publish his results. Evaluate this study in terms of the concepts discussed in this chapter.

**8.3**   *Field Project: Your Coincidence Diary*
One person's trivial coincidence might be another person's divine message. For a week, list all the things that happen that seem like a coincidence. How might someone view your coincidences as evidence of the paranormal? Save your list for the next chapter and see if that chapter offers additional interpretations for your discovered coincidences.

**8.4**   *Internet Search*
- A. Search "Believe it or not," "strange facts," or "weird facts." Find a fact or actually observed phenomenon that could inspire a paranormal explanation. What might that explanation be? Provide an alternative nonparanormal explanation.
- B. Search the internet for examples of coincidence. (Search "coincidences," "strange coincidences," "spooky coincidences.") Do either a video or a simple web search. Describe the most surprising coincidences. How might each invite a paranormal interpretation? For each provide a non-paranormal interpretation.
- C. Search the internet for paranormal explanations of coincidences. Discuss alternative explanations. I recommend a video (YouTube) search of these topics:
  - Number 23 coincidences
  - God Winks coincidences

- ○ Deepak Chopra coincidences
- ○ Benny Hinn dream prophecy
- ○ Birthday paradox
- ○ Monkeys typing Shakespeare
- ○ Gambler's fallacy
- ○ Bible code (Bible code Michael Shermer)
- ○ Jung synchronicity
- ○ Synchronicity skeptic

### 8.5  *Conversation with a Classmate*

> FROM: Jadoz Tassi
> SUBJECT: My dream
>
> ---
>
> I had a prophetic dream that I can't explain. It was so impressive that I can only believe there is more to the universe than meets the eye. Therefore there is a higher realm, a psychic dimension that validates astrology, the mind-reading of psychics, and the ability of meditators to levitate. Here's what happened. Last month I had a dream that the Pope (yes, we Klingon's have a religious leader we call the "Pope") had a heart attack and nearly died. In this dream he was hospitalized, and after a month of treatment thankfully recovered. The dream was so upsetting that I sent an email to my girlfriend Elana, which she kept. Then about a month later my Pope actually got sick, with a serious problem in his abdominal region, just below his heart. He had appendicitis and nearly died from the infection! But after a week in the hospital he recovered. My dream was incredibly accurate! A prophecy! I have proof that I predicted it a month ahead!

> TO: Jadoz
> SUBJECT: My dream
>
> ---

# 9

# Perceptual Error and Trickery

*Critical Thinking: Pseudoscience and the Paranormal*, Second Edition. Jonathan C. Smith.
© 2018 John Wiley & Sons, Inc. Published 2018 by John Wiley & Sons, Inc.

The fact that you are reading this book says something about you. Quite likely you're a college student curious about critical thinking and the paranormal. You may be surprised that surveys of other readers and students have revealed an interesting and remarkably detailed portrait. See how well it fits you:

> You have a need for other people to like and admire you, and yet you tend to be critical of yourself. While you have some personality weaknesses, you are generally able to compensate for them. You have considerable unused capacity that you have not turned to your advantage. Disciplined and self-controlled on the outside, you tend to be worrisome and insecure on the inside. At times you have serious doubts as to whether you have made the right decision or done the right thing. You prefer a certain amount of change and variety and become dissatisfied when hemmed in by restrictions and limitations. You also pride yourself as an independent thinker, and do not accept others' statements without satisfactory proof. But you have found it unwise to be too frank in revealing yourself to others. At times you are extroverted, affable, and sociable, while at other times you are introverted, wary, and reserved. Some of your aspirations tend to be rather unrealistic.

Time for a reality check. If you found these assessments uncomfortably close to the mark, you're not alone. In 1948 psychologist Bertram R. Forer gave his students a personality test, and a few days later personality profiles presumably based on the results. Students rated the accuracy of their profiles on a 5-point scale (0 = "very poor," 5 = "excellent"). The average rating was 4.26. However, the whole demonstration was a trick. In fact, Forer gave all students the same generic personality profile based on horoscopes he had read. The profile Forer used is actually the same as the "detailed portrait" presented above. It has nothing to do with your personality. The Forer demonstration has been given hundreds of times and the average accuracy score is always about 4.2, or 84% accurate (Carroll, 2003). Try giving it to friends at a party. Chances are they will marvel at your psychic powers.

## Top-Down Processes and Perception

Yes, often things are not what they seem. Our eyes can fool us. Others can trick us. In this chapter we consider these two types of trickery, perceptual error and the manipulations of magicians and psychics. We begin with perception.

Perception is fundamentally biased and constructive. We do not see exactly what is "really out there," but a selective and distorted picture. At any moment, the real world provides far too much information to be assimilated. Our attention is something like a *spotlight* (Crick, 1984) that targets and intensifies some stimuli and ignores others. Our *emotions and motivations* guide this spotlight; we perceive what is consistent with how we feel as well as our wants and needs. A starving person notices food. Our *past experiences, beliefs, and expectations* guide us to notice some things, ignore others, and even conjure up perceptions that may not accurately reflect reality. At times we *monitor* our perceptions in an attempt to evaluate their accuracy. In Chapter 2 we noted that this involves reality checking. The attentional spotlight; emotions and motivations; past experiences, beliefs, and expectations; and reality checking constitute *top-down* (or "internal cognitive") *processes* that mold perception.

## The Barnum Effect (Forer Effect)

The **Barnum effect** (also called the **Forer effect**, **personal validation fallacy**, or **subjective validation**) is the tendency to rate a statement as personally accurate even though it could apply to nearly anyone. Studies (Dickson & Kelly, 1985) show that this effect can be aggravated if (a) you are misled to believe that a statement applies only to you (if you read a newspaper horoscope or see one on television, it's fairly obvious that it wasn't written just for you), (b) you believe the authority of the person making the statement, and (c) the statement lists mainly positive traits.

I propose that the Barnum effect may be enhanced by the **transparency illusion** (Vorauer, 2001). We tend to overestimate the extent to which our internal states and characteristics are obvious to others. In studies in which participants were asked to negotiate, 60% of the time they believed that observers could tell what their hidden goals were, when in fact observers could correctly guess only 26% of the time (Vorauer & Claude, 1998). In other studies, participants instructed to deliberately lie incorrectly believed that observers could see through their attempts to hide deception. Similarly, anxious public speakers unrealistically believed that audience members could see through their calm facades (Gilovich, Savitsky, & Medvec, 1998). Perhaps when we believe that a psychic reads our internal states, traits, and future, we again are assuming too much personal transparency.

## Confirmation Bias

**Confirmation bias** is a special type of selective thinking in which one looks for and notices what confirms one's beliefs, and ignores or does not look for or undervalues what contradicts. Confirmation bias is a preference for supportive over conflicting information (Nickerson, 1998; Watson, 1960). It can be a powerful factor reinforcing prejudice and discrimination. In reading a long horoscope, one might skim past a list of statements until one chances upon one that appears to fit. When confronting a mass of information, we tend to notice what appears to fit our expectations. This process can be quite automatic, and partly explains why you can quickly pick out a friend's voice in a noisy crowd, known as the cocktail party effect (Cherry, 1953).

We see examples of confirmation bias every day. A fervent advocate of the value of a college education will notice all the job notices for college graduates. An advocate of entering the workforce without a college degree will notice all the job notices for those with experience, not education. Those advocating support for gays adopting children will selectively notice reports of successful gay adoptions (and perhaps heterosexual child molestation), whereas those opposing will notice examples of gay couples breaking up and gay child molestation. Those supporting abstinence before marriage will notice all the singles couples in taverns who go home alone. Those who believe otherwise will notice all the couples going home together. Chicago fans of the Chicago Cubs will notice all the people wearing Cubs hats. Chicago Sox fans will not. Obviously one way to directly counter our automatic tendency for confirmation bias and selective attention is to deliberately seek contrary evidence. As we say again and again throughout this book, look for alternative explanations.

**Denial** is the refusal to accept the facts. One of the most dramatic historic instances of this is that of the Millerites, a religious group in the 1800s who, on more than one occasion, predicted the end of the world. In 1818, William Miller figured out mathematically that the Bible predicted the world would come to an end between March 21, 1843, and March 21, 1844. This was refined to January 1, 1844. With the help of some newspaper publicity, Miller attracted a flock of eagerly awaiting followers. However, when the end date came and went, his followers awaited March 21, the final date. Again, nothing happened. Miller redid his calculations and concluded a new date, October 22. Of course, nothing happened. The Millerites eventually founded the Adventist movement and Jehovah's Witnesses, groups that exist today. (See religioustolerance, 2007.)

### Reasons for the Barnum Effect and Confirmation Bias

I suspect that the Barnum effect and confirmation bias persist for many reasons. Confirming evidence provides apparent **positive reinforcement**. When such evidence is professed by a group, we might experience communal reinforcement, a desire to accept claims because of others who are important to us. Confirming evidence requires the least effort to understand and assimilate because it fits what we already think we know. Such evidence is least likely to evoke **cognitive dissonance** (Festinger, 1957), the discomfort coming from having two conflicting thoughts at the same time, or from engaging in behavior that conflicts with personal beliefs. (Dissonant thoughts: "I am an intelligent person, yet an astrologer fooled me into paying good money for a bogus horoscope." Dissonance resolution: "Actually, the horoscope looks like it could eventually be true, if I wait a few weeks.") Cognitive dissonance can prompt one to accept what one expects to see and rationalize away disconfirming evidence. For a good discussion see Carroll (2007). Finally, people tend to believe that their own perceptions and introspections are based on what is "really out there," but believe that others are more vulnerable to the distortions of bias. Such a **bias blind spot** (Pronin, Lin, & Ross, 2002; Pronin, Gilovich, & Ross, 2004) might lead you to question the accuracy of horoscopes of others, and yet accept a horoscope as true for you.

### Everyday Illusions and Distortions

We have seen that the Barnum effect and confirmation bias can contribute to false and distorted perceptions. We conclude with an everyday process that is happening right now as you read this paragraph.

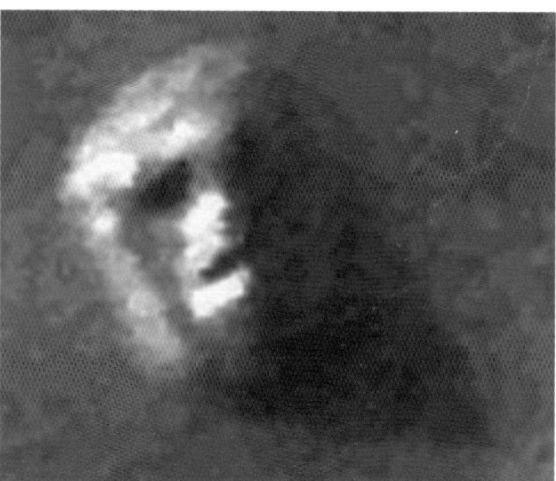

**Figure 9.1** NASA photo of the face on Mars.

**Figure 9.2** Mars smiley face.

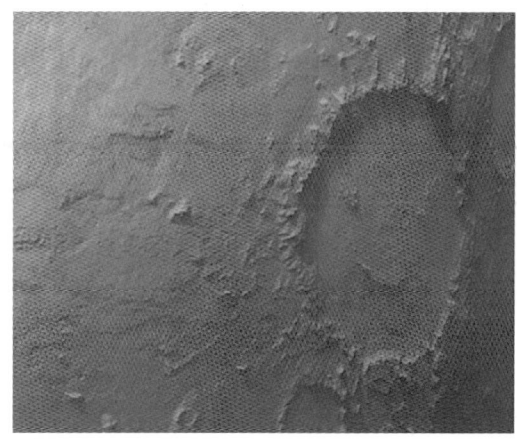

**Figure 9.3** Virgin Mary in a grilled cheese sandwich.

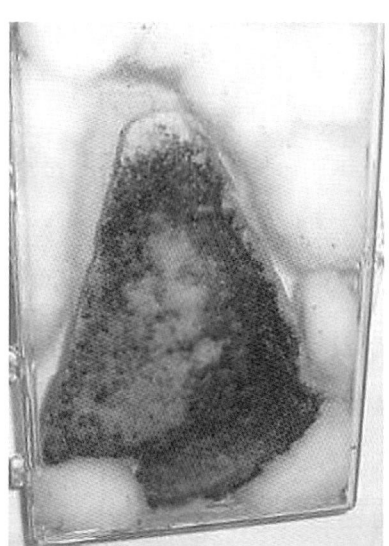

**Figure 9.4** The nun bun.

**Figure 9.5** Moon.

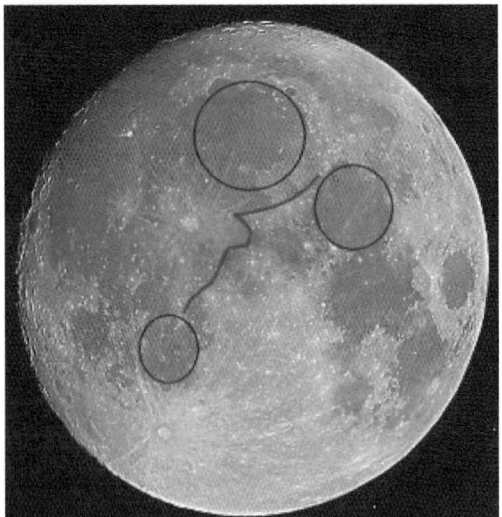

**Figure 9.6** Man in the Moon.

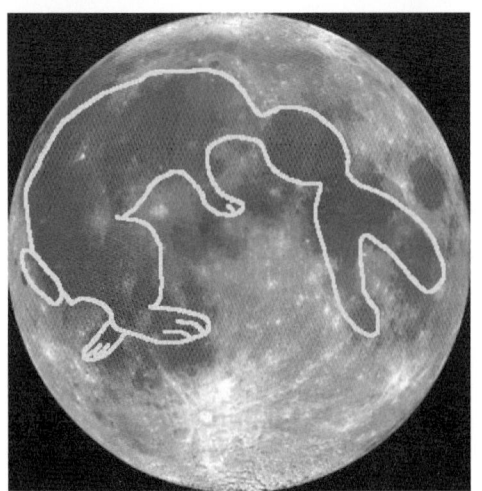

**Figure 9.7** Rabbit in the Moon.

### Illusions, Pareidolia, Apophenia

Perception is constructive. We unconsciously adjust ambiguities in our world by filling in missing details, connecting the dots, sometimes blatantly hallucinating something that just isn't there – often to fit our expectations (Sternberg, 2006). Perhaps the most familiar examples of this are optical illusions and magic. Less familiar is **pareidolia,** seeing recognizable forms in an ambiguous object. For example, many see a man in the Moon. East Indians see a rabbit in the Moon, Samoans see a woman weaving, and the Chinese a monkey pounding rice (Schick & Vaughn, 2005). And, of course, people see Jesus Christ or the Virgin Mary in window reflections, shadows, grilled cheese sandwiches, wood doors, tree stumps, and urine stains on freeway embankments. Similarly, through the process of **apophenia** we see connections and find meaning in unrelated things. The ancients connected the stars to form meaningful constellations. The Chinese and Indians have named constellations quite differently from Western astrology.

### Patternicity and Agenticity

Recently, Shermer (2012) has coined two similar terms, **patternicity** and **agenticity**. Patternicity refers to "the tendency to find meaningful patterns in meaningless noise," and agenticity is "the tendency to infuse patterns with meaning, intention, and agency." Our brains are hard-wired to find meaning in ambiguity, and have evolved to this end. Indeed, one could argue that natural selection favored our forest-dwelling ancestors who were prone to see patterns and conscious intent lurking in the shadows. Although they may tend to overreact, they were at least less likely to miss actual threats. In terms of evolution, ancestors possessing the capacity for patternicity and agenticity would be more likely to survive and contribute their genes to future generations. Although "patternicity" and "agenticity" are recent inventions and more or less synonymous with "pareidolia" and "apophenia," they have the advantage of being easy to remember.

### Perceptual Constancy

One of the simplest examples of constructive perception is the phenomenon of **perceptual constancy**. We tend to see objects as having a certain expected shape, size, color, and place regardless of whether they are close or far away, brightly or dimly lit, viewed directly or from an angle, and so on (Goldstein, 2007). For example, if you were on an open plain and saw some buffalo grazing a few miles away, they would appear very small. Are they really small? Of course not, and you would probably observe that the buffalo are about the size of large cows. But what if you brought along someone from an African tribe who had no experience with vast plains or buffalos? Anthropologist Colin Turnbull (1961) actually did just that. He was in Africa studying the BaMbuti, a people who live their entire lives in the dense Ituri Forest of the Rwenzori Mountains. Turnbull had a companion, a 22-year-old youth named Kenge, who introduced him to various tribes. One week they both traveled farther than before, to an area cleared by a missionary group. From there they could see things Kenge had never witnessed before. Of particular interest were some strange forms in the distance. Were they clouds? Turnbull explained that they were mountains, and to the mountains they drove. Then they viewed buffalo miles away. Kenge asked what kind of insects they were, because they appeared so small. Turnbull explained they were in fact buffalo, twice the size of the animals back home. Kenge laughed in disbelief and told him not to tell "such stupid stories." When Turnbull persisted, his companion started talking to himself "for want of more intelligent company." However, as the two approached the buffalo, the apparent size of the animals magically grew, and Kenge was frightened. Eventually, Kenge accepted the actual size of the buffalo, but his overall view of the world had not changed. When returning home, Kenge observed, "This is bad country, there are no trees." Perhaps it is stretching things only a bit to say that Kenge speaks the anxiety we all experience when we stick to our false and distorted perceptions and fail to entertain challenging hypotheses.

### Magic

Through basic perceptual processes, we often trick ourselves. In addition, trickery can be a deliberate manipulation of a magician or psychic. Magic is an ancient practice in which skilled sleight of hand evokes convincing errors in perception. From the simple card trick to escaping locked jails, magicians never cease to amaze. Indeed, unscrupulous magicians can and have convinced PhD physicists under laboratory conditions that they can bend metal rods locked in Lucite and read pictures sealed in envelopes using presumed paranormal powers. When confronting what appears to be a paranormal phenomenon, an Open-Minded Critical Thinker needs to perform perhaps the most basic of reality checks and ask: Is this a magic trick? (Martinez-Conde & Macknik, 2008)

## The Psychic's Toolkit: How to Be a Convincing Psychic

One of the easiest, and potentially most lucrative, applications of this chapter is the psychic reading. Here a seer appears to use paranormal powers to supply a willing stranger with personal information. Readings can provide descriptions of a deceased relative, personality observations, predictions, and identification of objective facts in one's life and history.

A **cold reading** is a prophecy, observation, or interpretation of a total stranger (whereas a **hot reading** involves simple cheating, such as secretly obtaining information on the "stranger" ahead of time). For the best discussion of cold reading techniques, see Ian Rowland's (2005) *The Full Facts Book of Cold Reading*.

Let me share with you one of the most widely cited examples of this very process. Psychologist Ray Hyman is one of the most outspoken critics of those who profess to have psychic powers of perception. In a review of research on psychic mediums, he recalls an experience he had as a student (Hyman, 2003).

> Now it so happens that I have devoted more than half a century to the study of psychic and cold readings. I have been especially concerned with why such readings can seem so concrete and compelling, even to skeptics. As a way to earn extra income, I began reading palms when I was in my teens. At first, I was skeptical. I thought that people believed in palmistry and other divination procedures because they could easily fit very general statements to their particular situation. To establish credibility with my clients, I read books on palmistry and gave readings according to the accepted interpretations for the lines, shape of the fingers, mounds, and other indicators. I was astonished by the reactions of my clients. My clients consistently praised me for my accuracy even when I told them very specific things about problems with their health and other personal matters. I even would get phone calls from clients telling me that a prediction that I had

made for them had come true. Within months of my entry into palm reading, I became a staunch believer in its validity. My conviction was so strong that I convinced my skeptical high school English teacher by giving him readings and arguing with him. I later also convinced the head of the psychology department where I was an undergraduate.

When I was a sophomore, majoring in journalism, a well-known mentalist and trusted friend persuaded me to try an experiment in which I would deliberately read a client's hand opposite to what the signs in her hand indicated. I was shocked to discover that this client insisted that this was the most accurate reading she had ever experienced. As a result, I carried out more experiments with the same outcome. It dawned on me that something important was going on. Whatever it was, it had nothing to do with the lines in the hand. I changed my major from journalism to psychology so that I could learn why not only other people, but also I, could be so badly led astray. My subsequent career has focused on the reasons why cold readings can appear to be so compelling and seemingly specific.

Many students have had convincing encounters with psychics (astrologers, spiritualists, intuitives, mystics, and the like) and find it difficult to accept that they use, perhaps unknowingly, the tools of perceptual distortion outlined in this chapter. I assure believing students that as Open-Minded Critical Thinkers we must be open to the possibility that each psychic reading could indeed be the most important event in the history of science. However, I invite students to consider more modest alternative hypotheses (at least before spending hundreds on cold readings).

To this end, I often begin class by performing cold readings on random students. After 20 minutes, about 60% of a typical class votes (secret ballot) that they are convinced I am a genuine psychic, "at least as genuine as the most famous TV psychics." I can easily increase my reputation by bending steel cafeteria spoons with a simple touch to my forehead. (Instructions are readily available from James Randi on the web.)

However, students find it even more useful to try on their own the following Psychic's Toolkit. They view online videos of actual readings from famous psychics and identify the tools used. Students then practice performing cold readings on each other, and then on friends and relatives. As far as I know, no student has charged money for their readings (although I suspect some could make far more than I if they were so inclined).

My Psychic's Toolkit organizes cold reading techniques into five groups. First are attempts to maximize the Barnum effect and confirmation bias. Second are sneaky strategies for tricking a subject into telling you things about themselves, which you can then feed back as a "reading." Third are ways of drawing inferences from information other than what a subject tells you. Fourth are ways of making less than perfect readings seem accurate. Fifth, and most important, make a good show. Let's consider each.

### Techniques for Enhancing the Barnum Effect and Confirmation Bias

#### Multiple Out

This is simply a vague statement that can have several interpretations or "outs." Make the statement. Elaborate based on your subject's response. Avoid elaborations that seem not to be true, pursue elaborations that seem to evoke a positive response. Finally, offer a complex statement; clients will tend to ignore what doesn't fit and notice what does fit.

PSYCHIC: You seem to be at a crucial junction in your life, a time of transition that involves significant other people, finances, and a major medical decision.
CLIENT: Yes, I'm worried about what to do after school.
PSYCHIC: Just as I thought. You have concerns about career, education, marriage – those things that confront us at this time of life.
CLIENT: Yes! I'm looking for a wife!

### Double-headed Statement
Make a prediction or observation that includes its opposite:

PSYCHIC: At times you are a bit shy and sometimes surprise yourself with how forward you can be.
PSYCHIC: You will find riches, but for each silver lining there will be a cloud.

Here a statement contains a claim and its opposite. One has to be true, so you can't lose. And if you appear genuine enough, your subject will selectively ignore the part of your statement that is wrong.

### Shotgunning
This is similar to using a double-headed statement. However, you inundate your subject with so many questions and claims that some are bound to be true. Again, if you appear sincere and knowledgeable, your "misses" will be ignored (especially if you talk quickly).

### Drop and Return
This bit of deception works best with shotgunning. While pelting your subject with questions and claims, make a mental note of any that seem to evoke a positive reaction (a fleeting smile, a glance up, a blink, or shake of the head). Give your subject time to forget your shotgunning. Then, with solemn certainty utter the claim that seemed to evoke some interest.

### Have the Subject Feed You Facts

#### Questions (Direct, Incidental, and Veiled)
Once you have establish rapport and cooperation it is amazing how much personal information a subject will tell you if you simply ask. You can do this **directly**, providing you talk quickly and distract the subject from thinking about the fact that they have actually given you personal facts. When you feed this information back, disguise it a bit so you aren't caught.

You might obtain information on the sly by slipping in a quick **incidental question** after a lot of talk.

PSYCHIC: In this day and age we're all working harder … I can tell that you are not immune from the pressures of today … how does this relate to you?
CLIENT: You sure are right. I'm working harder at home and school. Dealing with three kids is a bit much!

Try asking a **veiled question** by making a question sound like a tentative reading. Here's a relatively direct question that might evoke suspicion:

PSYCHIC: Is there stress between you and a certain significant other?

Turn this into a reading:

> PSYCHIC:  I am picking up a very faint impression that there might be some heat, no, maybe some type of tension in your life, perhaps between you and a certain significant other? ...
>
> CLIENT:  Yes, my boyfriend and I are discussing breaking up.

### Encourage Cooperation

Make it clear that doing a reading is a cooperative venture, and that readings work only to the extent that the reader and subject "connect." To do this "both you and your reader have to be very honest and open, hiding nothing."

### Ask for Interpretation of an Esoteric Reading

Give a vague, jargon-laden reading that sounds very mystical. Offer a vague interpretation. Ask the subject to elaborate.

> PSYCHIC:  I'm picking up something strange, and maybe very important. But it's very weak. It involves a large mythological creature who lives in a strange land. Help me out. Is there someone or something new in your life?
>
> CLIENT:  Yes! I just started college, and it is the threatening "beast" in my life!

### Draw Inferences

If a subject gives you any facts ("I am a student, married, live alone, busy shopping"), think about logical inferences one might make from these facts. For example, students have to buy books and deal with schedules. Those who live alone are responsible for a lot of finances. Then feed back these inferences, first as abstract generalizations, and then as specific readings. For example, for a subject who has earlier shared that he has been busy shopping, you might later observe:

> PSYCHIC:  I sense your awareness of your limitations (inference: a shopper often has to be concerned about not spending too much) ... perhaps of a financial nature (getting more specific, a shopper has to be concerned with finances).

### Twenty Questions

Twenty questions is a childhood guessing game in which one systematically narrows one's options through the process of elimination. See how Josh figures out what Tony is thinking of:

> JOSH:  Are you thinking of something living or inert?
>
> TONY:  Inert.
>
> JOSH:  Is it man-made or natural?
>
> TONY:  Man-made.
>
> JOSH:  Is it larger than a chair, or smaller?
>
> TONY:  It's smaller than a chair.
>
> JOSH:  Is it a high-tech device or a mechanical device?
>
> TONY:  A high-tech device.

JOSH:   Is it an appliance or entertainment device?
TONY:   Entertainment device.
JOSH:   Ah, is it a DVD player?
TONY:   Yes.
TOSH:   Do you have the purchase receipt?

This can easily be transformed into readings that sound astrological:

PSYCHIC:   You are thinking of something … inert …
CLIENT:    Not quite …
PSYCHIC:   Yes, I can tell, it is a living thing that sometimes is inert, possibly an animal.
CLIENT:    Yes!
PSYCHIC:   The animal is wild …
CLIENT:    Not quite …
PSYCHIC:   I know, you misunderstand, in the past the animal was once wild, and now has a wild streak in it. Of course, it is domestic, like a pet.
CLIENT:    Yes.
PSYCHIC:   I know you are the kind of person who would have either a dog or a cat, am I right?
CLIENT:    Yes.
PSYCHIC:   Which is it?
CLIENT:    A dog.
PSYCHIC:   Yes, it is a dog. That is what I was thinking of.

### Drawing Inferences from Other Sources of Information

You don't have to wait for a subject to tell you personal information in order to make informed readings. There are many other sources of information you can tap.

#### Read Subtle Cues and Body Language

A good observer will note that clothes, demeanor, posture, and gestures can be very revealing. A devout person may wear religious jewelry. A student may carry books. Someone with money may have expensive clothes. However, do not directly state your immediate conclusions ("you are devout," "you are a student," "you are rich"). Instead, start with observations that are logical inferences if your observation is true. So, if your subject has a book bag and several pens in his pocket, do not blurt out "you are a student" (which may arouse suspicion); say "I sense you are often tired at the end of the day, perhaps because you are doing many things at once and using your brain a lot." (Probably true if the subject is a student.) Indirect inferences protect you from being found out, and make it seem as if you are struggling to make your observations correct.

#### Base Prediction on a Probable but Unexpected Statistic

Here you will have to do your homework and find some fact that is unexpectedly common. Rowland (2005, p. 54) provides a catalog of good high-probability guesses. For example, people generally do not realize that in most homes one would likely find:

old unsorted photographs;
some toy or book that dates to childhood;
jewelry from a deceased relative;
a pack of cards (with one or more cards missing);
some electronic device that no longer works;
a note that is significantly out of date;
some books or instructions on a hobby or interest one no longer has;
a drawer or door that sticks or doesn't work properly;
a key no longer used (or you don't know what lock it works on);
a number "2" in their home address, or they know someone who does.

Rowland suggests that most men:

have tried learning a musical instrument as a child, but quit;
have had a beard or moustache at least once;
have an old suit that doesn't fit.

Most women:

have an item of clothing which they have never worn;
have more shoes than they need;
wore their hair longer as a child;
have at least one earring for which they have lost its pair.

Most people:

have or have had a scar on their left knee;
have been in a childhood accident involving water.

   Psychics often acquire vast listings of unexpected statistics that apply to most people. In a pinch, almost any reading can be pulled out of the hat and a client is impressed with the uncanny specificity of the reading. You might take the probable fact that one has unused medical supplies or outdated drugs somewhere at home. With a little flair, this can be woven into a plausible psychic reading:

I detect at home energy from an old, and possibly ongoing, medical concern. You have stopped using those pills, or that medical device. It or they are just sitting around gathering dust. Maybe they are dated. Perhaps you no longer need them. Am I right?

**Predict a Body Change that is Probable (but Unexpected)**
When most people breathe deeply and rapidly they feel a bit dizzy. This is called hyperventilation, a normal physiological process resulting from rapid decreases in carbon dioxide in the brain. You could have someone breathe deeply, and then predict

"The spirits are making your head light. Do you feel it?" Or have someone stare at a candle flame without blinking. In time their eyelids will get heavy, a simple physiological process of fatigue. Describe this in psychic terms: "The spirits of the flame are pulling your eyelids closed. You can actually feel the heaviness as the spirits work."

### Base a Prediction on Pareidolia or Apophenia

Find a simple ambiguous object that you know can readily evoke pareidolia or apophenia. Quickly show this object to your subject. Then, using a ritualistic incantation, suggest how this object is really something else (something which can be readily seen by most people). Show the object again, suggesting the vision. This works especially well with visions of Jesus or the Virgin Mary. Find any oddly shaped sidewalk stain, reflection of light, or pattern of wood grain. With great sincerity and emotion, proclaim your vision.

## Dealing with Less than Perfect Readings

### Divert Attention

Do anything to prevent your subject from generating alternative hypotheses, or looking more deeply into what you are doing. Divert attention by talking continuously, chanting, introducing a colorful environment, performing interesting rituals, evoking emotion, and so on.

### Shoehorning

Simply force the facts to fit your claim. If you are creative enough, you can make a claim fit nearly anyone. Shoehorning is the same as using *ad hoc* hypotheses.

### Turn Misses into Hits

If you have made a prophecy or interpretation that is off the mark, reinterpret it so it fits. You can see this in the following:

ASTROLOGER:  You are an Aries. You are very assertive and impulsive.
CLIENT:  No, I'm not. I am very shy. I have no friends.
ASTROLOGER:  I was picking up on your mood right now. Right now you are very assertive, assertive enough to challenge me!

An easy way to turn a miss into a hit is to assert that your claim refers to something that will happen in the future. Of course, that can never be verified at the moment, and can be made to appear very profound.

ASTROLOGER:  You have many friends.
CLIENT:  I am alone.
ASTROLOGER:  Let me reassure you that I see a time in the near future when you will have many friends.

### Blame the Client

If you get something wrong, blame your subject. "Help me out. We need to work together on this. I sense a certain negativity and skepticism in you, which is getting in the way. You are thinking too much, which is blocking my reading."

## Make a Good Show

### Create a Context Conducive to Confirmation Bias and the Barnum Effect

Take care to create a setting that is appropriate to and suggests the validity of the psychic claims you are making. Use soft, mysterious music; incense; photos of ancient saints; globes and crystals; strange animals; and perhaps a cat.

### Make a Few Errors

Getting everything right arouses suspicion. Make a few errors, and then claim that because your powers are not magic tricks, they come and go (depending on certain astrological factors, etc.).

### Flatter the Client and Tell them What they Want to Know

"You have more creative talent than you give yourself credit for." "Your friends respect and love you more than you might expect."

## Hypnotic Suggestion Enhancers

We have seen how cold readings and expectations can alter how we view ourselves and the world. In its simplest form, hypnosis is just a verbal suggestion, a verbal "command" to do or experience something. Hypnosis is not a zombie-like trance state. You cannot be forced to do something against your will during hypnosis. You don't even have to be told you are participating in hypnosis in order to respond to a hypnotic suggestion (Baker, 1990).

There has been much debate as to how to define hypnosis. I prefer a simple behavioral definition: hypnosis is responsivity to a set of standardized suggestions (Baker, 1990) as presented in various scientific scales, including the Harvard Group Scale of Hypnotic Susceptibility (Shor & Orne, 1962) and the Stanford Hypnotic Susceptibility Scale (Kihlstrom, 1962). In measuring how hypnotizable one is, a researcher often begins with a pre-induction ceremony in which hypnosis is defined as heightened suggestibility and then proceeds to instructions to close one's eyes, focus, and relax. Suggestions are then read, progressing from easy to difficult. A person "responds" to a suggestion if he or she involuntarily experiences the suggested effect, that is, without deliberately willing it. One's hypnotic susceptibility score is defined in terms of the number of suggestions that "take." Simple suggestions, passed by most people, include:

> Postural sway (your body is slowly swaying).
> Eye closure (your eyelids are getting so heavy they cannot stay open).
> Hand lowering (your hand – stretched in front of you – is getting so heavy you can't hold it up).
> Mosquito hallucination (you hear a mosquito buzzing).
> Taste hallucination (you can taste lemon in your mouth).

Slightly more challenging are:

> Arm immobilization (your arm is so stiff you can't bend it).
> Waking dream (right now you will have a dream).
> Age regression (you are going back to your grade school days. Giggle and talk like a little kid).

Most challenging are:

Hallucinated voice (you hear someone calling your name).
Insensitivity to ammonia (inability to smell a glass of ammonia placed under nose).
Finger lock (you can't separate hands clasped together).
Verbal inhibition (can't say your name).
Amnesia (you can't remember something simple, like your address).
Post-hypnotic suggestion (time-delayed suggestion in which you automatically and unconsciously do something, like change chairs).

Perhaps the simplest suggestion is the **ideomotor effect** in which one suggests a minor body movement (swaying, for example), which then unconsciously takes place. This effect is so powerful that the simple expectation that one might make a movement can be enough to evoke the movement.

It is important to realize that these scale items have been developed through careful research on thousands of individuals. This means that if someone passes a few highly challenging suggestions, it is very likely they will also pass other suggestions, especially those that are easier. Conversely, if someone displays no response to simple suggestions, it is very unlikely that they will respond to those that are more challenging.

This is a useful piece of information for students of the paranormal. For example, imagine that you have a headache and are participating in an elaborate "psychic healing ritual" complete with exotic music, incense, and a psychic dressed in a flowing lavender robe. As part of the ritual, the psychic suggests that you will hear the sound of a bell in the distance. There is no bell, and what you hear is a minor hallucination. However, the fact that you hallucinated reveals that you will probably respond to other suggestions, including that your pain will go away, and will respond to a post-hypnotic suggestion to speak favorably of your psychic to your friends. Indeed, research shows that the best predictor of such susceptibility is not personality, mental health, or brain functioning, but simply whether or not one responds to suggestions (Kirsch & Braffman, 2001).

Remarkably, most of the easier hypnotic behaviors can be elicited without initially closing one's eyes, focusing, or relaxing. A growing body of research on alert (or waking; Wark, 2006) hypnosis shows that one can respond hypnotically while fully aware, even while riding an exercise bicycle (Bányai & Hilgard, 1976). Suggestions to focus (probably required for inducing more advanced suggestions) can be woven into various eyes-open activities, such as preparatory stretching and breathing exercises.

Hypnosis is augmented when one is instructed to (a) close one's eyes, (b) focus on a simple stimulus (ideally in an environment of restricted stimulation, such as a quiet and dim room), and (c) relax. Furthermore, I propose that any suggestion, whether explicit or implicit, to suspend reality checking (Chapter 1) is an essential ingredient. It may help to establish a suggestive environment (an elaborate "hypnotic chamber" or the presence of a crowd that reinforces suggestions) and select a suggestible recipient (an imaginative person who can be completely "absorbed" in something such as a book or movie).

I find it useful to consider such "hypnotic suggestion enhancers" as ways of boosting the effects of expectation and manipulation considered in this chapter. For example, a psychic could perform a cold reading by simply looking at your palm and saying something like "Your life line indicates that this year will be very challenging, but you will grow from your difficulties." This might be moderately persuasive. Another psychic may give you the same reading, augmented to enhance expectation:

> I am about to perform a deep psychic reading. You need to come into my special silent-reading chamber. Close your eyes. Focus on the mysterious powers of the fragrances flowing from the candles. Attend to the soothing music and with every breath relax more and more deeply. Let me hold your hand. Your life line indicates that this year will be very challenging, but you will grow from your difficulties.

## Perceptual Bias in the Mental Health Professions

The possibility of perceptual bias exists throughout the mental health professions (Garb et al., 2002). It is beyond the scope of this book to consider pop psychology, psychoanalysis, humanistic therapies, "New Age" philosophy, questionable or "crazy" psychotherapies, or debated assessment strategies such as the Rorschach inkblot test, graphology (handwriting analysis), or lie detectors. First, some are legitimate topics of scientific debate, with qualified scientists arguing for and against. This is particularly true for psychoanalysis, humanistic therapies, the Rorschach test, and lie detectors. Here good scientists disagree, and they are not pseudoscientists or paranormalists. Also, to include such topics would require we include a discussion of every current controversy in psychology, not the task of this book. See Lilienfeld, Ruscio, & Lynn (2008).

That said, let me indulge in few observations. Clinical psychologists and other helping professionals must entertain hypotheses about their clients. What is the cause of a student's depression? What might be the best strategy to help a suicidal war veteran talk about her traumatic experiences? Should this patient receive medication or behavioral treatment for his anxiety? Hypotheses are evaluated on the basis of theory, research, and practice. However, uninformed fictional accounts of therapists often portray the act of generating hypotheses as something similar to that of making a psychic reading. Your dream about a bear reveals your fear of your father. The fact that you see blood in a red ink blot suggests you have concerns about death. If your doodles include a tiny human figure next to a big house, you have low self-esteem. Such psychic reading is bad psychology, and is not taught in any credible clinical training program approved by the American Psychological Association.

## Nostradamus: Sixteenth-Century Astrology Superstar

Nostradamus was a sixteenth-century French physician and perhaps history's most famous astrologer. I found 8,450,000 Google hits on Nostradamus, and 3,887 books. He is most known for his 942 prophetic quatrains, or four-line poems.

Nostradamus wrote his quatrains claiming to use ideas from astrology. He made them a bit vague so as not to provoke attacks from religious fanatics. People continue to read astonishing prophecies from the quatrains of Nostradamus. He is claimed to have predicted Napoleon, World War I, World War II, aircraft fighters, the French Revolution, the atom bomb, submarines, the deaths of both John F. and Robert Kennedy, the nuclear destruction of Hiroshima and Nagasaki, the Moon landings, the death of Princess Diana of Wales, the Space Shuttle *Challenger* disaster. Perhaps his most famous is his prediction of the rise of Hitler (Randi, 1993):

> Beasts ferocious from hunger will swim across rivers:
> The greater part of the region will be against the Hister,
> The great one will cause it to be dragged in an iron cage,
> When the German child will observe nothing.

*(II, 24)*

Believers claim that "Hister" refers to "Hitler," a lawless leader, and that the "Beasts" refer to Nazi armies crossing rivers, hungry for conquest. This is shoehorning at its best. Hister is actually the name of the Danube River. "German" at the time of Nostradamus did not refer to any country, but to an ancient region of Europe, or possibly part of the Roman Empire.

Imagine the mischief you could get into if you had all 942 of the Nostradamus quatrains to play with! Indeed I found one website that will randomly give you a genuine Nostradamus prophecy. All you have to do is type in a question and press the button (http://www.getodd.com/stuf/nostradamus.html).

For your edification, I typed in: "Will the reader of this page find true love this year?" After six attempts, I found your prophecy:

> When the lamp burning with an inextinguishable fire
> Over the walls to throw ashes, lime chalk and dust
> It will be seized and plunged into the Vat
> Drinking by force the waters poisoned by sulfur.

My apologies. I hope next year turns out better for you.

## Study Questions

**9.1** *Definitions (Define, differentiate, and provide an example for each of the following)*
- A.   Top-down processes
- B.   Forer effect
- C.   Personal validation fallacy
- D.   Subjective validation
- E.   Transparency illusion
- F.   Confirmation bias
- G.   Denial
- H.   Cognitive dissonance
- I.   Bias blind spot
- J.   Pareidolia
- K.   Apophenia
- L.   Patternicity
- M.   Agenticity
- N.   Perceptual constancy

- O. Cold reading
- P. Hot reading
- Q. Multiple out
- R. Shotgunning
- S. Drop and return
- T. Veiled question
- U. Twenty questions
- V. Ideomotor effect

**9.2** *Simple Thought Questions*
- A. How do top-down processes mold perception? How is this "constructive perception"? Give an example.
- B. How can the transparency illusion explain one's tendency to believe the observations of a psychic or astrologer?
- C. Explain how the Barnum effect and confirmation bias persist.

**9.3** *Essay Questions*
- A. How might an unscrupulous psychic use pareidolia as evidence for the paranormal?
- B. Explain how cold reading techniques might enhance the Barnum effect and confirmation basis. Use specific examples of cold reading techniques.
- C. Describe how a reflective thinking style might protect one from any of the perceptual errors described in this chapter.

**9.4** *Internet Psychic/Astrologer Analysis*
- A. Past support for psychic reading powers has been indirect word of mouth and print media. Today things are different. We now have available a lasting record of psychics caught in the act of doing their thing, with transcripts, videos, and firsthand accounts duly posted on the internet. The following are the twenty-first-century psychic superstars. Search the web for examples of each performing psychic readings. Using The Psychic's Toolkit (p. 142), identify which techniques they apply.
  - John Edward
  - Uri Geller
  - Sylvia Browne
  - Allison DuBois
  - James van Praagh
  - Rosemary Altea
  - Theresa Caputo
  - Dorris Collins
  - Joseph Tittel
  - Derren Brown (a magician who illustrates cold reading tricks)

**9.5** *Field Projects*
- A. With a classmate, go to an actual publically advertised psychic or astrologer. Simply let them perform readings on you. Using The Psychic's Toolkit (p. 142), identify which techniques they apply.

- B. At a party, attempt this "party game." Suggest that you have the ability to read the palms of feet (feet bottoms). Explain that this makes perfect sense. Traditional *palm reading* involves reading the palms of ones hands. However, "foot reading" is more valid, given that we carry the entire "weight" of our lives on the bottoms of our feet. If you examine the typical foot bottom you will find hundreds of lines, fissures, cracks, and wrinkles, all the result of the repeated foot pounding of our lives.

   I recommend performing foot-bottom reading on bare feet, so you can actually see the "character lines." In your reading, see how many of the "cold reading tools" you can apply. After your reading, come clean and explain that your "foot reading" is actually a class exercise in cold reading techniques. Prepare to buy your victims a nice apologetic dinner! Discuss your results in an essay.

- C. You can bend spoons with your mind! There are at least five techniques for doing this. Search the web and find them. I recommend the spoon-prebending technique. Then acquire a bunch of steel spoons (about 15) and practice. (Steel soup spoons are available on the internet for pennies each.) I took me about 10 spoons before I developed my skill. Then perform at your next party (assuming you are still welcome after your cold reading stunt!).

**9.6** *Videos*

- A. Search the internet for video examples of "confirmation bias." Typically, the first hits are useful and entertaining. Then suggest how confirmation bias can be combated.

- B. For fun, explore the internet for entertaining examples of pareidolia. Useful search phrases include:
  - "patternicity"
  - "Jesus in a dog"
  - "examples of pareidolia"

- C. The tricks of professional magicians can be more than entertainment. Often they provide very useful lessons of how our eyes can fool us, and how trickery must be ruled out before applying a paranormal explanation for a mystery. Search the web for magic tricks which (1) you can't explain and (2) an unscrupulous magician could use as evidence for paranormal or psychic powers. Useful search phrases include:
  - "Paul Daniels mind-reading"
  - "magic and the brain"
  - "James Randi magic"
  - "magic tricks paranormal"

# 10

# Memory Errors

| OUTLINE |
| --- |
| 1) Memory Myths |
| 2) What is Memory? |
| 3) Memory Errors |
|    a) False Memory |
|        i) Source monitoring error (or cryptomnesia) |
|        ii) Misinformation effect and pseudomemories |
|        iii) Familiarity (from repetition) is truth |
|        iv) Imagination inflation and saying is believing |
|    b) Déjà Vu |
|    c) The Déjà Vu Reality Check |
| 4) Repressed Memory Therapy |

Holly Ramona was a 23-year-old psychotherapy patient suffering from bulimia. Her therapist assisted the recall of repressed memory through hypnosis and sodium amytal ("truth serum"). In numerous sessions Holly vividly recalled a childhood trauma of being raped again and again by her father. Subsequently, her father was accused of incest. He lost a well-paying job as an executive of a large winery and his reputation was ruined. However, he sued the therapist, and won a settlement of half a million dollars. The rape incidents never happened. But the memories were real.

*(Johnston, 1998)*

Barney and Betty Hill were abducted by space aliens in rural New Hampshire in 1961. Their recollections were vivid and confirmed under hypnosis by a psychiatrist. Riding down the road at night Betty observed what she first thought was a star. It grew larger into an odd-shaped craft with flashing lights. Inside were over a dozen human-like creatures all with no ears, small mouth slits and noses, cat-like eyes, and broad foreheads. The Hills stopped their car, lost consciousness, and woke miles away. Later analyses of their dreams and hypnosis revealed they were abducted by the saucer creatures and taken to separate rooms, stripped and examined. One alien inserted a long needle into Betty's navel. A cup-like instrument was placed over Barney's groin and left a ring of warts. Betty spoke to one alien who showed her a star map and a book of mysterious writing. In time, the Hill Incident became the most famous account of an alien abduction.

*(Evans, 1987)*

The Ramona and Hill accounts are two famous stories of dramatic recollection. Some, such as accounts of alien abductions, strange déjà vu experiences, miracle cures, and recollections of past lives, are paranormal. Others, such as eyewitness testimony at criminal trials or psychotherapist explorations of childhood experiences, come from the world of the ordinary. Whenever a friend tells you of a paranormal incident, they are almost always sharing a memory. Memories can have consequences. Are they to be trusted?

Few things are as precious as our personal memories. Yet, few things are so immune from accurate review. Rarely do we need to check if personal cherished memories are entirely correct. It simply doesn't matter. You remember your dear Aunt Mimi, maybe her warm embraces, pink hat, green shoes, yellow flowers, and that awful sofa. All of these could be imagined embellishments, and no one would ever know.

## Memory Myths

Let's begin by debunking a few memory myths. First, many people believe that everything we experience is recorded in memory, as if we carried around a personal security camera that is always on. The fact is that very little of our experience is committed to memory. Our memory capacity is limited, and new memories can replace and corrupt old ones. This myth is perhaps a variant of a larger myth, that we use 10% of our brain. This myth may well have respected sources, perhaps one of the founders of psychology, William James, or even Albert Einstein. However, it is still false. Neuroscience shows that over the course of a day we use 100% of our brains. This should not be surprising. The brain is a relatively small organ, but it has much to do. It comprises 3% of the body's weight but uses 20% of its energy (Boyd, 2008; Radford, 1999).

The second myth is more serious. People believe that memory is accurate, like a video recording or photograph. The surprising finding of years of cognitive research is that memory is *reconstructive*, more like a historical fiction or docudrama than fact. Each memory may have nuggets of truth, but these are embellished by mental creations. Compare a memory with a movie of historical fiction, perhaps Cecil B. DeMille's *The Ten Commandments*, starring Charlton Heston. The movie was great entertainment, and even inspiring to those of faith. Is it based on fact? Very little.

Memories are more like such historical fictions than replays of the latest ball game. If you want to demonstrate the reconstructive nature of memory, try recalling your most recent encounter with a good friend. Close your eyes and conjure up as many details as you can. What was this brief mental snapshot like? Specifically, does it show what things were like as seen through your own eyes (called an **observer memory**)? Or did you picture this encounter as if you were looking at it from the outside (called a **field memory**)? Most people respond to this type of question with field memories. But if you think about it, field memories cannot be accurate because at the time of the event you were not hovering outside looking at what was happening. Your field memory has to be your own invention.

## What is Memory?

"Memory is the means by which we retain and draw on our past experiences to use that information in the present" (Sternberg, 2006, p. 157). The things we remember include personal experiences (our last date) and facts (the ideas in this chapter), as well as skills and habits (how to tie our shoes, how to program a digital video recorder). To do this we must encode, or process, what we want to remember, store it, and then retrieve or bring back memories or skills in response to a cue or command (Sternberg, 2006).

The traditional perspective considers three "memory stores" (Atkinson & Shiffrin, 1968; Squire, 2004). First, **sensory memory** is the fleeting registration of what we immediately experience. We look at something and for no longer than half a second a memory of it lingers, and then immediately fades.

Second, some of what's in sensory memory gets transferred to **short-term memory**, where it lasts from a few seconds to as long as a minute. If our initial perceptions are in error, clearly their registration in sensory and short-term memory will also be in error.

Third, with repetition and rehearsal, short-term memories can be transferred to **long-term memory**, the capacity of which is more extensive and enduring. Current memory theory focuses on **working (or active) memory**, the most recently activated portion of long-term memory. Here short-term memory is seen a little differently as a temporary storage place. Working memory theory provides a metaphor for how information moves in and out of memory:

> Information remains within long-term memory; when activated, information moves into long-term memory's specialized working memory, which actively will move information into and out of the short-term memory store contained within it.
>
> *(Sternberg, 2006, p. 170)*

Long-term memory can be declarative (explicit) or nondeclarative (implicit; Squire, 2004). Declarative or explicit memory consists of facts and event sequences we can deliberately and consciously recall. This includes **episodic memory**, or sequences of events such as the steps you took to get from home to school, and **semantic memory**, or abstract knowledge and facts (Tulving & Wayne, 1972).

If you are currently pondering the possibility that you have the paranormal ability to read thoughts, you are probably drawing upon your working memory of experiences. This may include recollections of times when you appeared to have read others' thoughts (episodic memory) as well as definitions and studies you have read about this psychic ability (semantic memory).

To continue, nondeclarative or implicit memory involves automatically remembering something without being aware where you learned it or even that you are remembering it (Schacter, 1996). These can be simple procedures, like riding a bicycle, or emotionally conditioned memories.

Although you may not know you have nondeclarative or implicit memories, they can influence your actions and experiences through a process called **priming**. To elaborate, in a **priming experiment**, you might be asked to identify words on cards briefly flashed in front of you. However, if you were previously flashed the word "hospital" you might more quickly recognize when the word "nurse" is flashed, whereas prior priming with the word "vehicle" would have no such effect. What is remarkable is that priming works even when you do not remember (and can't even recognize from a list) any of the priming words ("hospital" or "vehicle"). The entire effect is implicit, or unconscious. Advertising is often based on implicit memory. We are continuously exposed to ads and think we ignore them or tune them out. But in fact we are more likely to buy products featured in ad campaigns we might not even remember! And consider the many "docu-mentaries" and "reality shows" on cable television. Many present psychics, mediums, ghosts, and flying saucer chasers, blurring fact and fiction. At the very least, such shows prime you to notice paranormal claims.

Implicit memory is not like Freud's notion of the unconscious. According to Freud, we automatically bury memories of traumatic events through a process called repres-sion. Such events presumably are threatening to the ego. Freud claimed that repressed traumas create anxiety and depression, influence behavior, and are one source of night-mares. There is considerable debate about whether Freud was right. In fact, traumatic experiences are very much more likely to be remembered. Implicit memories are simply poorly encoded memory traces that still have a residual impact.

## Memory Errors

Many dramatic claims of the paranormal may simply be the result of memory errors. Recollections of alien abductions, past-life romances with famous emperors, and even everyday memories of fantastic psychic events years ago can be readily questioned. But some recollections have consequences. Some have destroyed lives and even led to death.

Memory, like perception, is reconstructive (Sutton, 2003). Indeed, many of the same processes that lead to perceptual distortion (Barnum effect, confirmation bias, etc.) can apply to our perception of memories (Moskowitz, 2005). An important point of this chapter is that when asked to recall a fact or event, you actually remember only bits and pieces and automatically fill in the missing details and add embellishments. Your final recollection is rarely a completely accurate record, but a partial fiction based on relevant fact, incidental information, suggestion, and sheer imagination.

### False Memory

The term "**false memory**" describes a wide range of episodic memory distortions (Hyman & Pentland, 1995; Wade et al., 2006). Generally, a false memory is an inaccurate recollection based on selective forgetting as well as mixing memories or memory frag-ments, dreams, fantasies, information from television or the movies, interrogations, or suggestions and manipulations of others. All these are potential sources of error accen-tuated by repetition, using imagery to "enhance" memory, and recalling in the presence of others who reinforce false recollections as true. Recent research suggests that those who believe in the paranormal and claim paranormal experiences are especially prone to display false memories (Wilson & French, 2006). As we shall see, research shows how surprisingly easy it is for distortions to occur.

### Source Monitoring Error (or Cryptomnesia)

If you could accurately determine the source of each part of a memory, you might determine to what extent the memory itself was false. Unfortunately, memories do not come with identification tags. Library books and emails generally have some record of where they came from, perhaps a return address or purchase record. Instead, in the process of recall, we evaluate our memories and attribute (accurately or inaccurately) what we think the sources are (Hicks & Marsh, 2001; Johnston, 2006; Johnston,

Hashtroudi, & Lindsay, 1993). We create source tags as needed, greatly compounding the difficulty in assessing the accuracy of recollections.

One widely cited example involves former president Ronald Reagan (Schacter, 1996). During a presidential campaign, Reagan told a heart-rending story of a World War II pilot who ordered his crew to bail out of their damaged bomber. One gunner was wounded and couldn't jump. Reagan, barely holding back tears, recalled the heroic pilot's promise: "Never mind. We'll ride it down together." A very touching memory, except it never happened – it's the ending of the 1944 film *Wing and a Prayer*.

It is important to note that a memory might have any of a number of sources, including actual fact, a dream, someone else's claim or dream, our desires, and our imagination. Without outside corroboration it can be impossible to determine whether your vivid memory of your Aunt Mimi's pink hat is accurate or based on what a friend claimed, a movie about an aunt, your wish that she wore clothes you prefer, a dream you had about your aunt, or simply your imagination. Furthermore, the degree of detail or vividness of your memory (although sometimes helpful) does not guarantee accuracy of its source. The best we can do is carefully consider our memories, for example, by reviewing their plausibility and objectivity (not part of what we want or expect).

Forgetting the source of a memory is more serious when we forget a source that might not be credible. A psychologist might claim to have conducted a research study that demonstrates that people can communicate with the dead. Later he might be exposed as a complete fraud. We might recall, "I remember a researcher who once demonstrated the validity of communication with the dead," completely forgetting the fraudulent source and recalling only the claim.

**Cryptomnesia** (from the Greek "kryptos" for hidden, and "mnesia" for memories, as in "amnesia") is another name for source memory error. As a nonparanormal phenomenon, cryptomnesia can lead to charges of plagiarism. Famous Beatle George Harrison moved millions with his song "My Sweet Lord," a deeply spiritual anthem for the Hindu Hare Krishna church. "My Sweet Lord" was the first hit by a Beatle after the group disbanded. Harrison was sued (and lost) when a competing record company claimed that his hit resembled another hit, "He's So Fine," composed by Ronald Mack and sung by the Chiffons. Harrison's plagiarism was likely unintentional; he fully believed his tune was new. In the literary world there are many examples of cryptomnesia. Helen Keller's "The Frost King" was an unintentional plagiarism of Canby's "The Frost Fairies." Bits of Robert Louis Stevenson's *Treasure Island* were taken from other books (Stevenson, 2004). Cryptomnesia is not an acceptable legal defense against accusations of plagiarism. If you're a student, don't try it on your professor. However, it is perfectly legal to remember your former life as an Egyptian queen (even though you have forgotten the book on Egyptian queens you read as a child). Many claims of reincarnation and alien abduction are quite likely examples of cryptomnesia.

### Misinformation Effect and Pseudomemories

Researchers have conducted over 200 studies involving over 20,000 individuals on the **misinformation effect**, in which exposure to misleading information can lead to the distortion of recollections (Loftus, 1996). In a typical study, one might observe a simulated event such as a crime or accident and, after a delay, be exposed to post-event information, some of which is accurate and some inaccurate. Later, accuracy of memory for the event is measured.

In a famous study (Loftus, 1996), participants watched a simulated auto accident that involved a crossing with a stop sign. Then, half received a suggestion that there was a yield sign, not a stop sign. Later, those who were given the false suggestion falsely remembered a yield sign rather than a stop sign. Participants in other studies have falsely remembered a suggested conspicuous barn in a scene that actually had no buildings, a white instead of a blue vehicle at a crime scene, and Minnie Mouse instead of Mickey Mouse. Loftus (1996) concludes that misinformation is especially likely to distort recollection when it comes from discussions we have with others, leading to aggressive interrogations ("did you steal the *six raisin oatmeal cookies in the glass jar over the refrigerator?*"), and exposure to media coverage about the event we have experienced.

The misinformation effect typically refers to the distortion of one or two details. It is possible to create more extensive memory errors with **implanted pseudomemories**. In one study Loftus (1996) created personalized information pamphlets for each of 24 participants. Each pamphlet described four childhood incidents, three of which actually happened to the participant (as determined from previous interviews with parents, older siblings, and close relatives). Unknown to the participants, the fourth event was fake, specifically a traumatic experience of getting lost in the shopping mall for an extended period of time.

Weeks later, participants were asked to recall and describe actual childhood experiences. Brief cues from each pamphlet story (real and fake) were presented to help cue and prod memory. About a quarter recalled as real the details presented for the shopping mall fiction. They were not just identifying a fake event as actual, but were recalling what they felt were real memories. Fake memories had been implanted. This effect occurs even when subjects had earlier correctly stated they did not recognize a fake event as having happened ("Getting lost in the shopping mall ... this is news to me."). In later interviews, 20% actually claimed remembering the fake event as factual, and actually provided details (all made up, of course).

Again, we can consider such memory errors as alternative hypotheses for what might seem like remarkable paranormal memories. For example, you and a friend attend a group reading featuring a famous psychic. The psychic gives one audience member a detailed personal reading, including: "you are a student, you have a respiratory disorder, your two pets miss you, and you are thinking about buying a new car." Immediately after the session, you and your friend go out for coffee. You recall the four specifics. Your friend adds, "but don't you remember that she correctly guessed that person's name, Bill?" You respond, "I don't recall this." In fact, your friend is in error. However, the stage has been set for an implanted pseudomemory. Months later you may well recall, and even remember details of, the psychic guessing one participant's first name.

As you might imagine, the implanted pseudomemory effect has the potential for compromising much eyewitness testimony in courts. Indeed, some have suggested that up to 10,000 individuals have been wrongly convicted because of such memory errors (Cutler & Penrod, 1995; Loftus & Ketcham, 1994). I am deeply skeptical of retrospective accounts of the paranormal, no matter how credible a witness may be.

### Familiarity (From Repetition) is Truth

We are more likely to believe a memory if it seems familiar and has been formed on the basis of repeated experience. However, familiarity is not a logical basis for truthfulness. This **illusion of truth effect** (Hasher, Goldstein, & Toppino, 1977) has been demonstrated in a number of startling experiments (Begg & Armour, 1991; Begg, Anas, & Farinacci, 1992). In a typical study, you first might be asked to study a list of general information statements, some of which happen to be true and some false. For example, the list might state that "Boston is the capital of Massachusetts" (true), "Los Angeles is the capital of California" (false), "Adams was president before Lincoln" (true), "Franklin was president after Jefferson" (false), "Edison invented the light bulb" (true), and "Einstein invented the television" (false). Note that in this case you are simply presented the statements, and not told that any are true or false.

If later on you are presented a larger list of statements, some repeating the true and false statements already presented, you are more likely to rate the previously presented statements as true – *regardless of whether they are true or false*. Furthermore, this effect is implicit and occurs even if subjects do not recall the actual previous statements. What happens if the initial statements were tagged as true ("It is widely known that ...") or false ("Few people believe that ...")? This makes little difference. Previous exposure to a statement, *even when labeled as true or false*, is enough to increase the likelihood that it will be subsequently rated as true.

There are many explanations as to why claims that seem familiar seem true (Begg et al., 1992). Perhaps once you have been exposed to a claim, it takes less time to process (and comprehend) when you encounter it again. The first time you read about "retroactive intercessory prayer," it may take you some time to learn that this actually refers to the claim that we can pray that people in the past be cured of illness. When you again encounter a claim of "retroactive intercessory prayer," you are familiar with it, and therefore more likely to feel it is true. In addition, we may erroneously believe that a quickly recognized claim is more likely to be true. Alternatively, when an event is clearly factual it may well be repeated with greater frequency. After living through dozens of cold and snowy winters in Michigan, you come to learn that this is a fact of life in Michigan. The one mild winter was never repeated and cannot be described as typical. From such experiences we may come to automatically label any repeated experience, factual or not, as based on actual evidence.

It is easy to identify many real-life examples that may well illustrate the familiarity-truth effect. Our media is saturated with advertisements claiming various "facts." Toothpaste X whitens teeth best, a specific diet works, and so on. Some of these claims may be challenged and thoroughly discredited by journalists. However, such debunking may have little effect. Simple repetition of the claim makes it seem familiar, and therefore true, regardless of whether it is presented as true or false. Indeed, in one study, warning older adults that a consumer claim is false can make them later mistakenly remember it as true (Skurnik et al., 2005).

Can you think of any paranormal claims that have been repeated so often that they are familiar? This might include flying saucers at Roswell, Uri Geller's psychic ability to bend spoons, ships lost in the Bermuda Triangle, sightings of the Loch Ness Monster, the Amityville haunted house, scientific studies proving the efficacy of prayer or healing touch, or the Nostradamus prediction of Hitler. The list grows if we add figures from antiquity and reports of individuals walking on water, levitating, turning water into wine, bringing the dead to life, and so on. Over time, the simple repetition of these claims (regardless of accompanying caveats or even disproof) contributes to their recollection as factual.

### Imagination Inflation and Saying is Believing

Asking someone to imagine or engage in a fantasy about an event that never happened increases the likelihood that later on they will remember the same event as having happened. This is called **imagination inflation** (Loftus, 1996). To elaborate, when we recall an experience, we are more likely to be confident that our memories are accurate when the perceptual details are vivid and detailed. Recalling a memory (false or otherwise) may well strengthen its vividness and detail, especially when relaxation and visualization strategies are used. One might as a consequence be increasingly convinced of the accuracy of one's recollection (Sternberg, 2006).

Sometimes **saying is believing** (Higgins, 1992; Ackil & Zaragoza, 1998), especially when we are addressing friends who agree with us. Consider this example. A politician who once supported the Iraq war proclaims to a cheering crowd of supporters that she opposes it. Another politician who derided extremist televangelists as "agents of intolerance" speaks glowingly of fundamentalists in front of warmly appreciative conservative Christians. Politicians are frequently accused of "flip-flopping" and adjusting their positions to fit those of their supporters. Nearly 30 years of research suggests that under certain conditions, we, and our politicians, actually come to believe what we say.

When we tune our message to fit our audience's beliefs, our later recollection and belief is of the tuned (and possibly distorted) message. Our perception of reality has been molded by our communications with others. This effect is strongest when there is an emotional and trusting connection between the speaker and the audience (Echterhoff et al., 2008). This is the glue that "fixes" the distorted memory. However, under some conditions this effect is much less pronounced, for example when trying to persuade skeptics, entertain, or simply comply mechanically with instructions.

Apply this to a paranormal belief. Imagine that you are an acupuncture buff in the company of other friendly believers. You are describing news reports of research on acupuncture. In fact the news accounts are complex and include observations from believers as well as scholarly skeptics. In your excitement you tune your report to what your listeners want to hear – the apparently supportive evidence. Later, when asked to describe the news reports, your honest recollection is distorted – you recall only the support for acupuncture.

### Déjà Vu

French for "already seen," déjà vu is the uncanny sense that you have experienced something before, when in fact you are experiencing it for the first time. About 60% of the population has had at least one déjà vu experience, and most people have them about once a year (Brown, 2004). This feeling is typically accompanied by an intense and convincing feeling of familiarity as well as a sense of "eeriness," "strangeness," or "weirdness." Such otherworldly feelings can readily suggest otherworldly interpretations. Given the prevalence and persuasiveness of déjà vu experiences in the paranormal literature, we will devote substantial space to this topic.

Let's imagine that you can remember specific details of a famous castle you have never visited. Why might one experience this strange and remarkable event? In a previous life, did you reside in the castle as a king or queen? Perhaps in sleep your spirit left your body and traveled to the castle. Is some supernatural entity, or worldly ghost, trying to communicate to you about the castle? Maybe one of your descendants traveled to the castle far in the future, and is telling you about it using time travel. Perhaps something very unfortunate, or fortunate, is going to happen in the castle, triggering a timely premonition. Could it be that the castle is on a quantum energy meridian that also connects to your house, giving you an occasional direct view? Maybe in an alternative universe you actually live in the castle, and this information is leaking through dimensional cracks to your mind. Could it involve wormholes? Maybe space aliens took you to the castle for their experimental probes, and then returned you, having botched the job of erasing your memory of the castle.

What does research say? Researchers have identified a few consistent patterns. Déjà vu is often associated with stress and fatigue (Brown, 2004). Logically, if you go to many places, the likelihood increases that you will evoke a déjà vu feeling just by chance. Stress, fatigue, and laws of probability may explain why soldiers going into battle and travelers are particularly likely to have déjà vu experiences since both face new environments and are under some stress and fatigue.

A few other patterns are worth noting. Those who recall their dreams are more likely to have déjà vu experiences. Zuger (1966) has suggested that some déjà vu experiences may be dream states intruding into waking consciousness. Also, a dream memory fragment may evoke a déjà vu experience when one encounters a similar situation while awake. Déjà vu is not consistently associated with psychopathology or brain-related illness; however, it is more common for head injury patients (who have lost consciousness). Finally, déjà vu has been associated with abuse of amphetamines, toluene-based solvents, use of mind-influencing medications (amantadine and phenylpropanolamine), and withdrawal from medication for bipolar disorder and herpes simplex encephalitis.

Theories of déjà vu experiences (Brown, 2004) suggest they reflect a temporary uncoordination of brain processes, moments of inattention, or simple memory error.

### The Déjà Vu Reality Check

What type of experiment would support a paranormal interpretation of a déjà vu experience? For the sake of illustration, imagine you are visiting a castle for the first time and have the strong feeling you have visited before, perhaps in a previous life. Here are some of the issues we should consider.

1) Your memories would have to be concrete and specific, as confirmed by neutral outside observers. You could not claim that a certain room in a castle is "creepy." You would have to name specifics, the number of tables and chairs, their composition and placement.

2) Your claimed recollections would have to be unique. You could not claim that the castle is made out of stone or is on a hill, characteristics that fit many castles.

3) Your recollections would have to be prospective and identify specific facts not available, otherwise your recollections could be based on conversations, what you've seen or read, or stimulus leakage. You might select a vault, sealed for hundreds of years, with no information concerning contents. Of course, you would have to identify the contents before (not after) the vault is opened.

4) You would have to rule out chance. Given that 60% of the population has had a déjà vu experience, one might suspect that many have had experiences that involve concrete and unique details. It is possible that a large number of people have had prospective déjà vu recollections involving long buried or hidden items. By chance alone we would expect some recollections to be right. To minimize chance identifications, we would have to publicly record a déjà vu-based prediction of hidden

information before the unveiling event. This might be hard to do given that déjà vu experiences occur unpredictably.

5) Finally, you would have to apply the FEDS Standard and ensure that each step is free from any possibility of fraud, error, deception, or sloppiness.

## Repressed Memory Therapy

The popular press abounds with cases of false memory. Some stories are amusing, such as those in which people recall living past lives as ancient slaves or kings. There can be only so many reincarnated Cleopatras or Napoleons. Then there are those poor souls who have been abducted, and probed, by aliens from outer space. Appropriately, these stories are particularly popular in science fiction. Many people have been falsely accused and incarcerated because of erroneous witness recollections. Today, juries are wisely suspicious of testimonies based only on recollection. But perhaps the most instructive examples are from the pseudoscientific world of **repressed memory therapy**.

Repressed memory therapy (RMT) derives from Freud's notion that threatening memories are automatically repressed in the unconscious, where they can do great harm. Specifically, RMT claims that traumatic childhood memories of sexual abuse are repressed, but can be uncovered and released through special therapeutic techniques including imagery and hypnosis. This approach is highly controversial, partly because its basic idea is probably false. Traumatic memories are actually more likely to be remembered than buried. But RMT therapists claim again and again that their patients recall vivid incidents of sexual abuse. Critics claim that many of these recollections are simply cases of **false memory syndrome**.

Repressed memory therapy has led to some very costly tragedies. Elizabeth Loftus (1997) has recounted numerous cases. For example, in 1986 a Wisconsin nurse's aid, Nadean Cool, was in therapy with a psychiatrist. Cool claimed she had buried memories of childhood sexual abuse, and indeed, after several sessions of hypnosis, she recalled fantastic memories of rape, being in a satanic cult, eating babies, and having sex with animals. Eventually Cool realized that her memories were false and sued. In 1997 she settled for $2.4 million.

In a similar example, in 1992 a Missouri church counselor helped Beth Rutherford uncover childhood memories of being repeatedly raped by her father, a pastor. On further exploration, she recalled that she had two pregnancies, both of which were terminated by her father through abortion. When these accusations were made public, Rutherford's father resigned as pastor. However, it was eventually determined that she was a virgin at age 22. She sued the counselor and received $1 million in 1996.

From 1986 to 1992, Patricia Burgus underwent psychiatric therapy in a major Chicago hospital by a respected psychiatrist. Through drugs and hypnosis, she recovered a variety of memories, including participating in a satanic cult, rape by her father and cult members, and cannibalizing body parts of up to 2,000 people, including her own aborted children (Belluck, 1997). These recollections were so convincing that her husband had a hamburger from a family picnic tested for human content. Burgus grew suspicious of her own recollections and searched for corroborative evidence. Finding none, she decided that her recollections were false, sued, and won the lawsuit, including a settlement of $10.6 million (the largest ever). The director of the trauma unit called the settlement a "travesty."

In general, cases such as these have a number of features in common:

- lack of accurate external corroborative evidence for a memory claim;
- use of imagery or hypnosis to evoke or "enhance" memories;
- instructions to recall after a time delay;
- initial suggestion (even indirect, through media accounts) of specific memory content and source;
- encouragement, group support, and reinforcement for accepting memories as true;
- failure to request critical and skeptical reconsideration of memory claims and their sources.

In the waning years of the twentieth century, repressed memory therapy was in its heyday. However, after hundreds of successful lawsuits, this approach waned in popularity. Today the consensus is that the foundations of repressed memory therapy are a "pernicious bit of psychiatric folklore" (McNally, 2004).

## Study Questions

**10.1** *Definitions (Define, differentiate, and provide an example for each of the following)*
- A. Reconstructive memory
- B. Observer memory
- C. Field memory
- D. Sensory memory
- E. Short-term memory
- F. Long-term memory
- G. Working memory
- H. Episodic memory
- I. Semantic memory
- J. Priming
- K. False memory
- L. Source monitoring error
- M. Cryptomnesia
- N. Misinformation effect
- O. Pseudomemories
- P. Familiarity from repetition is truth
- Q. Illusion of truth effect
- R. Imagination inflation
- S. Saying is believing
- T. Déjà vu
- U. Repressed memory therapy
- V. False memory syndrome

**10.2** *Essay Questions*
- A. How is priming like selective perception? How are they different? Can you think of a case where both might work together?
- B. Numerous psychics and faith healers have been repeatedly and publicly revealed as frauds. Yet their popularity persists and grows. What memory processes might explain this?

**10.3** *Internet Search*

The internet abounds with sites reviewing evidence for reincarnation. Examples of evidence include: transferred birthmarks, child born with bullet wounds, reincarnated handwriting, an individual born knowing Swedish, memories of past lives in monasteries, cat memories. Take a tour of supportive sites by searching the following phrases:

- "evidence for reincarnation"
- "proof of reincarnation"
- "past-life memories and reincarnation"

List the most popular forms of evidence. Discuss alternative explanations for each. If you have difficulty, go to skepdic.com.

**10.4** *Videos*

- A. You can find many superb examples of memory error on the internet. First focus on Elizabeth Loftus and her research on false memory. Search "Elizabeth Loftus false memory," "false memory research," and "implanted memory." Describe the most impressive research you can uncover. How was the study conducted? What were the results? What are the implications of this research?
- B. One serious implication of false memory research concerns the reliability of eyewitness testimony. Numerous convictions may well have been based on memory error. Search "false memory and eyewitness testimony." What are the most dramatic examples you can find? For your best example, describe (1) how convincing the memory was and (2) the psychological processes (using this text) that contributed to the false memory.
- C. False and implanted memories may be a part of repressed memory therapy. Find examples on the internet. Search "repressed memory therapy false memory."
- D. You can see for yourself how unreliable memory can be. For simple self-demonstrations search "eyewitness test," "accuracy of visual memory," and "memory error eyewitness." Search for examples that illustrate the principles illuminated in the research of Loftus.
- E. The "invisible gorilla" is a popular video illustrating selective attention and memory error. For fun, search "invisible gorilla" and take the test.
- F. The magician and psychic explainer Derren Brown has produced a very entertaining minute-long video on priming and memory. Search "Derren Brown applies the psychology of memory."
- G. Some accounts of alien abductions illustrate the possibility of false memory. Search the internet for accounts of people claiming to have been abducted into space by aliens from other worlds. Search "alien abductions." Identify the conditions in these dramatic encounters that may well foster perceptual distortion and memory error.

# 11

# The Placebo Effect

---

**OUTLINE**

1) What Are Placebos?
2) Do Placebos Work?
3) Weak and Strong Placebos
4) Suggestion and Expectation
5) Nonspecific Effects (Not Necessarily Placebos)
   a) Nonspecific Effects with No Agent
   b) Nonspecific Effects with an Agent
      i)   Self-stressing
      ii)  "Mediating" neurophysiological mechanisms
           1) The opioid system
           2) Other neurophysiological mechanisms
      iii) Classical conditioning
6) Placebos and Superstitious Beliefs
7) Placebos, Psychotherapy, and Stress Management
8) Placebos and Performance
9) How to Pump Up Your Placebo: The Placebo Checklist

---

Every decade has its cancer fad. In the 1950s it was Krebiozen, a worthless treatment made from horse blood. I am particularly fond of the Krebiozen story because it involves a treatment administered by a doctor whose Chicago office was in the very same building I have worked in for decades. In fact, it all happened just under my office. This story has been presented with little modification in many medical texts, although its source is Klopfer (1957).

We begin with Mr Wright, a desperate patient suffering from cancer of the lymph nodes (lymphosarcoma) who was not responding to traditional treatment. Orange-sized tumors were growing on his neck, armpits, chest, abdomen, and groin. They had metastasized. His spleen, liver, and chest were filled with fluid, requiring two quarts of draining a day. Mr Wright had little time left and demanded the new wonder drug Krebiozen.

His skeptical physician relented. The pace of recovery was unexpected, indeed miraculous. After one dose, tumors "melted like snowballs on a hot stove" to half their size. After 10 days, Mr Wright appeared to be cured and was able to return to most of his normal duties. He remained cancer free for about two months until the media reported that Krebiozen may not work.

*Critical Thinking: Pseudoscience and the Paranormal*, Second Edition. Jonathan C. Smith.
© 2018 John Wiley & Sons, Inc. Published 2018 by John Wiley & Sons, Inc.

Mr Wright was despondent and his cancers returned. In desperation, his physician decided on a placebo and a bit of deception. He claimed that Krebiozen worked but some of the initial shipments had deteriorated. He went on to say that he had a new and concentrated supply. Then, using an elaborate procedure, he injected his patient with a placebo, simple water. The experiment worked dramatically. Again, tumor masses melted and Mr Wright enjoyed life free of symptoms. But it was a short cure. Two months later the American Medical Association announced that nationwide research had shown that Krebiozen was completely worthless. Mr Wright's cancer returned and he died two days later (Klopfer, 1957).

The story of Mr Wright is practically a legend in medicine. It illustrates a potent dimension of treatment called the placebo effect. Alternatively, it may illustrate how perceptions, of patients, physicians, and presumed outside experts, distort the facts and contribute to pseudoscientific medical myths. Indeed, we will probably never know if Mr Wright's treatment in fact lengthened his life (Carroll, 2008).

## What Are Placebos?

Most experts define a **placebo** as a physiologically or psychologically inactive substance, treatment, procedure, or activity that can have a therapeutic physiological and psychological effect if administered to a patient who is not only conscious of the agent, but has the expectation that it is effective (Bausell, 2007; Benedetti, 2009; Shapiro & Shapiro, 1997). Put simply, **a placebo is an inactive agent that works through expectation**. A placebo is the proverbial "sugar pill," "dummy treatment," or in Mr Wright's case, water injection. It is an inert intervention whose medical effect, the placebo effect, is due to expectation. The core placebo effect can be diagramed:

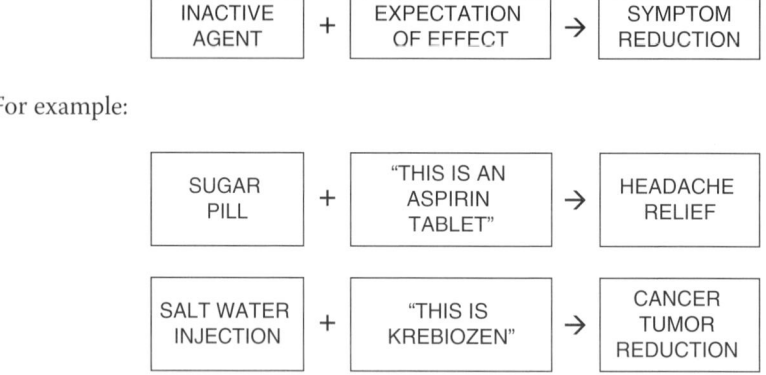

| INACTIVE AGENT | + | EXPECTATION OF EFFECT | → | SYMPTOM REDUCTION |

For example:

| SUGAR PILL | + | "THIS IS AN ASPIRIN TABLET" | → | HEADACHE RELIEF |

| SALT WATER INJECTION | + | "THIS IS KREBIOZEN" | → | CANCER TUMOR REDUCTION |

A placebo doesn't have to be a pill or a liquid. It can include any intervention, whether it be a form of psychotherapy, ritual, dietary prescription rehabilitation activity, or surgery. However, the intervention must be inactive. Sometimes, with complex treatments like psychotherapy, this might be impossible to demonstrate.

All placebos are **nonspecific** in that the same inactive agent could be applied to nearly any malady, providing the patient expects the agent to be effective. In contrast, medical drugs or procedures are **specific** in that they are carefully designed to work for targeted conditions independent of any expectations a patient may have. This distinction is easy to miss. *All placebos are nonspecific.* But, as we shall see later, *not all nonspecific interventions are placebos.* This point is often confused, even by top experts.

## Do Placebos Work?

The word placebo derives from the Latin word for "I shall please." The term entered English by way of a mistranslation of the 16th Psalm as "I will please the Lord" (correct version: "I will walk before the Lord."). In medieval times, this psalm was sung at religious ceremonies honoring the dead. In time, you could avoid such dreary duties by hiring professional mourners to sing your placebos for you. Not surprisingly, the "placebo" acquired a derogatory connotation that continues today – something superficial and not genuine. In the 1800s the term "placebo" entered the medical vocabulary as a treatment given "more to please than to benefit the patient" (Hooper, 1822). But it is misleading to say that placebos are simply tools for pleasing patients.

Contrary to popular opinion, placebos can work. As seen with Krebiozen, the effects can appear miraculous. But just how effective are treatments based on expectation? In medical lore, about one-third of the medical effect of a therapeutic intervention is attributable to the placebo effect. This claim is generally attributed to Beecher (1955). In fact, placebo response rates vary considerably from a low of 0% to up to 100% (Benedetti, 2009).

The placebo effect appears stronger for problems with a strong psychological component, such as pain or depression. However, research suggests that the effect is broad. Physicians have removed warts by painting the skin with harmless dye, induced airway dilation in asthmatics through fake bronchodilators, and reduced intestinal inflammation in colitis patients using simple placebos (Talbot, 2000). Some evidence appears to show a placebo effect for "postoperative swelling, movement disorders, vital signs such as oral temperature and pulse, blood pressure, weight loss, exercise tolerance among heart patients, healing of ulcers, cholesterol reduction, blood sugar ..." (Bausell, 2007, p. 138). Placebo surgery ("sham surgery") may also be effective in some cases. Here one group might receive actual surgical incisions plus treatment, and other group the same incisions without treatment. Patients would not know if a treatment was actually performed. Although sham heart surgery (Cobb et al., 1959) and knee surgery has been attempted (Moseley et al., 2002), the results are controversial because of the absence of adequate controls for the passage of time and nonspecific effects. We don't know if the sham worked, or if the problem would have gone away on its own. Placebos can even evoke the negative side effects of the drugs they are claimed to be, including headaches, drowsiness, decreased respiration, and altered cortisol levels (Bausell, 2007).

Most research on placebos has focused on pain reduction or depression. Here we find very high levels of efficacy, with up to 60% reporting significant improvement (again, different studies report different numbers). Given the huge pain and antidepressant medication industry, drug companies take considerable care to compare new medications with placebos. This is becoming increasingly difficult. So much rides on the magnitude of the placebo effect that disputes often arise.

## Weak and Strong Placebos

Not all placebos are equal. It is not enough simply to compare an experimental treatment with a sugar pill. Placebos appear to work better for patients highly motivated to improve their health. That is, patients who are conscientious about complying with treatment have better recovery rates, even with worthless treatments. Similarly, patients do better if they have been given strong reasons to expect that a placebo will work. Placebos presented in an "authoritative and/or positive" way work better than those given with a neutral or equivocal message (Bausell, 2007).

Even the type of pill can make a difference. Color pills work better than white pills, capsules better than pills, big pills better than small pills, and injected placebos better than oral placebos. Placebos administered frequently are more effective than those given infrequently (Bausell, 2007). Expensive placebos work better than cheap placebos (Waber et al., 2008).

Placebos are actually more effective if those giving them have been deceived into believing they work. This necessitates what is termed a **double-blind** design. Here neither the patient nor the person giving the drug knows if the treatment they are giving is the drug under question or the placebo. Failure to adequately "blind" research participants is one of the most serious problems plaguing placebo research, especially for studies on approaches to complementary and alternative medicine such as acupuncture (Interlandi, 2016; Madsen, Gøtzsche, & Hróbjartsson, 2009). For example, the rituals of "correct" acupuncture needle insertion are quite complex, requiring a trained acupuncturist. However, when such an expert administers treatment, it is no longer blinded. His or her enthusiasm could be a potent nonspecific therapeutic ingredient. It is extremely difficult to control for such enthusiasm. Could you have treatments given by experimenters who don't know if it is real or placebo? But then one could argue that the experimenter is then not really an expert in the treatment and one would not expect it to work. The more you think about it, the more difficult it is to create a true double-blind study.

Placebos with built-in negative side effects are more effective. These are called **active placebos** and can be created by spiking sugar pills with harmless substances designed to produce symptoms such as sweatiness. Such side effects can be perceived as "signs" that the placebo is actually working. (A placebo accompanied by a verbal suggestion of a negative effect is sometimes called a **nocebo**.)

The complexity and plausibility of a placebo treatment can influence its efficacy. A good placebo has a complicated explanation as to why it works (the explanation can be complete rubbish, but it has to sound plausible, with lots of technobabble; see Chapter 6). Similarly, placebo procedures are more effective than placebo pills (Bausell, 2007).

Finally, (at least for pain) the recalled effect of a placebo may well be greater than the actual effect experienced at the time of treatment. In one study, pain was induced artificially by a special heat pad. As expected, a placebo could reduce the pain. However, a few minutes after the end of the experiment, participants were asked how much their pain was relieved. Recollections of degree of pain reduction were greater than the actual reductions reported while the placebo was administered (Price et al., 1999). The implications of such findings are considerable, especially in light of what is known about the distorting effects of memory (Chapter 10).

When considering the possibility of a placebo effect, it is useful to understand underlying mechanisms that might make placebos work. Armed with these tools you can examine the conditions associated with a claimed treatment and ask if "placebogenic" mechanisms may be at play.

## Suggestion and Expectation

First, by definition, if there is no *expectation of relief*, there is no placebo. Must someone suggest that a treatment works, or is it enough that a patient expects it to work regardless of what the doctor says? It is conceivable a nurse may administer a placebo and suggest that it is effective, but the patient does not believe the nurse. The patient does not expect the treatment will work. Here we do not have a placebo. Conversely, a nurse may administer a placebo and suggest it is inactive and will not work. However, the patient may well expect the placebo is indeed effective (because he trusts the nurse would only act in his interest). Here we have a placebo. By definition, *expectation* is a necessary component for every placebo effect.

Second, if there is no *inactive agent*, there is no placebo. There may be simply suggestion or expectation. The suggestion/expectation effect can be a powerful *nonspecific agent* on its own. It is often confusingly described as a "placebo effect." By definition it is not:

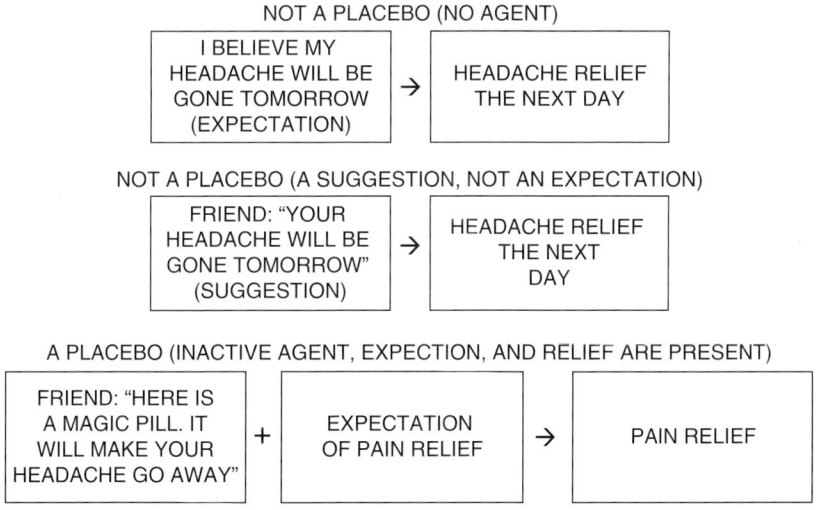

Given how often students and learned experts get confused about placebos, I repeat our basic formula:

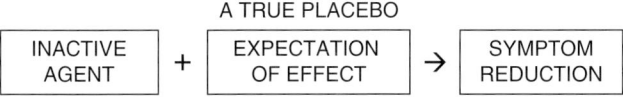

## Nonspecific Effects (Not Necessarily Placebos)

Sometimes patients improve without receiving an agent targeted to a specific problem. This can happen two ways: the problem goes away on its own and no agent whatsoever is involved; or the patient receives a substance, treatment, procedure, or activity, but its effects are general and not restricted to one outcome. In both instances, the literature describes the effect as **nonspecific**.

### Nonspecific Effects with No Agent

Sometimes a problem goes away on its own through **spontaneous remission**. The rates of spontaneous recovery vary considerably and are difficult to determine. For cancer they may be 1 in 100,000. For breast cancer, it may be 22% (Zahl, Maehlen, & Welch, 2008).

Patients can appear to improve because of **initial misdiagnosis**, that is, they may not have been seriously ill to begin with. (Indeed, one might argue that Mr Wright, our dramatic opening example, may have suffered from problems different from or in addition to the reported cancer.) The **normal recovery pattern** is such that most people get better over time. If you present an inactive treatment before a person is about to spontaneously recover, it might look like the treatment worked. Similarly, many serious diseases display a **cyclical course** in which patients improve for weeks, months, and even years, and then get worse.

**Repeated test taking** can give an erroneous impression that a treatment is working. Imagine that a nurse measures your blood pressure several times during an experiment testing the effects of a hypertension drug. Your first measure is high, partly because of the excitement of starting the experiment and unfamiliarity with the blood pressure cuff. After three or four measures, you get used to all of this and your blood pressure is no longer elevated. If you happened to be taking the experimental drug, you might be fooled into thinking that the drug, rather than adaptation, caused your blood pressure to decline.

Statisticians refer to a phenomenon called **regression to the mean** (Gilovich, 1991). Put simply, it means that if you have an extreme run of bad or good luck, chance alone says this won't continue. If you score high because of a statistical "fluke," chances are this won't be immediately repeated – that's why it's called a "fluke." If you pick three winning lottery tickets in a row, the laws of probability haven't changed a bit; the odds that your next ticket will be a winner are the same as for every other ticket, perhaps one out of a million. At this time, if your witch doctor friend casts a spell for you to lose the lottery, you might be fooled into believing that the spell actually caused you to lose when in fact your scores simply display regression to the mean.

Finally, medical science is always making new discoveries. A patient might improve because of an **undiscovered ordinary extraneous variable**. Perhaps it was the change of seasons, something in the drinking water, atmospheric pressure, a dietary change, fluctuations in the immune system due to sunlight, and so on – the list of potential extraneous variables is immense.

### Nonspecific Effects with an Agent

Some interventions are broadly effective and seem to have an impact regardless of what they are used for. These are nonspecific agents, again not placebos (because, again, expectations of efficacy are not required).

### Self-stressing

**Aggravating external conditions** can contribute to a variety of illnesses. Removing such conditions is a nonspecific procedure, one with general efficacy. Asthma is worse for those who live in polluted cities. People with digestive problems may suffer when eating a fat-rich diet. Simply removing an aggravating external condition may lead to symptom relief. An asthma patient may try a new drug while vacationing in unpolluted Arizona, and attribute her improvement to the drug.

**Stress** is one of the most common aggravating conditions, and the link between stress and illness is profound and well documented (Grady, 2007; Sapolsky, 2004). Chronic activation of our body's stress trigger (sometimes called the hypothalamus–pituitary gland–adrenal arc) evokes a primitive and pervasive physical "fight or flight" response, involving the release of dozens of stress hormones (such as adrenalin and cortisol). This response has a measurable impact on physiological wear and tear and immune system functioning, potentially impacting just about any medical condition. Stress increases your risk of getting, and the rate you recover from, heart disease, the common cold, some forms of cancer, ulcers, allergies, and so on. Stress even slows your rate of recovery from surgery. All of this has been carefully documented in thousands of well-designed medical studies (Lehrer, Woolfolk, & Sime, 2007; Sapolsky, 2004).

What has not been clearly articulated is how placebos may be part of the picture. I have devoted over 30 years of my professional life to researching and writing on stress management. Recently, I developed a theory that might help us understand placebos. *Self-stressing theory* (Smith, 2005, 2007, 2018) states that there are six ways that people trigger and maintain their physiological "fight or flight" stress response. These six forms of self-stressing include:

*Stressed posture and position.* When confronted with stress, people often assume a variety of defensive or aggressive postures or positions (standing, crouching, bending over a desk) for an extended time. This, combined with sustained immobility, can evoke skeletal muscle tension, joint stress, and reduced blood flow and contribute to tension, fatigue, and decreased energy.

*Stressed skeletal muscles.* When threatened, one clenches, grips, and tightens skeletal muscles to prepare for attack or escape. When chronic, such tension can contribute to pain and fatigue.

*Stressed breathing.* Under stress one is more likely to breathe in a way that is shallow, uneven, and rapid, deploying greater use of the intercostals (ribcage) and trapezius (shoulder) muscles and less use of the diaphragm.

*Stressed body focus.* Simply attending to and evoking thoughts and images about a specific body part or process can evoke related neurophysiological changes. An individual facing a threat may notice her rapidly beating heart or churning stomach. Attending to and thinking about these somatic reactions can aggravate them.

*Stressed emotion.* We often motivate and energize ourselves for a stressful encounter with affect-arousing cognitions. We entertain fantasies and repeat words and self-statements that can evoke anxiety, anger, or depression.

*Stressed attention.* When dealing with a threat, we actively and effortfully concentrate on attacking, defending, or running. In addition, we often direct our attention to multiple targets, including competing tasks (as in multitasking), a targeted task vs. worried preoccupation, or self-stressing efforts (thinking how one is breathing, maintaining a stressed posture or position, thinking about relaxing fantasies or negative emotions, etc.) rather than the task at hand. (2005, pp. 42–43)

Self-stressing theory proposes that professional relaxation techniques (the most widely used approaches in stress management) reduce different types of self-stressing, and thereby reduce stress arousal. Indeed, most forms of professional relaxation can be described in terms of which specific form of self-stressing they address. For example, stretching reduces stressed posture and position; simply letting go, stressed muscles; slowly and deeply breathing, stressed breathing; entertaining positive and pleasant images or thinking positive thoughts, stressed emotion; and quietly diverting attention from a source of stress to a simple nonstressful stimulus can reduce stressed attention. The effects of professional relaxation on stress have been well documented (Lehrer et al., 2007).

Of interest to us is the possibility that many nonspecific activities may reduce self-stressing in the same way as professional stress-management treatments. This would result in a limited reduction of stress arousal and stress-related symptoms. It is very important to note that professional relaxation techniques do much more than turn off stress arousal by moderating stress triggers; in addition, they bring about a profound physiological state of deep relaxation called the *relaxation response* as well as important psychological relaxation states of mind (called *R-States*) (Smith, 2005). Here a placebo can be seen as a form of *negative reinforcement*; the relaxation response and deep relaxation states are forms of *positive reinforcement* (Skinner, 1974). Negative reinforcement involves getting rid of something aversive or unwanted ("It felt so good when I walked out of the stuffy, overheated office!"). Positive reinforcement involves getting something that is desired ("It felt so good when I jumped into the cool, refreshing pond!").

The next time you encounter a treatment that seems like a placebo, ask if it might reduce any of the six forms of self-stressing. Let's consider Mr Wright's experience with Krebiozen (assuming his reported improvement was genuine). Before treatment we might suspect he was quite worried about his dire condition (stressed emotion). Indeed, he may well have devoted much of his attention to this condition (stressed attention). It is conceivable that the resulting self-stressing subjected his body to substantial wear and tear and may have contributed to suppressed immune system functioning. Reading about and receiving a "miracle cure" could have reduced his stressed emotion, eased and diverted his stressed attention, resulting in a rebound of physical health and immune system activity. This in turn may have contributed to his astonishing patterns of improvement and deterioration. In other words, if a placebo enables you to cease self-stressing, that in itself may be enough to free your body's self-healing powers to do their job. We can summarize the nonspecific effect of self-stressing:

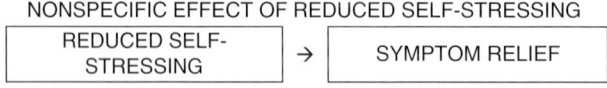

NONSPECIFIC EFFECT OF REDUCED SELF-STRESSING

| REDUCED SELF-STRESSING | → | SYMPTOM RELIEF |

### "Mediating" Neurophysiological Mechanisms

Are there specific brain or neurophysiological mechanisms that underlie the placebo effect (Benedetti, 2009)? Research is in its infancy and has identified some possibilities, although they may not apply to all placebos. Furthermore, such processes may evoke nonspecific effects apart from the placebo effect. We take a look at this frontier research.

*The opioid system.* Different neurophysiological mediating mechanisms may contribute to the placebo response for different medical conditions (Benedetti, 2009). Recent research suggests that the brain's reward system, the **opioid system** (and perhaps dopamine activation), may at times mediate the placebo effect for pain and perhaps anxiety and depression. The role of the opioid system in interventions for conditions with few overt symptoms (glaucoma, some early cancers, HIV infection) and surgical treatments is much less clear.

I find it most useful to diagram this complex effect:

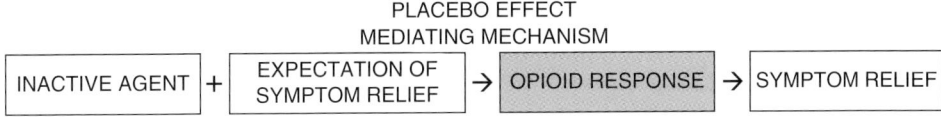

PLACEBO EFFECT
MEDIATING MECHANISM

| INACTIVE AGENT | + | EXPECTATION OF SYMPTOM RELIEF | → | OPIOID RESPONSE | → | SYMPTOM RELIEF |

First, a bit of pharmacology. Morphine is an extremely powerful analgesic and falls into the same class of addictive opioid drugs as heroin. The brain's opioid system produces its own morphine-like substances, called endorphins, which can block pain and evoke feelings of euphoria. This is one reason why long-distance runners can persist in spite of fatigue, and football players can continue playing in spite of painful injury.

**Naloxone** is an opioid antagonist, which means it can block the effects of opioids. Indeed, naloxone is sometimes used to treat heroin overdose. If an addict takes naloxone, heroin won't work.

When a placebo effect is associated with the brain's opioid system, then naloxone should block this effect. Often the effect is dramatic. For example, Benedetti, Arduino, and Amanzio (1999) injected capsaicin (the substance that makes chili peppers hot and burn) under the skin in the left and right hands and feet of participants in a study. Participants were then given a placebo cream for one burning body part. The cream was described as a powerful local anesthetic. The cream worked as expected and eliminated the pain in the one hand or foot to which it was applied. However, when naloxone was injected, the effect was completely eliminated, illustrating a purely expectation-driven effect mediated by the opioid system.

However, the opioid system may not be involved in all types of pain. Vase et al. (2005) injected patients suffering from irritable bowel syndrome with either a saline solution (placebo) or naloxone. Both worked equally well. Here, if pain-reduction were mediated by the opioid system, the naloxone group should have reported no effect.

Is it possible to actually see the placebo opioid effect in the brain? Researchers are coming close (Lidstone & Stoessl, 2007). A number of studies have used advanced brain-imaging techniques to examine what happens in individuals who are experimentally subjected to pain and then given a placebo. Positron emission tomography (PET) is an advanced technique for producing a three-dimensional image of processes in the body and brain. A small amount of a radioactive substance is injected into the body and, as it decays, it releases subatomic particles called positrons and eventually photons. These are detected and sophisticated computers produce an ongoing image of what happens in the body or brain as it occurs. Zubieta et al. (2005) applied a type of PET scan to participants subjected to experimental pain (produced by immersing a hand for about an hour in icy salt water). At times participants were informed that they were also receiving an analgesic (actually a placebo). When individuals were told they were receiving a painkiller, their pain was reduced through the placebo effect. This was expected. Remarkably, PET scans revealed increased activity in those parts of the brain associated with the release of opioids. Similar brain changes have been observed in individuals receiving fake acupuncture (Kong et al., 2006).

Many things can trigger the brain's nonspecific opioid system, including the positive loving care and attention provided by an empathic health provider. To this we can add conceivably any form of exertion, stress, or strong positive affect. Running up a flight of stairs can do it. So can good music or a good joke. If a claimed medical treatment requires effort or simply feels very good, there's a good chance it is triggering the brain's reward or opioid system. None of these are necessarily placebos.

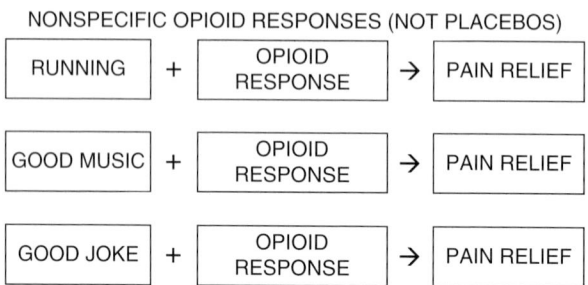

*Other neurophysiological mechanisms.* Perhaps too much has been written about the relationship between placebos and the opioid system. There are doubtless other brain processes and mechanisms that may be equally important. Focusing on the sensations of an inserted acupuncture needle may contribute to relief by blocking pain nerve impulses to the brain (gate control theory; Melzack & Wall, 1965). Or, focusing on a singular meditation stimulus, such as a repeated word or "mantra," may evoke a localized burst of slow and rhythmic "alpha" brain waves that blanket and soothe areas of the brain associated with pain (Gaspar & McDonald, 2014). This may well be a mechanism explaining why meditation sometimes helps pain and depression patients. Autogenic treatments have, for example, patients passively think the words "hands are warms and heavy" over and over (Smith, 2005). This in turn may evoke increased blood flow in the hands, resulting in an improvement for Raynaud's syndrome, a painful condition of reduced blood flow in the hands. Conceivably, each of these neurophysiological processes could work outside of the opioid response. If research discovers expectation is required for gate control processes, mantra repetition, or hand-warming verbalizations to work, then we have placebos:

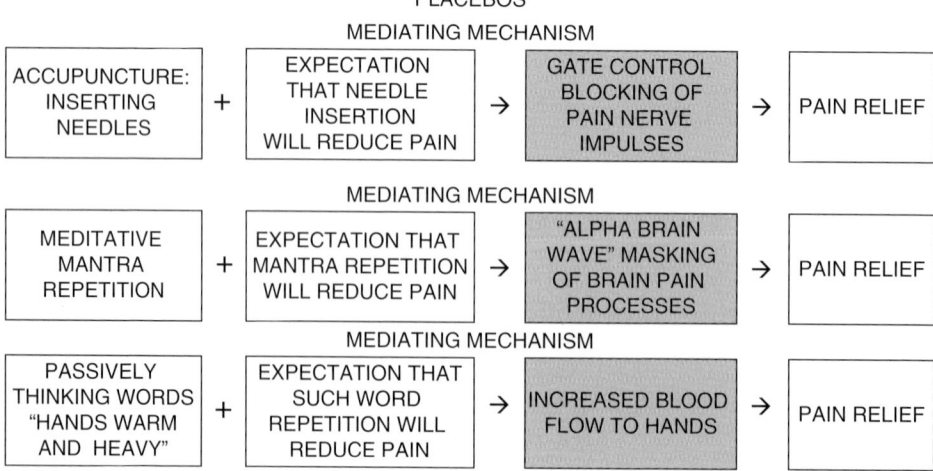

Conversely, if research shows that expectation is not necessary, then these are not placebos.

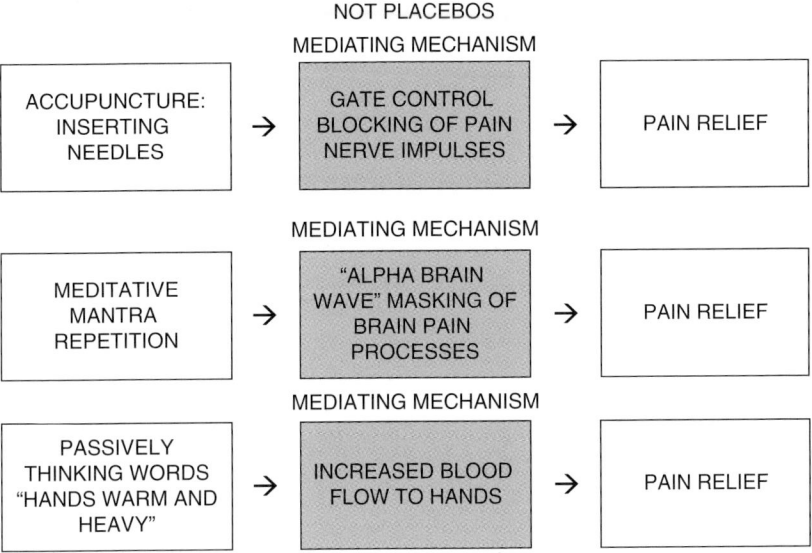

### Classical Conditioning

Famous Russian researcher Ivan Pavlov **classically conditioned** dogs to salivate to a bell simply by ringing a bell whenever they were fed (STEP 1). Eventually, the bell was enough to trigger salivation (STEP 2).

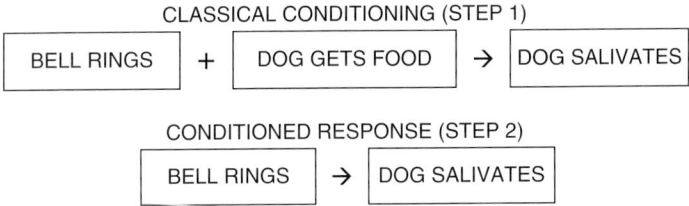

Similarly, classical conditioning may mediate some placebo effects. If you feel better after taking a prescribed medication in a paper cup, anything a doctor gives you in a similar paper cup might become a conditioned stimulus and evoke feelings of improvement.

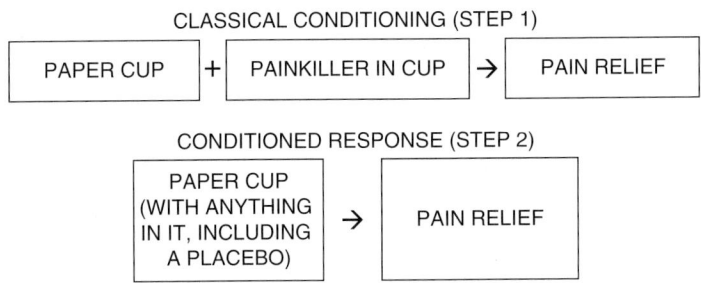

Nitroglycerine is a heart medication that induces changes in heart rate. When participants are first given actual nitroglycerine pills, and then similar pills not containing nitroglycerine, they continue to display changes in heart rate (Lang & Rand, 1969). Mice injected with harmless sugar water, and then with an immunosuppressive drug, display a reduced immune response (fewer antibodies). Then, when sugar water is injected alone, they display a classically conditioned immunosuppressive response (Cohen, Moynihan, & Ader, 1994). Classically conditioned placebos have been demonstrated to evoke the physiological effects of caffeine, nicotine, alcohol, interferon, bronchodilators and bronchoconstrictors, stimulants, and immunosuppression and nausea associated with cancer chemotherapy (Bausell, 2007; Benedetti, 2009). Benedetti (2009) suggests that classical conditioning is a central component to placebo effects when unconscious physiological processes are involved, such as with hormone secretion and the immune system. Does this mean that mice (and sleeping humans) can display an "unconscious placebo response?" I take a slightly different stance. There is no such thing as an "unconscious placebo." "Unconscious" means there is "no expectation." *A placebo involves an inactive agent and works through expectation.* If there is no presumed agent, and no expectation, there is no placebo. Instead, we may well have a nonspecific effect, which may well be classical conditioning.

Our lives are filled with thousands of instances in which stimuli evoke classically conditioned responses, including relief from various pains and discomfort. Sirens sound and we look around and forget our pains. A friend smiles and our hearts flutter in happiness. We see a TV ad for a hamburger and our stomachs growl. I see no value in calling every alarm, smile, or TV ad a "placebo." It is enough to describe them as classically conditioned effects. No more labels are necessary. Eschew technobabble.

To summarize, the impact of a treatment can be the result of a combination of three variables: specific effects, nonspecific effects, and the placebo (expectation) effect:

| SPECIFIC EFFECTS | NONSPECIFIC EFFECTS | PLACEBO EFFECT |
|---|---|---|

## Placebos and Superstitious Beliefs

Psychologist B. F. Skinner (1948) has suggested that **operant conditioning** may explain why people may mistake placebos and nonspecific treatment variables for actual treatment. Skinner did much of his research on caged pigeons (and in World War II invented a pigeon-piloted suicide "smart bomb"). Caged pigeons sometimes display strange repetitive behavior, such as nonstop pecking, flapping their wings, and turning their heads over and over. Skinner discovered that this was actually a type of superstition. If a pigeon happened to display a certain behavior, pecking for example, accidentally just before feeding, the bird would associate this behavior with food and do it again. Eventually, when more food is given, the behavior is reinforced (through "operant conditioning"). Soon, pigeons are pecking, flapping, and turning all the time, as if they were expecting food. (Of course, they had no way of knowing that food was randomly presented.)

Skinner believed that such repetitive pigeon behavior was analogous to superstitions in humans. An accidental reinforcement fools one into believing a causal link. Imagine you are suffering from the flu. Eventually just about everyone gets over the flu, in a week or two. Let's say that one week into your illness you start consuming chicken soup, and get better. Of course, this is the natural course of the disease. However, you may be fooled into thinking that the chicken soup cured your flu, just as Skinner's pigeons behaved as if compulsive pecking produced food.

## Placebos, Psychotherapy, and Stress Management

Often it is difficult to differentiate a placebo effect from nonspecific therapeutic, stress management, and self-improvement strategies that involve modifying thoughts and behaviors (Wampold et al., 2005). For example, perhaps you have burned your hand and wish to reduce the pain. Psychologists may recommend a variety of strategies, including redefining the pain sensation as a more tolerable sensation ("imagine the burn as the sensation of cold ice touching the skin"), giving the pain a meaningful interpretation that makes it more bearable ("this pain will teach you to tolerate adversity," "give the pain to God"), or simply focusing on the pain ("meditate on the sensation of pain, without trying to push it away or think about it").

Are these placebos? Such imagery may well be nonspecific. However, as long as there is no explicit or implied attribution of the pain-reduction to an agent or activity that theoretically should have no effect, there is technically no placebo effect. So, if a nurse says, "Take this pill [a sugar pill] and it will reduce your pain. Imagine a peaceful place so you can swallow the pill more easily," he has given a placebo. He has claimed that an inert agent (the sugar pill) will have an effect (pain reduction). However, if a nurse says, "Take this pill [a sugar pill] and imagine a peaceful place. At the very least, imagining a peaceful place may evoke brain opioids which might counter your pain [or block pain, trigger alpha filtering, etc.]" he has not administered a placebo (at least in pure form), but a nonspecific cognitive-behavioral pain-reduction strategy.

All mental health professionals, including cognitive-behavioral therapists, must entertain hypotheses about their troubled clients. What is the cause of a student's depression? What might be the best strategy to help a suicidal war veteran talk about her traumatic experiences? Should this patient receive medication or behavioral treatment for his anxiety? In a typical therapy session, a good counselor may entertain hundreds of specific hypotheses. Obviously, it would be impossible for every one to be subjected to a double-blind placebo study. Such real-life hypotheses are informed by theory, research, and practice, and an awareness of popular interventions that simply do not survive the empirical test (Norcross, Koocher, & Garofalo, 2006; Lilienfeld, Lynn, & Lohr, 2003; Lilienfeld, Ruscio, & Lynn, 2008). A good therapist is always cognizant of the possibility that his or her prized insight or intervention may in part be a placebo. Or it might work. He or she must not be paralyzed by such possibilities when the well-being, even the life, of a client may be at stake.

## Placebos and Meditation/Mindfulness

Some have claimed that placebo studies of psychological treatments are simply impossible. Although this claim has been made for most types of psychotherapy, its most recent and aggressive application has been to meditation and mindfulness. Since 2001, psychology has witnessed an explosion of interest in meditation and mindfulness among both researchers and therapists. These techniques are relatively simple, and involve effortlessly restricting attention to a simple stimulus task. Specifically,

> Some practices and trainings involve maintaining mental focus on a particular sensation (e.g., of the breath), while others involve focus upon a sound or auditory mental image, the silent repetition of particular words or phrases (e.g., as in loving-kindness meditation), a visual object, or a visual mental image. Other approaches attempt to broaden the attentional field without a preference for selection of any focus, releasing attention gently and without judgment whenever it is pulled to any particular mental experience.
>
> *(Davidson & Kaszniak, 2015, p. 358)*

Is it possible to create a meditation/mindfulness placebo? Davidson and Kaszniak (2015) unambiguously conclude and recommend:

> Unfortunately, this kind of design simply is not possible with meditation-based interventions because of the obvious fact that participants will know if they are assigned to a meditation condition and thus cannot possibly be kept blind to the nature of the intervention.
>
> *(p. 583)*

I highlight this claim because it appeared in the most prominent journal for psychologists (*American Psychologist*), was penned by top researchers, and is typical of the lack of understanding of placebos by experts who should know better.

In 1976 (Smith, 1976) I published an elaborate placebo study of transcendental meditation (TM), the most popular approach to meditation at the time. This study may well be the most elaborate placebo investigation of meditation/mindfulness (and perhaps psychotherapy) ever conducted.

I randomly assigned 49 anxious college students to TM and 51 to a placebo meditation, which I called "periodic somatic inactivity" (PSI). PSI was carefully designed to match the form, complexity, and expectation-fostering aspects of TM but involved sitting twice daily rather than sitting and focusing on a meditation mantra.

Complete TM instruction includes two introductory lectures that outline a credible-sounding supporting theory as well as research, a 15-day drug-free fast, standardized individual initiation, and three days of follow-up discussion. The technique involves passively attending to a mantra, effortlessly attending as it repeats in one's mind, and quietly returning attention after every distraction or instance of mind wandering.

PSI was a placebo control treatment specifically contrived to match every aspect of TM with one exception: instead of sitting and meditating, one simply sits with eyes closed for 15–20 minutes twice daily. One is instructed to "Let your mind do whatever it wants. Whatever you do mentally will have little or no impact on the effectiveness of the technique."

The technique was claimed to work automatically as long as one sits for 15–20 minutes twice daily. In other words, one may worry, daydream, plan one's day, or do anything. In contemporary meditation/mindfulness theory, PSI "mind wandering" and "default network" activity is seen as the opposite of meditative focus.

Considerable effort was made to make PSI as credible as TM. Liberal use was made of "official" logos, sign-up books, questionnaires, contrived testimonials, professional-looking slides, and the like. Like TM, PSI instruction began with two introductory lectures that outlined a highly credible yet contrived theory explaining why sitting twice daily should be an immensely effective cure for most forms of psychopathology. In addition, bogus research was presented supporting the claims made. Between lectures subjects participated in a 15-day fast from illegal drugs. After the fast and the lectures, each subject was scheduled for technique initiation. During initiation each subject was ushered into a small, quiet room and sat facing his instructor. After a few introductory remarks the instructor presented the PSI instructions. Subjects were given further instruction if it appeared they were practicing incorrectly.

PSI was taught by an undergraduate selected from 30 candidates for the degree to which he resembled the TM instructors (clean-cut, conservatively dressed, no facial hair, cheerful disposition). He was given the 71-page PSI instruction manual, which detailed all aspects of PSI theory, technique, and answers to "frequently asked questions."

One feature that makes PSI unique in the universe of placebos is its deployment of a credible and complex faux rationale. Notably, "PSI theory" includes not a single misstatement of existing psychological theory or research. (One might see it as an object lesson that the literature of psychology, like many holy books and the Pastafarian Quatrains, can be cherry-picked to support nearly any claim. However, among these, only the Pastafarian Quatrains can legitimately claim to contain not a single error or distortion.)

More to the point, "PSI theory" is an elaborate exercise in technobabble, weaving actual psychological constructs to explain how daily sitting would cure nearly any disease (or "dis-ease"). Incidentally, it took me three months of library research to concoct PSI theory.

### PSI Theory

Behavior theory explains that all physical inactivity (such as just sitting) triggers the release of a generalized product of all activity, reactive inhibition. PSI classically conditions brief periods of reactive inhibition dissipation to specific temporal zones in one's circadian rhythm pattern. These appear as physiological signatures or "little dips." (For example, a 7 a.m. sitting would trigger a small 7 a.m. dip.) Classical conditioning continues as long as the regimen of daily sitting continues and is practiced the same time (ensuring dip placement at the same time slot on one's circadian cycle). This results in the overlay of additional conditioned dissipation signatures so that "little dips" accumulate to "bigger dips." (7 a.m. initiates a brief period of significantly lower physiological arousal.) Such accumulated dips in generalized physiological arousal have cross-circadian impact, touching rhythm cycles for numerous physiological processes. As such they serve as profound autonomic zeitgebers, or time-regulating stimuli that serve to keep ones overall pattern of circadian rhythms synchronized and normalized. Normalization of circadian rhythms leads to enhanced well-being and physiological health.

To continue with my meditation study, the PSI instructor practiced each aspect of instruction until he could proceed fluently without notes. The instructor was deliberately misinformed that PSI was highly effective and well researched and that the main purpose of the project was to determine if PSI is effective for different people for different reasons. He enthusiastically accepted this rationale. (p. 632)

I submit this is a credible placebo control study of a meditative technique, one that meets the criteria specified by Davidson and Kaszniak (2015) and the Placebo Checklist at the end of this chapter. It may well be one of the most elaborate meditation/mindfulness placebos (and perhaps psychotherapy placebos) in the literature.[1]

## Placebos and Performance

Can placebos affect your performance? Can a worthless pill help you study better? The impact of placebos on performance is currently an important issue in sports psychology. Astonishingly, up to 75% of athletes can recall instances in which their performance actually improved after a hyped-up food supplement, procedure, or preparative ritual later revealed to be a worthless placebo (Beedie, 2007). On the internet you can find a football season's worth of enhancement products that go beyond power shakes and herbal supplements. These include an assortment of magnets, tapes, copper bands, crystals, computer chips, and electronic skin zappers. For the truly adventurous, a similar catalog of toys can be found for sexual enhancement.

Some of the variables that may underlie enhanced sports performance parallel research on the placebo effect. In hypnosis research, archers display improved performance when given active suggestions for increased body awareness, imagery, appropriate task focus, and smooth automatic execution of activities (Robazza & Bortoli, 1994; Wark, 2006). Brain-generated opioids may give long-distance runners extra endurance (and evoke a "runner's high"). One can easily hypothesize the involvement of classical conditioning. A cheering coach may motivate a basketball player to do her best. Eventually, simply the presence of the same coach may evoke the same effect. Athletes routinely engage in various breathing and stretching rituals before a contest, activities which may minimize the interference of self-stressing.

There is actually a growing lore of sports placebos. We have space for what is perhaps the most infamous account. Willy Voet is a well-known Belgian sports physiotherapist deeply involved in the notorious 1998 Tour de France. Voet tricked French cyclist Richard Virenque into taking a placebo injection, claiming it to be a performance-enhancing drug. Here is Voet's (1999) account:

> I was supposed to inject this rubbish into Richard's backside one hour before the start … At the given moment I gave Virenque his injection. That day he rode the time trial of his life, finishing second on the stage to Ullrich. The German started three minutes after Richard and caught him, after which the pair had a memorable ding-dong battle all the way to the finish. "God I felt good! That stuff's just amazing" he bubbled. "We must get hold of it." His result did have something to do with the magic capsule – but there is one thing he doesn't know, unless he reads this. I had got rid of the fabulous potion and swapped it for one which contained a small amount of glucose. There is no substitute for self-belief …"
>
> *(p. 104)*

This is an anecdotal account. What does the research show? I count six published empirical studies on the placebo effect in sports. These have involved fake anabolic steroids (Ariel & Saville, 1972; Maganaris, Collins, & Sharp, 2000), fake carbohydrates (Clark et al., 2000), fake caffeine (Beedie et al., 2006), a fake nostrum called the "new ergogenic" (Foster et al., 2004), or a fake respiratory training device (Sonetti et al., 2001). In each instance, those receiving a placebo performed better than baseline or controls.

## How to Pump Up Your Placebo: The Placebo Checklist

Imagine that you are considering to what extent a treatment might be a placebo. Here's a checklist of what to look for. The more a treatment incorporates these features, the more powerful its placebo effect.

☐ Does the therapist motivate the patient to want to get better? Does he give exciting testimonials of others who have benefited from the treatment? Does he cite some supportive research and experts? Does he give a motivational pep talk on the hidden powers in all of us?

☐ Does the therapist use a capsule rather than a pill, and make it large and colored? Better yet, does she have a nurse inject salt water? Does she give the treatment frequently?

☐ Is the belief and enthusiasm of the therapist or person giving the treatment high?

☐ Does the therapist give his treatment a complicated explanation or rationale that sounds plausible and use scientific-sounding terms? For example, "The esoteric elixir in this vial [note the jargon] may appear clear, but it has been formulated to disrupt molecular discordances that contribute to what is commonly known as 'itchy feet.' The clarity of this elixir is caused by the fact that its ingredients are in perfect biometric harmony. Science says that we experience a sensation of 'itchiness' whenever two neurophysiological processes exist in convolution, thereby contributing to subdural irritation, or the itch. This is the reason we giggle when tickled, and why it is so hard to tickle yourself."

☐ Does the therapist introduce a complicated and sophisticated procedure? For example, does she put the water in a chemistry flask, surrounded by tubes that run through an imposing electronic device with lots of knobs, dials, and lights (maybe an old VCR player)? Does she explain that this device is an "extractor/purifier"?

☐ Does the therapist alter the treatment so that it has a slight negative side effect? She might spike the water with vodka so it stings a bit when applied to the itch, or give it a slightly unpleasant medicinal odor. The sting means it is working. No pain, no gain.

☐ Does the therapist enhance the treatment with hypnotic suggestion [optional]? Does she have victims close their eyes, focus, and relax?

☐ When the treatment is over, does the therapist wait a few minutes before asking how well it worked? Delayed feedback is more likely to be positive than immediate feedback.

## Study Questions

**11.1** *Definitions (Define, differentiate, and provide an example for each of the following)*
- A. Placebo
- B. Nonspecific effect

- C.   Specific effect
- D.   Double-blind
- E.   Active placebo
- F.   Spontaneous remission
- G.   Initial misdiagnosis
- H.   Cyclical course of disease
- I.   Repeated test taking
- J.   Regression to the mean
- K.   Undiscovered ordinary extraneous variable
- L.   Self-stressing
- M.   Stressed posture and position
- N.   Stressed skeletal muscles
- O.   Stressed breathing
- P.   Stressed body focus
- Q.   Stressed emotion
- R.   Stressed attention
- S.   Relaxation reinforcement
- T.   Negative reinforcement
- U.   Positive reinforcement
- V.   Opioid system
- W.   Classical conditioning
- X.   Operant conditioning
- Y.   Superstitious operant conditioning effect

## 11.2   *The Placebo Quiz*

### The Placebo Quiz

*The literature on placebos is often confused and contradictory. Hopefully this chapter lends some clarity. To check if you've got the main points, here's a quiz. Which of the following are examples of a placebo effect, nonspecific effect, or expectation effect? (Please don't read the answers until after you've provided your own.) In each situation, Ebek Hogur suffers from stomach discomfort. His doctor could find no cause.*

1) *Ebek has been suffering for days. His doctor could find no cause. Ebek's wife gives him lemon tea, which she describes as a "powerful Chinese stomach soother." It's actually worthless. Ebek trusts his wife and is very happy and relieved that finally someone has a cure. Indeed, the tea works. IS THIS A PLACEBO EFFECT?*

   *ANSWER: YES. THIS IS A PLACEBO EFFECT. IT FOLLOWS THIS FORMULA:*

PLACEBO EFFECT

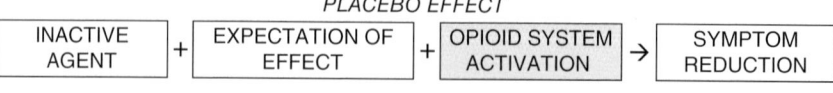

2) *Ebek's wife gives him lemon tea, which she describes as a "powerful Chinese stomach soother." It's actually worthless. Ebek does not believe his wife. He is thoroughly convinced the tea has no medicinal value. But the tea works. IS THIS A PLACEBO EFFECT?*

*ANSWER: NO. THIS IS A SUGGESTION EFFECT. THERE IS NO EXPECTATION OF RELIEF.*

SUGGESTION EFFECT

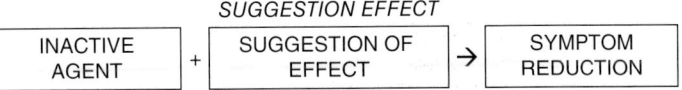

3) *Ebek's wife gives him lemon tea, expecting nothing. Ebek is thirsty, and drinks it, expecting nothing. His stomach feels better. IS THIS A PLACEBO EFFECT?*

> *ANSWER: NO. THIS IS A NONSPECIFIC EFFECT (NOT A PLACEBO). Maybe it involved classical conditioning (how?). IT FOLLOWS THIS FORMULA:*

NONSPECIFIC EFFECT

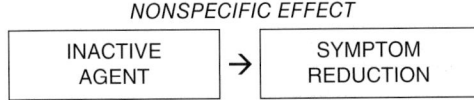

4) *Ebek's wife gives him lemon tea. The tea is remarkably delicious, and Ebek is very happy his wife was so loving to give him such a treat. His stomach feels better. IS THIS A PLACEBO EFFECT?*

> *ANSWER: NO. THIS IS A NONSPECIFIC OPIOID EFFECT (NOT A PLACEBO). IT FOLLOWS THIS FORMULA:*

NONSPECIFIC OPIOID EFFECT

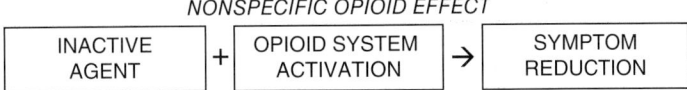

5) *Ebek's wife gives him a big hug, but does not give him any of her lemon tea. His stomach feels better. IS THIS A PLACEBO EFFECT?*

> *ANSWER: NO. THIS IS A NONSPECIFIC OPIOID EFFECT (NOT A PLACEBO). IT FOLLOWS THIS FORMULA:*

NONSPECIFIC OPIOID EFFECT

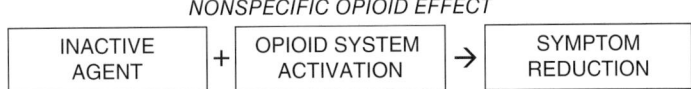

6) *Ebek is in his doctor's office, waiting to see the doctor again. While in the waiting room, the receptionist asks Ebek if he is thirsty and gives him a paper cup of lemon tea. There is no suggestion that this is any treatment, and Ebek has no expectation that it will do anything for his stomach distress. However, in the past his doctor has given him various medications in the same sort of paper cup. Ebek's stomach feels better. IS THIS A PLACEBO EFFECT?*

> *ANSWER: NO. THIS IS A NONSPECIFIC CLASSICAL CONDITIONING EFFECT (NOT A PLACEBO). IT FOLLOWS THIS FORMULA:*

NONSPECIFIC OPIOID EFFECT

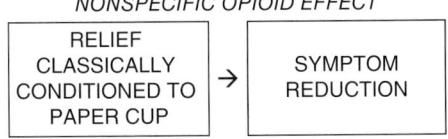

7) *Ebek's wife gives him lemon tea because she has some extra. Ebek remembers seeing something on TV about lemon tea being good for stomach discomfort. He was convinced by what he saw. He drinks the tea and feels better. IS THIS A PLACEBO EFFECT?*

*ANSWER: YES.*

*PLACEBO EFFECT*

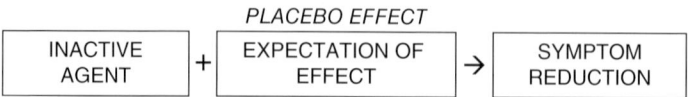

| INACTIVE AGENT | + | EXPECTATION OF EFFECT | → | SYMPTOM REDUCTION |

8) *Ebek's wife gives him lemon tea and she laughingly says: "Here's a placebo. It's like a sugar pill. Maybe it will stir your mind to heal itself!" He drinks it. His stomach feels better. IS THIS A PLACEBO EFFECT?*

*ANSWER: ??? THIS IS A TRICK QUESTION. IT SEEMS TO FOLLOW THIS FORMULA:*

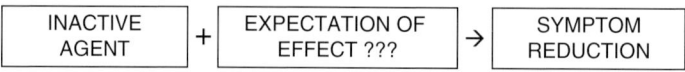

| INACTIVE AGENT | + | EXPECTATION OF EFFECT ??? | → | SYMPTOM REDUCTION |

*This was actually tried in research. Kaptchuk et al. (2010) gave patients suffering from irritable bowel syndrome a treatment described as "placebo pills made of an inert substance, like sugar pills, that have been shown in clinical studies to produce significant improvement in IBS symptoms through mind-body self-healing processes." The placebo worked better than no treatment. Is the placebo effect still in operation? What do you think?*

## 11.3 *Simple Thought Questions*

- A. "Placebo effects work only for psychological problems." Evaluate this claim.
- B. Explain Skinner's definition of superstition in terms of operant conditioning.

## 11.4 *Essay Questions*

- A. Is it ethical for a physician to give a patient a placebo? Some doctors knowingly prescribe a placebo without informing the patient, especially where a strong placebo effect is known to be a factor for that particular illness. Others believe such deception is wrong. Often practitioners of complementary and alternative medicine (CAM) have little interest in whether or not a treatment is a placebo, just as long as it works (skepdic.com/placebo). What do you think?
- B. Autogenic training (Smith, 2005) is a widely used therapy technique. In one simple beginning exercise patients think the words "hands are warm" over and over. They are instructed to do this passively, with utterly no expectation that anything will happen. Indeed, to emphasize this point, therapists often suggest patients repeat "warm and heavy" as if they were meaningless words from another language, or words of a pointless nursery rhyme. In fact, autogenic treatments have some effect. For example, the "hand warming" exercise indeed warms the hand, a useful tool for patients who suffer from Raynaud's syndrome, a painful condition in which blood vessels in the hands and feet narrow. Design an experiment that would

show that this complete autogenic training "hand warming exercise" is not a placebo. This is tricky because patients are instructed to practice "without expectation," seemingly ruling out a placebo effect.

- C. "Cupping" is an ancient Chinese treatment that involves placing two-inch circular cups over the skin and using a pump or heat to draw out air. The resulting suction pulls a small dome of skin and underlying muscle into the cup. Presumably, this draws blood into muscles, relieves pain, and enhances healing. The suction also ruptures small blood vessels leaving two-inch hickey-like circular purple dots. Cupping is popular among athletes and explains the purple dots that sometimes adorn their thighs, chests, and backs. This can be seen even for world-famous athletes such as Michael Phelps (google "Phelps cupping"). Is cupping a placebo? How would it score on the "Placebo Checklist"? If you were to run an experiment to compare actual cupping with a placebo, what kind of placebo would you deploy? (Why would it be unwise to compare cupping with a sugar pill?) You would have to create something that would fool patients and therapists into thinking actual cupping was involved, even though it was not. That is, you would compare "real cupping" with "fake cupping."

- D. How might memory errors described in Chapter 10 increase distorted recollections of the effectiveness of a placebo?

- E. Some positive thinking self-help books such as *The Secret* (Byrne, 2006) claim that positive thinking can create life-changing financial gain, cures, and happiness. All that is required is that you cultivate an intense expectation that the result will indeed occur. On the internet you will find stunning motivational videos showing large sums of money and beautiful love partners falling into the hands of those who simply believe. Is this a placebo? Why or why not? Are there any risks to such positive thinking?

- F. Explain the placebogenic features of PSI as described in the text. Apply the "Placebo Checklist" at the end of the chapter.

**11.5** *Internet Search*
- A. Most treatments have both active and placebo effects. Below is a list of some popular procedures often discussed in courses of critical thinking. We are not interested in whether or not they have any active treatment effects. Instead, what aspects of each treatment might contribute to a placebo effect? Find a complete description of the treatment on the internet. Select one treatment. Using your "Placebo Checklist," identify how each might "pump up" the placebo effect.

  - Acupuncture
  - Aromatherapy
  - Chiropractic
  - Crystal therapy
  - EMDR (eye movement desensitization and
  - reprocessing)
  - Healing touch
  - Homeopathy
  - Tai chi

- o Magnet therapy
- o Reflexology
- o Reiki
- o Thought field therapy

- B. What's the harm? Search the web to find an answer to "what's the harm" for any of the previously described treatments. Possible search phrases: "what's the harm" "21st Century Snake Oil."

**11.6** *Videos*

- A. Penn & Teller are two magicians who have done much to offer alternative explanations to extraordinary and paranormal claims. Their Showtime series *Bullshit!* offers some entertaining (and shocking) examples of placebos. Look for Season 1, Episode 2 (alternative medicine, reflexologists, magnet therapy, chiropractic, snail mucus facials) and Season 1, Episode 7 (feng shui, bottled water). Explain each example in terms of the "placebogenic" factors discussed in this chapter. How are the placebo treatments augmented?
- B. Magician Derren Brown has produced a short video that illustrates some basic concepts of suggestion and hypnosis. Search for "Derren Brown: How to get drunk without drinking." What placebo-augmenting factors can you detect?
- C. Episode 43 of the popular Discovery Channel science show *Mythbusters* focuses on placebos and seasickness. Search "Mythbusters Seasickness: Kill or Cure."

**11.7** *Conversation with a Classmate*

---

FROM: Lurinn Urni
SUBJECT: So what if it's a placebo!

---

Frankly, this chapter annoys me. My Klingon Natural Healer recommended I rub Klingon pebbles[2] on my foreheads to cure headaches. It works. She says the rocks contain a special Klingon quantum field energy that entangles with the dark energy pain of my brain's frontal lobes, reversing their photon spin, lightening the painful heavy dark matter of my brain, thus eliminating my headache, and any medical condition that can be associated with negative dark energy, ranging from cancer to heart disease. It works, so there must be something to what she says. Professor Smith may say it's a placebo. So, that just proves my point. A placebo is in the mind. Quantum field energy is also in the brain. So aren't we talking about the same thing? And another thing. Even if the rocks are completely placebos, there's nothing wrong in my Natural Healer prescribing pebbles to her patients. She's curing a lot more headaches than Professor Smith and his book!

---

TO: Lurinn
SUBJECT: So what if it's a placebo!

---

# 12

# Sensory Phenomena, Hallucinations, and Psychiatric Conditions

| OUTLINE |
|---|
| 1) Sensory Phenomena |
|     a) Autokinetic and Ideomotor Effects |
|     b) Pupil Response |
|     c) Entoptic Phenomena |
|     d) Synesthesia |
|     e) Migraines |
|     f) Tunnel Experiences |
| 2) Hallucinations |
|     a) Sleep and Rest-Related Hallucinations |
|     b) Out-of-Body Experiences |
|     c) Hallucinations in General |
|     d) Conditions Conducive to Hallucinations |
|         i) Food deprivation |
|         ii) Anoxia, hypercapnia, and hypocapnia |
|         iii) Sensory deprivation |
|     e) Are Hallucinations "Real"? |
|         i) Attentional searchlight |
|         ii) Reality checking |
|         iii) Emotions, motivations, expectations, and prior knowledge |
|     f) Hallucinations and the Critical Thinker's Toolkit |
| 3) Psychiatric Conditions and Disorders |
|     a) Seizures |
|     b) Tourette's Syndrome |
|     c) Schizophrenia |
|     d) Dissociative Disorders |
|         i) Dissociative amnesia |
|         ii) Depersonalization/derealization disorder |
|     e) Dissociation: Cognitive Failures and Reality Testing |
|     f) Dissociation and the Paranormal |

Most people realize that certain drugs can distort perception and trigger hallucinations. Schizophrenics sometimes hear voices. A patient suffering a severe fever can become delirious. A parched desert hiker may have visions of an oasis. Sometimes the brain and senses can go awry and lead us to experience things that are not there. Sensory phenomena, hallucinations, and various psychiatric conditions can be mistaken for the paranormal.

*Critical Thinking: Pseudoscience and the Paranormal*, Second Edition. Jonathan C. Smith.
© 2018 John Wiley & Sons, Inc. Published 2018 by John Wiley & Sons, Inc.

## Sensory Phenomena

One clear night go outside and look at a darkened area of the sky, one with only one or two stars. Now gaze at a star for five minutes. In time you will see it move. Of course, the star isn't actually moving. And it isn't a flying saucer or a winking ghost. Here is a famous literary example of this from H. G. Wells's *War of the Worlds* (1898):

> Looking through the telescope, one saw a circle of deep blue and the little round planet swimming in the field. It seemed such a little thing, so bright and small and still, faintly marked with transverse stripes, and slightly flattened from the perfect round. But so little it was, so silvery warm – a pin's-head of light! It was as if it quivered, but really this was the telescope vibrating with the activity of the clockwork that kept the planet in view.
>
> As I watched, the planet seemed to grow larger and smaller and to advance and recede, but that was simply that my eye was tired. Forty millions of miles it was from us – more than forty millions of miles of void. Few people realize the immensity of vacancy in which the dust of the material universe swims.
>
> *(p. 9)*

Perhaps you have figured out that H. G. Wells was not witnessing an incredible astronomical event. Something was happening to his eyes. Ordinary neurophysiological states can cause experiences easily misidentified as paranormal.

### Autokinetic and Ideomotor Effects

H. G. Wells actually described a sensory phenomenon called the **autokinetic effect**. Here a small point of light on a dark and featureless background appears to move because of minor involuntary eye movements, eye fatigue, and simple suggestion.

The autokinetic effect is a perfectly ordinary and minor aberration of physiological functioning. But it can easily trigger extraordinary paranormal experiences. Imagine that you are outside at night. You have read about UFO sightings. The sky is slightly overcast, and only one star appears. With great curiosity you stare at it for many long moments. Perhaps uncomfortable with your persistent observation, it moves. Others with you also see it move. Or imagine that you are in an old and dark abandoned house, again at night. A small light shines through a crack in the walls. You hold your breath, so as not to scare anyone away. The light moves. Or a friend claims that it is possible to move small distant objects by simply looking at them. She stares at a shiny penny on the sidewalk several yards away. You stare too. Both agree it moves. In none of these cases did anything move.

The autokinetic effect refers to a mistaken perception of movement outside of your body. When you erroneously think an outside force is causing you to move, we call it the **ideomotor effect**. Formally, the ideomotor effect refers to involuntary (or unconscious) movement caused by suggestion or expectation. You can demonstrate this any time in an elevator:

> The elevator doors have closed. You have three or four companions. The elevator has stopped between floors. Here's your cue to demonstrate the ideomotor effect. Slowly and subtly begin to sway back and forth. Continue this for about a minute.

(Don't be too obvious, or your companions might think you've been drinking!) Then quietly observe, "I think the elevator is beginning to move just a little." Continue swaying, just a little. "Yes, I think I can feel it swaying just a little." You've succeeded in your ideomotor demonstration if your companions begin to sway a little.

Many dramatic paranormal phenomena can be linked to such suggestion. Examples include the spontaneous movement of hands over ouija boards (presumably revealing the communications of individuals who have passed away), as well as various spontaneous twitches, body movements, or vocalizations caused by mysterious energies or spirits.

### Pupil Response

The autokinetic effect is one of many unusual sensory phenomena most of us experience. Another is the eye's **pupil response**. In darkness the pupils dilate to let in light and in bright conditions they constrict to keep light out. This is a simple reflex to protect the retina from overexposure. However, sounds, positive or negative emotion, relaxation, and focused attention are also factors that can cause dilation or constriction (Bradshaw, 1967; Partala & Surakka, 2003). An unexpected noise, someone whispering, fear, surprise, interest, a decision to focus one's attention, or simply uttering a sigh of relief after a few words of assurance can unexpectedly trigger a pupil response. When pupils constrict and less light enters the eyes, it might seem as if the lights were being turned down or the shades drawn. Shaded areas may suddenly emerge, and dark areas grow darker. Lacking an explanation, one might readily think of shadowy ghosts, spirits, or other paranormal goings-on. When pupils dilate and let in more light, shaded areas may disappear or shrink, as if they were moving. One might notice things previously obscured in darkness. I suspect this process is accentuated in conditions of poor illumination. Here the retina's black-and-white detectors, the rod cells, are dominant while color detectors, cone cells, are relatively inactive. As a result, in conditions of low illumination our eyes are much more sensitive to subtle changes in shading brought about by the pupil response. So, the next time you are in a haunted house and someone surprises you by whispering "look, a ghost!" you may well see a shadowy form emerge and move, all because of the pupil response. And if, when looking at the night sky, you suddenly think you see a flying saucer, bright shining objects may well appear from nowhere because an excitement-triggered pupil response has let in more light.

### Entoptic Phenomena

**Entoptic phenomena** are visual experiences caused by what happens in the eye itself rather than by external light. For example, **floaters** are slowly drifting translucent strings or dots that appear when one looks at the sky. They are caused by harmless debris in the eye's fluid. When looking at a blank blue screen you may notice the **blue field entoptic phenomenon**, points of light that dart about. Actually, the lights are white blood cells in retinal blood vessels. During an eye exam, an ophthalmologist may shine a light into your eye. Briefly you might actually see your own retinal blood vessels, the **vascular figure**. This image quickly disappears because of adaptation. By gently pressing against your closed eyes, you can evoke spots of light, **phosphenes**, simply caused by pressure-induced retinal activation. Serious paranormal investigators routinely attempt to rule out the possibility of entoptic phenomena when exploring various psychic visions.

### Synesthesia

Do you have an aura? Some psychics are convinced that people possess an energy glow or halo that may reflect important spiritual attributes. I hesitate to confess this fact, but in the 1970s my aura was detected by a teenage psychic and I will now reveal it for the first time.

*I was travelling the hills of Northern California, exploring various Zen monasteries and yoga retreats. One retreat caught my interest. High in a beautiful and isolated forest east of San Francisco, a successful American poet had changed careers and decided to devote his life to a spiritual path. He created an idyllic retreat with lovingly constructed wood cabins and meeting houses. Everything was ecologically friendly and open to all. A perfect place for self-discovery.*

*One evening about a dozen visitors sat around the beginning embers of a campfire for an introductory session. Our guide was an attractive woman in her early twenties. She wore a delicate white cotton dress, flowing and tastefully modest, adorned with a stunning star-like golden jewel of mysterious origin.*

*We began by introducing ourselves and describing our backgrounds. I shared that I was a student of psychology interested in using science to uncover the mysteries of the world. After about an hour our guide's voice changed. She began to speak slowly and knowingly, an octave lower than one might expect from a woman so young. The aura-readings were about to begin.*

*First was the thin young computer student wearing thick glasses and a backpack carefully filled with new camping supplies and more than a few books. Our guide revealed, "I detect you have a green aura ... meaning that you are careful and intelligent." Next was a woman, in her thirties, very attractively dressed, and wearing a bit more jewelry than might be needed for a simple hike in the woods. "I can see that your aura is a bright pink ... single and ready for love." The gentlemen to her right was in his late twenties and very muscular. He wore sweat pants and a tank-top. "Your aura is red. Your aura reveals you are athletic and are active on the dating scene." Then she turned to me, paused for a long, uncomfortable minute, and announced, "You have a gray aura." Quickly she moved to the next person.*

*I was a bit stunned. Gray? Why not silver, or titanium? At least a trendy off-white or eggshell. Perhaps she was distracted by the campfire smoke floating behind my head. Alas, I still remember this reading. Today, I suspect it reflected something going on in my guide's brain. Of course, I might be completely mistaken, an interpretation less critical readers of this text might readily accept.*

**Synesthesia** is an unusual neurological condition in which stimulation of one sense can evoke a response in another sense. In letter–color ("grapheme → color") synesthesia one actually sees different black-and-white letters tinged in color, each letter colored differently. In music–color synesthesia different tones (or even timbres or keys) trigger the perception of color. In emotion–color synesthesia, emotional states (often brought about by other people) trigger colorful auras. A synesthetic might see an irritating person as surrounded by an aura of red light, a friendly person by blue light, and so on. Day–color synesthesia (seeing days as colors) is most common (Ward, Huckstep, & Tsakanikos, 2006).

Synesthesia is caused by "cross-talk" between brain centers responsible for sensation and emotion. In other words, for an emotion–color synesthetic, brain centers responsible for the experience of emotion and color might be somewhat cross-wired. Although occasionally associated with drugs and strokes, synesthesia is harmless, and is sometimes a useful tool in creativity. Of course, to the uninformed, having a synesthetic experience might seem like evidence that one can see paranormal "auras," or has "X-ray vision" (Ward, 2004). Synesthesia is relatively common, perhaps occurring in 1 out of 23 (Simner et al., 2006). It is inherited and is more common among women.

### Migraines

Just in case you question the psychic credentials of your silver-aura author, let me indulge in another revelation. First, let me assure you that my brain and eyes work fine. I don't get headaches. Yet five years ago I was struck with an incredible vision.

> *It was an ordinary summer day in Chicago. The sky was clear and skyscrapers could be seen for miles. Suddenly the sky cracked. An enormous jagged crystal line spread the distance of four moons. It was brilliant, as bright as a shimmering string of carnival LED lights. This vision hovered for about five minutes and then disappeared. Every day that week the same shining crack appeared, sometimes taking mysterious geometric shapes, always precisely formed with crisp edges.*
>
> *Concerned, I visited my eye doctor. A number of hypotheses floated through my mind. Was I having a stroke? Some strange brain infection? Was this a religious experience? Maybe a flying saucer or a rift in the space-time continuum? The doctor immediately asked about my diet. No change. Nothing unusual. Then I remembered, a friend had given me a bottle of red wine, and I had a glass every night before retiring. Wine is not my preferred beverage. My eye doctor smiled and said, "you were having a scintillating scotoma, a visual phenomenon that can come before migraine headaches." I noted that I don't get headaches. No matter. These scintillating visions can occur on their own. No stroke. No brain disease. And they can be triggered by red wine. Alas, no UFO or rift in the space-time continuum.*

A migraine headache is characterized by intense pulsing or throbbing pain, usually with extreme sensitivity to light and sound, nausea, and vomiting (NINDS, 2007). Students of the paranormal are interested not so much in the migraine, but in the preceding aura, reported by 20–30% of patients (Evans & Matthew, 2005; Young & Silberstein, 2004). The aura lasts 5–20 minutes and typically includes changes in visual and sensory experience, and on occasion minor involuntary movements. Visual experiences can include **photopsia**, or flashes (usually white or black), **scintillating scotoma**, or brilliant neon-like zigzag lines, or **fortification illusion**, or brilliant abstract shapes of lights shaped like the battlements of a castle or fort. All of these dramatic visual aura experiences can occur on their own, without a subsequent headache. All can readily be misinterpreted as psychic energies, UFOs, ghosts, and the like. Religious visions at times look very much like fortification illusions (Sacks, 1999, 2008).

**Figure 12.1** Tunnel experience.

**Tunnel Experiences**

> You are resting in bed sinking into a state of deep relaxation. Your eyes are closed. Suddenly you have the sensation of sinking. Your attention turns to your eyes. Even though they are closed, faint lights appear. They seem to move. As you sink deeper, the lights move away as if you were floating deep into space, down a deep tunnel.

Such an eyes-closed visual light show is known as a tunnel experience. The precise form of this experience can vary and includes soaring through space, sinking, or moving through a hallway. The whole world may be seen as rushing past as one races toward a bright light. One might even have the sensation of leaving one's body. You may clearly recognize it as something happening "in your head," although, given the right context and suggestion, you might be convinced of a more paranormal interpretation (moving to a different dimension, moving into someone else's mind, etc.). Tunnel experiences can emerge while relaxing, falling asleep, or simply applying pressure to the eyeballs. They can be associated with fainting, migraines, epileptic seizures, and ingestion of drugs such as LSD, psilocybin, mescaline, or ketamine.

Although there are several theories of tunnel experiences, Blackmore and Troscianko's (1989) explanation has received considerable attention. Central to their idea is the basic visual illusion that lights flickering in sequence can be seen as apparently moving, even though they are not. You can see this illusion in banner advertising in which arrows, images, and words seem to move across a sign, even though the light bulbs are completely stationary.

Nerve signals from the retina are transmitted to and processed by the brain's visual cortex. What we see is actually not in the eye, but caused by nerves firing in the brain (like flashbulbs). Fortunately, these nerve cells do not fire all at once, but are kept in order by nerve cells that inhibit unnecessary activity. Trauma, oxygen deprivation, too much $CO_2$, drugs, sleep, meditation, and even relaxation can prevent inhibiting nerve cells from functioning. As a result, more visual neurons are *disinhibited* and start firing. With all these neural light bulbs going off, you might expect your visual world would turn into a blinding bright light (as if thousands of camera flashes went off at once). This isn't quite what happens. Gradually, more and more neurons fire in a cascade (imagine a "wave" of flashbulbs going off, moving down the bleachers in a football stadium as the home team enters the field). As more and more neurons fire, you experience concentric rings or spirals of light. This will look like a tunnel and you may experience movement.

## Hallucinations

I find that people often resist the notion that a treasured and vivid paranormal experience may actually be a hallucination.

> *I actually saw a flying saucer ... the holy statue really did bleed ... my astrologer correctly predicted I would fail this class ... my rash disappeared after I rubbed it with a rabbit's foot." How do you know it's real? "It was as vivid as real life ... I could see, hear, and taste it ... I do not hallucinate ... One hallucinates weird things, like in dreams; this was very realistic ... I was not drunk or on drugs ... I am not crazy ... I am actually very skeptical ... I know what it's like to hallucinate. Other people might hallucinate. But I'm not prone to such mistakes.*

Most people have an incorrect view of what hallucinations are, and how common they are.

The word *hallucination* (from the Latin *hallucinari* for "to wander in mind" or "to talk idly") was first used in English to refer to "ghostes and spirites walking by nyght" (Sarbin & Juhasz, 1975). Today, hallucinations are generally defined as false perceptions that occur while awake. David (2004) offers a formal popular contemporary definition:

> A sensory experience which occurs in the absence of corresponding external stimulation of the relevant sensory organ, has a sufficient sense of reality to resemble a veridical [accurate perception of what is real] perception, over which the subject does not feel s/he has direct and voluntary control, and which occurs in the awake state.

> *(p. 108)*

Hallucinations can occur in any modality, including auditory (hearing nonverbal sounds), verbal (hearing voices), visual (seeing visions), olfactory (smelling things), kinesthetic (sensed body position, movement, weight), gustatory (taste), tactile (touch and temperature), or multimodal (involving multiple senses).

Hallucinations appear in various clinical groups and are not restricted to one diagnostic category. Generally these include (a) psychotic disorders such as schizophrenia, severe forms of depression, and posttraumatic stress disorder; (b) neurological conditions such as brain tumors and injury, epilepsy, migraines; (c) degenerative (and ageing-related) disorders such as Parkinson's and Alzheimer's disease; (d) deficits in or injury and deterioration of sense organs such as blindness; and (e) substance abuse (Aleman & Larøi, 2008).

It is beyond the scope of this book to discuss the role of hallucinations in various clinical conditions. However, two very important points must be made. A significant minority of the nonclinical (normal) population has had hallucinations, with estimates generally ranging from 10 to 15% (Tien, 1991). Second, hallucinations in normal and disturbed individuals are *qualitatively the same* (Aleman & Larøi, 2008). There is essentially no difference between the hallucination of a schizophrenic patient and that of a normal college student who falsely hears his lover calling at night. Both involve the same processes and mechanisms. When differences appear they are *quantitative* and reflect how various groups react to their hallucinations. In other words, hallucinations exist along a continuum, perhaps defined in terms of how strongly one believes one's false perceptions are real, one's degree of preoccupation with the hallucination, the degree of distress associated with a hallucination, and how well one functions and copes (Aleman & Larøi, 2008).

## Sleep and Rest-Related Hallucinations

Among the most common and dramatic hallucinations are those that occur just before or after sleep, or while one is simply resting in a reclining position. Of course, dreams are false perceptions that occur during sleep; however, because we are not awake, they are generally not categorized as hallucinations. Similarly, we might engage in vivid fantasy while resting. Such imagery is voluntary and therefore not considered hallucination.

Sleep-related hallucinations occur in wakeful moments just before or after sleep. Consider this experience of a young anthropology student (who later became a noted scholar and scientist):

> As a college student in 1964, David J. Hufford met the dreaded Night Crusher. Exhausted from a bout of mononucleosis and studying for finals, Hufford retreated one December day to his rented, off-campus room and fell into a deep sleep. An hour later, he awoke with a start to the sound of the bedroom door creaking open – the same door he had locked and bolted before going to bed. Hufford then heard footsteps moving toward his bed and felt an evil presence. Terror gripped the young man, who couldn't move a muscle, his eyes plastered open in fright.
>
> Without warning, the malevolent entity, whatever it was, jumped onto Hufford's chest. An oppressive weight compressed his rib cage. Breathing became difficult, and Hufford felt a pair of hands encircle his neck and start to squeeze. "I thought I was going to die," he says.
>
> At that point, the lock on Hufford's muscles gave way. He bolted up and sprinted several blocks to take shelter in the student union. "It was very puzzling," he recalls with a strained chuckle, "but I told nobody about what happened."
>
> *(Bower, 2005, p. 27)*

Professor Hufford's experiences as a student illustrate several common sleep-related phenomena, including hallucinations and sleep paralysis. Just before falling asleep, some people experience auditory or visual **hypnogogic hallucinations**. These typically include faces, landscapes, and natural or social scenes and may be

**pseudohallucinations** (although they appear real, one senses they are not real) or actual hallucinations (falsely experienced as real). Hypnogogic hallucinations are typically static images. They can appear in daytime periods of drowsiness and fatigue, or in situations of reduced stimulation, and can be superimposed over what one really sees. They are relatively common, experienced frequently by 37% of the population. Similar **hypnopompic hallucinations** can emerge in the twilight state just before waking up. Typically such hallucinations are more often fragments of recent dreams.

    **Sleep paralysis** is a related and more dramatic condition in which one is unable to speak or move just before or after sleep. One might sense someone or something is "out there" and be unable to speak or scream. Visual, auditory, or tactile hallucinations are common. Physiologically, when we dream, our bodies become temporarily immobilized, our skeletal muscles (used for moving, gesturing, and speaking) are paralyzed. This is so that we don't actually act out our dreams. In sleep paralysis the brain awakens from a neurophysiological sleep state, but the body remains very briefly paralyzed. The person is fully aware, but can't move or talk. In addition, one might experience dream-like hallucinations. To the uninformed, sleep paralysis, as well as hypnagogic and hypnopompic hallucinations, can be quite terrifying. Many people experience sleep paralysis only a few times in a lifetime, although those suffering from the sleep disorder narcolepsy experience it more often. It is quite possible that many experiences of ghosts, alien abductions, and angels reported throughout history and around the world are actually examples of sleep paralysis and the terror sometimes associated with it.

**Figure 12.2** Out-of-body experiences. Reproduced with kind permission of Science Source.

**Out-of-Body Experiences**

An **out-of-body experience** (OBE) is the sensation of leaving and floating outside one's body, often while seeing one's body. Sometimes this experience is presented as evidence for a nonmaterial and disembodied "astral body," "spirit," or "soul," capable of paranormal journeying through "astral projection" or "spiritual travel."

OBEs are quite common. OBEs are common in dreams. Between 8 and 50% (for marijuana users) of the population have had waking OBEs (Blackmore, 1991, 2004; Schroeter-Kunhardt, 1993). Typically, one has the sensation of floating overhead, perhaps looking down on oneself.

Although an OBE can be spontaneous, it is more often associated with near-death experience, stroke, epilepsy, the ingestion of psychedelic drugs, or the emergence of hypnagogic states. Direct brain stimulation can evoke an OBE in waking subjects, and some can elicit OBEs through relaxed visualization and meditation. Researchers Ehrsson (2007), Lenggenhager (Lenggenhager et al., 2007), and their colleagues have achieved OBEs using little more than a set of virtual-reality goggles.

An OBE can seem more real than a fantasy or dream and many people actually believe that their "minds" or "souls" are leaving their body, perhaps to travel great distances. However, such ideas lack research support (Morris et al., 1978). Perhaps floating above the body one can see objects deliberately hidden in the ceiling. There is no evidence for this. A century ago, researchers attempted to measure the weight of the soul as it left a dying body. At first it appeared that the soul weighed about 21 ounces, although later research could detect no change in body weight at the moment of death. Recently, researchers have measured changes in ultraviolet and infrared light, magnet fields, temperature, and weight of living individuals having OBEs. Again, research has shown nothing.

**Hallucinations in General**

The range of hallucinations extends far beyond hypnagogic, hypnopompic, and out-of-body experiences. Most common are visions and voices. History provides us with many dramatic paranormal claims that some hypothesize can be interpreted as hallucinations, including the secular visions and voices of Galileo, Freud, Jung, Pascal, Pythagoras, and Mozart, as well as the spiritual visions of Joan of Arc, Martin Luther, St Paul, and Mohammed. Of course, one might claim that a hallucination, whatever its source, is an alternative window to truth. But then there are the guiding visions and voices of Attila the Hun, Idi Amin, and Charles Manson (Aleman & Larøi, 2008; Ritsher et al., 2004).

Hallucinations can occur in any sense modality and just about any hallucination can be mislabeled a paranormal experience. While exploring a haunted house you may hallucinate the sound of a breathing ghost (auditory hallucination). While you are deep in prayer, the divine may utter a loud command (complex auditory hallucination). When in the presence of someone you believe to be possessed by the devil, you may smell fire and brimstone (olfactory hallucination). While meditating in a cross-legged position, you may feel like you are becoming lighter and levitating in air (kinesthetic hallucination). You may relish the savory sweet flavor of tap water mislabeled as special exotic spring water (gustatory hallucination). While visiting a shrine, you may feel the touch of a departed holy person (tactile hallucination). You and your fellow believers may actually see and hear a flying saucer crash, feel the vibration of an explosion, and smell the smoke of burning metal (multimodal hallucination). While grieving a loved one, you may encounter your departed in a forest, engage in conversation, and even feel his touch and breath (multimodal hallucination).

Perhaps not quite a hallucination is the *sensed-presence effect* (Shermer, 2010). Here you experience a vague feeling that someone, an angel, alien, ghost, mystical force, or deity, is close by, an entity you cannot see, hear, smell, or feel. Even though there is no sensory confirmation, the experience can be quite real. Luhrmann (2012) has described how religious people often experience a sensed presence of God or Jesus, accompanied by hearing voices, and actually have what appears to be a working relationship and ongoing spiritual communication.

**Conditions Conducive to Hallucinations**

Some people are more likely to experience hallucinations than others. However, it is a mistake to think of some sort of hallucination trait, some type of latent attribute (like a defective heart valve) that, once manifest, can affect one for the rest of one's life. Instead, Aleman and Larøi (2008) prefer to use the term "hallucination proneness," a capacity one may have expressed from childhood, is generally controllable, and emerges only when triggered.

A substantial body of research has identified five types of hallucination triggers:

*Deprivation*
- Food deprivation and fasting
- Oxygen deprivation (and too much or too little carbon dioxide)
- Sleep deprivation and fatigue

*Reduced sensory input*
- Sensory loss (blindness, loss of hearing)
- Social isolation
- Sensory deprivation or isolation

*Stimulus overload*
- Increased external stimulation
- Prolonged and repetitive religious ritual
- Repetitive background noise

*Stressful and strenuous situations*
- Trauma
- Bereavement and grief

*Consumption of certain substances*
- Alcohol
- LSD, cannabis, mescaline
- Opiates
- Amphetamine, and cocaine

Hallucinations can occur while the substance is in one's bloodstream, or as a flashback memory of a previous "trip."
Of these, we focus on deprivation and reduced sensory input.

### Food Deprivation

A religious group requires a highly restricted fast for several weeks. Members report seeing visions. Campers searching for flying saucers track a mysterious sighting for two days. Involved in their quest, they eat little. They discover their elusive UFO, actually a vivid hallucination. A prisoner in solitary confinement hasn't eaten for days. He hears voices from ghosts of departed inmates.

When considering a paranormal report, sometimes one must rule out the psychological effects of starvation and extreme diet. Severe reductions in food intake can be accompanied by a number of physiological alterations in brain functioning and lead to hallucinations (Maddox & Long, 1999; Peterson & Mitchell, 1999).

### Anoxia, Hypercapnia, and Hypocapnia

The brain needs oxygen to survive and function. Deprivation of oxygen, **cerebral anoxia**, can lead to impaired functioning and hallucination. This can occur in many traumatic situations, including having a stroke, anesthesia, and drowning. And on the internet one can readily find NASA videos of astronauts training in whirling centrifuge merry-go-round devices in which rapid acceleration forces blood out of the brain, and triggers dramatic hallucinatory near-death experiences, including OBEs, tunnel experiences, sensations of seeing a brilliant light, and strong mystical feelings (Birbaumer et al., 2005; Lutz & Nilsson, 1997).

When we inhale, the body absorbs oxygen, and when we exhale, carbon dioxide ($CO_2$) is expelled. Oxygen is required for metabolism, and $CO_2$ is a waste product which in large quantities can be toxic. The brain detects how much $CO_2$ is in the blood. Excessive $CO_2$ is a condition called **hypercapnia**, whereas too little $CO_2$ (sometimes triggered by rapid deep breathing or hyperventilation) is called **hypocapnia**. $CO_2$ disruption can be triggered by anxiety and panic (where one "freezes," holds one's breath, or conversely breathes deeply and rapidly); deep breathing relaxation, yoga, and meditation exercises; and ritualistic dances. The effects vary and include dizziness, simple visual and auditory hallucination experiences (seeing lights, hearing roars and screams), impaired awareness, disorientation, weightlessness, detachment, and loss of control over one's muscles (Birbaumer et al., 2005). These can be aggravated by feelings of anxiety, including chest pain, numbness or tingling, fear of losing control, or loss of sense of self (depersonalization).

### Sensory Deprivation

In everyday life we are bombarded with stimulation. It is rare to encounter a situation in which sound, light, smell, and touch have been turned down. Even during sleep there is the pressure of the sheets, the weight of our bodies against a mattress, and if lucky, a partner. **Sensory deprivation** is an extreme condition in which sensory input is reduced to a minimum. In a similar condition, **sensory homogenization**, sensory input has been rendered bland, featureless, and unchanging. Instead of specific sounds, we hear the constant "woosh" of white noise. We see nothing but a blank, colorless screen. If in outer space, or in a special tank of water, we might feel weightless.

Something interesting happens in situations of reduced sensory input. The brain attempts to compensate for low levels of sensory stimulation by creating more. We think and fantasize more. Things seem more vivid. Hypnagogic imagery is more likely to appear. When reality testing is compromised, these experiences may become full-blown hallucinations (Grassian, 1993).

When an individual claims a paranormal experience, especially one that is described as vividly experienced and resembles hypnagogic hallucinations, look for signs of reduced sensory input. Consider these examples:

- Channelers sit silently in a darkened quiet room waiting for communications with the dead.
- UFO watchers sit in a quiet field at night silently awaiting the arrival of spacecraft.
- Haunted house investigators sit in the basement, at night, with all the lights turned off so as not to scare off expected ghosts.
- A psychic healer sits silently with a patient engaged in healing meditation.

**Are Hallucinations "Real"?**

Perhaps the biggest misunderstanding students have about hallucinations is that they somehow seem "less than real," somewhat "dreamlike," or are easily distinguished from "reality." Not true. What is the difference between a false and a real perception, an accurate percept vs. something you incorrectly experience and believe to be "really out there"? One obvious place to look is in the brain. Perhaps a hallucinated voice involves a different part of the brain than a voice you actually hear. Remarkably, advanced brain imaging studies have shown that hallucinations of one modality involve the same sensory cortical areas (that is, brain areas) as those linked to processing actual sensations of that modality (Aleman & Larøi, 2008). Indeed, *regardless of whether you are having a deliberate fantasy, spontaneously hallucinating, or actually seeing something that really exists, the same sensory cortical areas are active.* Auditory parts of the brain are linked to auditory hallucinations as well as to the perception of actual sounds. Vision areas are linked with both visual hallucinations and sensations.

This was demonstrated more than half a century ago in a dramatic and classic experiment. While performing surgery on an epileptic patient, Penfield (1955) inserted a small electrode in the brain's temporal lobe and stimulated it with a faint and harmless electric current. Immediately the patient vividly heard orchestral music. When another area was stimulated, the patient saw a man and a dog walking along a road, as clear as if it were actually happening. The point again is that a percept, whether a deliberate image, hallucination, or reality-based perception, is the same in the cortex. Instead of saying "I saw it with my very own eyes," one might more accurately say "I saw it with my very own brain" (Beyerstein, 1996). So what causes a hallucination? The same thing that triggers any percept, a "Penfield patch" or specific cortical area responsible for a sense experience.

However, most hallucinations, as well as deliberate fantasy images, are primarily the result of *top-down* perceptual processes or conceptual processes in the brain. Real percepts are externally (or *bottom-up*) driven. Disruption of the balance of bottom-up and top-down processes can set the stage for, or lead to, false percepts, hallucinations. Note that the processes involved are also associated with errors of perception and memory: (a) the *attentional searchlight* (what we focus on) (b) *reality checking*, and (c) *emotions, motivations, expectations*, and *prior knowledge*. These processes can actually lead us to see things that are not there.

**Attentional Searchlight**

Our brain's attentional searchlight focuses on and highlights specific external stimuli, and ignores others. Ordinarily this process is driven by our sense organs (and parts of the brain directly linked to the sense organs), modified by beliefs, expectations, and past experiences. However, there are times when the searchlight can be directed away from the external world to internal sensory experiences such as memories and fantasized images. For example, under conditions of sensory deprivation, our sense organs simply present insufficient data to process. Our searchlight must point inward in a search for cues as to what is real. Blindness, loss of hearing, or degradation of any sense organ can have a similar effect. Strong emotion, motivation, stress arousal, extreme external stimulation, or the ingestion of psychoactive substances can disrupt how the searchlight operates. Overcharged, like a blinding headlight, it may target stimuli and leave us unaware of informative contextual cues that may be useful in revealing if a percept is imagined. For any of these reasons, the attentional searchlight may target and stir a memory or image, making it as vivid as real.

### Reality Checking

In Chapter 10 we saw that through source monitoring we identify whether a memory is internally or externally based. Hallucination-prone individuals display an external source-monitoring bias. That is, they tend to misattribute experiences they have conjured up as having an external source. I propose that such a person does not or cannot deploy the reality checking outlined in our text. For example, a shaman priest may come from a spiritual tradition that teaches that a healer's soul can temporarily leave their body and accompany the soul of a newly deceased individual to the afterlife. Firmly accepting this traditional source, the priest may uncritically hallucinate, leaving his body during a spiritual ritual. A college student may visit a haunted house and hallucinate what appears to be a ghost walking through a wall, not realizing the logical error in believing that two objects can be at the same place at the same time. A grieving widower may have a hypnagogic hallucination of his spouse standing next to him. He may not think of performing a simple experiment to see if the image is real (like tossing a book at the figure).

### Emotions, Motivations, Expectations, and Prior Knowledge

In previous chapters we have considered how our emotions and motivations as well as our expectations and prior experiences (or knowledge) can lead to perceptual and memory errors. These very same processes can contribute to hallucinations. One may experience emotions of strong love toward the Virgin Mary, joy over the prospects of living in heaven, fear toward the Devil, and excitement toward the prospect of visitations of alien spaceships. Such strong emotions might prime one to experience hallucinations of the Virgin, voices from the afterlife, attacks from the Devil, and alien abductions. These hallucinations may be intensified by strong motivations to serve the Virgin Mary, do what is necessary to go to heaven, fight the Devil, and discover aliens. One may be in the presence of like-believers or belong to a group or culture that assumes the reality of the Virgin, afterlife, Devil, and aliens, all contributing to expectations and prior knowledge that further enhance one's hallucinations. Finally, strong emotion or motivation (positive and negative) can distract and disrupt strategies that one might ordinarily deploy to discern whether a hallucination is internal or external. Under conditions of high stress arousal, attention narrows to information that is simple and concrete, and complex verbal processing is reduced. The hallucinator under stress may be struck by the vividness of the hallucination and be less likely to engage in reality checking.

Cross-cultural research provides interesting support for the role of emotions, motivations, expectations, and prior knowledge. Some non-Western cultures prize hallucinations and do not make a rigid distinction between reality and fantasy (Aleman & Larøi, 2008). Bourguignon (1970) studied anthropological data from 488 societies and found that hallucinations play an important part in 62% of religious and healing rituals. Here hallucinations were best understood in terms of local beliefs and expectations rather than the ingestion of psychoactive substances. Other studies have found auditory hallucinations to be more common in the West and visual hallucinations in Africa and Asia. Auditory hallucinations in Saudi Arabia have religious and superstitious content, whereas hallucinations by those in the United Kingdom involve instruction and running commentary. Perhaps the most vivid illustration of the role of emotional and cognitive factors in hallucination is the frequent finding that hallucinations involving the loss of loved ones typically involve the deceased individual.

### Hallucinations and the Critical Thinker's Toolkit

Research on hallucinations shows dramatically that we see with our brains, not our eyes. A paranormal claim may be vivid and convincing, based on something genuinely experienced as "really real." A pseudoscientific misuse of sources, logic, and scientific observation may well provide spurious support for such claims. However, common sense suggests that we carefully consider alternative explanations. To what extent can our convincing visions be explained as misperception and misunderstanding of oddities of nature and numbers, errors of perception and memory, the placebo effect, and workings of the brain and body? Before betting the farm on some gambling superstition, making dating decisions on the basis of psychic forecasts, forgoing medical treatment for an ancient herbal nostrum, enlisting the assistance of a priest to exorcise evil spirits, voting to restrict the rights of a currently unfavored minority group, or engaging in yet another holy war, let us at least take pause and question with an open mind. There may be more to the world than what we see.

## Psychiatric Conditions and Disorders

A number of recognized psychiatric conditions have been mislabeled as paranormal phenomena, particularly as demon or spirit possession. I will not go into these in detail because today the risk of such mislabeling is less than in the past. For example, although the Catholic and some Protestant churches accept that individuals can be possessed by the Devil, they routinely require that the possibility of a psychiatric disorder first be explored professionally and ruled out. Also, I am not sure it is helpful for readers of this book to run around labeling UFO and ESP believers as schizophrenics.

### Seizures

An epileptic seizure is a neurological event involving rapid and extensive neuroelectrical activity in the brain. Seizures may have a variety of causes, including injury or stroke. Most often the cause is unknown. Many seizure patients experience a pre-seizure aura. Auras can include unusual body sensations, feelings of derealization, déjà vu, depression, irritability, nausea, and headache. Mild seizures are described as partial, whereas more severe seizures are generalized. Partial seizures can cause sense distortions, repetition of certain actions or utterances, or staring blankly without awareness. One might report an experience of "tunnel vision" or reduced awareness.

Partial seizures in different parts of the brain can evoke different experiences. For example, if you have a seizure in the part of the brain linked with sense experience, you might experience smells, hear music, or see flashes of light. If part of the motor cortex is involved, you may experience involuntary movement or spasms in various muscle groups. Temporal lobe seizures can evoke extremely pleasant mystical and ecstatic peak experiences. Indeed, individuals who report religious and mystical experiences are more likely to have a history of seizures. Such seizure patients are more likely to report numerous religious conversions (Geschwind, 1983).

Generalized seizures are more severe and often involve an interruption of consciousness. One might appear to be vacant or unresponsive, and display twitching for half a minute. In more severe forms, muscles may contract involuntarily and rhythmically ("epileptic fit" or "convulsions"). In primitive times, those suffering generalized seizures might have been tagged with a diagnosis of demon possession. Because such seizures are time-limited, they would invariably cease after a ritual incantation or exorcism, perhaps contributing to a superstitious placebo-like belief in the efficacy of such rituals.

### Tourette's Syndrome

Tourette's syndrome is a neurological disorder characterized by various types of involuntary tics, vocalizations, coughing, throat clearing, sniffing, and movement. On rare occasions it is associated with the uncontrollable and inappropriate exclamation of obscenities and insults. Many examples of demon possession may well involve Tourette's syndrome. During the Inquisition, the defining characteristics of witches resemble the diagnostic criteria for Tourette's syndrome (Goodman & Murphy, 1998). Even today, many Tourette's syndrome patients have been subjected to exorcisms (Shapiro et al., 1988).

### Schizophrenia

The official manual of mental illnesses used by most psychologists and psychologists is the *Diagnostic and Statistical Manual of Mental Disorder* (Beidel, Frueh, & Hersen, 2014; *DSM-5*, APA, 2013). Schizophrenia is the most debilitating of psychiatric disorders. *DSM-5* defines it in terms of severe problems in daily living, including work, social relations, and self-care. The most common additional symptoms include "positive symptoms" such as hallucinations, delusions, and disorganization; "negative symptoms" such as social withdrawal, apathy, and a profound dulling of emotion; cognitive impairments such as memory problems, planning problems, difficulty thinking; and problems with depression, anxiety, and anger.

Schizophrenics are seriously impaired and often withdraw or do not function or communicate well in social settings. For this reason I suspect it is rare that public advocates of paranormal phenomena are schizophrenic. It should be noted that schizophrenics may experience frightening and mysterious alterations in perception and mood. In a desperate attempt to make sense out of such unexplained events, they may resort to paranormal explanations ("I hear voices because … aliens are communicating with me," "Things seem strangely vivid because … I am possessed by ghosts."). However, given the complexity and severity of the disorder, it is perhaps wise for students of critical thinking to be careful when applying the label "schizophrenic" to questionable reality testing.

## Dissociative Disorders

*DSM-5* defines **dissociative disorders** as psychiatric conditions "marked by a disruption of and/or discontinuity in the normal integration of consciousness, memory, identity, emotion, perception, body representation, motor control, and behavior" (APA, 2013, p. 291). Although there are several forms of this disorder, all happen in the wake of trauma. *DSM-5* identifies three categories of dissociative disorder: *dissociative amnesia*, *depersonalization/derealization*, and *dissociative identity disorder*. Our discussion relies heavily on the excellent presentation of Lynn et al. (2014).

*Dissociative amnesia* is characterized by an inability to recall important information about oneself and one's life history (autobiographical information).

*Depersonalization/derealization disorder* is defined by a curious set of symptoms that might easily draw paranormal interpretation. Symptoms of depersonalization include feelings of "unreality," detachment or being an "outside observer" of one's thoughts, feelings, sensations, or actions, and out-of-body experiences. Additional depersonalization experiences might include an unreal or absent sense of self, physical or emotional numbing, or time distortion.

Consider the following accounts from a website of a community of individuals dedicated to those seeking to understand depersonalization in themselves and others (www.dpselfhelp.com):

> *In a split second, the world seems to tilt. I am suddenly a stranger in my own neighborhood.*
>
> *Reality seems to vanish, or is closing in, as if the literally the edge of the world is right beyond the horizon.*
>
> *Everything looks "off," like it turned into a stage set or fake replica of how it should really look ...*
>
> *The world looks like I'm dreaming, or like I have unwittingly taken LSD ...*

Derealization is somewhat different and can be hard to understand. Technically, it involves feelings of "unreality or detachment with respect to one's surroundings and includes the experience of individuals or objects as unreal, dreamlike, foggy, visually distorted, or lifeless" (Lynn et al., 2014).

Many experience mild episodes of derealization. Have you ever seen a long, engaging, and strange movie, walked into the daylight sun, and found that things and people seemed different – perhaps more vivid, perhaps unfamiliar, strange, unreal, dreamlike, or mechanical? Your perception of what's real has been slightly altered, and you experience derealization. Maybe you overslept, and when waking up felt a little confused. You may have wondered, "What day is this? What time is it?" Again, you have tasted a bit of derealization, in that parts of the normal ordinary world seem different. And perhaps you have witnessed a friend having a mildly distressing reaction to marijuana or some other drug. They may say they feel detached from their familiar world. Things might seem like they are not real, or not really happening. They may feel like they are a stranger or an outsider, even in familiar places. Maybe events seem speeded up or slowed down. Again, one's reality has been altered, and one is experiencing a type of derealization.

Symptoms of depersonalization and derealization are often associated with severe stress, sometimes (but not always) as a psychological way of distancing oneself from or becoming less aware of a trauma. Milder manifestations are relatively common, and not considered defining of pathology (although they may invite paranormal interpretations).

*Dissociative identity disorder (the "multiple personality")* exists when one experiences distinct personalities, or "personality states," and gaps in memory beyond the ordinary. In the "possession form" one may have the experience of being possessed or taken over by a spirit, supernatural being, or outside person. Such manifestations are not uncommon in other cultures and can be associated with accepted cultural/religious practices, and are not considered by *DSM-5* to be pathological.

### Dissociation: Cognitive Failures and Reality Testing

Giesbrecht and others (Giesbrecht et al., 2008, 2010) have proposed that **dissociation** is associated with a propensity to experience pseudomemories (especially false memories of early trauma), possibly mediated by suggestibility, fantasy, and various cognitive failures (Lynn et al., 2014). To elaborate, dissociatives tend to misremember, and even unconsciously invent memories for nonexistent events. This is aggravated by difficulties discriminating accurate perception from vivid imagery, and a tendency to unwittingly fabricate answers to leading or suggestive questions. To add to the mix, those prone to dissociation are also prone to hypnagogic and hypnopompic imagery, which could in turn feed the generation of pseudomemories, and augmentation of depersonalization and derealization. In sum, this paints a portrait of dissociation-related difficulties in reality testing.

### Dissociation and the Paranormal

As we can see in our examples, dissociation, especially derealization or depersonalization, can readily be misconstrued as paranormal. For example, we might consider dissociation as an alternative hypothesis for the following:

> After intense chanting, a medium enters a "trance" and is no longer aware of his surroundings (dissociation). He then communicates with a dead relative.
>
> A gifted psychic holds a pointer over the alphabet printed on the surface of a ouija board. Automatically her hand is guided over the board (dissociation; loss of awareness of deliberately moving hand) and the touched letters spell a message.
>
> A psychic is taken over by a spirit from her past life as an Egyptian queen (dissociation; ordinary experiences are outside of awareness). She puts on a convincing show and is herself quite convinced of the validity of her experience.
>
> A victim of an alien abduction vaguely remembers fragments of this weird, otherworldly encounter (dissociation; one is cut off from familiar everyday experiences and is immersed in memories that feel strange).
>
> After repeating a special magical chant, you feel like you have been transported into a strange and unknown world. Nothing seems familiar.

## Study Questions

**12.1**  *Definitions (Define, differentiate, and provide an example for each of the following)*
- A.  Autokinetic effect
- B.  Ideomotor effect
- C.  Pupil response
- D.  Entoptic phenomena
- E.  Floaters
- F.  Blue field entoptic phenomena
- G.  Vascular figure
- H.  Phosphenes
- I.  Synesthesia
- J.  Migraine
- K.  Photopsia
- L.  Scintillating scotoma
- M.  Fortification illusion
- N.  Tunnel experiences
- O.  Hallucination
- P.  Hypnagogic hallucinations
- Q.  Pseudohallucinations
- R.  Hypnopompic hallucinations
- S.  Sleep paralysis
- T.  Out-of-body experience
- U.  Anoxia
- V.  Hypercapnia
- W.  Hypocapnia
- X.  Sensory deprivation
- Y.  Seizures
- Z.  Tourette's syndrome
- AA. Schizophrenia
- BB. Dissociative disorder
- CC. Dissociative amnesia
- DD. Depersonalization/derealization disorder
- EE. Dissociative identity disorder

**12.2**  *Essay Questions*
- A. Advocates of some forms of Buddhist and Hindu meditation and yoga claim that long practice sessions can lead to the cultivation of psychic, paranormal, and supernatural powers, called "siddhis." These can include:
  - o dramatically reducing or expanding the size of one's body (even to the size of an atom),
  - o becoming weightless,
  - o moving anywhere instantly,
  - o seeing into the future,
  - o accessing past lives,
  - o reading the minds of others,

o influencing matter through thought, and

o turning any desire into reality.

However, development of siddhi powers requires discipline, including long sessions of solitary practice, immersing oneself in sacred texts, isolating oneself from others, practicing with expert "masters," and engaging in fasting (see http://www.esalen.org/ctr-archive/yogic_capacities.html). What alternative explanations do you have, from this chapter and this entire text?

- B.  Most religions are of two minds concerning paranormal claims. At times they view "siddhi" powers as positive, and at times negative. To elaborate, religions typically value three goals: (1) "coming close to God," (2) viewing the world realistically while putting aside distorting personal desires, expectations, prejudices, and wishes, and (3) living a life that is "unselfish" with little focus on "personal gain." How might paranormal claims contribute to these three religious goals? How might they interfere with these goals?

- C.  What is an "exorcism"? Are they performed today? What is the traditional religious interpretation? What alternative explanations can you provide?

- D.  Here are some remarkable paranormal claims, often collaborated in groups. Offer an alternative explanation for each.

  o A group of flying saucer enthusiasts have read accounts of UFO sightings over a secluded forest late at night. They take a long hike to this spot and quietly wait for hours, careful not to give evidence of their presence. Suddenly, with great excitement, all start noting strange lights in the sky. The lights are described as tiny, glowing particles of dust, and they seem to move and change direction very fast, especially when viewed from different angles.

  o Hundreds of worshipers of the Flying Spaghetti Monster have descended upon the small city of Corvallis, Oregon, for a special spiritual retreat. Last year retreat visitors reported actually seeing the FSM in the clouds. Excitement was high that the deity would reveal him or herself. After hours of devout chanting, singing, and two days of fasting, a few members shout out, "there it is!" Others look up, and indeed a sighting has been confirmed.

  o The old Macmillan house down the street is known to be haunted. Years ago its sole resident, Father Macmillan, disappeared, never to be seen again. Many suspect foul play, given the good Father cavorted with an unsavory group of individuals. Some even suspect he was buried in the basement. Every week an enterprising group conducts a ghost tour of the Macmillan house. The tour starts late at night, and concludes at midnight in the notorious basement. At the stroke of midnight all tour participants are instructed to remain completely silent for 30 minutes. Lights are turned off, except for a tiny candle over an unpaved section of floor. As advertised, the good Father reveals himself – at first to one, and then to all, usually with an ambiguous sign such as an unexplained flow of cold air on the back of one's neck, a movement in an empty corner, or an ambiguous sound heard by all.

○ Gizwald is mourning the passing of his uncle, Klurf. One night Gizwald had a particularly vivid vision that changed his life. While falling asleep, a dark figure appeared next to his bed. Gradually, it took the form of Uncle Klurf. Gizwald wanted to yell, but he could not speak. He wanted to get out of bed, but he could not move. His uncle was freezing him in bed so he would hear his message – "take good care of the family." The next day, Gizwald hugged his wife and children, promising to be the best father and husband possible.

**12.3** *Internet Search*

- A. What brain changes might happen in those who have deep religious or mystical experiences? (Search "God in the brain.") Some argue that such brain correlates diminish the validity of religious experience, claiming such experiences are "not real" and "just in the brain." Others argue that such neurological foundations lend to their credibility. What do you think? (Hint: Consider this chapter, and the section "Messing with Reality: Ontological Errors" in Chapter 6.

- B. Search videos on the internet for "dowsing." Explain what it is and the claims for its effects. How might it involve the ideomotor effect? What perceptual errors might be involved?

- C. Search the internet for accounts of out-of-body experiences. Useful search phrases include: "virtual out-of-body experience," "Michael Shermer Out-of-Body Experiment," "James Randi Out-of-Body Experience," or just "out-of-body experiences."

    After viewing what you have uncovered, what common features can you find for out-of-body experiences? What paranormal claims do those who have these experiences make? What alternative explanations seem most plausible?

- D. Magicians Penn & Teller (*Bullshit!*, Season 1, Episode 12) discuss "Ouija Boards/Near Death Experiences." View this episode and discuss what textbook concepts are illustrated.

- E. Search for "sleep paralysis AND alien abductions." What paralysis experiences do alien abductees sometimes report? How might these be related to sleep paralysis?

- F. How do psychics interpret "psychic auras"? Search the web for "auras" and "psychic auras." What are the meanings psychics attribute to various aura colors? How might you interpret an aura experience in terms of concepts of this chapter?

- G. Search the internet for "migraine art." How might such a migraine experience be interpreted as a paranormal event?

- H. Search for "Tourette's syndrome" AND "witches" or "demonic possession." What characteristics of Tourette's syndrome might be interpreted as evidence of witchcraft or evidence of demon possession? What is the most recent example of this you can find?

- I. "We see with our brains, not our eyes." How is this perspective different from subjective relativism?

**Part IV**

**Paranormal Challenges**

# 13

# Claims of Extraordinary Cures

---

**OUTLINE**

1) Vitalistic Energy Treatments and Complementary and Alternative Medicine (CAM)
   a) Concepts of Vitalistic Energy in Children and Western History
   b) Acupuncture
   c) Examples of Western Approaches: Homeopathy and Therapeutic Touch
2) Shamanism, Faith Healing, and Covert Physical Intercessory Prayer
   a) Shamanism
   b) Pentecostalism and Faith Healing
   c) Covert Physical Intercessory Prayer
   d) Sample Research: The Benson Study

---

We have used the paranormal as our practice arena for applying the tools of open-minded critical thinking. Our journey has been a bit strange, perhaps even breathtaking. But you may wonder, as we have said before, "What's the harm?" Does it really matter if people believe in angels, astrology, communicating with the dead, dream prophecy, fortune-telling, or reincarnation?

Of course it does. If you think the universe of the paranormal is simply a treasure chest of plot lines for TV and movie entertainment, I encourage you to review Chapter 3. However, there is one category of claim that rises above all others and has had lasting and substantial consequences. It continues to cost society millions of dollars a year, and contributes to needless misery and death. However, it is a notion that, if true, could revolutionize human life. I am referring to the claim that some undetectable energy or spirit can cure illness and extend human life. We shall consider two versions of this claim: vitalistic energy and the worlds of shamanism, faith healing, and distant intercessory healing prayer.

Let me warn you that the material in this chapter is quite controversial, and stirs more heated discussion than any other topic we have considered. However, I insist on including it for several reasons: Claims of extraordinary cures have substantial impact; Such claims are routine fare in most texts, journals, and serious popular magazines and websites on critical thinking; A student of critical thinking simply must be aware of the ongoing discussion.

*Critical Thinking: Pseudoscience and the Paranormal*, Second Edition. Jonathan C. Smith.
© 2018 John Wiley & Sons, Inc. Published 2018 by John Wiley & Sons, Inc.

# Vitalistic Energy Treatments and Complementary and Alternative Medicine (CAM)

As we noted in Chapter 3, complementary and alternative medicine (CAM), sometimes called "integrative medicine," includes a wide range of treatments not generally accepted as part of traditional medicine or taught in traditional medical schools. This includes a truly diverse assortment of approaches ranging from vitamin supplements, herbal treatments, and massage to yoga, acupuncture, tai chi, homeopathy, chiropractic, therapeutic touch, fasting, prayer, healing shrines, faith healing, and urine therapy. Some forms of CAM (such as massage, yoga, meditation, exercise, and some vitamins) have solid scientific support. But the consumer of CAM needs to be an Open-Minded Critical Thinker.

Many (but not all) forms of CAM are based on the paranormal belief in a special vitalistic life energy that supports and maintains living organisms. Acupuncture involves releasing blockages of life energy in the body. Feng shui involves balancing and optimizing life energies of the environment through architecture and interior design. A priest may use therapeutic touch to transfer healing energy to a patient.

To understand how such notions are paranormal, we need to understand what energy is. Life could not exist without energy. We need it to run our factories, fuel our cars, and heat our homes. You feel it when you wake up refreshed and your body is excited and ready for action. On some days you may be brimming with energy, ready to conquer the world. When sick, you're listless and drained.

The paranormal use of the term "energy" bears little resemblance to its use in any of the sciences. In physics, energy is the capacity for doing work. To say that a party is "energized" is a way of saying that lots of people are mingling, talking, and dancing. You can't take this "party energy" and put it in a bottle. (Although you could put the guests to work to clean up their mess when the party is over.) Put a rock in a fire and it will get hot, that is, energized. Put several energized rocks in a pile and they can do work, like bake potatoes. Energy can exist in several forms, such as mechanical, thermal, electromagnetic (including light, microwaves, radio waves), chemical, and nuclear. Energy cannot be created or destroyed. It cannot be bottled. It is not a "thing." It is not "living," and in no way has "consciousness," a "will," or "intentionality."

But there is one sense in which the term "energy" can apply to life. Living systems do metabolize (or "burn") the chemicals in food into other chemicals (wastes), an example of chemical energy. Such metabolism fuels our capacity for all types of "work." As a byproduct, infrared radiation energy is released. The nervous system generates electromagnetic radiation energy that can be detected by very sensitive equipment, electroencephalographs (EEGs). However, such electromagnetic waves are very weak and indistinguishable from electromagnetic waves that can be generated by inanimate objects such as computers and cell phones.

### Concepts of Vitalistic Energy in Children and Western History

Children think differently from adults. In attempting to make sense of the world they may erroneously think of objects as possessing consciousness and agency or intentionality (Lindeman & Saher, 2007). A lucky charm has a magical "energy" that gives you luck. The clouds "want" to rain on the parade, they have intentionality. Eventually, children outgrow such simplistic thinking patterns and learn to explain the world more accurately in physical, biological, and psychological terms. Rocks don't fall because they want to touch the Earth, but because of gravity.

The idea that objects possess energy and intentionality is **vitalistic causality** or **vitalism**, a type of thinking. Vitalistic thinking also characterized early human thought and philosophy. Aristotle believed that living things possessed a life-giving soul (Schubert-Soldern, 1962). In the nineteenth and twentieth centuries physiologists proposed a vital force underlying all living things. This force was given various names, including *life force, vis essentialis, vis viva, entelechy, élan vital*, and *soul atoms* (Lindeman & Saher, 2007). Somewhat similar vitalistic concepts permeated early Eastern thoughts.

Once again, vitalism is clearly a paranormal concept. There is no evidence of vitalistic energy, much less a thinking energy with intentionality, outside the energies physics has discovered. Children give up primitive vitalistic ideas as they mature. On a larger scale, civilization abandoned vitalistic explanations for those based on science. However, vitalism persists in energy treatments of complementary and alternative medicine. We consider major approaches that have developed in the East and West.

Many oriental practices rely on vitalistic concepts. In India, yoga incorporates prana (breath energy) and chakras (energy centers in the body). However, we will focus on an ancient Chinese philosophy of two basic principles of complementary "forces," yin and yang.

Things that are passive are described as yin, whereas yang is active. Additional attributes of yin include "earth, absorbing, cold, female, dark, inward, and downward." Yin is present in even numbers, valleys and streams, the color orange, and a broken line. Yang is "heaven, penetrating, hot, male, bright, outward, and upward" and exists in odd numbers, mountains, the color azure, and an unbroken line.

Everything is in constant and cyclical change. Yin eventually produces yang, and yang leads to yin. The dominance of one principle is always temporary. Illness follows health, and health follows illness. Strength leads to exhaustion, and exhaustion (and a good nap) leads to strength. Yin and yang exist in harmony, as symbolized in the popular yin/yang symbol in which dark and light halves are separated by a wavy "S" line. If you study a proper yin/yang symbol, you will note a dark dot in the light (yang) segment, and a light dot in the dark (yin) segment. This symbolizes that in every yin is the seed of yang.

Yin and yang work through a vitalistic energy, **chi** (**qi** or **ch'i**) (pronounced "chee" as in "cheese"). At first chi had a very simple and oderiferous meaning – the noxious vapors that arise from a corpse not buried deep enough (Watson, 1963). The term evolved to refer to universal vitalistic energy, one that fills the universe and is responsible for all life. It is in the environment, sunlight, and the very food we eat. Chi travels in the body through 12 major channels called **meridians**. Why 12? In Chinese thinking, there are 12 primary organs: the heart, lungs, stomach, small intestines, large intestines, spleen, urinary bladder, kidney, liver, gallbladder, pericardium, and the upper torso. Each organ has chi.

When a person is ill, yin and yang are out of balance. For example, someone with high blood pressure might have too much yang in the heart, requiring a treatment that would reduce heart yang and increase yin (yinyang, 2008). More concretely, disease is caused by a blockage or unhealthy flow of chi from one organ to another. Chinese interventions to adjust yin/yang and chi include various herbal medicines and diet (see also Ayurvedic medicine, an approach from India), physical training, martial arts, and massage.

**Figure 13.1** I Ching (8 trigrams in yin/yang). Reproduced with kind permission of Superstock.

The yin/yang school provides a foundation for many paranormal systems, including Chinese astrology and the *I Ching* or *Book of Changes*. Chinese astrology is quite different from Western astrology, and is rarely applied in the West. However, the *I Ching* is popular. This book provides a way of understanding and predicting change in the universe by randomly selecting and reading combinations of eight trigrams each of which is made of a different combination of one or two broken (yin) or unbroken (yang) lines. Each trigram has a different forecast, much like an astrological horoscope. Trigrams are often arranged in clockwise fashion around a yin/yang symbol.

Four major Chinese approaches have gained popularity in the West. **Feng shui** ("wind water") is the art of arranging objects (from furniture to buildings and cities) in harmony with the environment to achieve health, energy, and balance. It is primarily a practice of urban planning, architecture, landscaping, and interior design (Wu, 2000). Major cities of China have been developed according to the rules of feng shui. Generally, the goal is to build or place structures (or furniture) in "perfect spots," places with good chi.

**Qigong** (pronounced "chee gung"), or **chi kung** (Lin, 2000), is an ancient Chinese practice that freely mixes thousands of exercises, including postures and stretches, martial arts training, deep breathing, imagery, and focused meditations. Many are borrowed from yoga and Buddhism. All are designed to cultivate and balance one's chi.

**Tai chi** is an ancient Chinese exercise involving slow and graceful dance and yoga-like movements and postures. Although originally developed as a form of self-defense, it is increasingly used in the West as an approach to stress management and a tool for enhancing balance and flexibility. Like qigong, tai chi is based on chi.

Perhaps the most popular Chinese technique is **acupuncture**.

### Acupuncture

Acupuncture is a medical technique for unblocking chi by inserting needles at special points on body meridians. It is typically claimed to be from 2,500 to 5,000 years old.

Up to 15 million Americans spend about a half billion dollars a year on acupuncture treatments for AIDS, allergies, asthma, arthritis, bladder and kidney problems, bronchitis, constipation, depression, diarrhea, dizziness, colds, eye disorders, fatigue, flu, gynecologic disorders, headaches, high blood pressure, migraines, paralysis, PMS, respiratory problems, sciatica, sexual dysfunction, smoking, stress, stroke, tendinitis, and vision problems. It has even been used for cancer and alcoholism (Fleischman, 1998). According to the American Academy of Medical Acupuncture, about 1,300 US physicians are trained in acupuncture (www.medicalacupuncture.org).

Acupuncture procedures vary among practitioners. Generally, after an interview, an acupuncturist will identify organs (from the 12 mentioned earlier) that suffer imbalance. Along the associated 12 meridians there are about 2,000 potential target acupuncture points, of which 200 are used more frequently. Needles are inserted to manipulate chi in the appropriate meridians. Target points often have no relationship to the presumed affected organ. Sometimes needles are twirled, heated, and stimulated by mild electric current. In acupressure, pressure is applied to meridian

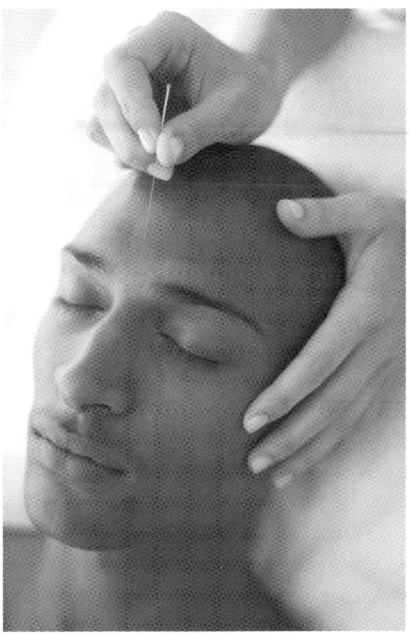

**Figure 13.2** Acupuncturist inserting needles in patient. Reproduced with kind permission of Superstock.

points. An acupuncture session lasts from 20 or 30 minutes up to an hour. After an initial prick there is generally no discomfort or pain. An acupuncturist will take great care to insert needles at special meridian points. Six to 12 needles are inserted during a session (Lewith, Kenyon, & Lewis, 1996; Pelletier, 2002).

Acupuncture appears to have some effect (NIH Consensus Development Program, 1997). However, evaluation of medical claims is beyond the scope of this book and many studies are conflicting. The most important issues in acupuncture research are:

- Is any claimed success of acupuncture due to placebo or other nonspecific effects? This is currently the most likely explanation for the effects of acupuncture (Madsen, Gøtzsche, & Hróbjartsson, 2009). Of the thousands of scientific studies on acupuncture, only a handful have attempted rigorous placebos that approach the criteria we have suggested in Chapter 11. The best have used **sham acupuncture**. Sham or fake acupuncture controls are designed to mimic the appearance and sensation of an acupuncture needle without the required insertion. This might be done with a clever skin-clicking device designed to look like a needle-inserter. Even this research is flawed because it does not deploy a truly rigorous double-blind protocol, which would require that neither the person giving nor the patient receiving the treatment knew if it was real acupuncture or a placebo. No matter how elaborate a sham needle may seem, if the person giving it knows it is a sham, then the procedure is not double-blind, and the administrator's lack of belief or enthusiasm may impact treatment results. To prevent patient exposure to such interpersonal effects, a researcher would have to completely block a patient from the individual giving the treatment (real or placebo).

Put a patient in a box with holes over meridian points? Have a surgery robot administer sham and authentic needle insertion to a blindfolded patient? A convincing double-blind placebo study of acupuncture has yet to be conducted.

- When an acupuncture success is not due to placebo or nonspecific effects, are there any other scientific explanations? Yes, gate control theory of pain states that a stimulus in one part of the body can send nerve impulses to the spine which switch off a neurological "pain gate," preventing pain sensations from reaching the brain. A more popular hypothesis is that sticking needles into someone evokes painkilling chemicals such as endorphins, enkephalins, and serotonin, some of which bear a chemical resemblance to morphine.
- Is needle insertion necessary? No, one can use touch, heat, or lasers.
- Must needles be inserted at precise acupuncture points? No. Poking just about anywhere works.
- Do meridian points correspond to human physiology? No consistent correspondence has been found between meridian points and any feature in human anatomy. However, with 2,000 potential needle insertion points, by chance alone one might expect some to correspond to areas of the skin dense with nerve endings.
- Do meridian points correspond to channels of chi? There is absolutely no evidence for this whatsoever. As Felix Mann (1993), founder of the Medical Acupuncture Society, has stated:

> The traditional acupuncture points are no more real than the black spots a drunkard sees in front of his eyes… The meridians of acupuncture are no more real than the meridians of geography. If someone were to get a spade and tried to dig up the Greenwich meridian, he might end up in a lunatic asylum. Perhaps the same fate should await those doctors who believe in [acupuncture] meridians. *(pp. 14, 31)*

**Examples of Western Approaches: Homeopathy and Therapeutic Touch**

Many Western vitalistic approaches have emerged over the century. These include chiropractic, reflexology, reiki, and therapeutic touch. We consider homeopathy and therapeutic touch.

**Homeopathy** is a clear example of an ineffective treatment supplement based on paranormal energy explanations. Nineteenth-century medicine was primitive by today's standards. Treatments were often based on ancient Greek humoral theory, which claimed that all illnesses were due to an imbalance of the four basic fluids (blood, phlegm, black bile, and yellow bile). Humors were balanced by treating symptoms with "opposites," for example, by attempting to cool a feverish patient by draining blood. German physician Samuel Hahnemann (1755–1843) rejected this brutal approach in favor of treating symptoms with "similars" through homeopathy.

Hahnemann believed that a vitalistic energy directs healing, a process that can be triggered by giving a patient a minute amount of the substance presumed to be causing an ailment, the "Law of Similars." His "Law of Infinitesimals" states that the more you dilute a treatment, the more effective it becomes. Indeed, a treatment can be so diluted that not even a molecule of the single presumed active ingredient remains in solution. This is because the original ingredient leaves a sort of "memory" in the solution, and this "memory" has a curative effect. To treat arsenic poisoning, one would dilute a drop of arsenic hundreds of times, so none of the poison remains, and give the resulting water to the patient. (One can enhance, or awaken, the spiritual potency of a bottle of such watery solutions with a good slap, a process called "dynamization.")

Homeopathy has been subjected to substantial research. Although it is clearly better than blood-letting, there is no evidence that it is any more effective than a placebo (Barrett, 2007; Hines, 2003; National Health and Medical Research Council, 2015). The idea of an undetectable "memory" that balances spiritual powers, can be slapped into activity, and can even be transmitted over phone lines is vitalism (Jarvis & The National Council against Health Fraud, 2002). There is no evidence that it exists (Goldacre, 2007).

**Therapeutic touch** (TT) involves manipulating vitalistic energy without needles. Instead one relies on placement of hands. Created by nurse Dolores Krieger (1979), TT involves moving hands over a patient's energy field and aura in order to free the flow of energy and bring it into alignment and balance. Techniques involve initial centering meditation, sweeping one's hands over the patient's body from head to feet to "unruffle stagnant energy," and actual intervention in which the healer repatterns the patient's energy field by removing "congestion," replenishing depletion, and smoothing out energy. When the patient's energy is balanced, the body can heal itself.

There is no evidence that TT works (Rosa et al., 1998). Its claims are purely paranormal. In spite of this, TT is widely accepted in the nursing profession. The American Nurses' Association holds TT workshops at national conventions, publishes articles on TT, and even grants continuing education credit for TT training.

In a classic study, 11-year-old Emily Rosa became the youngest person to publish an article in the prestigious *Journal of the American Medical Association* (Rosa et al., 1998). Emily wanted to determine if 21 expert practitioners of TT could detect the presence of her hand by simply feeling its aura. To do this she sat behind a cardboard screen with one hand-sized opening. She then tossed a coin to determine whether or

**Figure 13.3** Emily Rosa's therapeutic touch experiment. By Pat Linse.

not to place her hand next to the opening. A TT practitioner would then reach through an opening in the screen and (without touching) determine through aura energy if Emily's hand was present. TT practitioners were able to detect Emily's hand only 44% of the time, worse than chance. Emily was subsequently recognized by the *Guinness Book of World Records* as the youngest published scientist, and appeared on the *Today Show* and *Good Morning America*, as well as on major television news programs and in major newspapers.

## Shamanism, Faith Healing, and Covert Physical Intercessory Prayer

In France, a young woman suffering from breast cancer seeks faith and healing at the shrine in Lourdes. An elderly woman in Malaysia has swollen feet. She seeks the assistance of a shaman, who, through ritual dance, enters a trance, communicates with departed souls, and attempts a cure by cutting a hole in her ankle. In Kansas a middle-aged man with arthritis attends a popular big-tent faith healing revival led by a famous televangelist. With great excitement, the evangelist invokes the power of the Holy Spirit, reaches out to his flock, and pronounces all healed. A noted researcher has brain cancer. Experts in healing prayer from Christian, Jewish, Buddhist, shaman, and secular healing energy traditions converge at her bedside to intervene. A Presbyterian congregation in Ohio prays for the rapid recovery of a family at home with the flu.

Some of these examples may resemble experiences you have had. Some may seem foreign and even laughable. However, all illustrate the same thing: a special energy outside of the world of physics is claimed to effect a cure in this world. As such, this energy is vitalistic and paranormal. Often such energy is wielded by an entity larger or greater than ourselves that has thoughts and intentions. This supernatural entity may be a deity, the soul of a departed loved one, or a spirit.

At this point we must make an important distinction. Many of us invoke higher powers and spirits for many reasons: love, support, moral guidance, courage, forgiveness, insight, community, comfort for the departed, preparation for the afterlife, and so on. For the most part, such objectives are intangible and unfalsifiable. How could one possibly conduct a scientific or logical test of God's love, successful comforting of the spirit of a departed relative, forgiveness, or advancement into heaven? These objects are far beyond the reach of our text and we note them with respectful silence. However, whenever we use a higher power or spirit to effect a measurable cure in this world, we enter the arena of paranormal claim. We consider three such claims: shamanism, faith healing, and the healing petitions of mainstream religion.

### Shamanism

**Shamanism** is an ancient tribal religious phenomenon that emerged around the end of the stone age (8500 BC) in central Asia and Siberia. It appears around the world, including in North and South America, southeast India, Southeast Asia, Oceania and Malaysia, and Australia (Levinson, 1998; Lewis, 2003). Although it is unfair to treat diverse religious cultures as equivalent, a few central features are worth noting. Most important is the shaman (Manchu-Tungus for "he who knows"), a special and revered member of the community who has the power to cure illness and communicate with gods and spirits of the dead (Krippner, 2002).

Central to many forms of shamanism are dramatic rituals in which the shaman enters an ecstatic state, induced and supported by intense and prolonged drumming, dance, fasting, intense sauna-like sweat lodges, and ingestion of alcohol and other mind-altering substances (see Chapter 12). In such altered states the shaman may quiver, struggle, yell in rage, and eventually enter an unconscious "trance." Both the shaman and participants view such displays as evidence of spirit possession, or even as a sign that the shaman's soul has temporarily departed and entered the world of the spirits.

By directly contacting spirits and gods, the shaman acquires remarkable paranormal powers. He may heal, foresee the future, retrieve lost or stolen souls, escort souls of the dead (a process called "psychopomp"), communicate and work with spirits, and appease malevolent spirits. In everyday life the shaman has great priestly authority and supervises sacred rituals, interprets dreams, finds lost animals, and assists fishing and hunting (Krippner, 2002).

Shamans are often quite comfortable using deception and sleight of hand (Krippner, 2002; Warner, 1980) and at times use tricks well known to magicians (Sternfield, 1992). Some positive reviewers view this as a gift that can be used to help others acquire a deeper understanding of reality, specifically by enhancing perception, and temporarily lifting constraints of a consensus worldview of cause and effect (Krippner, 2002; Hansen, 2001).

### Pentecostalism and Faith Healing

The invocation of supernatural cures is a part of Christianity. Healing is one of the nine gifts of the spirit described in 1 Corinthians 12. Jesus and his Apostles performed 40 healings. For millennia Christians have celebrated miraculous cures brought about by saints. Healing shrines, including the famous shrine of Lourdes in France, attract millions every year. In the nineteenth century, Mary Baker Eddy founded Christian Science, a denomination that stresses that illness is the result of erroneous beliefs and that faith in the healing power of God largely eliminates the need for physicians.

We focus on a particularly conspicuous example of faith healing, the American healing revival. Faith healing revivals are part of contemporary American Pentecostal Christian culture, frequently attracting huge television audiences. Many faith healers are household names and television personalities, including Oral Roberts, A. A. Allen, Ernest Angley, Kathryn Kuhlman, Richard Rossi, Benny Hinn, Peter Popoff, and Pat Robertson. One, Pat Robertson, actually ran for President.

Close examination reveals that these public displays of faith healing have some similarities to the flamboyant cures of shamans. Both are tainted with fraud and self-deception. One can find on the internet frequent outings of fake healers. James Randi's *The Faith Healers* (1989) is one of the classic exposés. Astonishingly, even faith healers who have been repeatedly and publically exposed as frauds continue to attract huge followings and make millions. Google "Peter Popoff."

Faith healing can have a dark and cruel side. Arthritis patients have discarded crutches, only to discover that their pain returns after the adrenalin (and endorphin) rush subsides. Seriously ill patients have died after putting their faith in prayer rather than medicine. At least 200 children have died because they received healing prayer rather than standard medicine (Offit, 2015). (See whatstheharm.net.)

Does faith healing work? Randi (1989) and Hines (2003) have summarized a half-dozen scientific reviews; those who have investigated claims of cure have not found a single case that stands up to scrutiny. Stephen Barrett, founder of quackwatch.com, sees a problem (Barrett, 2003) and argues:

- Laws to protect children from medical neglect in the name of healing should be passed and enforced. In states that allow religious exemptions from medical neglect, these exemptions should be revoked. Maybe the practice of faith healing on minors should be illegal.
- Faith healing should no longer be deductible as a medical expense.
- Reporters should be encouraged to do follow-up studies of people acclaimed to have been "healed."
- "Healers" who use trickery to raise large sums of money should be prosecuted for grand larceny. *(2003)*

## Covert Physical Intercessory Prayer

*Is any one of you sick? He should call the elders of the church to pray over him and anoint him with oil in the name of the lord. And the prayer offered in faith will make the sick person well.*

(James 5:14–16; New King James Version)

*If a prophet speaks in the name of the Lord and what he says does not come true, then it is not the Lord's message.*

(Deuteronomy 18:22)

Most Americans believe that healing prayer works. Does it? This is a fair question and one that believers should not be embarrassed to ask. Both the Old and New Testaments provide numerous accounts of God-sanctioned objective tests of miracles.

The Old Testament reports at least one miracle that is actually a credible attempt at a control-group experiment. In 1 Kings (18:20–40) the prophet Elijah challenged the prophets of Baal (a local false deity) to a test. In accordance with custom, two bulls were sacrificed, one for Baal and one for the Lord. Traditionally, worshipers would build a fire under a sacrificial bull; however, in this test no fires were set. Instead, both Baal and the Lord were called upon to provide ignition. Making the test more stringent, Elijah stood aside and exhorted the Baalites to do whatever they could to evoke supernatural intervention. They failed. Elijah even drenched his own bull with 12 barrels of water (thereby reducing the risk of accidental spontaneous combustion or trickery). Then, in full view of everyone, skeptics and believers of both faiths, the Lord sent fire from the sky and ignited his bull. (In another experiment, reported in Daniel 1:1–16, a vegetarian diet was found superior to a more regal meat diet. However, the involvement of the Lord in the design of this study is unclear.)

This tradition continues in the New Testament. When Thomas demanded to feel Jesus's wounds as evidence of His resurrection, Jesus had no trouble complying (John 20:24–29). Indeed, Jesus did not command his disciples to be content with conjecture or hearsay and felt free to offer many evidential signs of His post-resurrection presence (John 20:31). Many miracles were performed in front of hostile skeptics (even scholarly priests), with multiple witnesses, and follow-up to confirm authenticity. In sum, the Bible counsels "Seek and ye shall find" (Matthew 7:7).

We have seen throughout this book that testimony is not the best type of evidence. Just as "doubting" Thomas sought a verifiable empirical test, both believers and skeptics have looked beyond testimonials for evidence of the efficacy of prayer. Some of this research has appeared in serious scientific journals. Indeed, journals that have devoted special issues to spirituality and health include the *American Psychologist, Annals of Behavioral Medicine, Health Education & Behavior, Journal of Health Psychology, Psychological Inquiry*, and *Research on Aging*. Many professional organizations have special divisions devoted to spirituality and health. A surprising number of health professionals use prayer with their clients. Surveys show that a majority of US social workers use intercessory prayer as a professional intervention (Hodge, 2007), a number that exceeds the number of nurses who use magical therapeutic touch. I never cease to be amazed by the number of licensed healthcare professionals who believe that research has proven that distant prayer works.

Now for a reality check. What does the research say? First, we will not consider studies that examine the impact of prayer on the prayer-giver. The act of prayer may well contribute to relaxation, stress-relief, community, and personal insight in ways that do not challenge physics. Similarly, we are not interested in the psychologically mediated effects the praying individual may have on the recipient. Recipients who know they are supported in prayer may experience reduced stress, greater relaxation, enhanced insight, and increased hope and optimism. These effects may be quite real and may have powerful nonspecific physical impact (Chapter 11).

Instead, we are interested in **covert physical intercessory prayer (CPIP)**. Such prayer is covert or secret; the recipient does not know he or she is being prayed for. It is physical in that the prayer-giver is asking for an objective measurable change in the physical condition of the recipient. CPIP is among the most widely practiced forms of alternative medicine (Barnes et al., 2002). It is very much a legitimate subject for serious students of the paranormal.

There are at least 16 published studies on CPIP. Researchers have examined rheumatoid arthritis, leukemia, heart disease, substance abuse, kidney disease, fertilization, and psychological health (Masters, 2005). Masters, Spielmans, & Goodson (2006) examined 15 studies in the most comprehensive meta-analysis to date. To make a long story short, *empirical evidence does not support a CPIP effect.*

However, the popular press (and occasionally scholars who should know better) at times actually misreport negative findings as supportive (see Gerhardt, 2000; Posner, 1998; Wallace, 1996; Chopra, 2008). Indeed Chopra (2008) reports there are 11 scientific studies that state that CPIP works. Reporters often select studies of questionable merit and ignore those of quality. More frequently, the press uncritically accepts conclusions of primary authors, unaware of subsequent criticisms. Perhaps such distortions are understandable, given the emotionally charged nature of the topic and the fact that the vast majority of Americans believe in the efficacy of prayer.

### Sample Research: The Benson Study

Herbert Benson is a well-known Harvard cardiologist, author of over 175 scientific articles and 11 books, including a number of bestselling popularizations. He is also one of the most influential scholars in stress management. Benson (1975) conducted his early work on mechanisms underlying professional relaxation techniques, arguing that clinical benefits may be due to a general anti-stress "relaxation response." Recently, he has become a passionate advocate of techniques integrating relaxation and prayer.

Given his popularity and reputation for careful, honest research, paranormal researchers took note when the Templeton Foundation honored him with a $2.4 million grant to study the effects of prayer. Aware of the criticisms of previous studies, Benson decided to conduct the most comprehensive and best-designed study ever (Benson et al., 2006). He succeeded. Indeed, David Myers, a respected scientist and self-avowed practicing Christian, summarized the excitement surrounding what could be the definitive study on prayer. Before the study was conducted, Myers proclaimed that it would be "the mother of all prayer experiments," one that "dwarfs all the others in both size and credibility" (Myers, 2000).

Benson decided to study the effects of prayer for cardiac bypass patients in six hospitals. Patients were randomly assigned to three groups: 604 received intercessory prayer but were told that they may or may not receive prayer; 597 did not receive prayer and were also told they may or may not get prayer; and 601 were told they would receive prayer and indeed were prayed for. If there is a CPIP effect, Group 1 should do better than Group 2. Group 3 should do best.

Prayers were provided by three Christian groups who agreed to pray for "successful surgery, no complications, and quick recovery." The results were unambiguous. Groups 1 and 2 (prayer and no prayer) *did not differ* on any of the measured outcomes, including death rate and complications. However, something interesting happened in Group 3, those who received prayer and knew it. They were 14% *more likely to experience complications* than those who received prayer but were not so informed. This study does not suggest a CPIP effect.

What are we to make of research on CPIP and the Benson study? Are the negative results due to bad design? Probably not. Perhaps the results are due to the placebo effect? Not likely, given that many participants were unaware that they were being prayed for. Furthermore, in the Benson study, those who knew they were receiving prayers actually did worse. Did the presence of skeptical researchers introduce a type of "negative energy" that blocked the effects of prayer? Most of the prayer researchers cited are passionate believers. Perhaps these findings call for a theological interpretation. What is God trying to tell us?

Before Benson performed his experiment, Myers (2000) predicted (as did other Christians) that he would find no prayer effect. Myers (and many learned theologians) remind believers that God is not a "celestial vending machine whose levers we pull with our prayers." The gifts we ask in prayer should be of a "spiritual" and not a "material" nature. After all, both the Old and New Testaments admonish us to "not put the Lord your God to the test" (Deuteronomy 6:16; Matthew 4:7).

## Retroactive Intercessory Prayer and a Concluding Thought on Science

One unusual prayer study deserves special note. It was published in a major medical journal by a leading and highly respected medical researcher. The study is one of the largest prayer projects ever conducted. Furthermore, it deployed a remarkable methodology that eliminates any possibility of a placebo effect and absolutely guarantees that the participants are unaware of the intervention they are receiving.

Yet this study has been ignored by some reviews, and celebrated by others. Indeed, the two most recent meta-analyses take opposite stances. Hodge (2007), publishing in *Research on Social Work Practice*, embraces the study, while Masters et al. (2006), in the equally respected *Annals of Behavioral Medicine*, ignore it.

Leibovici (2001) examined the effects of *retroactive* intercessory prayer, that is, praying for a change to take place in the past. This intervention is a relatively recent idea and does not appear in any major holy book. It is based on the notion that an all-powerful God is not limited by the Western view that time is linear and unidirectional (past to future). In other words, God can travel (and answer prayers) back and forth in time.

Leibovici was interested in whether prayer could retroactively influence the course of bloodstream infections. First, he obtained the medical files of 3,393 patients hospitalized 4–10 years previously. The files were randomly divided into two groups, one of which received a short prayer requesting full recovery and well-being. The patients, being in the past, were unaware that they were the recipients of prayer (a possible ethical problem because informed consent was not retroactively obtained). When Leibovici analyzed the files for both groups he found that the prayer group had spent less time in the hospital and had infections of shorter duration.

What are we to make of this strange study? Here are some clues. Leibovici (1999) has frequently argued that much paranormal research, particularly human trials on energy and prayer-based treatments, is unethical and should not be done. He rejects the notion that all hypotheses are fair game, regardless of their origin or plausibility. To explain, the logical consequence of such a relativistic perspective is that researchers would be distracted by an unconstrained avalanche of trivial questions, and fruitful areas of study would suffer. Furthermore, empirical science was not designed to work in such an unconstrained universe and is here not particularly effective in guarding against the possibility of chance findings, bias, and fraud. Spurious yet slightly significant findings (such as the impact of a single retroactive prayer on blood infection) are inevitable.

What protects science from wasting its time with false leads is the prevailing deep model of the world as described by physics. The deep model helps us pick which hypotheses to test, what tests to use, and how to interpret results. For example, a headache patient may benefit from acupuncture. The prevailing deep model of the physical universe rules out a magical energy, chi, or divine intervention, and prompts us to look for explanations consistent with the natural world, for example, the possibility of a placebo effect, distractions, or pain-reducing endorphins. The deep model does not guide us to spend millions attempting to develop a device to detect a new form of energy or consult with a shaman, televangelist, or Christian preacher for explanations.

Subjective relativists (Krippner & Achterberg, 2000) sometimes describe contemporary Western medicine as **biomedicine**, a term invented to suggest the possibility of alternative and equally valid forms of medicine not consistent with the prevailing deep model.

Leibovici rejects such thinking and reminds us that Western medicine is best described as **scientific medicine**, medicine based on empirical testing and the prevailing deep model of the physical universe. He goes on to state that the deep model for paranormal alternative medicine is at best magical thinking, a strange and empty model that specifies no agreed-upon measurable entity or force (chi? God? the Devil? ghosts? quantum entanglement? the Flying Spaghetti Monster?). As such, the paranormal deep model offers little help in screening hypotheses, suggesting new hypotheses, or telling us when to stop hypothesizing. This has one fatal consequence. The paranormal deep model fails to tell us when we cannot explain away unwanted findings with a never-ending flood of *ad hoc* rationalizations. Whereas the prevailing physics-based deep model permits disconfirming tests, the paranormal model renders a paranormal hypothesis unfalsifiable.

## Study Questions

**13.1**  *Definitions (Define, differentiate, and provide an example for each of the following)*

*Energy Treatments and Complementary and Alternative Medicine (CAM)*
- A. Complementary and alternative medicine
- B. Energy
- C. Vitalism
- D. Chi
- E. Feng shui
- F. Quigong or chi kung
- G. Tai chi
- H. Acupuncture
- I. Homeopathy
- J. Therapeutic touch

*Faith Healing and Distant Intercessory Prayer*
- A. Shamanism
- B. Pentecostalism
- C. Faith healing
- D. Covert physical intercessory prayer

**13.2**  *Essay Questions*
- A. What logical errors can you find in the concept of vitalism?
- B. What aspects of acupuncture might contribute to the placebo effect?
- C. Teachers of tai chi, acupuncture, and other energy treatments persist in believing vitalistic explanations. Using the concepts of this text, discuss why vitalistic thinking persists, even in face of contrary evidence.
- D. Using the tools of this text, how might you explain the tendency of the press to misreport prayer research?
- E. Is it appropriate to conduct research on religious claims?

**13.3** *Internet Search*

Here are some popular forms of CAM. Search the web and identify how each invokes the idea of vitalistic energy. Hint: if a treatment violates what we know about the laws of physics (is paranormal), by definition it must involve a paranormal form of energy, even if implied.

- Angel therapy
- Aroma therapy
- Aura therapy
- Chiropractic
- Healing touch
- Homeopathy
- Psychic surgery
- Reflexology
- Reiki
- Thought field therapy
- Urine therapy

**13.4** *Internet Videos*

There are many videos on the internet that illustrate key ideas in this chapter. I invite you to search and view the following. Explain what terms are illustrated. Which illustrated "open-minded critical thinking"? Why or why not?

*Energy Treatments and Complementary and Alternative Medicine*
- Penn & Teller the placebo effect
- Penn & Teller alternative medicine
- Penn & Teller feng shui
- Michael Shermer acupuncture
- Skeptic homeopathy
- Therapeutic touch *Scientific American*
- Emily Rosa healing touch

*Faith Healing and Distant Intercessory Prayer*
- James Randi
- Peter Popoff
- Benny Hinn
- Psychic surgery
- James Randi psychic surgery

**14**

# From the Paranormal Sampler: Four Claims of Consequence

*There are more things in heaven and earth, Horatio,*
*than are dreamt of in your philosophy.*

Hamlet (I, v, 166–167)

*All things bright and beautiful,*
*All creatures great and small,*
*All things wise and wonderful,*
*The Lord God made them all.*

Famous Anglican Hymn (Monk, 1875)

*'Extraordinary claims require extraordinary evidence'*
Popularized by Carl Sagan (Truzzi, 1976)

---

**OUTLINE**

1) Astrology
   a) History of Astrology
   b) The Zodiac
   c) Questions and Contradictions
   d) Science and Astrology
   e) Sample Research: The Gauquelin Study
   f) Sample Research: The Carlson Study
   g) The Lessons of Astrology
2) Spiritualism and the Survival Hypothesis
   a) History of Spiritualism
   b) Impact of Spiritualism
   c) How to Test a Medium
   d) Sample Research: Reincarnation
3) Parapsychology
   a) A Dictionary of Parapsychology
      i) Extrasensory perception (ESP)
         1) Precognition
         2) Retrocognition
         3) Telepathy/remote viewing
         4) Clairvoyance/remote viewing
      ii) Psychokinesis (PK)

---

*Critical Thinking: Pseudoscience and the Paranormal*, Second Edition. Jonathan C. Smith.
© 2018 John Wiley & Sons, Inc. Published 2018 by John Wiley & Sons, Inc.

The full spectrum of paranormal claims is a wonder to behold, a source of much entertainment and casual debate. However, some claims are more important than others, and go beyond the paranormal curios found in circus sideshows, Halloween parties, horror movies, and comic book superheroes. This text chooses not to waste time with such trivia and indulge in paranormal entertainment. However, even if you are a True Believer in fairies, pixies, or whatever, I invite you to practice your skills at open-minded critical thinking.

We conclude with four extraordinary **claims of consequence**, phenomena with historical, individual, social, philosophical, and political significance. These are taken from my companion text, *The Paranormal Sampler: Extraordinary Claims of Consequence* (Smith, in press, createspace.com), a text I use in my courses on critical thinking. In addition, I encourage the intrepid student or instructor to venture beyond the safe confines of our practice textbook arenas and explore the raw, astonishing, and often quite persuasive outer limits of the paranormal web.

Here is our roadmap. **Astrology** is important because it is the "grandmother" of paranormal beliefs, offers a prototype for prophecy and psychic readings popular to this day, and provides a vivid contrast to the view of the universe offered by pseudoscience and science. Historically, **spiritualism** and channeling the dead helped trigger and shape current interests in the paranormal. Most famous "TV psychics" and popular paranormal movies come from this tradition. The science of **parapsychology** offers the best methodology for studying paranormal claims. Indeed, parapsychologists have come tantalizingly close to providing evidence for some extraordinary claims. The debates over **creationism** and evolution have influenced American politics for decades. Perhaps more than any other set of claims, creationism has entered the public arena of critical thinking and has forced a broad consideration of the appropriate standards of scientific inquiry. I conclude with a personal thought.

## Astrology

Astrology is an ancient form of divination, a way of acquiring information, seeing into the future, or seeking interpretation. It is based on the idea that the positions and movements of the stars, planets, Sun, and Moon are associated with personal, political, and even geological events on Earth.

## History of Astrology

Western astrology can be traced to the Babylonians more than 4,000 years ago. At first they made use of omens such as dreams, disemboweled animals, and heavenly bodies. Many people also worshiped the Sun, and to a lesser extent the Moon. Eventually non-theistic astrology won out over other omens and the sky gods, perhaps because of the obvious links between seasonal warmth and the positions of the Sun and Moon (Culver & Ianna, 1984; Hoskin, 2003; Tester, 1989). Although the Babylonians developed many astrological concepts, at the time of Alexander the Great, the Greek geographer, mathematician, and astronomer Ptolemy was responsible for creating the system familiar today. Note that Ptolemy's view of astronomy was primitive. He viewed the universe as consisting of enormous spheres within spheres, a notion that persisted for centuries.

In Europe astrology grew in popularity during the renaissance, because of interest in science and astronomy. In the sixteenth and seventeenth centuries Christian theologians and popes condemned astrology as challenging free will and the prevailing views of an all-powerful God. However, even the founders of modern astronomy, Copernicus, Tycho Brahe, and Galileo, held astrology in high esteem (van Gent, 2007).

## The Zodiac

The Zodiac is a narrow horizon-to-horizon window divided into 12 window panes called *houses* or *signs*. Think of the Zodiac as a gigantic belt surrounding the Earth. Each house is defined by one of 12 (out of a possible 88) constellations of stars. Constellations are named for the animals or people they seemed to resemble. In fact, the word "zodiac" means "circle of animals" and is based on the same root as the word "zoo"; both the zodiac and zoos are filled with animals.

Your *Sun* or *natal sign* in *natal astrology* (the type used in newspaper horoscopes) is the house or window pane that the Sun is in at the moment of your birth. If the Sun is near the constellation of stars that define the house of Sagittarius ("The Archer"), you will be called a Sagittarius. Almost of equal importance is the *ascendant* or *rising sign*. This is the zodiac house rising on the eastern horizon at the moment you are born. So if the constellation of stars that defines Sagittarius appears on the eastern horizon, your rising sign is Sagittarius.

Each sign (and its Sun sign date) is associated with a different set of attributes, some of which are described below:

Aries (The Ram; March 21–April 19): Free, assertive, impulsive ...
Taurus (The Bull; April 20–May 20): Resourceful, patient, affectionate, stubborn ...
Gemini (The Twins; May 21–June 20): Logical, lively, sociable ...
Cancer (The Crab; June 21–July 22): Protective, clinging, nurturing, crabby ...
Leo (The Lion; July 23–August 22): Generous, proud, noble ...
Virgo (The Virgin; August 23–September 22): Practical, modest, fussy, lovable ...
Libra (The Scales; September 23–October 22): Cooperative, fair, charming ...
Scorpio (The Scorpion; October 23–November 21): Passionate, secretive, sadistic ...
Sagittarius (The Archer; November 22–December 21): Free, careless, optimistic ...
Capricorn (The Sea-Goat; December 22–January 19): Cautious, rigid, competent ...
Aquarius (The Water-carrier; January 20–February 18): Democratic, humanitarian, objective ...
Pisces (The Fishes; February 19–March 20): Imaginative, spiritual, lazy ...

**Figure 14.1** Sagittarius (the centaur). Reproduced with kind permission of Superstock.

These attributes were not obtained through any sort of scientific observation but simply reflect the shapes ancient people thought they saw in various patterns of stars, and popular associations to these shapes. So the house of Sagittarius is defined by a set of stars thought to look like a centaur, a half-human half-horse creature wielding a bow and arrow. The centaur was an untamed beast characterized as "free, careless, and optimistic." If you were born under Sagittarius you may also possess these attributes. There isn't agreement as to what constellations look like. Different systems of astrology have developed on different continents, each with their own cosmic set of animals and heroes.

### Questions and Contradictions

Astrology raises many unanswered questions. By what forces do celestial bodies influence human affairs? Gravity? Electromagnetism? Something related to dark energy? If the influence is through some unknown force, why do we have no evidence of it, especially if it is so strong as to produce accurate horoscopes, even for nations? Why is the Sun sign so important? When is upbringing more important than the positions of the stars?

More seriously, astrology conflicts with many facts already demonstrated by careful science. Distant stars have no measurable impact on the inhabitants of Earth. How could they have an astrological effect? The electromagnetic and gravitational forces of the gravity of the book you are now reading are millions of times stronger than the force of Mars on you, so how can the movement of Mars in the zodiac have any effect? Some heavenly objects once thought to be stars are actually galaxies combining billions of stars. Should they have greater astrological effect? Two stars that appear in the same constellation may not be close together, but huge distances apart. How could they possibly have an equal impact?

Going deeper, the houses of the zodiac are not of equal size. It takes the Sun seven days to pass through Scorpio and 44 days for Virgo. In addition, there are not 12, but 13 constellations in the zodiac. Ophiuchus (the "serpent bearer") has been left out. Also, Earth slowly wobbles over thousands of years. This process, called **precession**, means that the apparent positions of the Sun and constellations on January 1, 2007, were not the same as their positions on January 1, 2,000 years ago. If you are an Aries, you should read the Pisces horoscope. When astrology was developed 2,000 years ago, the Sun was in the house of Pisces, not Aries, when you were born. Newspaper horoscopes routinely ignore or use strange *ad hoc* explanations to discount this odd fact.

### Science and Astrology

Some astrologers are unconcerned with the contradictions and questions we have noted, and simply assert that it works, and therefore must be true (how does this demonstrate the "pragmatic logical error"?). How does astrology fare when subjected to scientific questioning? First, the fact that the basics of astrology have changed little for thousands of years suggests a system that is not particularly productive. This has not been for a lack of research (for summaries, see Blackmore & Seebold, 2001; Culver & Ianna, 1984; Dean, Mather, & Kelly, 1996; Eysenck & Nias, 1982; and Jerome, 1977). Indeed, there's so much research on astrology that even the summaries have been summarized (Hines, 2003; Schick & Vaughn, 2005). For an excellent recent review, check Dean (2016).

### Sample Research: The Gauquelin Study

Astrologers frequently cite the apparently supportive research of Michel Gauquelin, a French scientist who looked at astrological signs of various professions (Gauquelin, 1974; Irving, 2003). After examining 2,000 champions and thousands of nonchampions, he concluded that champions are more likely to be born when Mars is rising (the planet Mars appearing at the horizon at the time of one's birth). Examples include Babe Ruth, Mohammed Ali, Tiger Woods, and Venus Williams (but not her sister, Serena). Indeed, this observation earned its own technobabble label, "Mars Effect" or "Gauquelin effect," as if it were a fundamental law of physics.

Actually, some type of link between Mars and athleticism makes sense to astrologers. Mars was the god of war. Warriors are active and aggressive. Athletes are also active. So where the planet Mars appears in the sky at the time of one's birth should be associated with athleticism. Is it?

There are problems (Dean et al., 1996). First, it is misleading to claim that Gauquelin looked at Mars as a rising sign. More precisely, he divided the path that Mars travels from rising to setting into six equal parts, or sectors (a strange strategy typically not used by astrologers). Sectors 1 (the actual point of rising over the horizon) and 4 (Mars is in mid-sky) are most associated with athleticism. Why is this a problem? There are thousands of possible astrological patterns. The Sun, Moon, and all of the planets have their rising signs. If we include additional sectors, the possible signs multiply quickly into the tens of thousands. If you have enough time (Gauquelin devoted much of his life) and enough subjects (Gauquelin had thousands), eventually you will find a sign somewhere that fits what you expect. This is fishing in a cosmic sea of possibility. Why might this cause problems for the Open-Minded Critical Thinker?

Second, Gauquelin was very personally involved in his research. From a huge list of athletes (whose signs he knew), he selected those he personally considered to be champions.

His list did include a number of quite ordinary basketball and soccer players, and even aviators, as athletic champions. Most researchers have failed to agree on his selection of champions, or to replicate these findings when more controlled procedures are used.

### Sample Research: The Carlson Study

Carlson (1985) conducted an extensive study that answers the methodological problems that have plagued the work of Gauquelin and other researchers. One of the most frequent *ad hoc* critiques leveled at astrology studies has been their use of simplistic and mechanical horoscopes. Astrology is a complex enterprise, and casting a horoscope can indeed be as sophisticated as performing a complete medical assessment. A horoscope is only as good as the person creating it.

To meet such objections, Carlson sought the assistance of the National Council for Geocosmic Research (NCGR: www.geocosmic.org/). The NCGR is the nation's most prestigious professional astrological organization. It includes serious astrologers, medical professionals, and scientists, and offers a certification program as well as a scientific journal. With the advice of the NCGR, Carlson incorporated prominent American and European astrologers, all of whom agreed that his research procedures were fair before the study began. Astrologers were asked to construct horoscopes for 177 subjects and match them with detailed personality profiles from standard psychological tests. They couldn't do it.

### The Lessons of Astrology

The science of astronomy has made discoveries about our universe, some involving the same constellations considered by astrologers. I am particularly fond of one finding because it teaches us how the awe and wonder of science can outshine the fantasized mysteries of the paranormal. Indeed, for those so inclined, there may be something of a deeper message in all of this.

For thousands of years astrologers have written about the constellation Sagittarius. Unknown to astrologers, most of the 20 stars of Sagittarius aren't stars at all, but huge clusters of stars. However, one "star," *Sagittarius A\** (pronounced "A-Star"), isn't even a star or cluster. It is a mysterious invisible object which astronomers had no idea existed until the twentieth century. This object occupies a strangely unique position – the exact center of our galaxy. Indeed, the entire Milky Way is an enormous disk that rotates round Sagittarius A\*.

In 1999 astronomers made an astonishing discovery (Melia, 2007). Sagittarius A\* is a *supermassive black hole* more than four million times more massive than our Sun. Remarkably, it may be the closest black hole to Earth. To review basic physics, a black hole is one of the most mysterious objects in the universe, with gravity so massive that not even light can escape. Although black holes can be as small as an atom, or huge like Sagittarius A\*, generally they are of "stellar mass," about 10–20 miles in diameter, and having the mass of at least 3.8 suns. Sagittarius A\* is not alone. Incredibly, it may well be surrounded by a gigantic swarm of hundreds of thousands of stellar-mass black holes (Irion, 2008).

Unknown to astrologers, Sagittarius A\* is very much central to our lives. Every object in the Milky Way orbits it. The Earth travels around this black hole at 500,000 miles an hour. This enormous black hole and its companions may have been pivotal to the very formation of our galaxy and may well contribute to the complete destruction of humankind, the Sun, the solar system, and neighboring stars (when it gobbles up the neighboring Andromeda galaxy in a few billion years). Indeed, this process has begun and the Milky Way, with the help of Sagittarius A*, has already destroyed several galaxies. Sagittarius A* is very much the master of our galaxy and other galaxies as well.

There are important lessons in these contrasting stories from science and astrology. Astrologers had no idea of the significance of the little spot of light tagged as Sagittarius. Sagittarian horoscopes have provided no insight concerning our origins or long-term cosmic fate. And the claims of astrology have remained fossilized for thousands of years. In contrast, astronomy has revealed a breathtaking trove of discovery in less than a single decade. The story science reveals is truly one of immense and searing beauty, far more awesome than some fairy tale of a horse with a human head. This is something of a parable for much of the universe of paranormal claims. An Open-Minded Critical Thinker questions and looks deeper.

In spite of such apparent fatal problems, astrology still has an impact. Wars have been influenced by astrological forecasts. Presidents and popes have consulted astrologers. Horoscopes remain very popular and appear in nearly every newspaper. Hundreds of astrologers belong to serious international organizations and have their own serious, professional journals.

## Spiritualism and the Survival Hypothesis

Does some aspect of our humanity survive death? Perhaps there's an immaterial soul, one's personality, or consciousness? Such claims reflect the life-after-death or *survival hypothesis*. Although people have believed in life after death for thousands of years, we begin in the nineteenth century with a spiritual movement called spiritualism.

### History of Spiritualism

Spiritualism is a collection of beliefs based on the claim that spirits or departed souls live in a realm beyond our material universe. In the nineteenth century, **séances**, ceremonies in which **mediums** communicated with the dead, became fashionable winter-night parlor entertainment. Popular mediums would roam from city to city and amaze thousands with their astonishing communications with the departed.

In the United States, in time spiritualism became a social movement that offered hope of an afterlife for those grieving the slaughter of the civil war and skeptical of a Christianity newly challenged by science, especially Darwin. Spiritualists fought against slavery (in the afterlife all are equal) and the movement provided women with a rare public role not unlike that enjoyed by male priests (mediums were female). This movement set the stage for current widespread interest in channeling, psychics, parapsychology, and faith healing. Organized scholarly research into the paranormal began with serious investigations of spiritualist claims.

### Impact of Spiritualism

Although interest in spiritualism declined in the 1920s, it did have a major impact on the serious exploration of paranormal claims. Spiritualist research organizations, such as the Society for Psychical Research (formed in 1882), were among the first professional organizations dedicated to the paranormal. Similar societies exist to this day.

Magicians, with their unique insight into the tools of deception, acquired a new and important reality-checking role. One of the first, Harry Houdini, actually devoted the latter part of his life to stalking itinerant mediums and publicly debunking their readings by performing similar feats through simple sleight of hand. This role continues with such famous magicians as James (The Amazing) Randi, Banachek (Steve Shaw), Milbourne Christopher, Penn and Teller, Ian Rowland, Johnny Thompson (The Great Tomsoni), and Derren Brown. To this list we can add accomplished magicians Criss Angel, David Blaine, Apollo Robbins, and Lance Burton. Unfortunately, many physicists and psychologists, untrained in the skills of sleight of hand, continue to be duped.

**How to Test a Medium**

How does one test a medium? First attempts simply involved having a medium talk to a relative of the deceased, contact the deceased through channeling, and then report on the otherworldly communication. Television psychics, such as James van Praagh, Sylvia Browne, and John Edward, have made millions using this technique. Although their performances are often edited (introducing the opportunity to weed out failed reading), many transcripts and video clips are available online. Most deploy the cold reading techniques we have discussed in this text. Indeed, most of my students, after studying "The Psychic's Toolkit: How to Be a Convincing Psychic" in Chapter 9, can outperform famous TV psychics.

Research has been a bit more rigorous. A typical study deploys a **medium** and a **sitter**, usually a friend or relative of the deceased. The sitter provides the medium with the first name of the departed. The medium then contacts the departed and records any information obtained. This is presented to the sitter who determines whether or not it is accurate.

Hyman (2003) has pointed out one fatal flaw of this design. A sitter can easily distort a reader's "reading" to fit the departed, and selectively and erroneously recall information about the departed to confirm readings. For example, a reader might claim that the dearly departed reports having "died a painful death in the company of a few others, was not really understood in her community, was greatly respected, and had the capacity to evoke considerable irritation." The processes of perceptual and memory error could easily prompt a sitter to agree to the uncanny accuracy of this reading. Indeed, we can view it as a cold reading reflecting all the potential for manipulation of a psychic reading.

Clearly, any study on medium readings must introduce some basic controls. First, the medium and sitter should be prevented from viewing each other while the medium is presenting an improvised reading. The medium may even be in a different state and never communicate with or view the sitter. The medium could type out readings which are then presented to the sitter for evaluation. But there's an obvious flaw here. The sitter still gets only one reading and may selectively note only comments that fit his or her expectations.

A better strategy would be to give the sitter several names, one for the departed and the others randomly produced. He or she would produce a reading for each. The sitter would review all the readings and select which one is from the departed. What could possibly go wrong? Plenty. What if the departed was a sitter's English great-grandmother "Cordelia." Imagine this name is presented to the medium along with four dummy names, "Cynthia," "Chelsea," "Coco," and "Chris." Which name might evoke descriptions of an old woman of English descent? Coco? Probably not. Once generated, the sitter evaluates the readings for "Cordelia," "Cynthia," "Chelsea," "Coco," and "Chris." Any guess as to which reading might best fit great-grandmother? Unfortunately, there are numerous opportunities for stimulus leakage and fraud (Hyman, 2003). Frequently, controls are not carefully introduced and this is not reported. Researchers may well have discarded disconfirming trials, and reported only the successes (Hyman, 2003).

One study on mediums has made it into a mainstream journal. O'Keeffe and Wiseman (2005) enlisted five professional mediums and five sitters. Each sitter was given 25 readings, which included 20 fake and five genuine readings (one from each medium). Sitters then had to identify which of the 25 readings applied to them. Mediums were shielded from the sitters, and the sitters did not know each other. The design was rigorous and appeared to eliminate artifacts. The sitters were unable to identify readings that applied to them.

Even if an apparent genuine medium were uncovered, problems remain. How can we separate claimed communications of a deceased person from those of spirit guides, angels, other-worldly entities, space aliens, the Universal Intelligence, God, or the Flying Spaghetti Monster? Of course, many mediums attempt to solve this problem by asking the departed to confirm that they are indeed the targeted individual. Why would a dead person have any reason to lie? Perhaps recognizing the problem still remains, one famous medium reader researcher, Gary Schwartz, has expanded his efforts to people who claim to "channel or communicate with Deceased People, Spirit Guides, Angels, Other-Worldly Entities/Extraterrestrials, and/or a Universal Intelligence/God." (Schwartz, 2012). Can you figure out how this solves our problem? Incidentally, the motto of Professor Schwartz's new University of Arizona "Laboratory for Advances in Consciousness and Health" is reassuring: "If it is real, it will be revealed; and if it's fake, we'll find the mistake" (lach.web.arizona.edu).

## Sample Research: Reincarnation

Reincarnation is the belief that the spiritual essence of a person (and perhaps of animals, insects, plants, and even objects such as jars) lives beyond death and is reborn in a new body. We have found it to be one of the most controversial of paranormal claims (Chapter 3).

Traditions differ as to the nature of a reincarnated spiritual essence, sometimes describing it as "soul," "spirit," "higher self," or "selfless consciousness." Views of the attributes of what is reincarnated also vary widely and include immeasurable non-material attributes, personality and memories, even physical bodily characteristics such as scars and birthmarks. How one is reborn is determined by one's past actions, the overall effect termed "karma" in Hinduism. Misdeeds, or attachments to desires, lead to continued rebirth, perhaps in lower forms. Virtuous actions and freedom from attachment lead to better rebirthing outcomes or freedom from rebirth (Molé, 2002).

The concept of reincarnation is ancient and can be traced to Greek and Egyptian cultures. However, it has become a central doctrine in religions of India, including Hinduism, Buddhism, Jainism, and Sikhism. Christian leaders reject reincarnation, although a 2003 Harris poll found that 21% of Christians do believe (Taylor, 2003). Many biblical stories of the dead coming back to life (Jesus wasn't the only one) share some key attributes of reincarnation (a person dies, an essential part lives on and returns to life). More recently, spiritualists and followers of many new age movements believe in reincarnation, focusing more on the process of rebirth than ultimate release.

Believers in reincarnation often cite the work of Ian Stevenson (1980, 1997), who devoted over 40 years to tracking down leads and claims. Many have criticized this research, including Edwards (1996) and Roach (2005). The most popular evidence includes child prodigies, strange birthmarks, déjà vu, and past-life regression. His arguments include the following (see if you can figure out the criticism before reading what skeptics say):

- History provides numerous accounts of unexceptional parents who have children of extraordinary talent and genius. Where did they get their talent? Perhaps they were reincarnated from ancient geniuses. (Skeptics say such events are perfectly consistent with what we know about genetics. Genes may well be recessive and not emerge for many generations.)
- There are numerous accounts of infants born with wounds that appear similar to those relatives recall of long deceased relatives. (But wounds are like inkblots, clouds in the sky, or craters on the Moon. One can see in them what one wants.)
- A déjà vu experience is the uncanny feeling that one has been somewhere before. A reincarnationist might explain that your hunch that you've been somewhere is evidence that you have actually been there. (Such an uncanny feeling proves nothing and can be readily evoked by suggestion or in laboratory settings.)
- Much of Stevenson's evidence for reincarnation is based on simple memories, usually of individuals who already believe strongly in reincarnation. A mother might claim that her infant daughter acts very much like her great-grandmother, or that her son is afraid of rats, just like a great-grandfather. Such memories can be quite vivid suggesting their veracity. (Humans are quite prone to memory error and false memory. Clarity of a memory and event is no proof that it is accurate.)

## Parapsychology

Parapsychology (Greek for "beyond/beside" the "mind/soul/reason") is the scientific study of paranormal psychological claims. Although parapsychologists also study paranormal healing and life-after-death claims (mediums, ghosts, reincarnation), they often consider basic parapsychological processes as alternative explanations (are you actually receiving thought messages from a dead relative, or thoughts from a living acquaintance of the relative?). Many parapsychologists passionately dissociate themselves from astrology, witchcraft, and spiritualism (Irwin & Watt, 2007). Although early parapsychological research involved much pseudoscience, current researchers often make a genuine attempt to deploy rigorous critical thinking and apply serious reality checks.

### A Dictionary of Parapsychology

Here are the terms parapsychologists use (Irwin & Watt, 2007). First, **psi** (and occasionally "anomalous cognition") is a general term for all parapsychological phenomena (Thouless & Wiesner, 1948). There are two types of psi:

1) **Extrasensory perception** (ESP, receptive psi, paranormal cognition, or psi-gamma) is the acquisition of information about, or response to, an external object or influence not using any known sensory channel.

A) **Precognition** (premonition, fortune-telling, prophecy) is a form of ESP in which the target is a future event that cannot be known from present data.

B) **Retrocognition** is a form of ESP in which the target is a past event that could not have been learned or inferred by normal means. It is seeing into the past.

C) **Telepathy** (thought-transference) is the paranormal acquisition of information concerning the thoughts, feelings, or activities of

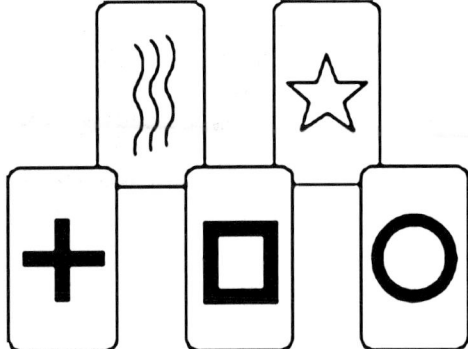

**Figure 14.2** Zener cards (used in ESP research).

another conscious person. When the source of information is out of range of the senses (in another room, in another country), telepathy of perceptions is often called **remote viewing**.

D) **Clairvoyance** is the acquisition of information directly from an external object or physical event (viewing a concealed photograph), not through the thoughts or perceptions of someone else. When the source of information is out of range of the senses, clairvoyance is also sometimes called **remote viewing**.

2) **Psychokinesis** (PK, expressive psi, paranormal action, or psi-kappa) is the direct influence of thought on physical objects or processes (moving things, bending spoons) or living systems.

### Research and History

In America, serious research on psi began with the card-guessing studies of Joseph Banks Rhine, wife Louisa Rhine, and other colleagues. Rhine coined the term "**extrasensory perception**." The Rhines were skeptical of the popular mediums of the day and chose a different path of investigation. They began their work at Duke University by examining the claims that a remarkable horse, Lady Wonder, could answer human questions by "typing" or kicking alphabet blocks. Rhine tested Lady Wonder and concluded she was genuine. However, he later concluded her powers were the result of trickery (Christopher, 1970).

Rhine began his research into ESP in 1930 with the help of his colleague, Carl Zener. Quickly the use of traditional cards was discarded (the images were too complicated), and Zener developed a deck of 25 cards (the now-famous **Zener cards**) in which each card had one of five simple symbols: star, cross, circle, wavy lines, and square. In a guessing experiment, by chance one would correctly pick 5 out of the 25.

Rhine's first experiments were the most successful; participants could guess slightly above chance. After 100,000 trials, Rhine announced to the world that he had finally made a world-changing discovery, a scientific demonstration of psi phenomena (Rhine, 1934).

Today, researchers discount the first decade of Rhine's work with Zener cards after noting that symbols embossed on card faces left slight indentations on card backs. In addition, subjects could see and hear the experimenter, and note subtle but revealing facial expressions or changes in breathing. (Do you see any possibility of stimulus leakage?) The psi effect would mysteriously disappear whenever a magician was present in the Rhine laboratory.

In the face of these and other failures, psi researchers attempted various explanations, notions that quickly rose to the level of established scientific theory. Remarkably, they present an illustration of how technobabble can evolve into apparent fact. Rhine suggested that psi studies are difficult to replicate because of a psi **decline effect**. Participants may initially score high, but through fatigue and boredom, eventually perform at chance levels. Students of statistics readily recognize that there is nothing paranormal about this example of **regression to the mean**. A more creative *ad hoc* explanation is that psi works only when researchers and participants are believers, termed "**sheep**." Somehow, skeptics and magicians, termed "**goats**," emit some sort of mysterious influence or vibration that negates any psi effect (Schmeidler, 1945). The resulting negative effect is termed **psi-missing**. Similarly, psi is described as a **jealous phenomenon**, one that disappears under close scrutiny, or is manifest only when tested by True Believers. Finally, the claimed psi **displacement effect** occurs when subjects predict the card that immediately *follows* or *precedes* each card being sent. Can you see how such explanations might render psi explanations unfalsifiable?

### Sample Research: Remote Viewing and the CIA Stargate Program

Conspiracy theorists sometimes claim the CIA funds psi research. Has this happened? Yes. Not only that, but early test subjects were high-level members of the Church of Scientology who used their Scientology techniques to develop paranormal powers. Between 1969 and 1971 there were reports that the Soviet Union was engaged in extensive psi research on a variety of exotic attempts, including using psychics for long-distance assassination. In 1972 the CIA enlisted the efforts of the SRI (Stanford Research Institute, which has no connections to the university) to investigate psi in a legendary project named Project Stargate. In 1990 the program was given to Science Applications International Corporation (SAIC). The overall goal of this research was to determine if talented psychics could be used as spies and obtain crucial military information not available through ordinary channels. The project was extensive and eventually cost $20 million.

Much of this research was conducted by Russell Targ and Harold Puthoff, himself a talented Scientologist. Their work focused on remote viewing and began with gifted "empaths" from the Church of Scientology who had progressed to OT (Operating Thetan) Level VII, a high achievement associated with extraordinary powers. Later, Stargate focused on subjects not involved with Scientology and ultimately tested over 20 individuals.

One can find numerous examples of remote viewing on the web. Although often dramatic, most illustrate cherry-picking, errors of very large numbers, confirmation bias, and pareidolia. Imagine a remote viewer (RV) walks into a classroom of 20 students. He asks students to make a simple drawing, and then turn their work over so it can't be viewed. The RV then takes a blank sheet of paper, closes his eyes in psychic contemplation, and announces he has remotely viewed one of the student's drawings, even though it is hidden. Smiling, he draws a three-inch stick with a circle on top, about the size of a quarter. With great excitement, a student waves her drawing and announces: "He got it right! See! I drew my bald grandfather, standing and waving to me." Another student waves his drawing, "Yes, here it is! A drawing of a sunflower!" Our psychic proclaims, "Very impressive! I have super

ESP! I read two drawings, and remotely fused them into my drawing! See the obvious similarities. This is truly an example of quantum entanglement!" Any alternative explanations? (Imagine another student chimes in, "I drew a flat cube." Our RV replies "Ah, you have negative energy, so I drew just the opposite of what you drew. I must be on a roll!")

Targ and Puthoff's remote viewing procedure was a bit more sophisticated than popular examples. For example, a sender might be instructed to visit a randomly selected series of locations such as an airport, bridge, park, or library (Hines, 2003) while a receiver remains in a laboratory. At specific times the sender attempts to mentally communicate to the receiver information concerning a site he or she is currently observing. The receiver immediately begins speaking and reports any impressions received. These (as well as comments from the attending experimenter) are tape-recorded and transcribed. Thus, at the end of this phase of the project the sender will have visited a specific number of sites, and the receiver will have produced the same number of impressions.

Then a rater, blind to the identity of the sender and receiver, might be taken to each site, given transcripts of impressions for all sites, and asked to determine which transcript was associated with each site. What could possibly go wrong with this design? Actually, one cannot tell by reading direct published accounts. Years of detective work have uncovered some unreported facts.

Targ and Puthoff (1977) report over 100 such experiments and claim spectacular support for remote viewing (Carroll claims up to 1,000; 2014). Marks (2000) examined the available transcripts and identified a serious flaw, stimulus leakage. For example, raters were told the specific order in which locations were visited. So they knew that the "university library" was visited/transmitted first and the "bridge" visited/transmitted last. You might think that this is a trivial matter, except that transcripts contained clues that gave away the order in which they were recorded. For example, one transcript might contain the phrase "Don't be nervous, you're just starting" (Hines, 2003). Thus, a rater would know this site was visited first. The Stargate project was compromised by several instances of stimulus leakage.

A distressing number of additional problems plagued the program. Occasional "hits" could have been chance occurrences, given the large number of trials. Reviewers have noted instances of researchers weakening claimed protocols (Marks, 2000). Finally, the fact that key researchers (in violation of accepted research ethics) refused to share raw data makes it difficult to examine possible lapses in design and analysis. Most important, claimed findings could not be replicated in independent laboratories when proper designs were deployed and possible stimulus leakage was removed (Marks, 2000; Randi, 1982). The program was abandoned in 1995 after 24 years of fruitless research. Note that even pro-psi reviewers are in disagreement. Radin (1997) views Project Stargate as a remarkable success. Irwin and Watt (2007), in their decidedly pro-psi text, mention the research in one short paragraph noting the conflicting conclusions we have mentioned. At the very least, Project Stargate emphasizes the importance of adhering to our FEDS Standard when doing psi research.

### Sample Research: New Directions

Early psi research relied on a handful of subjects, perhaps famous psychics, respected astrologers, channelers with an apparently impressive record, or everyday people reporting what they see while viewing images or taking a stroll. However, one might argue this is the wrong strategy. Perhaps we need to search for the strongest "psi signal" possible. This has been the new direction recent psi research has taken.

### Boosting the Signal and Reducing Noise

People who report paranormal events in everyday life frequently describe events of considerable emotional intensity (premonitions of the death of a loved one, messages of distress from a spouse, for example). Stimuli such as Zener cards have little emotional impact. In research, one might have psychics send emotionally strong, violent images (Moulton and Kosslyn, 2008) or images of strong sexual content (Bem, 2011). Such strategies have not produced convincing evidence, or have failed replication. Numerous "noise reduction" strategies have been deployed, including sensory deprivation or "ganzfeld" environments, sleep and dreams, hypnosis, and meditation, all with unimpressive results (Child, 1985; Honorton, 1985).

Researchers have even attempted to remove distraction by measuring subtle unconscious neurological brain activity through functional magnetic resonance imaging. In the best brain study of its kind, Moulton and Kosslyn (2008) attempted to maximize sensitivity. Specifically, they settled on a procedure that would detect not only precognition (such as guessing cards), but telepathy, clairvoyance, and even (although they fail to note this) psychokinesis. Furthermore, the study used emotionally related participants (e.g., twins, relatives, friends, roommates) and emotional stimuli, both features which previous psi researchers have speculated should enhance psi. In line with recommendations from psi researchers, senders were instructed to maintain a playful attitude and an active interest in their task. Target stimuli, those selected to be "transmitted," were chosen to differ as much as possible in emotional valence and intensity. That is, some stimuli were highly negative (e.g., eye surgery), positive (e.g., erotic couple), neutral (e.g., a simple face or tissue box), or low negative or positive. Finally, they deployed a measure of "unconscious" and "conscious" brain activity, functional magnetic resonance imaging (fMRI).

Let me attempt a simplified summary of the design of study. First, stimulus photos were assembled into pairs so that each pair included a positive and a neutral or negative photo. A sender and receiver were placed in different rooms, limiting the possibility of stimulus leakage. Then sender and receiver proceeded with 240 trials. The basic idea was simple. The sender viewed and transmitted a randomly selected image. The receiver viewed two images, one being the transmitted image. fMRI recordings could detect if the receiver unconsciously recognized which of the two was in fact the sent image.

Results revealed no differences in brain activity for images correctly and incorrectly identified. That is, the brains of participants reacted the same to psi and non-psi stimuli. Finally, participants were not able to select or guess transmitted images. It should be noted that some physiological studies do claim mixed results (for reviews see Beloff, 1974; Braud, Shafer, & Andrews, 1993a, 1993b). However, the most rigorous find nothing. Nonetheless, an open-minded critically thinking paranormal researcher might be advised to pursue this line of investigation over, say, less promising topics such as communicating with the dead, haunted houses, reincarnation, and pixies.

## Meta-analyses and Computerized Mass Studies

The most distant galaxies are invisible to the naked eye. However, they can be detected by groups of powerful telescopes together, taking thousands of photographs over weeks. Combining huge numbers of photographs enables astronomers to gather enough photons, or packets of light energy, to detect the faintest of stellar objects. Similarly, some subatomic forces are so tiny that huge particle accelerators must conduct millions of trials in order to detect their operation. Perhaps psi is a star or force so faint that evidence becomes clear only after examining a large number of participants. This can be achieved through meta-analysis.

Meta-analysis is a popular statistical method in which the results of many studies can be treated as a single large study. Bösch, Steinkamp, & Boller (2006) have conducted what may be the most comprehensive meta-analysis of random number generator research. In these studies a truly random process, such as the decay of a radioactive sample, triggers a sequence of numbers. They combined the results of 380 studies and found a very small but significant effect. However, they concluded that the results are likely the result of the file drawer effect. To review (Chapter 4), if researchers who obtain negative effects choose not to publish their results (and simply put them in the file drawer), and if journals tend not to publish negative findings, then the resulting literature will include a misleading number of positive findings. If all findings were included, the unpublished negative results would cancel out the published positive findings (Bausell, 2007, p. 198).

Meta-analysis is a controversial and quirky tool. It is statistically possible for a meta-analysis to combine 50 studies, none of which report significant results, and generate a spurious significant overall result (Alcock, 1981). Most researchers who conduct meta-analyses wisely either omit what they judge to be poorly designed studies, or at least give such studies less statistical weight. However, those who have attempted this in psi research rarely agree on how to rate the studies included. As a result, almost invariably two researchers who conduct meta-analyses on the same set of studies come up with quite different (and often opposing) results.

What if we created a test for psi that is completely automatic, run entirely by computers with no human involvement? First, we would eliminate the contaminating noise of human interaction. Also, we could conduct very large numbers of trials at very low cost, and increase the likelihood of detecting the faint signals of psi.

With large numbers, even small sources of error (slight problems in the design of random number generating machines, temperature, "clumpiness" of data) can have an apparent effect. It has actually been demonstrated that with a very large randomly generated sample, an effect can be extremely small, *entirely spurious*, yet statistically significant (see Alcock, 1981).

In conclusion, much research and discussion has focused on the effects of PK on random number generation. Irwin and Watt (2007) offer the most reasonable summary, one that is still applicable after more than a decade: It is too early to draw a firm conclusion as to the authenticity of PK from meta-analyses. Yet, an open-minded critical thinking reviewer must recognize that some studies come tantalizingly close to finding an effect. In light of this advice, our well-funded hypothetical paranormal researcher might be advised to focus his or her efforts on this line of study.

---

### How to Prove You Have Psi Ability without an Expensive Lab

If you have a psychic ability, there are ample ways you can demonstrate your talents, and get rich. Play the lottery. Go to a casino. Invest in stocks. Use your powers to find hidden treasures. Write a book on positive thinking and appear on television.

But where are the rich psychic lottery-winners? Perhaps they are hiding their winnings for security purposes. One might argue that selfish pursuits of questionable morality cannot work because they are contrary to the spiritual nature of psi phenomena. (However, this has not prevented the Roman Catholic Church from running bingo games, or hundreds of psychics from getting rich off their schemes and books.)

Fortunately, there is a way for truly selfless psychics to demonstrate their powers, and benefit humankind. Over the past two decades, over 35 public challenge tests have offered substantial rewards for a demonstrated paranormal ability (e.g., http://www.skepdic.com/randi.html). Wikipedia offers an updated "list of prizes for evidence for the paranormal."

Today, over $2 million is available. Perhaps the most famous was the James Randi $1 million challenge open primarily to those with claimed paranormal powers who have received media attention. The challenge lasted from 1964 to 2015 and had no winners.

Finally, for psychics who must operate in isolation, far from the intrusive observations of scientists or temptations of material gain, Beloff (1985) offers a simple challenge. Produce a "permanent paranormal object" that could not be created by any means known to science. One might create a block of wood that seamlessly blends two types of timber, a living rabbit's foot with gold toes integrated at the sub-cellular level, iron that is liquid at room temperature, or pure copper wire that is superconductive at room temperature. Such an object could be taken to a lab and tested, or if the psychic prefers, simply kept for personal contemplation.

---

## Creationism, Intelligent Design, and Evolution

In the contemporary annals of the paranormal, perhaps the greatest story being told is the debate over creationism and evolution. **Young Earth creationists** posit that God created the universe as described in the book of Genesis. The world is only 6,000–10,000 years old (or "young"), created in six days. Then came the Flood, Noah's Ark, and eventually Jesus. Creationist thinking has made considerable headway. Up to half of Americans believe its central claims. It is a view that dominates Christian publishing. Presidents Carter (2005), Reagan (Holden, 1980), G. H. W. Bush (Boston, 1988), and G. W. Bush (Mooney, 2005) have all espoused creationist views. However, creationism is controversial, rejected by serious scientific organizations, and even condemned by the European Union as a threat to individual rights (Council of Europe, 2007). Outside of Bible colleges, it is rarely taught in biology classes. But that is where the controversy resides, one that is required reading for any serious student of open-minded critical thinking.

Should creationism be taught in schools as a part of the science curriculum (rather than in classes on religion, theology, or history)? The US Supreme Court decided in 1987 that the direct instruction of creationism as a scientific theory in biology is a serious violation of the constitution's first amendment establishment clause that separates church and state ("Congress shall make no law respecting an establishment of religion,

**Figure 14.3** Charles Darwin. Reproduced with kind permission of Science Source.

or prohibiting the free exercise thereof."). Furthermore, the Court decided in 2005 that science classes cannot teach that the universe is so complex that it must have a supernatural, and intelligent, designer, such as God (or logically perhaps a space alien, a being from the future, or the Flying Spaghetti Monster). This was struck down as religion in disguise in 2005 by a landmark case in Dover, Pennsylvania. Currently, some creationists argue that science classes should "teach the controversy" and present the "strengths and weaknesses" of various theories, including creationism vs. evolution. Logically, such a perspective would permit introducing astrology in astronomy class, the flat Earth theory in geography, witchcraft brews in chemistry, extrasensory perception in communication class, ghost theory in architecture (haunted houses), chi in physical education, and the stork theory of reproduction in health class. If we follow this yellow brick road, there will be truly no time left for real science.

**Kitzmiller v. Dover Area School District: Evidence in the Courtroom**

It was a week before Christmas in the small and sleepy town of Dover, Pennsylvania. In a major courtroom clash between creationism and science, a federal judge barred a Pennsylvania public school district from introducing creationism in biology class. The trial was an international sensation, involving top creationists and scientists. In the end, it redefined a centuries-old debate.

Darwin and Evolution

Here is a synopsis of the debate. In 1859 Charles Darwin published his theory of evolution in *On the Origin of Species*. He proposed that different species evolve through a process of natural selection and survival of the fittest. In any particular generation, mutations can alter an organism, for example, adding a limb, subtracting an organ, modifying a process, and so on. Most mutations are fatal, but an occasional mutation is an improvement. When sea creatures mutated with fins, they could swim. Because these improved organisms were better able to survive, they were more likely to have offspring, which in turn would carry on the mutation. Over hundreds of millions of years, bad mutations are sorted out and improved mutations add up, resulting in organisms remarkably fit for their environments. The evidence for evolution is considerable, including recently unearthed fossils of transitional "missing link" creatures (such as fish-like animals that evolved from fish and eventually into land animals), and complex genetic similarities between related species. Indeed, humans (including both evolutionists and creationists) share 98.8% of their DNA with chimpanzees.

### Creationists and Species Diversity

Intelligent design (ID) creationists (including Darwin at one time) argue that their God created each species independently and that different species are not linked through a common ancestry. As evidence, creationists often invoke a variety of arguments. First is the **argument from design: grand watchmaker version**:

> Anything that is complicated must be the product of an intelligent designer.
> The universe is complicated.
> Therefore the universe was created by an intelligent designer.

A grand watch requires a grand watchmaker. This was first posed by the Roman philosopher, lawyer, and statesman Cicero (1972), who argued that the complexity of a sundial implies a purposeful and intelligent sundial designer.

The argument from design can actually be applied to many paranormal claims. For example, only a remarkable mystical nonphysical energy, chi, can explain such diverse treatments as healing touch, acupuncture, tai chi, psychic surgery, and kundalini yoga.

Those on the other side of this argument might view the universe as a "cosmos half empty" and note all the mistakes in creation, such as sickness, ignorance, species extinction, and computers that never work right. God would have to be quite inept, or malicious, to create the universe we are stuck with.

ID creationists focus on a subtle theological variation of the argument from design, **irreducible complexity**. The notion of irreducible complexity states that some biological structures are so complex that if you remove a single part they will cease to function. Furthermore, a component part is useless in itself, and therefore had no adaptive reason to survive, let alone be part of a larger evolutionary process. Thus, the complete structure must have emerged spontaneously in full final form. The most famous example presented by ID creationists is the bacterial flagellum, perhaps the only example of a living organism with an actual functioning propeller as a tail. For years this remarkable structure mystified scientists. Indeed, it appeared to be irreducibly complex. However, biologists eventually discovered that the ID creationists were wrong, and that the bacterial flagellum could indeed be partially taken apart and still work, not as a propeller but as a syringe (useful for injecting disease). ID creationists are prone to use a shotgun strategy, showering biologists with marvelously complex examples that defy explanation. How could evolution possibly lead to such miracles as the human eye or immune system? In every case, when biologists carefully study a claimed miracle of complexity, they discover how it is indeed not irreducibly complex but evolved from simpler structures.

Another variation of the argument from design is the **anthropic principle**, the notion that the universe is fine-tuned for life (Barrow & Tipler, 1988). To understand, one has to begin with the idea that in the universe there are certain constants that are the same everywhere. These include the speed of light, the amount of matter in the universe, and the strength of the force that binds atomic nuclei. Everywhere in the universe these are exactly the same. Rees (2000) argues that there are six such "cosmic numbers," and if any one of them were even slightly different, the universe could not permit life. Thus, the universe appears to be fine-tuned for life, suggesting a fine-tuning entity, a grand designer, a god at the control panel. This is a fascinating and important philosophical argument that belongs in a philosophy class, not in a science class. Skeptics argue that there is no experiment one could perform to test the cosmic effects of adjusting the constants of physics. And one can just as easily speculate that there are an infinite number of universes, and just by chance a few pop up fine-tuned for life. Or perhaps it is not an accident that the cosmic numbers are what they are; maybe some yet-to-be-discovered grand unifying theory will show that the values of cosmic numbers are what they are for a very good scientific reason.

Creationists also cite the theological **cosmological argument: the first cause**. Here one begins with the presumption that everything has to be caused by something. So considering the entire universe, what created it? Logically, this cause would have to be larger and greater than what it caused, that is, supernatural. Skeptics reply, "Who created the first cause? Who created God?" and argue that the argument of the first cause traps us in a logical black hole, an absurd **infinite regression**, and the only way out is to apply Occam's razor by accepting the simplest explanation. The universe just is. Or maybe there are multiple universes.

An important component of the debate is a consideration of what is science. First, we have seen that creationists frequently use untestable theological arguments to support empirical claims. The arguments from design, irreducible complexity, the anthropic principle, and the cosmological argument are purely theological notions that may well belong in high school or college classes. But they are not science and should not be taught in science class.

Second, creationists display a misunderstanding of the nature of science. Often they claim that Darwinian evolution is "only a theory" and should be presented fairly with other equally worthy theories, notably ID creationism. This confuses everyday and scientific uses of the term "theory." In everyday usage, a theory is a hunch. You may have a theory of who swiped the cookies. In science, a theory is the highest form of scientific explanation, one that has withstood numerous tests, and accounts for more facts than any competing theory. A theory is falsifiable (testable), productive, comprehensive, and simple. According to these criteria, the theory of evolution may well be among the best theories science has invented. It is falsifiable and productive, and has generated thousands of testable hypotheses. Sometimes these hypotheses involve real-time experiments (changing the environment for fruit flies, and observing them evolve through their fleeting generations) and careful observation of existing evidence (digging up fossils in search of missing-link transitional organisms). It is comprehensive, tying together mountains of evidence from geology, biology, chemistry, and even astronomy. As Isaac Asimov has stated, "the strongest of all indications as to the fact of evolution and the truth of the theory of natural selection is that all the independent findings of scientists in every branch of science, when they have anything to do with biological evolution at all, *always* strengthen the case and *never* weaken it" (Asimov & Gish, 1981).

In contrast, ID creationism fails miserably as a theory. It has difficulty producing testable hypotheses and some versions are probably untestable. Instead of generating hypotheses, ID creationism is essentially negativistic (arguing from ignorance), poking holes rather than proposing. Although ID creationism has wide scope in that God is posited to have created everything, this assertion explains nothing. What court would accept "the Devil did it" as a theory explaining a bank robbery? Any event, as well as its antithesis, can be explained as "God's will." Most seriously, ID creationism fails the test of simplicity. The God hypothesis begs more questions than it answers. When? Where? How? Which God? Furthermore, ID creationism has the troubling complexity that it cannot be adopted "without discarding all of modern biology, biochemistry, geology, astronomy—in short, without discarding all of science" (Asimov & Gish, 1981). In sum, ID creationism is a supernatural explanation, and as such it is a "science stopper" (Miller, 2007).

### Science and Religion

Mixing science and theology is a risky venture, pseudoscience at its worst. Biologist and paleontologist Steven Jay Gould (1999) has offered a popular way out, one that merits some discussion. Perhaps religion and science represent separate domains of authority, or Nonoverlapping Magisteria (NOMA). Specifically, science is a "magisterium" that covers the empirical world of scientific fact and theory; religion considers questions of meaning, beauty, and moral value. This position is similar to that taken by The National Academy of Sciences (Steering Committee on Science and Creationism, 2008). But this brings up more theological questions.

First, a good theory indeed can be immensely beautiful. Second, honesty, truth, and openness are powerful scientific values. Third, if religion doesn't deal with the physical world, then religious people shouldn't pray for changes in the physical world (healing, peace, etc.) or changes in the brains of distant leaders (wisdom, compassion). But they do in just about every house of worship I know.

## A Parting Thought

In the back pages of the current discussions of astrology, spiritualism, parapsychology, and even God, one occasionally finds an interesting point of agreement between passionate skeptics and believers, for example Sam Harris (*The End of Faith*, 2004) and Christian Bishop John Shelby Spong (*Jesus for the Non-Religious*, 2007). It is an invitation to take very seriously that which one experiences to be most profound and fills one with awe and mystery. Such ideas are beyond the scope of this book. However, let me conclude our journey of open-minded critical thinking with a personal thought.

In the darkness of night, we gaze into the eyes of Sagittarius, the constellation viewed by astrologers millennia ago. We feel awe and wonder. Mystery. Perhaps a touch of reverence. What do such feelings tell us? Does some quantum entanglement physically link us with heavenly forces? Does some secret spirit infuse us with magical psychic power? These may or may not be the case. However, the stars remain.

Perhaps the quiet night holds a message. Our deepest feelings need not be a distraction. Seen clearly, they can inspire a humble appreciation of our true place in the universe. They can guide us to handle life's onslaughts with greater equanimity. They can prompt us to care more generously for those in our human family. And perhaps, for one precious moment, they may awaken us from our daydreams of centaurs and open our eyes to things wise and wonderful. The searing beauty of the universe as it is.

**Figure 14.4** Centaur. Reproduced with kind permission of Fotolia.

## Study Questions

**14.1** *Definitions (Define, differentiate, and provide an example for each of the following)*

*Astrology*
- A. Divination
- B. Zodiac
- C. Houses
- D. Signs
- E. Sun sign
- F. Natal sign
- G. Natal astrology
- H. Sagittarius
- I. Sagittarius A*
- J. Ascendant sign
- K. Rising sign
- L. Precession
- M. Supermassive black hole

*Spiritualism and the Survival Hypothesis*
- A. Survival hypothesis
- B. Spiritualism
- C. Séances
- D. Mediums
- E. Channeling
- F. Sitter
- G. Reincarnation

*Parapsychology*
- A. Parapsychology
- B. Psi
- C. Extrasensory perception
- D. ESP
- E. Precognition
- F. Retrocognition
- G. Telepathy
- H. Remote viewing
- I. Clairvoyance
- J. Psychokinesis
- K. PK
- L. Zener cards
- M. Decline effect
- N. Regression to the mean
- O. Sheep
- P. Goats
- Q. Psi-missing
- R. Jealous phenomenon

- S. Displacement effect
- T. Stargate Program
- U. Ganzfeld
- V. Meta-analysis
- W. Random number generators
- X. Project Alpha
- Y. Million dollar challenge

*Creationism, Intelligent Design, and Evolution*
- A. Creationism
- B. Young Earth creationism
- C. The Kitzmiller v. Dover case
- D. Argument from design
- E. Grand watchmaker argument
- F. Irreducible complexity
- G. Anthropic principle
- H. Cosmological argument: the first cause
- I. Nonoverlapping Magisteria

**14.2** *Thought Questions*

*Astrology*
- A. Using the tools of logic, evaluate this astrological claim: Mars was the god of war. Warriors are active and aggressive. Athletes are also active. So where the planet Mars appears at a certain point in the sky at the time of one's birth should be associated with athleticism.
- B. Conduct an internet search for sites promoting astrology. What types of support do they use?

*Spiritualism and the Survival Hypothesis*
- A. A simple study of channeling should involve some basic controls. First, the medium and sitter should be prevented from viewing each other while the medium is presenting an improvised reading. The medium may even be in a different state and never communicate with or view the sitter. The medium could type out readings which are then presented to the sitter for evaluation. Is this the best way of preventing stimulus leakage? Can you think of any other strategies? How might a devious researcher, or medium, get around this design?
- B. A TV psychic claims to have communicated with the departed grandmother of an audience member. How could you determine that he was not actually communicating with the unconscious of the audience member (or another departed relative, or time-traveling alien)?

*Parapsychology*
- A. Your astrological horoscope accurately predicts what you will do tomorrow. Can you think of a nonparanormal alternative explanation? A paranormal explanation might invoke which psi phenomenon?

- B. Your psychic healer places his hands over your stomach and cures your stomach ache (no lemon tea is involved). What psi processes might be involved?
- C. Frequently, the first researchers of a paranormal claim obtain strong positive results, which are subsequently not replicated. In areas of scientific research not involving paranormal phenomena, the opposite pattern is common: first studies find a faint effect, and later studies report a stronger effect. How might you explain this difference?
- D. Think of alternative explanations for the remote viewing examples given in your text.
- E. Irwin and Watt (2007) acknowledge the skeptics' criticism that evidence for ESP may be the result of artifact. However, they go on to state: "This line of argument certainly should not be accepted without subjecting the specific claims to further empirical scrutiny" (p. 81). Where does this place the burden of proof? Compare this with "Sagan's Balance."
- F. How does the "decline effect" reflect regression to the mean?
- G. On the internet, find a site that presents arguments and evidence for one of the following claimed parapsychological phenomena:
  - ○ Precognition
  - ○ Telepathy
  - ○ Clairvoyance
  - ○ Psychokinesis

First, summarize the arguments and evidence given.

Second, provide an alternative explanation using one or more of the following:
  - ○ Misunderstanding of statistics
  - ○ Perceptual error
  - ○ Trickery, deception, and magic
  - ○ Memory error
  - ○ Unusual sensory phenomena or hallucinations

*Creationism, Intelligent Design, and Evolution*
- A. Is deception and trickery a proper tool for teaching the skills of open-minded critical thinking? How are the tricks of shamans any different from James Randi's Project Alpha described earlier?
- B. What are the logical problems with the argument from design and grand watchmaker argument.
- C. What is NOMA? Why is it popular? What are some of the problems with this perspective?

*Entire Chapter*
- A. All of the topics in this chapter have victims of hoaxes, fraud, and deception. On the internet, find an example of such trickery for each. Search "hoax astrology," "hoax parapsychology," "fraud faith healing," "deception creationism," etc. What are the incentives that motivate those who engage in such trickery?
- B. What's the harm? Search the internet for examples of harm caused by each of the paranormal claims discussed in this chapter. Search: "What's the harm?"

**14.3**   *Videos. Search the internet for videos on the following. Discuss textbook concepts illustrated.*

*Astrology*
- A. Precession and astrology
- B. Bill Nye on astrology
- C. Carl Sagan on astrology

*Spiritualism and the Survival Hypothesis*
- A. Babysitter cam
- B. Ghost hunters
- C. Harry Houdini

*Parapsychology*
- A. Pickover online ESP experiment
- B. Tittel remote viewing
- C. Moulton and Kosslyn experiment
- D. Michael Shermer remote viewing
- E. SRI experiments Uri Geller
- F. Uri Geller Johnny Carson
- G. Uri Geller James Randi
- H. Randi spoon bending
- I. How to bend a spoon, spoon bending tutorial
- J. Million dollar challenge Randi
- K. Randi Project Alpha

*Creationism, Intelligent Design, Evolution*
- A. BBC *Horizon* Dover trial
- B. NOVA PBS documentary Dover trial: "Judgment Day"
- C. Argument from design banana version
- D. Argument from design peanut butter version

# Appendix A

## Why Do You Believe?

*Nicholas Borgogna and Jonathan C. Smith[1]*

Perhaps the most popular question asked by researchers of the paranormal is "What do you believe?" For decades dozens of public opinion polls have tapped the popularity of beliefs from angels to zombies, and continue to do so.

How one asks such questions affects the answers one gets. Surveys usually deploy a simple dichotomous "yes/no" format. Using this format, huge majorities believe in angels (68–72%) and a literal Devil (60–70%). Nearly half believe in ghosts and extra-sensory perception. Nearly a majority reject evolution. The apparent popularity of paranormal claims has been a frequent observation of most, if not all, texts of critical thinking, prompting many anguished paragraphs about failures of our educational system, the dominance of anti-scientific thinking in politics, and the merging of religion and politics. But is such commentary justified? Indeed, an Open-Minded Critical Thinker might wonder if the popularity of certain paranormal claims suggests they merit serious research. Regardless of one's stance, the popularity of beliefs revealed by traditional polls obscures information important for both believers and skeptics.

First, polls rarely ask why one believes. For decades researchers have explored a variety of explanations (Newberg and Waldman, 2006; Shermer, 2012). For example, studies have looked at the role of unfalsifiable arguments (Friesen, Campbell, & Kay, 2014) and personality characteristics such as paranoia or openness to experience (Goertzel, 1994; Swami et al., 2013). But what do believers claim? What information do we gain when we replace yes/no questions with a more differentiated inquiry? What justifications do believers give for their acceptance of extraordinary claims?

## Procedure

We used the Belief Justifications Survey (BJS). This scale consists of 22 items that assess nine belief justifications derived through factor analysis of 64 item candidates assessing justifications considered in a popular text of critical thinking. Scales include:

1) *Argument from ignorance* ("This shows there's a lot science doesn't know about the world. This is real because there's no evidence against it. This is a mysterious truth science can't explain.")

*Critical Thinking: Pseudoscience and the Paranormal*, Second Edition. Jonathan C. Smith.
© 2018 John Wiley & Sons, Inc. Published 2018 by John Wiley & Sons, Inc.

2) *Conspiracy theory* ("The medical/scientific community doesn't want people to know about these things. The authorities are keeping this kind of information from us.")

3) *Eyewitness testimonial* ("This is something many people have experienced. This has been described in many eyewitness reports.")

4) *Family and culture* ("This is something my family has accepted for a long time. This is something I've been taught is true. This is something people in my culture generally believe.")

5) *Faith and religion* ("This is supported by my spiritual and religious teachers. This is supported by the existence of God. This is consistent with my faith.")

6) *Media support* ("This is supported on TV shows and documentaries. This has often been reported in the news media.")

7) *Personal experience/intuition* ("This is something I have personally experienced. This is true because it just feels right. This fits what my intuition tells me.")

8) *Science* ("This is supported by science. This is supported by research studies by scientists and experts.")

9) *Test of time* ("This has passed the test of time. If something has lasted this long, there must be something to it.")

The BJS asks one to indicate why one believes or does not believe in a single targeted belief, described in a box on the top of the inventory, for example "Astrology." One is first asked, "To what extent do you believe or disbelieve in the above?" (1 = I do not believe in this, 2 = I believe a little, 3 = I believe somewhat, 4 = I believe a lot). One is then asked, "Why do you believe or disbelieve in the above?" The nine justification items (plus three filler scales) are rated on a four-point Likert scale (1 = I do not believe, 2 = I believe a little, 3 = I believe somewhat, 4 = I believe very much).

We distributed 12 versions of the BJS to 554 undergraduates from a Midwestern university. Each individual received a randomly selected survey targeting one belief from the following list:

1) Acupuncture and other Oriental treatments cure through an invisible and mysterious energy field
2) Angels are literally real
3) Astrology
4) Communicating with the dead
5) Dream prophecy
6) Flying saucers from other planets have visited Earth
7) Fortune-telling and seeing into the future
8) Ghosts and haunted houses
9) Herbal medicine
10) Prayer can heal people from a great distance, even when they don't know they're being prayed for (distant healing prayer)
11) Psychic mind-reading and extrasensory perception (psychics/ESP)
12) Reincarnation and past lives

## Results and Discussion

We examined both level of belief and justifications applied to specific belief claims.

## Levels of Belief

Most belief surveys deploy dichotomous or "yes/no" rating scales. An important recent exception is the Chapman University Survey on American Fears (Chapman, 2014). We find that this obscures very important information, as discussed in Chapter 3. Table A1 shows the levels of belief for each belief claim.

**Table A1** Levels of belief by claim.

| (Numbers in brackets show percentages of "believers" in generic polls) | I DO NOT BELIEVE (%) | I BELIEVE A LITTLE (%) | I BELIEVE SOMEWHAT (%) | I BELIEVE VERY MUCH (%) |
|---|---|---|---|---|
| PATTERN 1: BELIEF | | | | |
| Herbal medicine [75] | 5.6 | 19.4 | 38.6 | 36.4 |
| PATTERN 2: OPEN-MINDED QUESTIONING | | | | |
| Astrology [23.1] | 9.8 | 43.9 | 34.1 | 12.2 |
| Acupuncture [1.5 claim to use[1]] | 14.3 | 40.5 | 35.7 | 9.5 |
| Psychic mind-reading/ESP [35.5] | 16.7 | 40.5 | 35.7 | 7.1 |
| Dream prophecy [55.2] | 19.1 | 26.2 | 45.2 | 9.5 |
| PATTERN 3: POLARIZATION | | | | |
| Ghosts/haunted houses [40.5] | 9.3 | 34.9 | 18.6 | 37.2 |
| Reincarnation [19.1] | 30.5 | 22.2 | 30.6 | 16.7 |
| Communicating with dead [21.3] | 28.1 | 37.5 | 21.9 | 12.5 |
| Prayer at a distance [83.0] | 24.4 | 19.5 | 26.8 | 29.3 |
| PATTERN 4: SKEPTICISM | | | | |
| Angels [71.7] | 33.3 | 22.3 | 16.6 | 27.8 |
| Fortune-telling [22.8] | 42.1 | 36.8 | 15.8 | 5.3 |
| Flying saucers [34.8] | 50.0 | 15.6 | 28.1 | 6.3 |

1 Clarke et al. (2015). Retrieved February 7, 2017, from: https://www.cdc.gov/nchs/data/nhsr/nhsr079.pdf

**Justifications Used by Believers**

A total of 354 indicated some level of belief in their assigned belief (that is, they indicated they "believed a little," "believed somewhat," or "believed a lot," by checking "2, 3, or 4" on the belief Likert scale.

What do students believe? Why do they believe? We found it depends very much on how you ask the question. A crude examination of mean justification scores for our sample reveals which justifications appear to be most popular overall:

1) Test of time (<u>mean</u> = 2.43, <u>standard deviation</u> = .87)
2) Eyewitness testimonial (2.41, .87)
3) Argument from ignorance (2.31, .73)
4) Media support (2.18, .83)
5) Personal experience/intuition (2.13, .83)
6) Family and culture (2.05, .97)
7) Faith and religion (1.92, .95)
8) Science (1.80, .86)
9) Conspiracy theory (1.79, .89)

But this metric is misleading because it fails to take into account *level of belief*. Some justifications become increasingly important as level of belief rises. That is, believers use different justifications than those who are more moderate in their belief.

By differentiating level of belief in a paranormal claim, we can apply a more refined statistic, stepwise multiple regression. Multiple regression tells us what combination of justifications most effectively predicts degree of belief. If we know what justifications a person values, we can begin to predict how strongly they hold their selected paranormal belief.

We entered as primary predictors test of time, eyewitness testimonial, argument from ignorance, media support, personal experience/intuition, family and culture, faith and religion, science, and conspiracy theory.[2]

Four justifications accounted for the largest portion of belief (40%). By far, students justify their paranormal beliefs by claiming *personal experience/intuition*. This accounts for 34% of belief in a claim. *Argument from ignorance* and *family and culture*, taken together add 5%, and *science* just about 1%.

These variables far outweigh variables that did not contribute to level of belief, including faith and religion, media support, test of time, and conspiracy theory.

An even more differentiated portrait of justifications emerges if we look at each paranormal claim individually. Are the justifications given by those who believe in astrology the same as those given by believers in dream prophecy? Here we conducted an overall MANOVA[3] and then pairwise comparisons for each claimed paranormal claim.

### Personal Experience/Intuition

Those who believe in angels are uniquely likely to justify their belief on personal experience/intuition, faith and religion, and family and culture. The only other group equally likely to justify belief on personal experience/intuition are those who believe in dream prophecy. With the exception of those who believe in angels, dream prophecy, astrology, herbal medicine, and flying saucers, those who believe in other paranormal claims display few differences in their relative likelihood of justifications for their beliefs.

### Faith and Religion; Family and Culture
Those who believe in angels are far more likely to justify their belief based on faith and religion as well as family and culture.

### Science
Those who believe in astrology and herbal medicine are similar in that they are particularly likely to base their beliefs on science.

### Conspiracy Theory
Those who believe in flying saucers are particularly likely to justify their belief based on perceived conspiracy theory.

### Additional Tentative Comparisons
The following comparisons are less robust, involving fewer beliefs. We mention them to encourage future research.

- Believers in fortune-telling, when compared to believers in herbal medicine, distant healing prayer, and reincarnation, are more likely to suspect their claim is the result of trick or delusion. This is consistent with our finding that 42.1% of our sample does not believe and 36.8% believe only slightly in fortune-telling. Fortune-teller believers appear to be among the most skeptical of our groups of believers.
- Believers in dream prophecy are somewhat more likely to justify their beliefs with personal experience/intuition than believers in fortune-telling, psychics/ESP, reincarnation, and flying saucers.
- Believers in astrology as well as fortune-telling are more likely to justify their belief as entertainment ("It's just fun to believe it.") than believers in herbs and distant prayer.
- Believers in acupuncture as well as fortune-telling are especially unlikely to justify their beliefs based on media support, especially when compared to believers in ghosts and herbs.
- However, believers in herbs are more likely to justify their belief based on media support than believers in distant prayer and reincarnation.
- Believers in herbs are more likely to justify their belief based on the test of time than believers in reincarnation or psychics/ESP.

Future researchers will likely uncover a richer portrait of justifications by restricting their attention to one or two belief claims.

# Appendix B

# Belief Justification Survey

*Jonathan C. Smith, PhD*

The Belief Justification Scale (BJS) is designed to assess reasons or justifications participants give for embracing or rejecting various paranormal claims. Development of the scale started with 64 item candidates, each reflecting a belief rationale obtained from Smith's text "Pseudoscience and Extraordinary Claims of the Paranormal." Through extensive factor analysis involving 600 participants, the initial list of 64 candidates was reduced to 12 orthogonal belief factors, each reflecting a reason one believes or doesn't believe in a particular paranormal claim: trick or delusion, personal experience or intuition, faith and religion, family and culture, argument from ignorance, coincidence or error, entertainment, media, popular witness, science, test of time, conspiracy theory.

The BJS asks if you believe or do not believe in a particular claim. We are interested in the extent to which one accepts a justification or rationale for believing in a certain claim. So instead of determining if someone affirms "I believe in ghosts," we want to know if "I believe because it just feels right." The BJS was developed using these targeted beliefs

1) Acupuncture and other Oriental treatments cure through an invisible and mysterious energy field
2) Angels are literally real
3) Astrology
4) Communicating with the dead
5) Dream prophecy
6) Flying saucers from other planets have visited Earth
7) Fortune-telling and seeing into the future
8) Ghosts and haunted houses
9) Herbal medicine
10) Prayer can heal people from a great distance, even when they don't know they're being prayed for
11) Psychic mind-reading and extrasensory perception
12) Reincarnation and past lives

© 2015, Jonathan C. Smith, PhD. Reprinted by permission.

## The BJS

```
INSERT TARGETED BELIEF HERE
```

To what extent do you believe or disbelieve in the above?
(Check one of these circles):

① I do not believe in this ② I believe a little ③ I believe somewhat
④ I believe very much

Why do you believe or disbelieve in the above? Below are some reasons people believe or disbelieve. Please check how much you agree with each reason. Please use this key:

① I do not agree ② I agree a little ③ I agree somewhat ④ I agree very much

① ② ③ ④    1. This is a delusion.
① ② ③ ④    2. This is something I have personally experienced.
① ② ③ ④    3. This is something my family has accepted for a long time.
① ② ③ ④    4. This shows there's a lot science doesn't know about the world.
① ② ③ ④    5. Who cares if it's true. It's just fun to believe it.
① ② ③ ④    6. This is supported on TV shows and documentaries.
① ② ③ ④    7. This has passed the test of time.
① ② ③ ④    8. This is the product of a trick or hoax.
① ② ③ ④    9. This is supported by my spiritual and religious teachers.
① ② ③ ④   10. This is something I've been taught is true.
① ② ③ ④   11. This is real because there's no evidence against it.
① ② ③ ④   12. I believe because this is entertaining.
① ② ③ ④   13. This is something many people have experienced.
① ② ③ ④   14. If something has lasted this long, there must be something to it.
① ② ③ ④   15. This is true because it just feels right.
① ② ③ ④   16. This is supported by the existence of God.
① ② ③ ④   17. This is something people in my culture generally believe.
① ② ③ ④   18. This is a product of accident or error.
① ② ③ ④   19. This has often been reported in the news media.
① ② ③ ④   20. This is supported by science.
① ② ③ ④   21. The medical/scientific community doesn't want people to know about these things.
① ② ③ ④   22. This fits what my intuition tells me.
① ② ③ ④   23. This is consistent with my faith.
① ② ③ ④   24. This is a mysterious truth science can't explain.
① ② ③ ④   25. This is a product of meaningless coincidence.
① ② ③ ④   26. This has been described in many eyewitness reports.
① ② ③ ④   27. This is supported by research studies by scientists and experts.
① ② ③ ④   28. The authorities are keeping this kind of information from us.

SCORING KEY. INSTRUCTIONS: Add responses for scale items, divide by number of items in scale.

TRICK OR DELUSION (FILLER ITEM; TYPICALLY NOT SCORED)
(Test-retest reliability = .88, N = 28) To score add the following items, divide sum by 2.
  Item # 1 "This is a delusion."
  Item # 8 "This is the product of a trick or hoax."

PERSONAL EXPERIENCE OR INTUITION
(Test-retest reliability = .93, N =28) To score add the following items, divide sum by 3.
  Item # 2 "This is something I have personally experienced."
  Item # 15 "This is true because it just feels right."
  Item # 22 "This fits what my intuition tells me."

FAITH AND RELIGION
(Test-retest reliability = .84, N =28) To score add the following items, divide sum by 3.
  Item # 9 "This is supported by my spiritual and religious teachers."
  Item # 16 "This is supported by the existence of God."
  Item # 23 "This is consistent with my faith."

FAMILY AND CULTURE
(Test-retest reliability = .79, N =26) To score add the following items, divide sum by 3.
  Item # 3 "This is something my family has accepted for a long time."
  Item # 10 "This is something I've been taught is true."
  Item # 17 "This is something people in my culture generally believe."

ARGUMENT FROM IGNORANCE
(Test-retest reliability = .88, N =28) To score add the following items, divide sum by 3.
  Item # 4 "This shows there's a lot science doesn't know about the world."
  Item # 11 This is real because there's no evidence against it."
  Item # 24 "This is a mysterious truth science can't explain."

COINCIDENCE OR ERROR (FILLER ITEM; TYPICALLY NOT SCORED)
(Test-retest reliability = .84, N =28) To score add the following items, divide sum by 2.
  Item # 18 "This is a product of accident or error."
  Item # 25 "This is a product of meaningless coincidence."

ENTERTAINMENT (FILLER ITEM; TYPICALLY NOT SCORED)
(Test-retest reliability = .82, N =28) To score add the following items, divide sum by 2.
  Item # 5 "Who cares if it's true. It's just fun to believe it."
  Item # 12 "I believe because this is entertaining."

MEDIA
(Test-retest reliability = .64, N =28) To score add the following items, divide sum by 2.
  Item # 6 "This is supported on TV shows and documentaries."
  Item # 19 "This has often been reported in the news media."

POPULAR WITNESS

(Test-retest reliability = .80, N =28) To score add the following items, divide sum by 2.

Item # 13 "This is something many people have experienced. "

Item # 26 "This has been described in many eyewitness reports."

SCIENCE

(Test-retest reliability = .73, N =28) To score add the following items, divide sum by 2.

Item # 20 "This is supported by science."

Item # 27 "This is supported by research studies by scientists and experts."

TEST OF TIME

(Test-retest reliability = .80, N =28) To score add the following items, divide sum by 2.

Item # 7 "This has passed the test of time."

Item # 14 "If something has lasted this long, there must be something to it."

CONSPIRACY THEORY

(Test-retest reliability = .73, N =28) To score add the following items, divide sum by 2.

Item # 21 "The medical/scientific community doesn't want people to know about these things."

Item # 28 "The authorities are keeping this kind of information from us."

# BJS Scoring Summary Sheet

**YOUR BELIEF:**

| SCORE | BELIEF JUSTIFICATION |
|---|---|
| | Trick or delusion |
| | Personal experience or intuition |
| | Faith and religion |
| | Family and culture |
| | Argument from ignorance |
| | Coincidence or error |
| | Entertainment |
| | Media |
| | Popular witness |
| | Science |
| | Test of time |
| | Conspiracy theory |

## Example of Completed BJS

| *Astrology* |
| --- |

To what extent do you believe or disbelieve in the above?

(Check one of these circles):

① I do not believe in this ② I believe a little ③ I believe somewhat
✕ I believe very much

Why do you believe or disbelieve in the above? Below are some reasons people believe or disbelieve. Please check how much you agree with each reason. Please use this key:

① I do not agree ② I agree a little ③ I agree somewhat ④ I agree very much

✕②③④   1. This is a delusion.
①②③✕   2. This is something I have personally experienced.
①②✕④   3. This is something my family has accepted for a long time.
✕②③④   4. This shows there's a lot science doesn't know about the world.
✕②③④   5. Who cares if it's true. It's just fun to believe it.
✕②③④   6. This is supported on TV shows and documentaries.
①✕③④   7. This has passed the test of time.
✕②③④   8. This is the product of a trick or hoax.
①✕③④   9. This is supported by my spiritual and religious teachers.
①②✕④   10. This is something I've been taught is true.
✕②③④   11. This is real because there's no evidence against it.
✕②③④   12. I believe because this is entertaining.
①✕③④   13. This is something many people have experienced.
①✕③④   14. If something has lasted this long, there must be something to it.
①②③✕   15. This is true because it just feels right.
✕②③④   16. This is supported by the existence of God.
①②✕④   17. This is something people in my culture generally believe.
✕②③④   18. This is a product of accident or error.
①✕③④   19. This has often been reported in the news media.
①✕③④   20. This is supported by science.
✕②③④   21. The medical/scientific community doesn't want people to know about these things.
①②③✕   22. This fits what my intuition tells me.
✕②③④   23. This is consistent with my faith.
①✕③④   24. This is a mysterious truth science can't explain.
✕②③④   25. This is a product of meaningless coincidence.
①✕③④   26. This has been described in many eyewitness reports.
①②✕④   27. This is supported by research studies by scientists and experts.
①✕③④   28. The authorities are keeping this kind of information from us.

SCORING KEY. INSTRUCTIONS: Add responses for scale items, divide by number of items in scale.

## TRICK OR DELUSION (FILLER ITEM; TYPICALLY NOT SCORED)
To score add the following items, divide sum by 2.
   Response for Item # 1 "This is a delusion." = 1
   Response for Item # 8 "This is the product of a trick or hoax." = 1
   COMPUTED SCORE: $(1 + 1) \div 2 = 1$

## PERSONAL EXPERIENCE OR INTUITION
To score add the following items, divide sum by 3.
   Response for Item # 2. "This is something I have personally experienced." = 4
   Response for Item # 15 "This is true because it just feels right." = 4
   Response for Item # 22 "This fits what my intuition tells me." = 4
   COMPUTED SCORE: $(4 + 4 + 4) \div 3 = 4$

## FAITH AND RELIGION
To score add the following items, divide sum by 3.
   Response for Item # 9 "This is supported by my spiritual and religious teachers." = 2
   Response for Item # 16 "This is supported by the existence of God" = 1
   Response for Item # 23 "This is consistent with my faith" = 1
   COMPUTED SCORE: $(2 + 1 + 1) \div 3 = 1.3$

## FAMILY AND CULTURE
To score add the following items, divide sum by 3.
   Response for Item # 3 "This is something my family has accepted for a long time." = 3
   Response for Item # 10 "This is something I've been taught is true." = 3
   Response for Item # 17 "This is something people in my culture generally believe." = 3
   COMPUTED SCORE: $(3 + 3 + 3) \div 3 = 3$

## ARGUMENT FROM IGNORANCE
To score add the following items, divide sum by 3.
   Response for Item # 4 "This shows there's a lot science doesn't know about the world" = 1
   Response for Item # 11 "This is real because there's no evidence against it." = 1
   Response for Item # 24 "This is a mysterious truth science can't explain." = 2
   COMPUTED SCORE: $(1 + 1 + 2) \div 3 = 1.3$

## COINCIDENCE OR ERROR (FILLER ITEM; TYPICALLY NOT SCORED)
To score add the following items, divide sum by 2.
   Response for Item # 18 "This is a product of accident or error." = 1
   Response for Item # 25 "This is a product of meaningless coincidence" = 1
   COMPUTED SCORE: $(1 + 1) \div 2 = 1$

## ENTERTAINMENT (FILLER ITEM; TYPICALLY NOT SCORED)
To score add the following items, divide sum by 2.
   Response for Item # 5 "Who cares if it's true. It's just fun to believe it." = 1

Response for Item # 12 "I believe because this is entertaining." = 1
COMPUTED SCORE: $(1 + 1) \div 2 = 1$

## MEDIA
To score add the following items, divide sum by 2.
Response for Item # 6 "This is supported on TV shows and documentaries." = 1
Response for Item # 19 "This has often been reported in the news media." = 2
COMPUTED SCORE: $(1 + 2) \div 2 = 1.5$

## POPULAR WITNESS
To score add the following items, divide sum by 2.
Response for Item # 13 "This is something many people have experienced." = 2
Response for Item # 26 "This has been described in many eyewitness reports" = 2
COMPUTED SCORE: $(2 + 2) \div 2 = 2$

## SCIENCE
To score add the following items, divide sum by 2.
Response for Item # 20 "This is supported by science." = 2
Response for Item # 27 "This is supported by research studies by scientists and experts." = 3
COMPUTED SCORE: $(2 + 3) \div 2 = 2.5$

## TEST OF TIME
To score add the following items, divide sum by 2.
Response for Item # 7 "This has passed the test of time." = 2
Response for Item # 14 "If something has lasted this long, there must be something to it." = 2
COMPUTED SCORE: $(2 + 2) \div 2 = 2$

## CONSPIRACY THEORY
To score add the following items, divide sum by 2.
Response for Item # 21 "The medical/scientific community doesn't want people to know about these things." = 1
Response for Item # 28 "The authorities are keeping this kind of information from us." = 2
COMPUTED SCORE: $(1 + 2) \div 2 = 1.5$

# BJS Sample Summary Sheet

## (Highest scores circled)

YOUR BELIEF: *Astrology*

| SCORE | BELIEF JUSTIFICATION |
|-------|----------------------|
| 1 | Trick or delusion |
| (4) | Personal experience or intuition |
| 1.3 | Faith and religion |
| (3) | Family and culture |
| 1.3 | Argument from ignorance |
| 1 | Coincidence or error |
| 1 | Entertainment |
| 1.5 | Media |
| 2 | Popular witness |
| 2.5 | Science |
| 2 | Test of time |
| 1.5 | Conspiracy theory |

# Notes

## Chapter 2: The Paranormal Spectrum

1 To understand this definition, you must possess a minimal level of scientific literacy and understand the basics of science at a high school level. If you are unaware of what science says is possible, you are also unaware of what is most likely impossible. If you think science has shown that objects can travel faster than the speed of light, that thoughts can travel outside of the human brain like TV transmissions, that the afterlife is proven fact, or that the mind can cure all disease, then the concept of the "paranormal" makes no sense, because nothing is unlikely or impossible. If you accept one paranormal claim as proven fact, you are obligated to accept all claims with comparable support as fact.

2 Of course, one could propose that there may be observed events that have absolutely no explanation, and could never be explained by anyone or anything at any time, now or ever. Such hypothetical events may not be supernatural or godlike in that they may well be restricted, simple, and lacking any particular internal organization. Put differently, if such events have an explanation, it is beyond the capacity of any conceivable sentient being. Such "islands of inexplicability" would indeed merit the label "paranormal." However, I suspect they are a logical impossibility based on the untestable claim that there are specific limits to what any being or entity could ever understand.

## Chapter 5: Logic (Bonus: The Big Four Informal Logical Fallacies)

1 Final search was conducted 2/7/2017. Specific search terms (including quotation marks): "appeal to fear" AND "irrational"; "*ad hominem*" AND "irrational"; "red herring" AND "irrational"; "cherry-picking" AND "irrational"; "appeal to emotion" AND "irrational"; "argument from ignorance" AND "irrational"; "poisoning the well" AND "irrational"; "appeal to pity" AND "irrational"; "false dilemma" AND "irrational"; "false equivalence" AND "irrational"; "appeal to pride" AND "irrational." This represents a snapshot of irrational as seen through the eyes of the Google search engine on 2/7/2017. Some philosophers argue that "irrational" and "illogical" are not quite the same, that a claim that is "irrational" may not be the same as a claim that is "logically fallacious." However, most dictionaries consider these terms to be loosely synonymous. In our searches we consistently find far more hits for errors listed as "irrational" than for "illogical," "logical error," or "logical fallacy." For example, the error "red herring" yields 320,000 hits when searched as "'red herring' AND 'irrational'" and only 44,900 hits when searched as "'red herring' AND

'logical fallacy.'" Future researchers might consider entering these exact same search terms and examining any consistencies and changes over time.

2  Received fewer than 30,000 hits. For purposes of illustration, I have added several low-hit fallacies throughout this discussion.

## Chapter 8: Oddities of Nature and the World of Numbers

1  For the spiritually inclined, this can be a tricky point. Mystics of all religions often note deep mysteries that exist outside of our bubble (perhaps "delusion") of what we think we can deliberately control. These can range from the explosion of stars or the fall of meteors, to a sudden breeze or the smile of a child. The unexpected wonder and beauty of the ever unfolding universe can be a source of genuine awe and reverence. This is not paranormal synchronicity. It is an honest acknowledgement of something more than oneself. In one sense, it is taking perspective. Those of religion might use such terms as "grace," "tao," and "dharma." In my humble opinion, interpreting such wonders as "paranormal" can be a distraction.

## Chapter 11: Placebos

1  There are many simpler ways to construct a meditation/mindfulness placebo. For example, package instructions for both meditation/mindfulness and placebo default-network mind wandering ("let your mind worry or ruminate in any way you want") in a way that makes no mention of meditation or mindfulness. Both would be described as Cortical Cingulate Conditioning (CCC). Or we could indeed package both as "meditation/mindfulness," stating that they reflect core processes involved in the technique.

2  A Klingon Pebble is smooth, black, and about the size of a flattened egg.

## Appendix A: Why Do You Believe?

1  Sammantha Chin distributed 300 questionnaires in completion of her work as a research assistant in Chicago's Roosevelt University doctoral (PsyD) program in clinical psychology.

2  Multiple Regression Results. Multiple stepwise regression was used to determine if justifications predicted level of belief. The results of the regression indicated the four predictors explained 40.2% of the variance ($R^2 = .402$, F (4, 330) = 55.49, $p = .000$). It was found that the following variables significantly predicted level of belief: personal experience/intuition ($\beta = .361$, $p \le .0009$), argument from ignorance ($\beta = .210$, $p \le .0009$), family and culture ($\beta = .145$, $p \le .006$), and science ($\beta = .108$, $p \le .015$).

3  Wilks' Lambda (N = 352, subsample excluding those who do not believe)

| Value | F | df | Error df | sig | Partial Eta Squared |
|---|---|---|---|---|---|
| .235 | 3.718 | 132 | 2537.942 | .00 | .123 |

Given the large number of comparisons, we limited ourselves only to those comparisons significant at least $p \ge .009$ for at least three comparisons.

# References

## Chapter 1: Your Survival Kit

Bouvet, R., & Bonnefon, J.-F. (2014). Non-reflective thinkers are predisposed to attribute supernatural causation to uncanny experiences. *Personality and Social Psychology Bulletin, 41*, 955–961.

Frederick, S. (2005). Cognitive reflection and decision making. *Journal of Economic Perspectives, 19*(4), 25–42.

Nicholas, N., & Strader, A. (2000). *Hamlet Prince of Denmark by William Shakespeare*. New York: Pocket Books.

Okrand, M. (1992). *The Klingon dictionary*. New York: Pocket Books.

Oreskes, N., & Conway, E. M. (2010). *Merchants of doubt*. New York: Bloomsbury Press.

Scriven, M., & Paul, R. (2014). Critical thinking as defined by the National Council for Excellence. Retrieved February 4, 2017, from: http://www.criticalthinking.org/pages/defining-critical-tthinking/766

Shenhav, A., Rand, D. G., & Greene, J. D. (2011). Divine intuition: Cognitive style influences belief in God. *Journal of Experimental Psychology: General, 141*(3), 423–428.

Smith, J. C. (in press). *The paranormal sampler*. Charleston, SC: createspace.

Stanovich, K. E., & West, R. F. (1998). On the relative independence of thinking biases and cognitive ability. *Journal of Personality and Social Psychology, 94*, 672–695.

Tassi, J. (2012). pagh bullshit-page vagh. *yuDHa' Liar, 6,342,112*(11), 12–12.1.

## Chapter 2: The Paranormal Spectrum

Bauer, H. H. (1996). Cryptozoology. In G. S. Stein (Ed.), *The encyclopedia of the paranormal* (pp. 199–214). Amherst, NY: Prometheus Books.

Frazer, J. G. (1911–1915). *The golden bough: A study in magic and religion* (3rd ed.). London: Macmillan.

Heuvelmans, B. (1962). *On the track of unknown animals*. London: Rupert Hart-Davis.

Hitchens, C. (2009). *God is not great: How religion poisons everything*. New York, Hachette.

Ludden, D. (2010). Reality check: A review of pseudoscience and extraordinary claims of the paranormal: A critical thinker's toolkit (J. C. Smith). *PsycCRITIQUES, 55*(16).

*Critical Thinking: Pseudoscience and the Paranormal*, Second Edition. Jonathan C. Smith.
© 2018 John Wiley & Sons, Inc. Published 2018 by John Wiley & Sons, Inc.

No pagination. Retrieved February 12, 2017, from: http://psycnet.apa.org/critiques/55/16/1.html

Monk, W. H. (1875). *Hymns ancient and modern* (2nd ed.). London: W. M. Clowes and Sons.

Truzzi, M. (1976). Editorial. *The Zetetic, 1*(1), *Fall/Winter*, 4.

## Chapter 3: What's the Harm?

Angell, M., & Kassirer, J. P. (1998). Alternative medicine – the risks of untested and unregulated remedies. *New England Journal of Medicine, 339*, 839.

Bader, C., Dougherty, K., Froese, P. et al. (2006) The Baylor religion survey. Waco, TX: Baylor Institute for Studies in Religion. Retrieved February 20, 2017, from: http://www.baylor.edu/content/services/document.php/33304.pdf

Barnes, P. M., Powell-Griner, E., McFann, K., & Nahin, R. L. (2004). *Complementary and alternative medicine use among adults: United States*. Washington, DC: National Center for Health Statistics.

Bausell, R. B. (2007). *Snake oil science: The truth about complementary and alternative medicine*. Oxford: Oxford University Press.

Chapman (2014). The Chapman University Survey on American Fears. Retrieved February 2, 2017, from: https://blogs.chapman.edu/wilkinson/2016/10/11/americas-top-fears-2016/

Clarke, T. C., Black, L. I., Stussman, B. J. et al. (2015). Trends in the use of complementary health approaches among adults: United States, 2002–2012. National health statistics reports, no. 79. Hyattsville, MD: National Center for Health Sciences. Retrieved February 7, 2017, from: https://www.cdc.gov/nchs/data/nhsr/nhsr079.pdf

Dawkins, R. (2006) *The God delusion*. New York: Bantam Books.

Farha, B., & Steward, G. (2006). Paranormal beliefs: An analysis of college students. *Skeptical Inquirer, 30*(1), 37–40.

Fontanarosa, P. B., & Lundberg, G. D. (1998). Alternative medicine meets science. *Journal of the American Medical Association, 280*, 1618–1619.

Gallup (2014). Evolution, creationism, intelligent design. Retrieved February 20, 2017, from: http://www.gallup.com/poll/21814/Evolution-Creationism-Intelligent-Design.aspx

Gilovich, T. (1991). *How we know what isn't so*. New York: Free Press.

Glenday, C., & Friedman, S. T. (1999). *The UFO investigator's handbook*. Philadelphia, PA: Running Press.

Gordon, J. E. (Ed.). (1967). *Handbook of clinical and experimental hypnosis*. New York: Macmillan.

Gould, S. J. (1999). *Rocks of ages: Science and religion in the fullness of life*. New York: Ballantine Books.

Hall, T. (1972). Sociological perspectives on UFO reports. In C. Sagan & T. Page (Eds.), *UFOs: A scientific debate* (pp. 213–223). Ithaca, NY: Cornell University Press.

Harris Poll. (2005). The religious and other beliefs of Americans, 2005. The Harris Poll #90, December 14. Retrieved February 4, 2017, from: http://www.prnewswire.com/news-releases/the-religious-and-other-beliefs-of-americans-2005-55544047.html

Harris Poll. (2009). Retrieved February 2, 2017 from: http://media.theharrispoll.com/documents/Harris_Poll_2009_12_15.pdf

Harris Poll. (2013). Retrieved February 2, 2017, from: http://www.theharrispoll.com/health-and-life/Americans__Belief_in_God__Miracles_and_Heaven_Declines.html

Harris, S. (2004). *The end of faith: Religion, terror, and the future of reason*. New York: W. W. Norton.

Harris, S. (2015). *Waking up: A guide to spirituality without religion*. New York: Simon and Schuster.

Hitchens, C. (2007). *God is not great: How religion poisons everything*. New York: Twelve.

Irwin, H. J., & Watt, C. A. (2007). *An introduction to parapsychology* (5th ed.). Jefferson, NC: McFarland.

Kroger, W. S. (1977). *Clinical and experimental hypnosis in medicine, dentistry, and psychology*. New York: Lippincott.

Lynn, S. J., & Kirsch, I. (2006). *Essentials of clinical hypnosis: An evidence-based approach*. Washington, DC: American Psychological Association.

Moore, D. W. (2005). Three in four Americans believe in paranormal. Gallup News Service, June 16. Retrieved February 20, 2017, from: http://www.gallup.com/poll/16915/Three-Four-Americans-Believe-Paranormal.aspx

Newport, F. (2007). Americans more likely to believe in God than the Devil, heaven more than hell. Gallup News Service, June 13. Retrieved February 20, 2017, from: http://www.gallup.com/poll/27877/Americans-More-Likely-Believe-God-Than-Devil-Heaven-More-Than-Hell.aspx

Newport, F., & Strausberg, M. (2001). Americans' belief in psychic and paranormal phenomena is up over the last decade. Gallup News Service, June 8. Retrieved February 20, 2017, from: http://www.gallup.com/poll/4483/Americans-Belief-Psychic-Paranormal-Phenomena-Over-Last-Decade.aspx

Newsweek/Beliefnet. (2005). Newsweek/Beliefnet poll results. Retrieved February 20, 2017, from: http://www.beliefnet.com/story/173/story_17353_1.html

New York Times. (2001). Massachusetts clears 5 from Salem witch trials. November 2. Retrieved February 20, 2017, from http://www.nytimes.com/2001/11/02/us/massachusetts-clears-5-from-salem-witch-trials.html

Niewyk, D. L., & Nicosia, F. R. (2000). *The Columbia guide to the Holocaust*. New York: Columbia University Press.

Offit, P. A. (2015). *Bad faith: When religious belief undermines modern medicine*. New York: Basic Books.

Pattie, F. A. (1994). *Mesmer and animal magnetism: A chapter in the history of medicine*. Hamilton, NY: Edmonston.

Pew Forum on Religion & Public Life. (2009). Many Americans mix multiple faiths. Retrieved February 2, 2017, from: http://www.pewforum.org/2009/12/09/many-americans-mix-multiple-faiths/

Rice, T. W. (2003). Believe it or not: Religious and other paranormal beliefs in the United States. *Journal for the Scientific Study of Religion, 42*, 95–106.

Robbins, R. (1959). *Encyclopedia of witchcraft and demonology*. New York: Crown Publishers.

Saher, M., & Lindeman, M. (2005). Alternative medicine: A psychological perspective. *Personality and Individual Differences, 39*, 1169–1178.

Vyse, (1997). *Believing in magic: The psychology of superstition*. New York: Oxford University Press.

## Chapter 4: Sources

Bausell, R. B. (2007). *Snake oil science: The truth about complementary and alternative medicine.* Oxford: Oxford University Press.

Brotherton, R. (2013). Towards a definition of "conspiracy theory." *PsyPAG Quarterly, 88*(3), 9–14.

Brotherton, R. (2015). *Suspicious minds: Why we believe conspiracy theories.* New York: Bloomsbury.

Carroll, R. T. (2005). Anecdotal (testimonial) evidence. *Skepdic.com.* Retrieved February 12, 2017, from: http://www.skepdic.com/testimon.html

Dickersin, K., Chan, S., Chalmers, T. C. et al. (1987). Publication bias and clinical trials. *Controlled Clinical Trials, 8*(4), 343–353. DOI:10.1016/0197-2456(87)90155-3.

Dickersin, K., & Min, Y. I. (1993). NIH clinical trials and publication bias. *Online Journal of Current Clinical Trials*, April 28. Doc No. 50. PMID 8306005.

Franco, A, Malhotra, N., & Simonovits, G. (2014). Publication bias in the social sciences: Unlocking the file drawer. *Science, 345*(6023), 1502–1505.

Gilbert, N. T., King, G., Pettigrew, S., & Wilson, T. D. (2016). Comment on "Estimating the reproducibility of psychological science." *Science, 351*, 1037a.

Goertzel, T. (1994). Belief in conspiracy theories: A pilot study. *Frontiers in Psychology, 15*(4), 731–642.

Groh, D. (1987). The temptation of conspiracy theory, or: Why do bad things happen to good people? In C. F. Graumann & S. Moscovici (Eds.), *Changing conceptions of conspiracy* (pp. 1–37). Berlin: Springer-Verlag.

Hines, T. (2003). *Pseudoscience and the paranormal.* Amherst, NY: Prometheus Books.

Hofstadter, R. (1964). The paranoid style in American politics. *Harper's Magazine, 229*(1374).

Hume, D. (1958). *An enquiry concerning human understanding.* Chicago: University of Chicago Press. Originally published 1758.

Janis, I. L. (1982). *Groupthink: Psychological studies of policy decisions and fiascoes.* Boston: Houghton Mifflin.

Jolley, D., & Douglas, K. M. (2013). The social consequences of conspiracism: Exposure to conspiracy theories decreases intentions to engage in politics and to reduce one's carbon footprint. *British Journal of Psychology, 105*, 35–56.

McCauley, C. (1989). The nature of social influence in groupthink: Compliance and internalization. *Journal of Personality and Social Psychology, 57*, 250–260.

Open Science Collaboration. (2015). Estimating the reproducibility of psychological science. *Science, 349*(6251), 943. DOI:10.1126/science.aac4716.

Robins, R. S., & Post, J. M. (1997). *Political paranoia.* New Haven, CT: Yale University Press.

Rosenthal, R. (1979). The file drawer problem and tolerance for null results. *Psychological Bulletin, 86*(3), 638–641. DOI:10.1037/0033-2909.86.3.638.

Seitz-Wald, A. (2013). Fairleigh Dickinson University's PublicMind survey on conspiracy theories. Retrieved February 20, 2017, from: https://www.scribd.com/doc/120815791/Fairleigh-Dickinson-poll-on-conspiracy-theories

Shermer, M. (2011). *The believing brain.* New York: Times Books.

Swami, V., Pietschnig, J., Tran, U. S. et al. (2013). The impact of informational framing and individual differences in shaping of conspiracist beliefs about the Moon landings. *Applied Cognitive Psychology, 27*(1), 71–80.

Uscinski, J. E., & Parent, J. M. (2014). *American conspiracy theories.* New York: Oxford University Press.

Wood, M. J., Douglas, K. M., & Sutton, R. M. (2012). Dead and alive: Beliefs in contradictory conspiracy theories. *Social Psychology and Personality Science, 3*(6), 7l67–773. DOI:10.1177/1948550611434786.

## Chapter 5: Logic (Bonus: The Big Four Informal Logical Fallacies)

Bennett, B. (2012). *Logically fallacious: The ultimate collection of over 300 logical fallacies (academic edition).* Sudbury, MA: eBookit.com.

*Oxford English Dictionary.* (2015). Oxford: Oxford University Press.

Truzzi, M. (1976). Editorial. *The Zetetic, 1*(1), *Fall/Winter,* 4.

## Chapter 6: Fallacies of Ambiguity

*American Heritage Dictionary of the English Language, Fourth Updated Edition.* (2003). New York: Houghton Mifflin. Retrieved February 22, 2008, from: http://www. thefreedictionary.com/faith

Carroll, R. T. (2006). False analogy. Retrieved February 20, 2017, from: http://www.skepdic. com/falseanalogy.html

Chaplin, S. (1900). The stained-glass political platform. *The Century Magazine,* June, pp. 305–308.

Davies, P. (2007). Taking science on faith. Op-ed contribution. *New York Times,* November 24. Retrieved February 20, 2017, from: http://www.nytimes.com/2007/11/24/ opinion/24davies.html?_r=1&oref=slogin

Ganter, V., & Strube, M. (2009). Finding hedges by chasing weasels: Hedge detection using Wikipedia tabs and shallow linguistic features. Proceedings of the ACL-IJCNLP 2009 Conference Short Papers, p. 175.

Irwin, H. J., & Watt, C. A. (2007). *An introduction to parapsychology.* Jefferson, NC: McFarland.

Lindeman, M., & Aarnio, K. (2007). Superstitious, magical, and paranormal beliefs: An integrative model. *Journal of Research in Personality, 41,* 731–744.

Nowak, R. M., & Walker, E. P. (2005). *Walker's carnivores of the world.* Baltimore: Johns Hopkins University Press.

Park, R. L. (2008). Two meanings of "faith" confuse even scientists. *Skeptical Inquirer, 32,* 14.

Radin, D. (1997). *The conscious universe: The scientific truth of psychic phenomena.* New York: HarperCollins.

Radin, D. (2006). *Entangled minds: Extrasensory experiences in a quantum reality.* New York: Simon & Schuster.

Randi, J. (1982). *The truth about Uri Geller.* Buffalo, NY: Prometheus Books.

Ryle, G. (1949). *The concept of mind.* Chicago: University of Chicago Press.

Schwartz, G. (2004). Feedback and systemic memory: Implications for survival. Survival of Bodily Death: An Esalen Invitational Conference, May 2–7, 2004. Retrieved February 20, 2017, from: http://www.esalenctr.org/display/confpage.cfm?confid=19&pageid=149&pgtype=1

Schwartz, G. E. R., & Russek, L. G. S. (1999). *The living energy universe.* Charlottesville, VA: Hampton Roads.

Sokal, A. D. (1996). Transgressing the boundaries: Towards a transformative hermeneutics of quantum gravity. *Social Text, 46/47,* 217–252. Retrieved February 20, 2017, from: http://www.physics.nyu.edu/faculty/sokal/transgress_v2/transgress_v2_singlefile.html

Svedholm, A., Lindeman, M., & Lipsanen, J. (2010). Believing in the purpose of events – why does it occur, and is it supernatural? *Applied Cognitive Psychology, 24*(2), 252–265.

Townes, C. H. (2005). Statement by Charles Hard Townes at the Templeton Prize News Conference, March 9. Retrieved February 20, 2017, from: http://www.templeton.org/newsroom/press_releases/archive/050309townes.html

## Chapter 7: Observation and Science

Associated Press (2007). Panic attacks may raise heart attacks. *Oakland Tribune,* October 8. Retrieved February 2, 2017, from: http://articles.latimes.com/2007/oct/08/health/he-briefly8.s3

Black, J. G. (1996). *Microbiology: Principles and applications* (3rd ed.). Upper Saddle River, NJ: Prentice Hall.

BBC News. (2003). Pill changes women's taste in men. January 20. Retrieved February 20, 2017, from: http://news.bbc.co.uk/1/hi/health/2677697.stm

BBC News. (2006a). Housework cuts breast cancer risk. December 29. Retrieved February 20, 2017, from: http://news.bbc.co.uk/2/hi/health/6214655.stm

BBC News. (2006b). Sex "cuts public speaking stress." January 26. Retrieved February 20, 2017, from: http://news.bbc.co.uk/2/hi/health/4646010.stm

Brooks, D. (2007). Goodbye, George and John. *New York Times,* August 7. Retrieved February 20, 2017, from: http://select.nytimes.com/2007/08/07/opinion/07brooks.html?hp

Burns, W. C. (1997). Spurious correlations. Retrieved February 20, 2017, from: http://www.burns.com/wcbspurcorl.htm

Carroll, R. T. (2007). Occult statistics. Retrieved February 20, 2017, from: http://www.skepdic.com/occultstats.html

CNN. (1999). Night-light may lead to nearsightedness. May 13. Retrieved February 20, 2017, from: http://www.cnn.com/HEALTH/9905/12/children.lights/index.html

Einstein, A. (1936). *Physics and reality.* Reprinted in A. Einstein (1950). *Out of my later years.* New York: Philosophical Library, p. 59.

Fox News (2006). Sexually explicit song lyrics prompt teens to have sex earlier. August 6. Retrieved February 12, 2017, from: http://www.foxnews.com/story/2006/08/07/study-sexually-explicit-song-lyrics-prompt-teens-to-have-sex-earlier.html

Friesen, J. P., Campbell, T. H., & Kay, A. C. (2014). The psychological advantage of unfalsifiability: The appeal of untestable religious and political ideologies. *Journal of Personality and Social Psychology, 108*(3), 515–529.

Gledhill, R. (2005). Societies worse off "when they have God on their side." *The Times.* September 27. Retrieved February 20, 2017, from: http://www.timesonline.co.uk/tol/news/uk/article571206.ece

Hartshorne, C., & Weiss, P. (Eds.). (1932). *Collected papers of Charles Sanders Peirce, Volumes I and II, Principles of philosophy and elements of logic.* Cambridge, MA: Belknap Press.

Huxley, T. H. (1880). *The crayfish: An introduction to the study of zoology.* London: C. Kegan Paul & Co.

Irwin, H. J., & Watt, C. A. (2007). *An introduction to parapsychology.* Jefferson, NC: McFarland.

Kuhn, T. S. (1970). *The structure of scientific revolutions.* Chicago: University of Chicago Press.

Metchnikoff, E., & Berger, D. (1939). *The founders of modern medicine: Pasteur, Koch, Lister.* New York: Walden.

Mueller, J. (2007). Correlations or causation. Retrieved February 20, 2017, from: http://jonathan.mueller.faculty.noctrl.edu/100/correlation_or_causation.htm

Paydarfar, D., & Schwartz, W. J. (2001). An algorithm for discovery. *Science Express*, *292*(5514), 13.

Peer trainer. (2007). New study sponsored by General Mills says that eating breakfast makes girls thinner. Retrieved February 20, 2017, from: http://www.peertrainer.com/LoungeCommunityThread.aspx?ForumID=1&ThreadID=3118

Popper, K. (1959). *The logic of scientific discovery.* New York: Basic Books.

Randi, J. (1982). *Flim-Flam!* Amherst, NY: Prometheus Books.

Randi, J. (1983). The Project Alpha experiment. In Frazier, K. (Ed.). (1986). *Science confronts the paranormal* (pp. 158–165). New York: Amherst, NY: Prometheus Books.

Reynolds, G. (2017). Get up and move. It may make you happier. *New York Times*, January 25. Retrieved February 2, 2017, from: https://www.nytimes.com/2017/01/25/well/move/get-up-and-move-it-may-make-you-happier.html

Schick, T., & Vaughn, L. (2005). *How to think about weird things: Critical thinking for a new age* (4th ed.). New York: McGraw-Hill.

Science Daily. (2007). Surgeons with video game skill appear to perform better in simulated surgery skills course. Retrieved February 20, 2017, from: https://www.sciencedaily.com/releases/2007/02/070220012341.htm

Springen, K. (2007). New findings on Alzheimer's. Newsweek online. Retrieved February 20, 2017, from: http://www.newsweek.com/id/41945

Vaughn, L. (2008). *The power of critical thinking: Effective reasoning about ordinary and extraordinary claims* (2nd ed.). New York: Oxford University Press.

## Chapter 8: Oddities of Nature and the World of Numbers

Bellos, A. (2014). *Through the looking-glass.* New York: Bloomsbury.

Blackmore, S., & Troscianko, T. (1985). Belief in the paranormal: Probability judgments, illusory control, and the "chance baseline shift." *British Journal of Psychology*, 76, 459–468. Retrieved February 20, 2017, from: http://www.susanblackmore.co.uk/Articles/BJP%201985.htm

Bollobás, B. (Ed.). (1986). *Littlewood's miscellany.* Cambridge: Cambridge University Press.

Bonferroni, C. E. (1935). Il calcolo delle assicurazioni su gruppi di teste. In *Studi in Onore del Professore Salvatore Ortu Carboni.* Rome, Italy: Bardi, pp. 13–60.

Chopra, D. (2003). *The spontaneous fulfillment of desire.* New York: Harmony/Random House.

Curl, M. (1996). *The anagram dictionary*. London: Robert Hale.

Drosnin, M. (1997). *The Bible code*. New York: Touchstone.

Frazier, K. (Ed.). (2009). The new UFO interest: Scientific appraisals. [Special issue]. *Skeptical Inquirer, 33*(1), January/February.

Gauquelin, M. (1974). *Cosmic influences on human behavior*. London: Garnstone Press.

Gilovich, T. (1991). *How we know what isn't so*. New York: Free Press.

Holt, J. (2004). Throw away that astrological chart. *New York Times,* April 29, D10.

Jung, C. G. (1960). *Synchronicity: An acausal connecting principle*. Princeton, NJ: Princeton University Press.

Leavy, J. (1992). Our spooky presidential coincidences contest. *Skeptical Inquirer, 16*, 316–320.

McGaha, J. (2009). The trained observer of unusual things in the sky (UFOs?). *Skeptical Inquirer, 33*(1), 55–56.

McKenna, F. P., & Albery, I. P. (2001). Does unrealistic optimism change following a negative experience? *Journal of Applied Social Psychology, 31*, 1146–1157.

Morewedge, C. K., & Norton, M. I. (2009). When dreaming is believing: The (motivated) interpretation of dreams. *Journal of Personality and Social Psychology, 96*, 249–264.

Murray, H. A., & Wheeler, D. R. (1936). A note on the possible clairvoyance of dreams. *The Journal of Psychology, 3*, 309–313.

Myers, D. G. (2004). *Intuition: Its powers and perils*. New Haven, CT: Yale University Press.

Paulos, J. P. (2001). *Innumeracy: Mathematical illiteracy and its consequences*. New York: Hill and Wang.

Redfield, J. (1993). *The Celestine prophecy*. New York: Warner Books.

Sanbonmatsu, D. M., Posavac, S. S., & Stasney, R. (1997). The subjective beliefs underlying probability overestimation. *Journal of Experimental Social Psychology, 33*, 276–295.

Schick, T., & Vaughn, L. (2005). *How to think about weird things: Critical thinking for a new age*. New York: McGraw-Hill.

Smith, J. C. (2011a). The Flying Spaghetti Monster and the Pastafarian Quatrains. *Skeptical Inquirer*, September/October, 2011, 54–56.

Smith, J. C. (2011b). *God speaks: The Pastafarian Quatrains*. Raleigh, NC: Lulu Press.

Tversky, A., & Kahneman, D. (1973). Availability: A heuristic for judging frequency and probability. *Cognitive Psychology, 5*, 207–232.

www.veegle.com. Substantiated true facts – the odds. Retrieved February 20, 2017, from: http://www.veegle.com/odds.htm?submit2=The+Real+Odds

Weinstein, N. D. (1980). Unrealistic optimism about future life events. *Journal of Personality and Social Psychology, 39*, 806–820.

Weinstein, N. D., & Klein, W. M. (1996). Unrealistic optimism: Present and future. *Journal of Social and Clinical Psychology, 15*, 1–8.

## Chapter 9: Perceptual Error and Trickery

Baker, R. A. (1990). *They call it hypnosis*. Buffalo, NY: Prometheus Books.

Bányai, É., & Hilgard, E. (1976). A comparison of active-alert hypnotic induction with traditional relaxation induction. *Journal of Abnormal Psychology, 85*(2), 218–224.

Carroll, R. T. (2003). *The skeptic's dictionary*. Hoboken, NJ: Wiley.

Carroll, R. T. (2007). Cognitive dissonance. In *The skeptic's dictionary*. Retrieved February 20, 2017, from: http://skepdic.com/cognitivedissonance.html

Cherry, E. C. (1953). Some experiments on the recognition of speech, with one and with two ears. *Journal of the Acoustic Society of America, 25*, 975–979.

Crick, R. (1984). Function of the thalamic reticular complex: The searchlight hypothesis. *Proceedings of the National Academy of Sciences USA, 81*, 4586–4590.

Dickson, D. H., & Kelly, I. W. (1985). "The Barnum Effect" in personality assessment: A review of the literature. *Psychological Reports, 57*, 367–382.

Festinger, L. (1957). *A theory of cognitive dissonance*. Stanford, CA: Stanford University Press.

Garb, H., Lilienfeld, S., Wood, J., & Nezworski, M. (2002). Effective use of projective techniques in clinical practice: Let the data help with selection and interpretation. *Professional Psychology: Research and Practice, 33*(5), 454.

Gilovich, T., Savitsky, K., & Medvec, V. J. (1998). The illusion of transparency: Biased assessments of others' ability to read our emotional states. *Journal of Personality and Social Psychology, 75*, 332–346.

Goldstein, E. B. (2007). *Sensation and perception*. Belmont, CA: Thomson Wadsworth.

Hyman, R. (2003). How *not* to test mediums: Critiquing the afterlife experiments. *Skeptical Inquirer, 27.1*. Retrieved January 30, 2017, from: http://www.csicop.org/si/show/how_not_to_test_mediums_critiquing_the_afterlife_experiments

Kihlstrom, J. F. (1962). *Stanford Hypnotic Susceptibility Scale*. Palo Alto, CA: Consulting Psychologists Press.

Kirsch, I., & Braffman, W. (2001). Imaginative suggestibility and hypnotizability. *Current Directions in Psychological Science, 4*, 57–61.

Lilienfeld, S. O., Ruscio, J., & Lynn, S. J. (Eds.). (2008). *Navigating the mindfield: A guide to separating science from pseudoscience in mental health*. Amherst, NY: Prometheus Books.

Martinez-Conde, S., & Macknik, S. L. (2008). Magic and the brain. *Scientific American, 299*(6), 72–79.

Nickerson, R. S. (1998). Confirmation bias: A ubiquitous phenomenon in many guises. *Review of General Psychology, 2*, 175–220.

Pronin, E., Gilovich, T., & Ross, L. (2004). Objectivity in the eye of the beholder: Divergent perceptions of bias in self versus others. *Psychological Review, 111*, 781–799.

Pronin, E., Lin, D. Y., & Ross, L. (2002). The bias blind spot: Perceptions of bias in self versus others. *Personality and Social Psychology Bulletin, 28*, 369–381.

Randi, J. (1993). *The mask of Nostradamus: The prophecies of the world's most famous seer*. Amherst, NY: Prometheus.

religioustolerance. (2007). Retrieved February 20, 2017, from: http://www.religioustolerance.org/end_wrld.htm

Rowland, I. (2005). *The full facts book of cold reading* (4th ed.). London: Ian Rowland.

Schick, T., & Vaughn, L. (2005). *How to think about weird things: Critical thinking for a new age* (4th ed.). New York: McGraw-Hill.

Shermer, M. (2005). *Science friction*. New York: Henry Holt.

Shermer, M. (2012). *The believing brain: From ghosts and gods to politics and conspiracies – how we construct beliefs and reinforce them as truths*. New York: St Martin's Griffin.

Shor, R. E., & Orne, E. C. (1962). *Harvard Group Scale of Hypnotic Susceptibility*. Palo Alto, CA: Consulting Psychologists Press.

Sternberg, R. J. (2006). *Cognitive psychology* (4th ed.). Belmont, CA: Thomson/Wadsworth.

Turnbull, C. M. (1961). Some observations regarding the experiences and behavior of the BaMbuti Pygmies. *American Journal of Psychology, 74,* 304–308.

Vorauer, J. D. (2001). The other side of the story: Transparency estimation in social interaction. In G. B. Moskowitz (Ed.), *Cognitive social psychology: The Princeton symposium on the legacy and future of social cognition* (pp. 371–385). Mahwah, NJ: Erlbaum.

Vorauer, J. D., & Claude, S. (1998). Perceived versus actual transparency of goals in negotiation. *Personality and Social Psychology Bulletin, 24,* 371–385.

Wark, D. M. (2006). Alert hypnosis: A review and case report. *American Journal of Clinical Hypnosis, 48,* 291–300.

Watson, P. C. (1960). On the failure to eliminate hypotheses in a conceptual task. *Quarterly Journal of Experimental Psychology, 12,* 129–140.

## Chapter 10: Memory

Ackil, J. K., & Zaragoza, M. S. (1998). Memorial consequences of forced confabulation: Age differences in susceptibility to false memories. *Developmental Psychology, 34*(6), 1358–1372.

Atkinson, R. C., & Shiffrin, R. M. (1968). Human memory: A proposed system and its control processes. In K. W. Spence & J. T. Spence (Eds.), *The psychology of learning and motivation: Volume 2. Advances in research and theory.* New York: Academic Press.

Begg, I., & Armour, V. (1991). Repetition and the ring of truth: Biasing comments. *Canadian Journal of Behavioral Science, 23,* 195–213.

Begg, I. M., Anas, A., & Farinacci, S. (1992). Dissociation of processes in belief: Source recollection, statement familiarity, and the illusion of truth. *Journal of Experimental Psychology, 121,* 446–458.

Belluck, P. (1997). "Memory" therapy leads to a lawsuit and big settlement. *The New York Times,* p. A1, November 6. Retrieved February 20, 2017, from: http://www.nytimes.com/1997/11/06/us/memory-therapy-leads-to-a-lawsuit-and-big-settlement.html

Boyd, R. (2008). Do people only use 10 percent of their brains? *Scientific American.* Retrieved January 30, 2017, from: https://www.scientificamerican.com/article/do-people-only-use-10-percent-of-their-brains/

Brown, A. S. (2004). *The déjà vu experiences: Essays in cognitive psychology.* Brighton, UK: Psychology Press.

Cutler, B. L., & Penrod, S. D. (1995). *Mistaken identification: The eyewitness, psychology, and the law.* New York: Cambridge University Press.

Echterhoff, G., Higgins, E. T., Kopietz, R., & Groll, S. (2008). How communication goals determine when audience tuning biases memory. *Journal of Experimental Psychology: General, 137*(1), 3–21.

Evans, Hilary (1987). *Gods, spirits, cosmic guardians.* Wellingborough, UK: Aquarian Press.

Hasher, L., Goldstein, D., & Toppino, T. (1977). Frequency and the conference of referential validity. *Journal of Verbal Learning and Verbal Behavior, 16,* 107–112.

Hicks, J. L., & Marsh, R. L. (2001). False recognition occurs more frequently during source identification than during old-new recognition. *Journal of Experimental Psychology: Learning, Memory, and Cognition, 27,* 375–383.

Higgins, E. T. (1992). Achieving "shared reality" in the communication game: A social action that creates meaning. *Journal of Language and Social Psychology, 11,* 107–131.

Hyman, I. E., & Pentland, J. (1995). The role of mental imagery in the creation of false memories. *Journal of Memory and Language, 35,* 101–117.

Johnston, M. K. (1998). *Spectral evidence: The Ramona case: Incest, memory, and truth on trial in Napa Valley.* Boston: Houghton Mifflin.

Johnston, M. K. (2006). Memory and reality. *American Psychologist, 61,* 760–771.

Johnston, M. K., Hashtroudi, S., & Lindsay, D. S. (1993). Source monitoring. *Psychological Bulletin, 114,* 3–28.

Loftus, E. F. (1996). *Eyewitness testimony.* Cambridge, MA: Harvard University Press.

Loftus, E. F. (1997). Creating false memories. *Scientific American, 277,* 70–75.

Loftus, E. F., & Ketcham, K. (1994). *The myth of repressed memory.* New York: St Martin's Press.

McNally, R. J. (2004). The science and folklore of traumatic amnesia. *Clinical Psychology: Science and Practice, 11,* 29–33.

Moskowitz, G. B. (2005). *Social cognition.* New York: Guilford Press.

Radford, B. (1999). The ten-percent myth. *Skeptical Inquirer, 23,* 52–53. Retrieved February 20, 2017, from: http://www.csicop.org/si/9903/ten-percent-myth.html

Schacter, D. L. (1996). *Searching for memory: The brain, the mind, and the past.* New York: Basic Books.

Skurnik, I., Yoon, C., Park, D. C., & Schwartz, N. (2005). How warnings about false claims become recommendations. *Journal of Consumer Research, 31,* 713–724.

Squire, L. R. (2004). Memory systems of the brain: A brief history and current perspective. *Neurobiology of Learning and Memory, 82,* 171–177.

Sternberg, R. J. (2006). *Cognitive psychology.* Belmont, CA: Thompson.

Stevenson, R. L. (2004). *Essays in the art of writing.* Adelaide: eBooks.

Sutton, J. (2003). Memory, philosophical issues about. In L. Nabel (Ed.), *Encyclopedia of cognitive science, Volume 2* (pp. 1109–1113). London: Nature Publishing Group.

Tulving, E., & Wayne, D. (1972). *Organization of memory.* Oxford: Oxford University Press.

Wade, K. A., Sharman, S. J., Garry, M. et al. (2006). False claims about false memory research. *Consciousness and Cognition, 16,* 18–28.

Wilson, K., & French, C. C. (2006). The relationship between susceptibility to false memories, dissociativity, and paranormal belief and experience. *Personality and Individual Differences, 41,* 1493–1502.

Zuger, B. (1966). The time of dreaming and the déjà vu. *Comprehensive Psychiatry, 7,* 191–196.

## Chapter 11: Placebos

Ariel, G., & Saville, W. (1972). Anabolic steroids: The physiological effects of placebos. *Medicine and Science in Sport and Exercise, 4,* 124–126.

Bausell, R. B. (2007). *Snake oil science: The truth about complementary and alternative medicine.* Oxford: Oxford University Press.

Beecher, H. K. (1955). The powerful placebo. *Journal of the American Medical Association, 159*(17), 24 December, 1602–1606.

Beedie, C. J. (2007). Placebo effects in competitive sport: Qualitative data. *Journal of Sports Science and Medicine, 6,* 21–28.

Beedie, C. J., Stuart, E. M., Coleman, D. A., & Foad, A. J. (2006). Placebo effects of caffeine in cycling performance. *Medicine and Science in Sport and Exercise, 38,* 2159–2164.

Benedetti, F. (2009). *Placebo effects: Understanding the mechanisms in health and disease.* New York: Oxford University Press.

Benedetti, F., Arduino, C., & Amanzio, M. (1999). Somatotopic activation of opioid systems by target-directed expectations of analgesia. *Journal of Neuroscience, 9,* 3639–3648.

Byrne, R. (2006). *The Secret.* New York: Atria Books.

Carroll, R. T. (2008). Book review: The cure within: A history of mind-body medicine (A. Harrington). In *The skeptic's dictionary.* Retrieved February 20, 2017, from: http://skepdic.com/refuge/harrington.html

Clark, V. R., Hopkins, W. G., Hawley, J. A., & Burke, L. M. (2000). Placebo effect of carbohydrate feeding during a 4-km cycling time trial. *Medicine and Science in Sport and Exercise, 32,* 1642–1647.

Cobb, L. A., Thomas, G. I., Dillard, D. H. et al. (1959). An evaluation of internal-mammary-artery ligation by a double-blind technic. *New England Journal of Medicine, 260,* 1115–1118.

Cohen, N., Moynihan, J. A., & Ader, A. (1994). Pavlovian conditioning of the immune system. *International Archives of Allergy and Immunology, 105,* 101–106.

Davidson, R. J., & Kaszniak, A. W. (2015). Conceptual and methodological issues in research on mindfulness and meditation. *American Psychologist, 70*(7), 581–592.

Foster, C., Felker, H., Porcari, J. P. et al. (2004). The placebo effect on exercise performance. *Medicine and Science in Sport and Exercise, 36*(Suppl.), S171.

Gaspar, J. M., & McDonald, J. J. (2014). Suppression of salient objects prevents distraction in visual search. *The International Journal of Neuroscience, 34*(16), 5658–5666.

Gilovich, T. (1991). *How we know what isn't so.* New York: Free Press.

Grady, A. M. (2007). Psychophysiological mechanisms of stress: A foundation for stress management therapies. In P. M. Lehrer, R. M. Woolfolk, & W. E. Sime (Eds.), *Principles and practice of stress management* (3rd ed., pp. 16–37). New York: Guilford Press.

Hooper, R. (1822). *Hooper's lexicon-medicum.* New York: Harpers and Brothers.

Interlandi, J. (2016). The acupuncture myth. *Scientific American, 315*(2), 24–25.

Kaptchuk, T. J., Friedlander, E., Kelley, J. M. et al. (2010). Placebos without deception: A randomized controlled trial in irritable bowel syndrome. *PLOS one.* December 22. Retrieved February 12, 2017, from: http://journals.plos.org/plosone/article?id=10.1371/journal.pone.0015591

Klopfer, B. (1957). Psychological variables in human cancer. *Journal of Projective Techniques, 21*(4), 331–340.

Kong, J., Gollub, R. L., Rosman, I. S. et al. (2006). Brain activity associated with expectancy-enhanced placebo analgesia as measured by functional magnetic resonance imaging. *The Journal of Neuroscience, 26,* 381–388.

Lang, W., & Rand, M. A. (1969). A placebo response as a conditional reflex to glyceryl trinitrate. *Medical Journal of Australia, 1,* 912–914.

Lehrer, P. M., Woolfolk, R. M., & Sime, W. E. (2007). *Principles and practice of stress management* (3rd ed.). New York: Guilford Press.

Lidstone, S. C. C., & Stoessl, A. L. (2007). Understanding the placebo effect: Contributions from neuroimaging. *Molecular Imaging and Biology, 9*, 176–185.

Lilienfeld, S. O., Lynn, S. J., & Lohr, J. M. (Eds). (2003). *Science and pseudoscience in clinical psychology.* New York: Guilford Press.

Lilienfeld, S. O., Ruscio, J., & Lynn, S. J. (Eds.). (2008). *Navigating the mindfield: A guide to separating science from pseudoscience in mental health.* Amherst, NY: Prometheus Books.

Madsen, M. V., Gøtzsche, P. C., & Hróbjartsson, A. (2009). Acupuncture treatment for pain: Systematic review of randomized clinical trials with acupuncture, placebo acupuncture, and no acupuncture groups. *British Medical Journal,* March, 3115. Retrieved February 20, 2017, from: http://www.bmj.com/cgi/reprint/338/jan27_2/a3115?maxtoshow=&HITS=10&hits=10&RESULTFORMAT=&fulltext=sham+acupuncture&searchid=1&FIRSTINDEX=0&resourcetype=HWCIT

Maganaris, C. N., Collins, D., & Sharp, M. (2000). Expectancy effects and strength training: Do steroids make a difference? *The Sport Psychologist, 14,* 272–278.

Melzack, R., & Wall, P. D. (1965). Pain mechanisms: A new theory. *Science, 150*(3699), 971–979.

Moseley, J. B., O'Malley, K., Petersen, N. J. et al. (2002). A controlled trial of arthroscopic surgery for osteoarthritis of the knee. *New England Journal of Medicine, 347,* 81–88.

Norcross, J. C., Koocher, G. P., & Garofalo, A. (2006). Discredited psychological treatments and tests: A Delphi poll. *Professional Psychology: Research and Practice, 37*(5), 515–522.

Price, D. D., Milling, L. S., Kirsch, I. et al. (1999). Analysis of factors that contribute to the magnitude of placebo analgesia in an experimental paradigm. *Pain, 83,* 147–157.

Robazza, C., & Bortoli, L. (1994). Hypnosis in sport: An isomorphic model. *Perceptual and Motor Skills, 79*(2), 963–973.

Sapolsky, R. M. (2004). *Why zebras don't get ulcers* (3rd ed.). New York: Henry Holt.

Shapiro, A. K., & Shapiro, E. (1997). *The powerful placebo: From priest to modern physician.* Baltimore, MD: Johns Hopkins University Press.

Skinner, B. F. (1948). "Superstition" in the pigeon. *Journal of Experimental Psychology, 38,* 168–172.

Skinner, B. F. (1974). *About behaviorism.* New York: Random House.

Smith, J. C. (1976). Psychotherapeutic effects of transcendental meditation with controls for expectation of relief and daily sitting. *Journal of Consulting and Clinical Psychology, 44*(4), 630–637.

Smith, J. C. (2005). *Relaxation, meditation, & mindfulness: A mental health practitioner's guide to new and traditional approaches.* New York: Springer.

Smith, J. C. (2007). The psychology of relaxation. In P. M. Lehrer, R. L. Woolfolk, & W. E. Sime (Eds.), *Principles and practice of stress management* (3rd ed., pp. 38–56). New York: Guilford Press.

Smith, J. C. (2018). *Stress & coping: The eye of mindfulness.* Dubuque, IA: Kendall-Hunt.

Sonetti, D. A., Wetter, T. J., Pegelow, D. F., & Dempsey, J. A. (2001). Effects of respiratory muscle training versus placebo on endurance exercise performance. *Respiration Physiology, 127*(2–3), 185–199.

Talbot, M. (2000). The placebo prescription. *New York Times Magazine,* January 9. Retrieved February 20, 2017, from: http://www.nytimes.com/library/magazine/home/20000109mag-talbot7.html

Vase, L., Robinson, M. E., Verne, G. N., & Price, D. D. (2005). Increased placebo analgesia over time in irritable bowel syndrome (IBS) patients is associated with desire and expectation but not endogenous opioid mechanisms. *Pain, 115*, 338–347.

Voet, W. (1999). *Breaking the chain: Drugs and cycling, the true story*. London: Random House/Yellow Jersey Press.

Waber, R. L., Shiv, B., Carmon, Z., & Ariely, D. (2008). Commercial features of placebo and therapeutic efficacy. *Journal of the American Medical Association, 299*, 1016–1017.

Wampold, B. E., Minami, T., Tierney, S. C. et al. (2005). The placebo is powerful: Estimating placebo effects in medicine and psychotherapy from randomized clinical trials. *Journal of Clinical Psychology, 61*, 835–854.

Wark, D. M. (2006). Alert hypnosis: A review and case report. *American Journal of Clinical Hypnosis, 48*, 291–300.

Zahl, P. H., Maehlen, J., & Welch, H. G. (2008). The natural history of invasive breast cancers detected by screening mammography. *Archives of Internal Medicine, 168*(21), 2311–2316.

Zubieta, J-K., Bueller, J. A., Jackson, L. R. et al. (2005). Placebo effects mediated by endogenous opioid activity on μ-opioid receptors. *The Journal of Neuroscience, 25*, 7754–7762.

## Chapter 12: Sensory Phenomena, Hallucinations, and Psychiatric Conditions

Aleman, A., & Larøi, F. (2008). *Hallucinations: The science of idiosyncratic perception*. Washington, DC: American Psychological Association.

American Psychiatric Association (APA). (2013). *Diagnostic and statistical manual of mental disorders* (5th ed.) *(DSM-5)*. Washington, DC: American Psychiatric Association.

Beidel, D. C., Frueh, B. C., & Hersen, M. (Eds.). (2015). *Adult psychopathology and diagnosis*. Hoboken, NJ: Wiley.

Beyerstein, B. L. (1996). Believing is seeing: Organic and psychological reasons for hallucinations and other anomalous psychiatric symptoms. *Medscape Psychiatry & Mental Health ejournal, 1*. Retrieved February 20, 2017, from: http://www.medscape.com/viewarticle/431517

Birbaumer, N., Gruzelier, J., Jamieson, G. A. et al. (2005). Psychobiology of altered states of consciousness. *Psychological Bulletin, 131*, 98–127.

Blackmore, S. (1991). Near-death experiences: In or out of the body? *Skeptical Inquirer, 16*, 34–45.

Blackmore, S. (2004). *Consciousness: An introduction*. New York: Oxford University Press.

Blackmore, S. J., & Troscianko, T. S. (1989). The physiology of the tunnel. *Journal of Near-Death Studies, 8*, 15–28.

Bourguignon, E. (1970). Hallucinations and trance: An anthropologist's perspective. In W. Keup (Ed.) *Origins and mechanisms of hallucinations* (pp. 83–90). New York: Plenum Press.

Bower, B. (2005). Night of the crusher. *Science News, 168*, 27. Retrieved February 20, 2017, from: http://www.sciencenews.org/articles/20050709/bob9.asp

Bradshaw, J. (1967). Pupil size as a measure of arousal during information processing. *Nature, 216*, 515–516.

David, A. S. (2004). The cognitive neuropsychiatry of auditory verbal hallucinations: An overview. *Cognitive Neuropsychiatry, 9*, 107–124.

dpselfhelp (Depersonalization Support Community). Retrieved February 20, 2017, from: www.dpselfhelp.com/

Ehrsson, H. E. (2007). The experimental induction of out-of-body experiences. *Science, 317*, 1048.

Evans, R. W., & Matthew, N. T. (2005). *Handbook of headache* (2nd ed.). Philadelphia: Lippincott Williams and Wilkins.

Geschwind, N. (1983). Interictal behavioral changes in epilepsy. *Epilepsia, 24*, 23–30.

Giesbrecht, T., Lynn, S. J., Lilienfeld, S., & Merckelbach, H. (2008). Cognitive processes in dissociation: An analysis of core theoretical assumptions. *Psychological Bulletin, 134*, 617–647.

Giesbrecht, T., Lynn, S. J., Lilienfeld, S., & Merckelbach, H. (2010). Cognitive processes, trauma, and dissociation: Misconceptions and misrepresentations (Reply to Bremner, 2009). *Psychological Bulletin, 136*, 7–11. (2014-06-30).

Goodman, W. K., & Murphy, T. K. (1998). Obsessive-compulsive disorder and Tourette's syndrome. In S. J. Enna & J. T. Coyle (Eds.), *Pharmacological management of neurological and psychiatric disorders* (pp. 177–211). New York: McGraw-Hill Health Professions Division.

Grassian, S. (1993). Psychiatric effects of solitary confinement. Declaration submitted September 1993 in Madrid v. Gomez, 889F. Suppl. 1146. Retrieved February 12, 2017, from: http://openscholarship.wustl.edu/cgi/viewcontent.cgi?article=1362&context=law_journal_law_policy

Lenggenhager, B., Tadi, T., Metzinger, T., & Blanke, O. (2007). Video ergo sum: Manipulating bodily self-consciousness. *Science, 317*(5841), 1096–1099.

Luhrmann, T. M. (2012). *When God talks back: Understanding the American evangelical relationship with God.* New York: Knopf.

Lutz, P. L., & Nilsson, G. E. (1997). *The brain without oxygen.* Austin, TX: Landes Bioscience.

Lynn, S. J., Berg, J. M., Lilienfeld, S. O. et al. (2014). Dissociative disorders. In D. C. Beidel, B. C. Frueh, & M. Hersen (Eds.), *Adult psychopathology and diagnosis* (pp. 407–449). Hoboken, NJ: Wiley.

Maddox, R. W., & Long, M. A. (1999). Eating disorders: Current concepts. *Journal of the American Pharmacological Association, 39*, 378–387.

Morris, R. L., Harary, S. B., Janis, J. et al. (1978). Studies of communication during out-of-body experiences. *Journal of the Society for Psychical Research, 72*, 1–22.

National Institute of Neurological Disorders and Stroke (NINDS). (2007). Migraine information page. Retrieved January 31, 2017, from: https://www.ninds.nih.gov/Disorders/All-Disorders/Migraine-Information-Page

Partala, T., & Surakka, V. (2003). Pupil size variation as an indicator of affective processing. *International Journal of Human-Computer Studies, 59*, 185–198.

Penfield, W. (1955). The twenty-ninth Maudsley lecture: The role of the temporal cortex in certain physical phenomena. *Journal of Mental Science, 101*, 451–465.

Peterson, C. B., & Mitchell, J. E. (1999). Psychosocial and pharmacological treatment of eating disorders: A review of research findings. *Journal of Clinical Psychology, 55*, 685–697.

Ritsher, J. B., Lucksted, A, Otilingam, P. G., & Grajales, M. (2004). Hearing voices: Explanations and implications. *Psychiatric Rehabilitation Journal, 27,* 219–227. Retrieved January 31, 2017, from: http://escholarship.org/uc/item/32x6g6zn#page-2

Sacks, O. (1999). *Migraine.* New York: Knopf.

Sacks, O. (2008). Patterns. *New York Times,* February 14. Retrieved February 20, 2017, from: https://migraine.blogs.nytimes.com/2008/02/13/patterns/index.html

Sarbin, T. R., & Juhasz, J. B. (1975). The historical background of the concept of hallucination. In R. K. Siegel & L. J. West (Eds.), *Hallucinations: Behavior, experience and theory* (pp. 214–227). New York: Wiley.

Schroeter-Kunhardt, M. (1993). A review of near death experiences. *Journal of Scientific Exploration, 7,* 219–239.

Shapiro, A. K., Young, J. G., Shapiro, E., & Feinberg, T. E. (1988). *Gilles de la Tourette syndrome.* Philadelphia, PA: Lippincott Williams and Wilkins.

Shermer, M. (2010). The sensed-presence effect. *Scientific American,* April 1. Retrieved February 12, 2017, from: https://www.scientificamerican.com/article/the-sensed-presence-effect/

Simner, J., Mulvenna, C., Sagiv, N. et al. (2006). The prevalence of atypical cross-modal experiences. *Perception, 8,* 1024–1033.

Tien, A. Y. (1991). Distribution of hallucinations in the population. *Social Psychiatry and Psychiatry Epidemiology, 26,* 287–292.

Ward, J. (2004). Emotionally-mediated synaesthesia. *Cognitive Neuropsychology, 21,* 761–772.

Ward, J., Huckstep, B., & Tsakanikos, E. (2006). Sound-colour: To what extent does it use cross-modal mechanisms common to us all? *Cortex, 42*(2), 264–280.

Wells, H. G. (1898). *War of the worlds.* New York: Bartleby.com.

Young, W. B., & Silberstein, S. D. (2004). *Migraine and other headaches.* St Paul, MN: AAN Press.

## Chapter 13: Claims of Extraordinary Cures

### Energy Treatments

Barrett, S. (2007) Homeowatch. Retrieved February 20, 2017, from: www.homeowatch.org/

Fleischman, G. F. (1998). *Acupuncture: Everything you ever wanted to know.* New York: Barrytown.

Goldacre, B. (2007). The end of homeopathy. *The Guardian,* November 17. Retrieved February 20, 2017, from: http://www.badscience.net/2007/11/a-kind-of-magic/

Hines, T. (2003). *Pseudoscience and the paranormal* (2nd ed.). Amherst, NY: Prometheus Books.

Jarvis, W. T., & The National Council against Health Fraud. (2002). Homeopathy. In M. Shermer (Ed.), *The skeptic encyclopedia of pseudoscience* (pp. 347–356). Santa Barbara, CA: ABC-CLIO.

Krieger, D. (1979). *The therapeutic touch: How to use your hands to help or to heal.* Englewood Cliffs, NJ: Prentice Hall.

Krippner, S. C. (2002). Conflicting perspectives on shamans and shamanism: Points and counterpoints. *American Psychologist, 57,* 962–977.

Levinson, D. (1998). *Religion: A cross-cultural dictionary*. New York: Oxford University Press.

Lewis, I. M. (2003). *Ecstatic religion: A study of shamanism and spirit possession* (2nd ed.). London: Routledge.

Lewith, G., Kenyon, J., & Lewis, P. (1996). *Complementary medicine: An integrated approach*. Oxford: Oxford University Press.

Lin, Z. (Ed.). (2000). *Qigong: Chinese medicine or pseudoscience?* Amherst, NY: Prometheus Books.

Lindeman, M., & Saher, M. (2007). Vitalism, purpose and superstition. *British Journal of Psychology, 98*, 33–44.

Madsen, M. V., Gøtzsche, P. C., & Hróbjartsson, A. (2009). Acupuncture treatment for pain: Systematic review of randomized clinical trials with acupuncture, placebo acupuncture, and no acupuncture groups. *British Medical Journal,* March, 3115. Retrieved February 20, 2017, from: http://www.bmj.com/cgi/reprint/338/jan27_2/a3115 ?maxtoshow=&HITS=10&hits=10&RESULTFORMAT=&fulltext=sham+acupuncture& searchid=1&FIRSTINDEX=0&resourcetype=HWCIT

Mann, F. (1993). *Reinventing acupuncture: A new concept of an ancient medicine*. Oxford: Butterworth-Heinemann.

National Health and Medical Research Council. (2015). NHMRC information paper: Evidence on the effectiveness of homeopathy for treating health conditions. Canberra, Australia: National Health and Medical Research Council.

National Institutes of Health (NIH) Consensus Development Program. (November 3–5, 1997). *Acupuncture – Consensus Development Conference Statement*. National Institutes of Health. Retrieved February 20, 2017, from: https://consensus.nih. gov/1997/1997Acupuncture107html.htm

Pelletier, K. R. (2002). *The best alternative medicine*. New York: Simon & Schuster.

Rosa, L., Rosa, E., Sarner, L., & Barrett, S. (1998). A close look at therapeutic touch. *Journal of the American Medical Association, 279*(13), 1005–1010.

Schubert-Soldern, R. (1962). *Mechanism and vitalism*. London: Burns & Oates.

Watson, B. (1963). *Mo Tzu: Basic writings*. New York: Columbia University Press.

Wu, B. (2000). *Lighting the eye of the dragon: Inner secrets of taoist feng shui*. New York: St Martin's Press.

yinyang. (2008). In *Encyclopædia Britannica*. Retrieved February 12, 2017, from: https:// www.britannica.com/topic/yinyang

## Shamanism, Faith Healing, and Distant Intercessory Prayer

Barnes, P., Powell-Griner, E., McFann, K., & Nahin, R. (2002). CDC Advance Data Report #343: Complementary and alternative medicine use among adults: United States, 2002. Washington, DC: US Government.

Barrett, S. (2003). Some thoughts about faith healing. Retrieved February 20, 2017, from: http://www.quackwatch.com/01QuackeryRelatedTopics/faith.html

Benson, H. (1975). *The relaxation response*. New York: Morrow.

Benson, H., Dusek, J. A., Sherwood, J. B. et al. (2006). Study of the therapeutic effects of intercessory prayer (STEP) in cardiac bypass patients: A multicenter randomized trial of uncertainty and certainty of receiving intercessory prayer. *American Heart Journal, 151*, 934–942.

Chopra, D. (2008). Taking the afterlife seriously. *Skeptic, 13*, 55–57.

Gerhardt, P. (2000). Saying a prayer for science: Studies of the healing power of prayer pose challenges some call divine. *Washington Post,* December 19. Retrieved February 20, 2017, from: http://pqasb.pqarchiver.com/washingtonpost/access/65284393.html?dids =65284393:65284393&FMT=ABS&FMTS=ABS:FT&date=Dec+19%2C+2000&author= Pamela+Gerhardt&pub=The+Washington+Post&edition=&startpage=Z.08&desc= FINDINGS+OF+FACT

Hansen, G. P. (2001). *The trickster and the paranormal.* New York: Xlibris.

Hines, T. (2003). *Pseudoscience and the paranormal.* Amherst, NY: Prometheus Books.

Hodge, D. R. (2007). A systematic review of the empirical literature on intercessory prayer. *Research on Social Work Practice, 17*, 174–187.

Krippner, S., & Achterberg, J. (2000). Anomalous healing experiences. In E. Cardeña, S. J. Lynn, & S. C. Krippner (Eds.), *Varieties of anomalous experience: Examining the scientific evidence* (pp. 353–395). Washington, DC: American Psychological Association.

Krippner, S. C. (2002). Conflicting perspectives on shamans and shamanism: Points and counterpoints. *American Psychologist, 57*, 962–977.

Leibovici, L. (1999). Alternative (complementary) medicine: A cuckoo in the nest of empiricist reed warblers. *British Medical Journal, 319*, 1629–1632.

Leibovici, L. (2001). Effects of remote, retroactive intercessory prayer on outcomes in patients with bloodstream infection: Randomised controlled trial. *British Medical Journal, 323*, 1450–1451.

Levinson, D. (1998). *Religion: A cross-cultural dictionary.* New York: Oxford University Press.

Lewis, I. M. (2003). *Ecstatic religion: A study of shamanism and spirit possession* (2nd ed.). London: Routledge.

Masters, K. S. (2005). Research on the healing power of distant intercessory prayer: Disconnect between science and faith. *Journal of Psychology and Theology, 33*, 268–277.

Masters, K. S., Spielmans, G. I., & Goodson, J. T. (2006). Are there demonstrable effects of distant intercessory prayer? A meta-analytic review. *Annals of Behavioral Medicine, 32*, 21–26.

Myers, D. G. (2000). Is prayer clinically effective? *Reformed Review, 53*, 95–102. Retrieved February 20, 2017, from: http://www.davidmyers.org/Brix?pageID=53

Offit, P. A. (2015). *Bad faith: When religious belief undermines modern medicine.* New York: Basic Books.

Posner, G. P. (1998). Has science proven the "divine" health benefits of religion? Retrieved February 12, 2017, from: https://www.infidels.org/secular_web/feature/1998/prayer-USAToday.html

Randi, J. (1989). *The faith healers.* Amherst, NY: Prometheus Books.

Sternfield, J. (1992). *Firewalk: The psychology of physical immunity.* Stockbridge, MA: Berkshire House.

Wallace, C. (1996). Faith and healing. *Time.* June 24. Retrieved February 20, 2017, from: http://www.time.com/time/magazine/article/0,9171,984737,00.html

Warner, R. (1980). Deception and self-deception in shamanism and psychiatry. *International Journal of Social Psychiatry, 26*, 41–52.

# Chapter 14: From the Paranormal Sampler: Four Claims of Consequence

Smith, J. C. (in press). *The paranormal sampler*. Charleston, SC: createspace.

**Astrology**

Blackmore, S., & Seebold, M. (2001). The effect of horoscopes on women's relationships. *Correlation*, *19* (2), 17–32.

Carlson, S. (1985). A double-blind test of astrology. *Nature*, *318*, 419–425.

Culver, R., & Ianna, P. (1984). *The Gemini Syndrome*. Amherst, NY: Prometheus Books.

Dean, G. (2016). Does astrology need to be true? A thirty-year update. *Skeptical Inquirer*, *40*, 38–45.

Dean, G., Mather, A., & Kelly, I. W. (1996). Astrology. In G. Stein (Ed.), *The encyclopedia of the paranormal* (pp. 47–99). New York: Prometheus.

Eysenck, H., & Nias, D. (1982). *Astrology: Science or superstition?* New York: St Martin's Press.

Gauquelin, M. (1974). *Cosmic influences on human behavior*. London: Garnstone Press.

Hines, T. (2003). *Pseudoscience and the paranormal*. Amherst, NY: Prometheus Books.

Hoskin, M. (2003). *The Cambridge concise history of astronomy*. Cambridge: Cambridge University Press.

Irion, R. (2008). Homing in on black holes. *Smithsonian Magazine*, April. Retrieved January 31, 2017, from: http://www.smithsonianmag.com/science-nature/homing-in-on-black-holes-31385827/

Irving, K. (2003). The Gauquelin planetary effects. *Planetos: An online journal*. Retrieved February 20, 2017, from: http://www.planetos.info/index.html

Jerome, L. E. (1977). *Astrology disproved*. Amherst, NY: Prometheus Books.

Melia, F. (2007). *The galactic supermassive black hole*. Princeton, NJ: Princeton University Press.

Monk, W. H. (1875). *Hymns ancient and modern* (2nd ed.). London: W. M. Clowes and Sons.

Schick, T., & Vaughn, L. (2005). *How to think about weird things: Critical thinking for a new age*. New York: McGraw-Hill.

Tester, J. (1989). *A history of western astrology*. New York: Ballantine Books.

Truzzi, M. (1976). Editorial. *The Zetetic*, *1*(1), *Fall/Winter*, 4.

van Gent, R. H. (2007). *Isaac Newton & astrology*. Retrieved February 12, 2017, from: https://www.staff.science.uu.nl/~gent0113/astrology/newton.htm

**Spiritualism**

Edwards, P. (1996). *Reincarnation: A critical examination*. Amherst, NY: Prometheus Books.

Hyman, R. (2003). How *not* to test mediums: Critiquing the afterlife experiments. *Skeptical Enquirer*, January/February 2003. Retrieved January 31, 2017, from: http://www.csicop.org/si/show/how_not_to_test_mediums_critiquing_the_afterlife_experiments

Molé, P. (2002). Reincarnation. In M. Shermer (Ed.), *The skeptic encyclopedia of pseudoscience* (pp. 204–212). Santa Barbara, CA: ABC-CLIO.

O'Keeffe, C., & Wiseman, R. (2005). Testing alleged mediumship: Methods and results. *British Journal of Psychology, 96*, 165–179.

Roach, M. (2005). *Spook: Science tackles the afterlife.* New York: W. W. Norton.

Schwartz, G. E. R. (2012). The Sophia Project. Retrieved February 12, 2017, from: http://www.spiritualistresources.com/cgi-bin/links/index.pl?read=69

Stevenson, I. (1980). Twenty cases suggestive of reincarnation (2nd ed., rev. and enlarged). Charlottesville: University of Virginia Press.

Stevenson, I. (1997). *Where reincarnation and biology intersect.* Westport, CT: Praeger.

Taylor, H. (2003). *The religious and other beliefs of Americans 2003.* The Harris Poll #11, February 26. Retrieved January 31, 2017, from: http://media.theharrispoll.com/documents/Harris-Interactive-Poll-Research-The-Religious-and-Other-Beliefs-of-Americans-2003-2003-02.pdf

**Parapsychology**

Alcock, J. E. (1981). *Parapsychology: Science or magic?* Burlington, MA: Elsevier.

Bausell, R. B. (2007). *Snake oil science: The truth about complementary and alternative medicine.* Oxford: Oxford University Press.

Beloff, J. (1974). ESP: The search for a physiological index. *Journal of the Society for Psychical Research, 47*, 403–420.

Beloff, J. (1985). Research strategies for dealing with unstable phenomena. In B. Shapin & L. Coly (Eds.), *The repeatability problem in parapsychology* (pp. 1–21). New York: Parapsychology Foundation.

Bem, D. J. (2011). Feeling the future: Experimental evidence for anomalous retroactive influences on cognition and affect. *Journal of Personality and Social Psychology, 100*(3), 407–425.

Bösch, H., Steinkamp, F., & Boller, E. (2006). Examining psychokinesis: The interaction of human intention with random number generators – a meta-analysis. *Psychological Bulletin, 132*(4): 497–523.

Braud, W., Shafer, D., & Andrews, S. (1993a). Reactions to an unseen gaze (remote attention): A review, with new data on autonomic staring detection. *Journal of Parapsychology, 57*, 373–390.

Braud, W., Shafer, D., & Andrews, S. (1993b). Further studies of autonomic detection of remote staring: Replications, new control procedures, and personality correlates. *Journal of Parapsychology, 57*, 391–409.

Carroll, R. T. (2014). A short history of psi research. From *The skeptic's dictionary.* Retrieved February 20, 2017, from: http://skepdic.com/essays/psihistory.html

Child, I. L. (1985). Psychology and anomalous observations: The question of ESP in dreams. *American Psychologist, 40*, 1219–1230.

Christopher, M. (1970). *ESP, seers & psychics.* New York: Thomas Y. Crowell Co.

Hines, T. (2003). *Pseudoscience and the paranormal* (2nd ed.). Amherst, NY: Prometheus Books.

Honorton, C. (1985). Meta-analysis of psi ganzfeld research: A response to Hyman. *Journal of Parapsychology, 49*, 51–86.

Irwin, H. J., & Watt, C. A. (2007). *An introduction to parapsychology* (5th ed.). Jefferson, NC: McFarland.

Marks, D. (2000). *The psychology of the psychic* (2nd ed.). Amherst, NY: Prometheus Books.

Moulton, S. T., & Kosslyn, S. M. (2008). Using neuroimaging to resolve the psi debate. *Journal of Cognitive Neuroscience, 20*, 182–192.

Radin, D. (1997). *The conscious universe: The scientific truth of psychic phenomena*. New York: HarperCollins.

Randi, J. (1982). *Flim-Flam*. Amherst, NY: Prometheus Books.

Rhine, J. B. (1934). *Extra-sensory perception*. Boston: Boston Society for Psychic Research.

Schmeidler, G. R. (1945). Separating the sheep from the goats. *Journal of the American Society for Psychical Research, 39*, 47–50.

Targ, R., & Puthoff, H. (1977). *Mind-reach: Scientists look at psychic ability*. New York: Delacorte Press.

Thouless, R. H., & Wiesner, B. P. (1948). The psi processes in normal and "paranormal" psychology. *Proceedings of the Society for Psychical Research, 48*, 177–196.

## Creationism

Asimov, I., & Gish, D. (1981). The Genesis war. *Science Digest, 89* (October), 82–87.

Barrow, J. D., & Tipler, F. (1988). *The anthropic cosmological principle*. Oxford: Oxford University Press.

Boston, R. (1988). God, country, and the electorate. *Church and State*, October, 8–15.

Carter, J. (2005). *Our endangered values: America's moral crisis*. New York: Simon & Schuster.

Cicero. (1972). *The Nature of the Gods* (trans. H. C. P. McGregor). Harmondsworth, UK: Penguin.

Council of Europe. (2007). *Resolution 1580, The dangers of creationism in education. Council of Europe Parliamentary Assembly*. Retrieved January 31, 2017, from: http://assembly.coe.int/nw/xml/XRef/Xref-XML2HTML-EN.asp?fileid=17592&lang=en

Gould, S. J. (1999). *Rocks of ages: Science and religion in the fullness of life*. New York: Ballantine Books.

Harris, S. (2004). *The end of faith: Religion, terror, and the future of reason*. New York: W. W. Norton.

Holden, C. (1980). Republican candidate picks fight with Darwin. *Science, 209*(4462), 1214.

Miller, K. (2007). In defense of evolution. Judgement day: Intelligent design on trial. Retrieved February 20, 2017, from: http://www.pbs.org/wgbh/nova/id/defense-ev.html

Mooney, C. (2005). *The republican war on science*. New York: Basic Books.

Rees, M. (2000). *Just six numbers: The deep forces that shape the universe*. New York: Free Press.

Spong, J. S. (2007). *Jesus for the non-religious: Recovering the Divine at the heart of the human*. San Francisco: HarperCollins.

Steering Committee on Science and Creationism, National Academy of Sciences. (2008). *Science, evolution, and creationism*. Washington, DC: The National Academies Press.

## Appendix

Chapman. (2014). The Chapman University Survey on American Fears. Retrieved February 12, 2017, from: http://www.chapman.edu/wilkinson/research-centers/babbie-center/survey-american-fears.aspx

Friesen, J. P., Campbell, T. H., & Kay, A. C. (2014). The psychological advantage of unfalsifiability: The appeal of untestable religious and political ideologies. *Journal of Personality and Social Psychology, 108*(3), 515–529.

Goertzel, T. (1994). Belief in conspiracy theories: A pilot study. *Frontiers in Psychology, 15*(4), 731–642.

Newberg, N., & Waldman, M. R. (2006). *Why we believe what we believe: Uncovering our biological need for meaning, spirituality, and truth.* New York: Free Press.

Shermer, M. (2012). *The believing brain: From ghosts and gods to politics and conspiracies – how we construct beliefs and reinforce them as truths.* New York: Times Books.

Smith, J. C. (2010). *Pseudoscience and extraordinary claims of the paranormal: A critical thinker's toolkit.* Chichester: Wiley-Blackwell.

Smith, J. C. (2015). Belief Justification Survey. Available from author.

Swami, V., Pietschnig, J., Tran, U. S. et al. (2013). The impact of informational framing and individual differences in shaping of conspiracist beliefs about the Moon landings. *Applied Cognitive Psychology, 27*(1), 71–80.

# Index

Page numbers in *italics* indicate figures; page numbers in **bold** indicate tables

*Critical Thinking: Pseudoscience and the Paranormal*, Second Edition. Jonathan C. Smith.
© 2018 John Wiley & Sons, Inc. Published 2018 by John Wiley & Sons, Inc.